WINNIPEG

D1012921

THE PARIS GAME

General Charles de Gaulle posed for Canadian photographer
Yousuf Karsh during an Ottawa visit, August 1944.

THE PARIS GAME

Charles de Gaulle, the Liberation of Paris,
and the Gamble that Won France

RAY ARGYLE

Foreword by Maurice Vaïsse

DUNDURN
TORONTO

Copyright © Ray Argyle, 2014

All rights reserved. No part of this publication may be reproduced, stored in a retrieval system, or transmitted in any form or by any means, electronic, mechanical, photocopying, recording, or otherwise (except for brief passages for purposes of review) without the prior permission of Dundurn Press. Permission to photocopy should be requested from Access Copyright.

Editor: Dominic Farrell
Design: Laura Boyle
Cover Design: Jennifer Gallinger
Front Cover Image: S2 Photo/S.M./ Bridgeman Art Library
Back Cover Image: Karsh
Printer: Webcom

Library and Archives Canada Cataloguing in Publication

Argyle, Ray, author
     The Paris game : Charles de Gaulle, the liberation of Paris, and the gamble that won France / Ray Argyle ; foreword by Maurice Vaïsse.

Includes bibliographical references and index.

Issued in print and electronic formats.

ISBN 978-1-4597-2286-6 (pbk.).--ISBN 978-1-4597-2287-3 (pdf).--ISBN 978-1-4597-2288-0 (epub)

     1. Gaulle, Charles de, 1890-1970. 2. Paris (France)--History--1940-1944. 3. France--History--German occupation, 1940-1945. 4. Generals--France--Biography. I. Title.

D762.P3A74 2014   940.53'44092   C2014-902126-7
                                                C2014-902127-54

1   2   3   4   5   18   17   16   15   14

We acknowledge the support of the **Canada Council for the Arts** and the **Ontario Arts Council** for our publishing program. We also acknowledge the financial support of the **Government of Canada** through the **Canada Book Fund and Livres Canada Books**, and the **Government of Ontario** through the Ontario Book Publishing Tax Credit and the **Ontario Media Development Corporation**.

Care has been taken to trace the ownership of copyright material used in this book. The author and the publisher welcome any information enabling them to rectify any references or credits in subsequent editions.

J. Kirk Howard, President

The publisher is not responsible for websites or their content unless they are owned by the publisher.

Printed and bound in Canada.

VISIT US AT

Dundurn.com
@dundurnpress
Facebook.com/dundurnpress
Pinterest.com/dundurnpress

Dundurn	Gazelle Book Services Limited	Dundurn
3 Church Street, Suite 500	White Cross Mills	2250 Military Road
Toronto, Ontario, Canada	High Town, Lancaster, England	Tonawanda, NY
M5E 1M2	LA1 4XS	U.S.A. 14150

Paris! Paris outraged! Paris broken! Paris martyred! But Paris liberated! Liberated by itself, liberated by its people with the help of the French armies, with the support and the help of all France, of the France that fights, of the only France, of the real France, of the eternal France!

— Charles de Gaulle, Paris,
August 25, 1944

CONTENTS

Foreword

Maurice Vaïsse

Writing a book about a historic figure, or a period in history, is somewhat like painting a portrait or a landscape. No two people will produce a work that looks exactly the same; we all project a little bit of ourselves into the work. The appeal of *The Paris Game* stems from the fact that its author reveals he is a lover of Paris and an admirer of Charles de Gaulle, and one can read these sentiments in every line. Every biographer of "the Man of the 18th of June" has chosen to emphasize a particular aspect of his character, and this is also the case for Ray Argyle.

I would first like to say why it was a pleasure to read him. He is an author who innovates and surprises, often resorting to lesser-known Canadian and American sources, alongside the better-known French documentation, such as Charles de Gaulle's own *Mémoires de guerre*. The detailed "Notes and Sources" that Argyle has included are particularly useful, revealing his knowledge of the culture and the life of France.

Although the book is well-documented, it pleases me especially because to read it is to enjoy a refreshing change from academic histories.

It is not cluttered with abstract references and considerations. Instead, it is distinguished by its practical approach and the liveliness of its depiction of the personalities. The author likes to portray people and things in their environment and in their everyday life; they are not mere abstract figures or intellectual entities. De Gaulle has a family, wife, children, and Argyle excels in giving them their proper place in the family environment.

The book places great importance on a variety of interesting figures, each of whom had a role in the liberation and recovery of France. They include such personalities as Jean Moulin, Elisabeth de Miribel, Philippe Leclerc, and de Gaulle's son, Philippe, along with Jean-Paul Sartre and Simone de Beauvoir. Less attention is paid to ministers, administrators, diplomats, and military figures — those that may be referred to as de Gaulle's entourage. Because we forget too often, it is worth remembering, as does the author, that de Gaulle did not transform France alone. He was aided by members of a supportive circle that extended from London to Algiers, and from de Gaulle's home in Colombey-les-Deux-Églises to the presidential suite at the Élysée Palace.

But men and women are not the only ones to play a role in this book. There is also the immortal Paris, which holds a place of prime importance. Paris is not merely the setting for the events described so well by the author, but a real actor in the story and the main stage on which General de Gaulle performed. As a lover and a connoisseur of the capital's different neighbourhoods, the author describes the principal scenes in which Charles de Gaulle acted out his career. This is a book full of interesting portraits and little-known facts that hook the reader with a sense of action and life.

To paraphrase Pirandello, who wrote, "To each his own truth," I could say, "To each his own de Gaulle." Argyle has made his choice: he has chosen to put "the Man of the 18th of June" on the stage — the man who rallied the French to fight on. For my part, I would have appreciated it if Argyle had described the following years of de Gaulle's career with the same precision he has applied to that era. But there you have it; it is his choice, which he illustrates by focusing on the period of the Second World War and the French Resistance (1939–1945), rather than on the presidency of General de Gaulle (1958–1969). In this sense, Argyle is in agreement with a majority of the French, for whom Charles de Gaulle remains the Man of the 18th of June and the man of legend.

Readers of *The Paris Game* will not find lengthy arguments on issues that continue to divide analysts: Was de Gaulle a republican or was he a Bonapartist — a man for the people or a would-be emperor? Was he a doctrinarian or was he a pragmatist? And if he was a doctrinarian, what was his doctrine? Was he a man attached to the nation-state, and as such, unable to understand the postwar world? Or was he a true European? Was he anti-American in the 1960s in reaction to his wartime experiences? Or was he merely enamoured of national independence and conscious of France's need to remain close to the United States? Was de Gaulle determined to preserve France's domination of its colonies and was his approach to decolonization thus a sham? Or did de Gaulle understand the new path that was opening up for France: the path to progress through co-operation? And what did the Gaullian call for the greatness of France really signify?

In his conclusion, Argyle briefly evokes some of these aspects. He insists precisely on the construction of the de Gaulle legend — the fruit of both dramatic events and of the general's own actions. He also sweeps aside the idea that Charles de Gaulle would have been something other than a democrat, or that he was merely a vain and prideful man in search of glory. Argyle has a sympathetic view of the man of whom he paints a rather favourable portrait. An exception comes in his discussion of the general's trip to Quebec in 1967. There is an implicit condemnation by the author of de Gaulle's verbal gaffe in his summoning, from the balcony of the Montreal City Hall, the image of an independent Quebec through his use of the expression, "Vive le Québec libre."

The title of this book, *The Paris Game*, at first surprised me. Argyle explains his choice by his reference to the "Great Game" played out on the borders of India and Afghanistan by the Russians and the British in the nineteenth century. This is a logical comparison, but one should not lose sight of the fact that in this very personal and lively book, there are two heroes: Charles de Gaulle and Paris.

Maurice Vaïsse
Sciences Po, University of Paris

Maurice Vaïsse is professor emeritus at the Institut d'études politiques de Paris (Sciences Po), University of Paris, where he has specialized in the history of international relations. He is the author of fourteen books, including La Grandeur: Politique étrangère du général de Gaulle (1958–1969). *Professor Vaïsse has been a counsellor to the Charles de Gaulle Foundation and is the recipient of many honours. He is an Officer of the Ordre national du Mérite and a Knight of the Légion d'honneur.*

Introduction

The air is sultry and the sky threatens rain as we reach the square in front of l'Hôtel de Ville, the city hall of Paris, for the ceremonies commemorating the liberation of the world's most celebrated city. Every year since 1944, Paris has paused on the 25th of August to remember the day that its citizens, having risen against their Nazi German occupiers, revelled in the arrival of their liberators, the Fighting French 2nd Armoured Division and the United States 4th Infantry Division. Parisians celebrated joyfully as tanks and armoured cars clattered across the bridges of the Seine, bringing to an end four years and four months of oppression, humiliation, and betrayal.

Many of the liberating soldiers of Charles de Gaulle's Free French Army — it included black colonials from French Equatorial Africa and haggard veterans of the Spanish Civil War — had never before set eyes on Paris. The city shimmered before them in the midsummer sun of that long-ago day, their presence a fulfillment of a fiercely held dream. That they were here was due in great measure to the towering arrogance and grandiose sense of self of one man, a man who had refused to bow to defeat after the catastrophic Battle of France in 1940. All the rivalries, divisions, and contradictions that would arise in Charles de Gaulle's long life — the rebellious soldier who brought discipline to a fractious army; the arch-conservative who launched the French welfare state; and the Empire loyalist who set free France's richest colony, Algeria — are now but postscripts to a legendary life. His memory is forever interred in the national myth he bestowed on his country — one that will be reaffirmed today — of France as a nation of resisters, a people capable of surviving gigantic trials and emerging to resume their march toward their destiny.

All my life I have come to Paris at every opportunity, either on assignment or simply for the joy of being here. This time I have arrived from Colombey-les-Deux-Églises, a village in eastern France where Deborah and I spent a week visiting La Boisserie, the general's country home, and the Charles de Gaulle Memorial Museum, with its huge Cross of Lorraine, high above the Marne countryside. My purpose in returning to Paris is to reassemble the story of the occupation, liberation, and rebirth of this great city — one of the most dramatic episodes of the Second World War, played out in a high-stakes game reminiscent of the Great Game between Russia and Britain for influence in Central Asia in the nineteenth century.

The game for Paris would prove even more critical, its outcome shaping national honour, personal glory, and the destiny of Western Europe. The players: Winston Churchill, faced with perilous odds but enthusiastic for de Gaulle's playing of "the card of France, a card now called de Gaulle"; President Franklin Roosevelt, suspicious of de Gaulle and wanting to put Paris under American military rule; General Dwight D. Eisenhower, who wanted to bypass Paris in the Allied plunge toward Nazi Germany; the once-heroic Marshall Philippe Pétain, who wanted Paris as the capital of a "New France" partnered with Germany; Adolf Hitler, who wanted Paris burned; and Charles de Gaulle, determined to see Paris liberated by the French, an act that would restore the honour of France in the eyes of his countrymen and the world.

To reach l'Hôtel de Ville this day, we have walked across Pont Royal from our apartment on Quai Voltaire and taken coffee on the rue de Rivoli near the Hôtel Meurice, wartime headquarters of General Dietrich von Choltitz, the German commander of *Gross Paris*. The anniversary ceremony has drawn a crowd of several thousand, small by Parisian standards, but it includes many young people curious to witness this renewal of their history. People chat quietly, content with their presence at what is the largest of several remembrances held on this day. Earlier, citizens had gathered at Gare de l'Est before a memorial etched into the wall of the station commemorating the deportation of Jews and others to German concentration camps. In front of Gare Montparnasse, at a statute of General Jacques Leclerc, commander of the 2nd Armoured Division, a ceremony recalled his taking the surrender of the German Occupation forces. It was at Gare Montparnasse that Charles de Gaulle had on that fateful day made his first stop in Paris.

Hundreds of chairs have been set out for veterans of the uprising and soldiers — *anciens combattants* — who took part in the liberation, as well as for military and political officials and their families. They arrive bearing invitations from the mayor of Paris, Bertrand Delanoë, and take their seats in front of a stage behind which has been erected a giant screen, flanked by French flags and a single American Stars and Stripes. There is no obvious sign of security in the square, no apparent presence of armed soldiers carrying assault guns as we'd seen on patrol near Notre Dame the evening before.

This year's ceremony — "*Memoire d'une insurrection — Hommage au Peuple de Paris*" — pays tribute to the men and women of the Paris uprising. It begins with police and firemen parading in honour of the Régiment de marche du Tchad, the infantry regiment of the 2nd Armoured Division. The crowd stands and sings pridefully when "La Marseillaise" is played.

The big screen shows close-ups of men and women present today, now aged and grey, who fought and saw their comrades die in the liberation of Paris. In a whispered aside, one helps his neighbour remember an incident of that long-ago day. It is no mere history they are recalling, but the mainstream of their lives, a remembrance of the most important thing they ever saw or did, no matter what has happened to them since. The Gaullist myth of a nation united against its occupiers has of course long since faded, dissolved in the hard truths testified to by survivors and recounted in films and books. The *résistants* who are being honoured today, however, are among that brave band of Parisians who dared to rise against their occupiers, and in so doing cleared the way for their Fighting French and American liberators.

Black-and-white images fill the screen, bearing dates and events of the uprising. We see the barricading of the streets, young men and women firing at German soldiers from open windows, and we hear the ringing of church bells that tell Parisians their city has been freed. Finally, the epochal scenes of Charles de Gaulle addressing members of the Resistance in l'Hôtel de Ville, declaring that while Paris had been outraged and martyred, Paris has now been liberated, by itself, and with the support of eternal France.

Next comes a solemn presentation of pictures of men and women of the Resistance who have died during the past year. The images serve as reminders that we will not much longer have among us those who bear personal witness to the events of August 1944. The voice of a young soprano fills the air, "Le Chant des Partisans," evoking the courage of those French who defied their German conquerors, unwilling to meekly accept the conquest of their homeland.

It is then that I meet Angela Irving, an elegant English woman who mistakes me for a Parisian and addresses me in impeccable French. I explain why I am here, and we talk. Her presence is a tribute to the universality of Paris. Elderly now, she has come in remembrance of her friend Pierre, a lieutenant in the Free French Army who helped liberate Paris. She draws a silk handkerchief from her purse and dabs at her eyes as she speaks of him. I wonder if they were lovers.

My thoughts of what it must have been like for Pierre and his comrades blur with the images before my eyes. I think of Captain Raymond Dronne of the 9th Company of the Regiment of Chad, whose reconnaissance squad of three tanks and nine armoured cars had entered this square late in the evening of August 24, 1944, the first liberators into Paris. Others of the Free French 2nd Armoured Division followed shortly after dawn, to find the Tricolour already flying over l'Hôtel de Ville.

More profoundly, the liberation marked a climactic date in Charles de Gaulle's enormous gamble to transform France from a defeated and dispirited nation into an equal among conquering Allies. As an American soldier told playwright Irwin Shaw while dodging shells from a tank battle on the rue de Rivoli, the liberation of Paris deserved to be remembered as "the day the war should end."[1] And why not? With the freeing of Paris in the west and the onward surge of the Red Army in the east, everyone knew the war could have but one outcome.

Paris was no Stalingrad, fought over from house to house, nor was it the victim, like London, of merciless aerial attack. It stood as a symbol of culture and freedom — of what had been lost to the Nazis and what must be regained for the world. From its subjugation by the Romans who gave it the name Lutétia, the history of this settlement founded on an island in the Seine by the Parisi, an ancient Celtic tribe, is filled with momentous occasions: its sacking by Viking raiders in 845; the laying of the foundation stone of Notre Dame in 1163; the storming of the Bastille on July 14, 1789, that set off the French Revolution; Napoleon's seizure of power ten years later; the city's surrender to the Prussian army on January 28, 1871; the brief but bloody life of the Paris Commune of that year; the belle époque of high art and culture of the years before the First World War; and the dreadful losses of that conflict that bequeathed France "*une génération perdue*," a term borrowed by North Americans such as Ernest Hemingway who saw themselves as members of that forsaken generation.

Of the legion of books about the Second World War, most provide only a partial understanding of the ordeal that France endured through defeat, occupation, and finally liberation. General de Gaulle's *Mémoires de guerre*, as might be expected, offer a perspective shrewdly tailored to support his life's mission to render France "some signal service." Our vantage point three-quarters of a century later allows us to present a more clearly etched picture of a man who on three occasions intervened decisively in his country's affairs: to save the honour of a defeated nation in 1940; to prevent its slippage into the Communist arc between 1944 and 1946; and to forestall civil war and military dictatorship between 1958 and 1962.

Because of the emphasis historians have placed on the particularities of de Gaulle's personality and their focus on such traits as vanity and arrogance, his significance as a transformative figure of the twentieth century has not been fully recognized. The British-born academic Niall Ferguson fails to mention de Gaulle in his massive (746-page) *The War of the World*. Ferguson credits his countryman Liddell Hart with developing the theories of mechanized warfare practised so successfully by the Germans, although de Gaulle had called, as early as 1934, for the use of tanks and planes in coordinated attack, a lesson Hitler said he learned from having de Gaulle's book, *Vers l'Armée de Metier* (*The Army of the Future*) read to him.

Because most of the commentary dealing with de Gaulle's actions and policies during and after the Second World War reflects a dominant Anglo-American bias, a more nuanced global perspective of his strategies and thinking has not always been offered. As I will show, for example, it took the forceful presence and persistent obstinacy of Charles de Gaulle, coupled with the realization by the Allies that he had the support of an overwhelming majority of the French people, to dissuade General Eisenhower from implementing President Roosevelt's ill-advised scheme to impose an American military government on liberated France. Trading one form of occupation for another could only have provided the Communist Party, then the country's largest political party, with a grievance it would have cleverly ridden to power — with shattering consequences for the future of Europe and the peace of the world.

De Gaulle again rescued France from catastrophe when he assumed power for the second time, in 1958. His actions as president of the Fifth Republic prevented the outbreak of a civil war over Algeria; he later saved France from a secret army plot to put the country under military dictatorship. Internationally, de Gaulle achieved reconciliation with Germany, creating a relationship that would become the bedrock for peace in Europe. He played a pre-eminent role in assembling the forerunner of today's European Union and launched France on an independent course on the world stage. His rejection of American supremacy — symbolized by France's withdrawal from NATO and the creation of its own nuclear *force de frappe* — raised the curtain on an era of robust diplomacy by middle powers, a state of affairs to which the world has become accustomed since the end of the Cold War.

Personal reminiscences, official records, books, letters, and diaries — from de Gaulle himself, but also from members of his family, those who knew him and who worked for him or against him, writers and diarists, as well as ordinary people — all these I have drawn on for insights into the personal experiences and intimate perceptions of those who were witness to these tumultuous times. The narrative follows the arc of de Gaulle's life through his hurried departure from a besieged Paris as the newly minted one-star general and undersecretary of defense of the French government, to his occupancy of the Élysée Palace as president of the Fifth Republic, an organism of his creation. It is then we hear him exult, "I have played my cards well. I've won!"[2]

I am conscious of the fact that France, one of the two European nations in which my country, Canada, is deeply rooted, holds an exceptional place in the history of Europe and the world. I hope this book will give the general reader a fuller understanding and a greater appreciation of the dramatic and profoundly important role that Charles de Gaulle has played in shaping the twentieth-century narrative that stands as his legacy.

Ray Argyle
Kingston, Ontario, 2014

The Players

Free French/Fighting French

General Charles de Gaulle: Undersecretary of national defense, June 1940; thereafter, leader of the Free French/Fighting French throughout Second World War; head of Provisional French Government, 1946; premier of Fourth Republic, 1958; president of Fifth Republic, 1959–69.

Geoffroy de Courcel: Aide-de-camp and private secretary to General de Gaulle, 1940–41; later deputy *chef du cabinet*, ambassador to London.

Elisabeth de Miribel: Volunteer and aide to General de Gaulle 1940–49; member Carmelite Order 1949–58; later a French diplomat.

General Marie-Pierre Koenig: Commander-in-chief, Free French Forces; later marshall of France.

General Jacques-Philippe Leclerc de Hautecloque: Commander, 2nd Armoured Division 1944–45; liberator of Paris.

Jean Moulin: Delegate-General to the French Resistance.

Henri Georges René Tanguy (Colonel Rol-Tanguy): Communist leader of the Resistance in Paris.

Georges Bidault: President, Comité National de la Resistance.

General Jacques Chaban-Delmas: Fighting French military delegate to the Resistance, 1944–45.

Government of France (1940)

Édouard Daladier: Premier and minister of defense.

Paul Reynaud: Premier, March–June 1940.

Albert Lebrun: President, 1932–40.

Vichy France (1940–44)

Marshall Philippe Pétain: First World War hero; surrendered France to Germany in Second World War; chief of state, 1940–44.

Pierre Laval: Premier during German occupation.

General Maxime Weygand: Minister of defense.

Admiral François Darlan: Minister for interior, defense, and foreign affairs, 1941–42; high commissioner in North Africa, 1942.

United Kingdom

Winston Churchill: Prime minister 1940–45, 1951–55.

Anthony Eden: Secretary of state for war, 1940–45; prime minister during 1956 Suez crisis.

Major-General Edward Spears: Personal representative of Winston Churchill to France, 1940.

United States

Franklin D. Roosevelt: President, 1933–45.

Cordell Hull: Secretary of State, 1933–44.

Robert Murphy: Chargé d'affaires, Vichy, 1940; special mission, Algeria, 1941–43.

General Dwight D. Eisenhower: Commander-in-chief, Allied forces in Europe, 1943–45; president 1953–61.

Admiral William D. Leahy: Ambassador to Vichy France, 1941–42.

William C. Bullitt: Ambassador to France, 1935–40.

Canada

William Lyon Mackenzie King: Prime minister 1935–48.

Major Georges Vanier: Ambassador to France 1940, 1944–53; governor general, 1959–67.

Jean Dupuy: Ambassador to Vichy France, 1941–42, later head of Expo '67, Montreal.

Nazi Germany

Adolf Hitler: Führer, head of Nazi Party, commander-in-chief of armed forces, 1933–45.

General Dietrich von Choltitz: Military governor of Paris, August 1944.

Otto Abetz: Nazi ambassador to France, 1940–44.

West Germany

Konrad Adenhauer: Chancellor, Federal Republic of West Germany, 1949–63.

Chronology

1890 **November 22** — Charles de Gaulle is born in Lille, France, son of schoolmaster Henri de Gaulle and Jeanne Maillot-Delannoy, daughter of a well-to-do factory owner.

1895 **January 5** — French officer Alfred Dreyfus convicted of treason, triggering worldwide charges of anti-Semitism. De Gaulle's father is sympathetic to Dreyfus.

1909 **October 10** — Charles de Gaulle enlists for one year's service as a private soldier in the 33rd Infantry Regiment.

1912 **October 1** — De Gaulle graduates from Saint-Cyr, 13th out of 211. Accepts commission to 33rd Infantry Regiment where the commandant is Colonel Philippe Pétain.

1914 **August 3** — Germany declares war on France as First World War envelops Europe.

1916 **March 2** — Serving under Pétain, de Gaulle is seriously wounded at Douaument; he is assumed killed. Taken prisoner of war, he spends the rest of the war in Germany and attempts five times to escape. He is later awarded the Légion d'Honneur.

1921 **April 6** — Wedding at Calais of Charles de Gaulle and Yvonne Vendroux.

1924 **March** — De Gaulle publishes first book, *La Discorde chez l'Ennemi*, arguing for civilian control of the military. Book sells fewer than a thousand copies.

1933 **January 30** — Adolf Hitler becomes chancellor of Germany.

1934 **May** — De Gaulle publishes *Vers l'Armé de Métier*, urging the modernization of the French army with tanks and a mobile striking force. Begins close relationship with future premier Paul Reynaud, who promotes his ideas.

1939 **September 3** — United Kingdom and France declare war on Germany.

1940 **May 10** — Following eight months of *la drôle de guerre* (phony war), German blitzkrieg conquers the Low Countries and France. The only successful French counterattack is that of de Gaulle at Montcarnot and Abbeville.

June 10 — After being named to the Cabinet, de Gaulle abandons Paris with Premier Reynaud as government moves to Bordeaux.

June 18 — De Gaulle issues famous "Appeal," urging French to join him in London to carry on the fight against Nazi Germany.

July 4 — Military tribunal in Vichy France sentences de Gaulle to death.

1942 **November 8** — An Anglo-American army invades North Africa. German and Italian troops occupy balance of France; the United States accepts Admiral Darlan as head of French administration in North Africa.

December — Resistance movement in France declares support for General de Gaulle.

December 24 — Admiral Darlan assassinated; replaced by General Giraud.

1943 **October 2** — French Committee of National Liberation appoints General de Gaulle as its head, with General Giraud named Inspector of the Armed Forces. Giraud later resigns.

1944 **June 6** — D-Day: American, British, and Canadian forces invade France; Fighting French elements take part.

June 13 — Charles de Gaulle returns to France, making first speech at Bayeux.

August 1 — French 2nd Armoured Division arrives in France, joins Allied attack.

August 15 — French 1st Army and U.S. 6th Corps invade southern France.

August 25 — Liberation of Paris. General de Gaulle returns to the War Ministry and gives a dramatic speech at l'Hôtel de Ville.

November 13 — De Gaulle is chosen as head of the government and forms a tripartite administration with representation from the Communist, Socialist, and Popular Republican parties.

1945 **May 8** — Unconditional surrender of Nazi Germany.

August 14 — Surrender of Empire of Japan following the dropping of two atomic bombs, August 5 and 6.

1946 **January 20** — Frustrated by political machinations, de Gaulle resigns as the head of the government; begins long "political exile" at Colombey-les-Deux-Églises.

1947 **April 7** — De Gaulle announces the formation of new party, Rassemblement du peuple français (RPF), in a speech in Strasbourg.

1948 **February 6** — Death of Anne, daughter of Charles and Yvonne de Gaulle.

1951 **June 17** — Despite solid municipal successes, RPF wins only 121 seats in National Assembly due to the system of apportioning seats. De Gaulle later announces the termination of RPF.

1954 **May 7** — The French defeat at Dien Bien Phu in Vietnam leads to Geneva Accords and French withdrawal from Indochina, with Vietnam divided at the 17th parallel.

1958 **May 15** — As France is gripped by crisis following the army's formation of a Committee of Public Safety in Algeria, de Gaulle announces he is prepared to "assume the powers of the Republic."

May 29 — President Coty asks de Gaulle to become premier, with powers to rule by decree and to oversee writing of a new constitution. National Assembly accepts appointment on June 1 by a vote of 329 to 224, with thirty-two abstentions.

September 28 — In a referendum, French voters give 80 percent approval of a new constitution and the creation of the Fifth Republic. The president is to be elected for seven years by an electoral college; the National Assembly, by popular vote for five-year terms.

December 21 — Electoral College chooses de Gaulle to be president; he is inaugurated on January 8, 1959.

1959 **March 15** — France withdraws military forces from NATO command.

August 22 — De Gaulle narrowly escapes death in an assassination attempt engineered by the OAS (Organisation de l'armée secrète) at Le Petit-Clamart. It is the eighteenth attempt to kill him.

September 16 — Referendum gives approval to Algerian self-determination.

1960 **February 13** — France tests its first atomic bomb, exploding it in the Algerian desert.

May 16 — The Big Four Summit meeting in Paris terminated after United States refuses to apologize to Soviet Union for May 1 spy-plane flight by U2 pilot Francis Gary Powers.

1961 **June 1** — De Gaulle warns President John F. Kennedy that armed intervention in Vietnam will cause the United States to "sink step by step into a bottomless military and political quagmire."

1962 **April 8** — Algerians vote 90 percent in favour of independence; Algeria becomes independent on July 3 and more than one million European-born Algerians commence departure.

October 16–28 — Cuban missile crisis; Nikita Khrushchev agrees to withdraw missiles from Cuba in return for American withdrawal from Turkey.

October 18 — Election of president by universal suffrage is approved with 66.25 percent support in a referendum.

1963   **January 14** — President de Gaulle rejects British application to join European Economic Community.

November 22 — Assassination of President Kennedy in Dallas, Texas.

1965   **December 19** — De Gaulle wins presidential election run-off vote, defeating François Mitterrand by 54.6 percent to 45.4 percent.

1967   **October 27** — For the second time, de Gaulle rejects British entry to European Common Market.

1968   **May** — Student demonstrations and general strike cause chaos in France; situation calmed only after public appeal from de Gaulle.

1969   **April 27** — De Gaulle–backed referendum on reform of the Senate, regionalization, and worker participation in management is rejected by 53 percent of voters. De Gaulle resigns.

June 15 — Georges Pompidou, prime minister under de Gaulle, is elected president.

1970   **October 23** — Publication of last of de Gaulle's memoirs, *Mémoires d'Espoir*.

November 9 — Charles de Gaulle dies at Colombey-les-Deux-Églises and is buried in local churchyard next to daughter Anne.

I

Days of Darkness: The Hand Is Dealt

We do not yet know what will happen in France.... However matters may go, we will never lose our sense of comradeship with the French people. If we are now called upon to endure what they have been suffering, we shall emulate their courage, and if final victory rewards our toils they shall share the gains, and freedom shall be restored to all.

— Winston Churchill
London, May 10, 1940

CHAPTER 1
The Débacle of Paris

The Battle of France has begun. The order is to defend our
positions without thought of retreat.... May the thought
of our wounded country inspire in you an unshakable
resolution to hold where you are.

— General Maxime Weygand
Commander-in-chief of Allied Forces in France
Order of the Day, June 5, 1940

In Paris that spring the lilac and wisteria bloomed early. Along the
Champs-Élysées, the chestnut trees blossomed gloriously but briefly,
their white flowers fading too soon before falling to the pavement.
The newspapers were filled with optimistic accounts of the war, and the
premier, Paul Reynaud, went on the radio to give assurances that France
was "calm and stood strong" in the face of the enemy. Crowds flocked
to theatres and cinemas. Polish émigré Alexandre Ryder premiered his

anti-German docudrama, *Après Mein Kampf, mes crimes,* at the Olympia, but *Goodbye Mr. Chips*, showing at Le Triomphe, played to far larger audiences. Maurice Chevalier and Josephine Baker entranced visitors at the Casino de Paris. Shoppers in chic outfits sunned themselves at sidewalk cafés. French couturier Lucien Lelong linked high fashion to patriotism: "The more French women remain elegant, the more our country will show foreigners it is not afraid."[1] In the Bois de Boulogne, the stands were filled at Auteuil racetrack for the annual spring meet. Some lucky winners enjoyed a celebratory dinner at the elegant Pré-Catalan café, first pausing to admire the elephant-skinned beech tree that stood nearby, said to have been planted before the French Revolution.

On the Left Bank, writers and artists gathered at such favoured cafés as the Dome, La Rotonde, and Café de Flore, debating whether to support the war. Simone de Beauvoir — her paramour Jean-Paul Sartre having been conscripted into the army — confessed her attachment to these places in a passage in her diary: "I feel as if I'm home with my family and that protects me against anguish."[2]

In the poor outer regions of Paris — later to be called the Red Belt — workers with families jammed into tiny walk-up apartments grumbled at again having to work six days a week, the forty-hour week introduced during the brief regime of the leftist Popular Front now all but forgotten. Communists in factories and foundries, and they were many, hewed to the party line that the war was a conspiracy among imperialist powers, undeserving of working-class support. Union members paraded as usual in the traditional May Day celebration of labour, but festivities were subdued. A front-page editorial in *Le Figaro* noted that employers and workers were each marking the day "on their own terms, in the interests of the national solidarity of France at war."

The diversions and labours of the citizens of Paris acquired a sudden urgency on Friday, May 10, 1940, when the German Wehrmacht unleashed a fearful armed attack — the *blitzkrieg*, or lightning war — across Holland, Belgium, and Luxembourg, and into France. A month later, Paris had suffered its first air raid, units of the German 9th Division were at the Seine River sixty kilometres below Paris, and, for the second time in the lives of many of its citizens, the capital became a besieged city. Sandbags were hastily piled up around Paris monuments. It was a city beset by rumours — that German parachutists had landed in the Tuileries Gardens and that poisoned chocolates had been dropped by air over Gare d'Austerlitz, with at least one child having died from eating them. Parisians who had not already fled were startled by the pall of acrid smoke and fumes that hung over the city, detritus from the burning of tons of government documents. Knots of retreating soldiers, some drunk, their rifles lost or thrown aside, clustered around felled trees and overturned buses and trucks, meagre barricades against oncoming German panzer tanks.

Parisians who had cars and could obtain gasoline clogged the roads to the south. Thousands shuffled in lines for hours at Gare Lyon and other stations, desperate for tickets on the last departing trains. Refugees from regions already overrun pushed carts and bicycles filled with pitiful belongings. A barge filled with fleeing civilians was seen making its way up the Seine. Government officials were in the forefront of those fleeing Paris. Yann Fouéré, an official with the Ministry of Information who took part in the evacuation, wrote of the panic on the routes leading out of the capital:

> The scene along the roads was staggering. The whole population was in full flight, on foot, on bicycles, by car and in carts. Most of the cars had mattresses on the roof. Having lost their regiments, a number of soldiers mingled with the crowds and fled with them. Struggles were breaking out around the petrol stations. Grocery shops and bakeries of villages along the way could no longer cope. Some people slept, exhausted, in the ditches. A massive exodus from Paris had begun as soon as the government's departure had been officially announced on the evening of the 10th of June. Why them and not us? If they are fleeing, we must also flee. At the time, it was estimated that there were ten million people on the roads. Paris was fleeing, distraught, causing the rest of the country insoluble problems.[3]

The literary icons of France also took note. Paul Valéry, poet, author, and a member of Académie française wrote of the flight of refugees in his journal, the *Cahiers:* "The impression of living, poignant disorder. Every possible conveyance, carts stuffed with children in the straw. They don't know, nobody knows, where they are going."[4]

✝

Out of five million Parisians, fewer than one million remained in the capital. The evacuation — *l'exode* — went on hour after hour, spurred by conflicting declarations from General Maxime Weygand: first, that there must be no retreat; then, his sudden pronouncement that Paris was an open city. French bureaucrats, recalling the chaos of 1914, when Paris emptied out in the face of a German advance, had made careful plans to manage the evacuation. It soon became a case of every man for himself. At the Ministry of War, housed in an eighteenth-century stone *hôtel particulier* on rue Saint-Dominique, a short distance north of the complex of military museums that make up Les Invalides and a kilometre east of another Paris landmark, the Eiffel Tower, officers debated who should leave first. The newly appointed undersecretary for defense, Brigadier General Charles de Gaulle, found an office filled with noise and confusion when he arrived to take up his charge on June 6. In a room filled with medieval armour, he called together his staff and, standing in front of a wall covered with a large map, gave a clear and honest account of the situation. His blunt presentation seemed to calm his listeners, even if it did not give them cause for optimism.

De Gaulle's arrival at the War Ministry came in answer to a summons he had received while leading the French 4th Armoured Division in a series of counterattacks northeast of Paris. Filled with a sense of fury that the war was beginning so badly, he had hurled his three tank battalions against the oncoming German panzer brigades, the only time during the Battle of France that the Wehrmacht had been forced to retreat. The French High Command, insistent on a strategy of defensive warfare, had failed to grasp the awesome offensive power of tanks. Their powerfully armed Renault, Hotchkiss, and FCM machines were the equal of, if not superior to, Germany's Mark I and II tanks. But rather than deploying them in forward-attack brigades, French commanders dispersed their tanks among regular divisions, rendering them largely ineffective for offensive purposes. De Gaulle had railed against this blindness in a stream of papers, memos, and books that argued the urgent need for France to master the new strategies of mechanized warfare.

Not everyone at the War Ministry approved of this ungainly figure with his imperious ways, who, at the age of forty-nine, was still relatively young as senior French officers went. De Gaulle was accustomed to ridicule and bullying, brought on as much by his unusual height — 1.9 metres (six feet, five inches) — and a face dominated by high cheeks and an enormous nose that led detractors to call him "the Great Asparagus," as by his behaviour. He smoked incessantly and you could see nicotine stains on his fingers and teeth.

Premier Reynaud had summoned de Gaulle to the Cabinet during a frantic reshaping of French leadership that saw two revered First World War leaders, General Weygand and Marshall Philippe Pétain, called back to service. Pétain, who had agreed to become vice-premier, was eighty-four years old when Reynaud summoned him from Madrid, where he had been ambassador to Spain. Weygand, seventy-four, was brought out of retirement to replace the disgraced General Maurice Gamelin, who had presided over the retreats and routs of eight hundred thousand Allied soldiers — French, British, Dutch, and Belgian — in the first days of the blitzkrieg.

De Gaulle's first meeting with Weygand after his appointment to the Cabinet had not gone well. He'd taken a room at the Hôtel Lutetia on Boulevard Raspail and had himself driven to the office of the commander-in-chief at Château de Montry, the army headquarters on the outskirts of Paris.

It took only a few words from Weygand to convince de Gaulle that the commander was resigned to defeat. "When I've been beaten here," Weygand told him, "England won't wait a week before negotiating with the Reich." He added despairingly: "Ah! If only I were sure the Germans would leave me the forces necessary for maintaining order!"[5]

Weygand was not the only voice of despair in the French capital that week. Marshall Pétain, revered for saving the French army in the Battle of Verdun in the First World War, also was ready to throw in his hand.

He had made it clear in a letter to Premier Reynaud that France was left with no choice but to ask for an armistice.

To hear these sentiments from the men charged with protecting the Republic was excruciatingly painful to de Gaulle. He was in favour of defending the capital, no matter the risk, and he clung to the hope that the French army could yet be rallied to resist the German tide, either in a closely defended redoubt in Brittany, or, if necessary, from bases in French North Africa. How could the nation live with itself if it had not done everything possible to save its most sacred precincts from the enemy? Officers de Gaulle talked to, however, were not so certain. To a man, they appeared convinced that in the upper echelons of the High Command "the game was considered lost." The surrender of Paris, these exasperated men reasoned, might offer the only means of saving it.[6]

The idea of capitulation was repugnant to de Gaulle. When he joined the army as a nineteen-year-old officer cadet in 1909 — 119th out of 221 candidates who wrote exams to enter Saint-Cyr that year — he had been swept up in an enormous sense of the grandeur of France. To be a soldier "was one of the greatest things in the world," he would write in his *Mémoires de guerre.*[7] Living in Paris as a young man, nothing struck him more forcefully "than the symbols of our glories; night falling over Notre Dame, the majesty of evening at Versailles, the Arc de Triomphe in the sun, conquered colours shuddering in the vault of the Invalides." Now that everything that meant so much to him was under threat, he could conceive of no other course than to exert every ounce of strength in the defence of these precious symbols.

In the early months of 1940, the symbols of the Third Republic were being challenged from within as well as without. The year had barely begun when all 294 members of the Senate, in a rare act of unanimity, voted to strip the seventy-two Communist members of the Chamber of Deputies of their parliamentary immunity. Vice-premier Camille Chautemps called the decision "a link in the chain against terrorism." It was one of a series of actions expressing France's revulsion at the German-Soviet non-aggression pact signed in August 1939, an accord that left Hitler free to make war as he chose, knowing his eastern flank was secure. The premier of the day, Édouard Daladier — head of one of forty-two French governments to play out their cards in the 1930s — immediately banned *L'Humanité* and other Communist newspapers. The party itself was outlawed and hundreds of its members were interned. The moves were generally applauded. After the German-Soviet pact, French Communists had indicated their strong support for the Moscow line, becoming vocal critics of the war. Some were said to have carried out acts of sabotage. After several warplanes blew up mysteriously shortly after takeoff, the young Communist Roger Ramband was accused of tampering with seventeen of them. His puncturing of gas lines was said to have allowed fuel to drip onto red-hot exhaust pipes, causing explosions.

At the opposite end of the political pole stood forces of the right. Hating what they saw as the moral decadence of the Third Republic and preferring fascist dictatorship to either liberal democracy or dictatorship of the proletariat, they were equally opposed to vigorous prosecution of the war. They drew their strength from the wealthiest segments of France's *grande bourgeois* class made up of industrialists, property owners, bankers, senior civil servants, and the larger *patronats.* Their abhorrence of Communism was often accompanied by a generous mixture of anti-Semitism, long a powerful force in France, with a dash of Anglophobia thrown in.[8] One of the most vicious anti-Semites, Charles Maurras, warned in his *L'Action Française* that the French people must not allow themselves "to be slaughtered unsuspectingly and vainly at the will of forces that are English-speaking Jews, or at the will of their French slaves."

Adding to the increasingly bitter social atmosphere were the actions and teachings of the Catholic Church, resolutely anti-Communist and supportive of laws to entrench traditional family values, and from whom Premier Daladier was assured of approval for his edict imposing heavy penalties against abortion.

The political right of France never forgave the anti-fascist Popular Front government — a coalition of Communists, Socialists, and Radicals that ruled from 1936 to 1938 — for its encouragement of sit-down strikes, and its enactment of higher wages for workers, the forty-hour week, the raising of the school-leaving age from thirteen to fourteen, and the nationalization of the railways and munitions factories. Most of all, the rightists hated the Popular Front for supressing their fascist-flavoured leagues, notably La Cagoule (literally, The Hood), which had terrorized Paris with bombings, and Croix de Feu (Cross of Fire), a veterans' organization of three hundred thousand members.

Financial support for right-wing conspirators came from the chief German agent in Paris, Otto Abetz, who cloaked his activities as an art dealer, publishers' representative, and founder of the Comité France-Allemagne. A familiar figure in the salons of right-wing society, Abetz paid off French writers with lucrative German publishing contracts and saw to the wining and dining of politicians and businessmen on expense-paid trips to Germany. He funded the notoriously fascist Parisian daily *La Liberté*, the organ of Jacques Doriot, an ex-Communist who would win a German Iron Cross for his services on the Eastern Front. When the criticism of Abetz's activities could be no longer ignored, Premier Daladier ordered his expulsion. At the same time, the Communist Party chief Maurice Thorez, having spent his boyhood in the coal mines of the *Nord*, found his citizenship revoked even though he was French-born. Conscripted into the army, he deserted and fled to Moscow. It would not be the last France would see of either Thorez or Abetz.

In the face of the quarrelsome factions that beset France, it nonetheless still met the test for nationhood set down by historian Ernest Renan in 1882 when he wrote in *Qu'est-ce qu'une nation? (What is a Nation?)*:

> Now, the essence of a nation is that the people have many
> things in common, but have also forgotten much together.
> To have the glory of the past in common, a shared will
> in the present; to have done great deeds together, and
> want to do more of them, are the essential conditions
> for the constitution of a people.... One loves the house
> which one has built and passes on. We love the nation in
> proportion to the sacrifices to which we consented, the
> harms that we suffered.[9]

More than most Europeans, the French clung to their traditions and continued to feel the tug of the soil.[10] Many Parisians identified more closely with the small towns or rural lands of their parentage than the city where they now lived but in which they often felt "de-rooted." A people of conservative and Catholic heritage — although agnosticism had been growing since the final split between church and state in 1905 — the French loved soccer, cycling, and the cinema. Cautious, sometimes devious, not entirely trustful of strangers, most French threw a wall of fierce protection around their private lives. Their women still belonged in the home and possessed neither the vote nor the right to enter into business without permission of their husbands. The average Frenchman didn't much care for priests, wrote the literary critic Jules Lemaître, "but he is not intolerant; he lets his wife and children attend Mass." The perilous economy of the 1930s drove multitudes into abject poverty; economic statistics showed workers spending 60 percent of their income on food, compared to 10 percent on housing (well-off bourgeois families spent only a third as much of their income on food, but the same proportion, a tenth, on housing). Many felt oppressed by bureaucracy and regarded taxes and military service as something to be avoided. But in one sentiment the French were united: their visceral fear of war. [11]

William C. Bullitt, the United States ambassador to France, a one-time journalist and novelist, was determined to stay in Paris despite the flight of the French government. On June 5, fearful the British were holding back aid for France in order to set the stage for a peace accord with Hitler, Bullitt sent a coded telegram to President Roosevelt: "It will mean that the British intend to conserve their fleet and air force and their army, and either before a German attack on England or shortly afterwards, to install eight Fascists trained under Oswald Mosley and accept vassalage to Hitler."[12] The message revealed his colossal ignorance of European affairs.

A veteran actor on the diplomatic stage, Bullitt had been the first American ambassador to the Soviet Union. He was remembered in Moscow for getting a bear drunk at an embassy party. He continued his partying ways after his posting to Paris in 1936. An ardent Francophile with fluent command of the language, he kept a cellar of eighteen thousand bottles of wine. He also followed the antics of the Paris press, whose editors were as adept at game-playing as the politicians and army commanders.

In a telegram to the State Department on November 17, 1939, Bullitt called Washington's attention to how "the French press remains confused … by shouts and alarms pointing one day to the certain danger of attack against Holland and Belgium, another time to the raid that is to be made [by France] on Hungary and Romania." The day after the attack on the Low Countries, *Le Temps,* France's most prominent daily, read in embassies and newsrooms around the world, credited the German war machine with the power to "break the resistance of the Allies and all those which M. Hitler views as his enemies."[13] What Bullitt did not have to mention, because it was so well-known, was the widespread corruption of the French press. *Le Temps* at one time was receiving payoffs from the embassies of five different countries. French government departments routinely gave out cash-filled envelopes to correspondents on their beats. Government officials wrote many of *Le Temps's* editorials.

As de Gaulle struggled to cope with the chaos enveloping the War Ministry, he would have found it difficult to push all thoughts of family from his mind. His wife, Yvonne, was with their handicapped daughter, Anne, at La Boisserie, their country home in Colombey-les-Deux-Églises, 240 kilometres east of Paris. He believed that it was time for them to go, though; they should by now be packed and on their way to her sister's home near the Loire Valley town of Orléans. If only he could be sure she had received his letters, the ones in which he'd addressed her as his "darling little wife," and congratulated her on her fortieth birthday. There was no telephone at La Boisserie and it was hopeless to try to leave a message with the village postmaster, as he'd sometimes done before the war.

He missed his little angel, Anne, who was just twelve years old and suffered from Down's syndrome, a condition that left her with little ability to walk or speak. He loved to get down on the floor to play with her, and when he was stationed at Metz, 140 kilometres away, he often ordered a car to take him home in the evening so he could rock her to sleep in his arms.

Then there were the older children. De Gaulle had given instructions to his son Philippe, attending Collége Stanislas in Paris, to collect his sister Elisabeth from her school, Notre-Dame-de-Sion, and make for their aunt's residence, where they might meet up with their mother and Anne. But travel was uncertain in the chaos that had overtaken much of the country. He had to get money to them somehow.

Charles de Gaulle spent the morning of Monday, June 10, overseeing the amassing of War Ministry files, some to be packed for removal but most to be burned. Those he chose for safekeeping were among the 7,700 tons of archival materials that would be sent out of Paris on fourteen special trains. De Gaulle also found himself fending off a stream of visitors bearing rumours of imminent disaster, while telephones in his office "rang without cease."[14] The Italian ambassador arrived to tell the undersecretary for foreign affairs, Paul Baudouin, that at midnight his country would be at war with France. "Much good will come of it," the Italian promised. Filled with agony on "this day of anguish," de Gaulle must have thought the man sly and deceitful.[15]

He managed a light lunch at his desk and had a mid-afternoon meeting with Premier Reynaud. It took place one floor up from de Gaulle's ground-floor office, in the War Ministry office that Reynaud maintained by virtue of also holding the Defense portfolio. While the two worked on a statement in response to the Italian declaration of war, they found themselves confronted by General Weygand. He burst into the room, claiming he had been summoned.

"Not by me," Reynaud and de Gaulle insisted in turn.

"A mistake, then, but a useful one," Weygand answered, handing Reynaud a note. It urged that France sue for an armistice. The room took on, de Gaulle would remember, "a most heavy atmosphere."[16]

That evening, de Gaulle received a phone call advising him it was time to leave Paris. The smell of cordite from German guns, added to the fumes from burning papers, made the night air even more suffocating. De Gaulle and his aide-de-camp, Lieutenant Geoffroy de Courcel, got into a staff car for the short drive to the Hôtel Matignon, official residence of the premier, on rue de Varenne.[17] Only twenty-seven, de Courcel was descended from a once-noble family in Lorraine. Despite being nearsighted — his thick glasses bearing testimony to the state of his eyes — de Courcel had seen duty with a cavalry regiment in the French protectorate of Lebanon and was on leave in Paris when he was picked for de Gaulle's staff.

After a simple meal accompanied by wine and ample servings of coffee, the two accompanied Reynaud to a waiting limousine. Shortly before midnight, the black Citroën, carrying the French Tricolour on its hood but with its headlights off due to the blackout, cleared Port de Châtillon and edged out of the Paris suburbs. It was bound for the Loire Valley and the temporary safety of the Touraine, the old French province of châteaus and vineyards 140 kilometres to the southwest. The French government was in flight. Paris would be sure to fall within days.[18]

We can imagine that the drive to Orléans would have seemed barely endurable. The night was hot, the car was stuffy, and one roadblock after another held up the premier's car. De Gaulle struggled to stretch his long legs in the Citroën's uncomfortable confines, but Reynaud, the "littlest man" in French politics (1.6 metres — five feet, three inches) had no such problem. Both, however, were angered by the sight of a convoy of luxurious American automobiles that swept by. They were filled with members of the *corps diplomatique*, with armed militiamen on the running boards and motorcyclists at their sides.

Premier Reynaud tried to reassure his new undersecretary of defense that he would not permit the surrender of France. One of Reynaud's last acts before leaving Paris had been to cable a passionate appeal to President Roosevelt for all possible aid short of troops: "Today the enemy is almost at the gates of Paris. We shall fight in front of Paris; we shall fight behind Paris; we shall close ourselves in one of our provinces to fight and if we should be driven out of it we shall establish ourselves in North Africa to continue the fight and if necessary in our American possessions."

De Gaulle was skeptical of the premier's protestations; he knew that as well as dealing with the defeatism of the High Command, Reynaud had to put up with the equally troubling interference of his appeasement-minded mistress, Countess Hélène de Portes. She was following close behind in a second car, accompanied by her retainers. It was common knowledge that the countess, while floating about Parisian high society, had enjoyed expounding on her fondness for fascism. The daughter of a wealthy Marseille dock contractor and a widow, she was much younger than Reynaud — thirty to his sixty-two — and was short, plain, and not especially attractive. She and Reynaud had lived together since before his divorce and they planned to wed as soon as a change in the law, permitting marriage a year after divorce, came into effect. De Gaulle perhaps thought it just as well that now, amid the turmoil of war, the change might never come. He would have agreed with Ambassador Bullitt who had predicted a few days before to President Roosevelt: "In the end, she will be shot."[19]

Jarred by constant stopping and starting in the clogged traffic, the official party were unable to get much sleep. Tired and disheveled, they reached Orléans, where the Loire River makes its great bend on its way to the Atlantic, shortly after five o'clock. Steeped in French history, it was a place that had seen Roman, English, and Prussian soldiers storm its streets, and was the site of the great victory over the English in 1429, said to have been engineered by the never to be forgotten Jeanne d'Arc. The war had so far left Orléans almost entirely untouched. All up and down the Loire, handsome châteaus, occupied by "surviving aristocrats and other country gentlemen," offered panoramic views of the shallow river. Arrangements had been made for the government to take over many of them, from Briare in the east where General Weygand was to take up residence, to Tours in the west where the departments would set up their offices.

Driving in off the old Boulevard Chemin de Fer, Reynaud's car pulled up in front of the Préfecture on rue de Bourgogne, a one-time Benedictine monastery that now housed the area's civil administration. At the Orléans post office, a stack of three hundred coded telegrams awaited the premier's attention. Ignoring the official papers, Reynaud sent for the *préfet* while he and de Gaulle shared coffee and croissants. After, they went to separate offices to make telephone calls. De Gaulle's took only a few minutes, and when he moved to the room where Reynaud was on the phone, he heard the premier speaking with Weygand. De Gaulle was shocked to hear that, unknown to anyone in the government, the general had arranged for

THE DÉBACLE OF PARIS · 43

Winston Churchill to arrive later that day for an emergency conference.

"Are you really going to allow General Weygand to invite the British prime minister on his own authority?" de Gaulle exploded. "Don't you see the generalissimo is pursuing a policy that is not yours?" He was convinced Weygand was working behind the premier's back to extract Churchill's blessing for a French surrender.

"You are right," Reynaud answered. "This situation must cease." Perhaps it was time to replace Weygand. "What is your view?" Reynaud asked.

De Gaulle had a candidate in mind. "The only one I can see now is Huntziger," de Gaulle replied, referring to General Charles Huntziger, commander of the 2nd Army, whose retreating forces were encamped at the village of Arcis-sur-Aube, 150 kilometres east of Paris. "He is not ideal, but he is capable."

Reynaud agreed. At first Reynaud thought they should both go to see Huntziger, but he then decided it was more important for him to stay in the Loire and prepare for the meeting later that day with Winston Churchill. "I'll see you in Briare," he told de Gaulle.[20]

It was now approaching seven o'clock, and de Gaulle faced a long drive back to the north, a perilous trip in the face of an advancing enemy. All this could have been avoided, he might have reflected, if the High Command had accepted even the most basic principles of the strategy for mechanized warfare that he had preached in his lectures and books. "At least," as he would later declare, "we would have had a battle instead of a débacle."[21]

CHAPTER 2
A Rebel at Heart

Early in his life, Charles de Gaulle acquired the conviction that France would someday endure "gigantic trials" and that the purpose of his life would be to render his country "some signal service." As a fifteen-year-old schoolboy in 1905, he wrote an essay set twenty-five years in the future in which he cast himself as "General de Gaulle ... at the head of two hundred thousand men and 518 guns," securing victory over a divided German army.

Whether his self-assurance sprang from the conceit of a precocious personality or as the consequence of an alert boy's appraisal of his country's vulnerability, de Gaulle would never allow his belief in himself to falter. His upbringing as the third of five siblings of the fifth generation of a respected Parisian family, known for its religious fealty and its intellectual repute, gave him a healthy appreciation for his position in life. Another factor also played into his self-image: his name, de Gaulle — *of France*. Once he became aware of his distinguished name, he was caught up in patriotic tales of his family's part in France's glorious achievements and its disastrous setbacks. At an early age, Charles created a vision of himself as the unflinching defender of his imperiled homeland.[1]

For centuries, de Gaulles had figured in French history.[2] A Chevalier de Gaulle helped his countrymen defend the Normandy town of Vire against English invaders, and a Jean de Gaulle is cited in the Battle of Agincourt.[3] The de Gaulle family's roots lay hundreds of years deep in Normandy, where their achievements in the legal profession assured them a role among the *petite noblesse d'épée* — the sword-bearing nobility of the region. Yet there is some uncertainty as to the origins of the de Gaulle name. One source cites it as a Flemish name evolved from a form of De Walle, meaning "the wall." There is also an Irish connection: the McCartans, who were forced to flee their homeland after the defeat of their Catholic king, James II, at the Battle of the Boyne in 1690. These "wild geese" fled to the continent and de Gaulle's great-grandmother was Marie Angelique McCartan. The linkage intrigued de Gaulle. His grandmother Josephine de Gaulle wrote a biography of the Irish nationalist Daniel O'Connor, and his uncle and namesake, Charles de Gaulle, was the author of a history of the Celts, of whom the Gauls, occupying much of the landmass of what is modern France, were an important component. The book advocated a union of the Breton, Scots, Irish, and Welsh peoples. De Gaulle, after his resignation as president of France, would visit Ireland with his wife in 1969. While there, he hosted a reception for members of the MacCartan *sept* (the Gaelic term for a branch of a clan).

Charles de Gaulle's great-great-grandfather Jean Baptiste de Gaulle started the Parisian branch of the family around 1740 when he moved to the capital from Châlons-sur-Marne in the Champagne district, where his branch had settled. A lawyer in the family tradition, he soon became a high-ranking civil servant in the capital. His son Jean Baptiste Philippe survived the French Revolution, but not before being cast into jail during the Terror. Julien Philippe, scion of the next generation, was a geographer who took up his pen to write a *Histoire de Paris et ses Environs*, and a *Life of King Saint Louis.* His son Henri — Charles's father — armed with degrees in French literature and the law, became a teacher of philosophy and mathematics.

He also served in the French army in the disastrous Franco-Prussian war of 1870. The loss of France's two eastern provinces, Alsace and Lorraine, burned forever in Henri's conscience. He would have preferred to have stayed in the military, but his modest income as a teacher left him without the funds he would need to supplement an army stipend of a franc or two a day. His distress at the outcome of that conflict was passed on to his sons, and for Charles, the defeat was but one of several calamities that denied France the greatness to which it was rightly destined. As well, there were the seven wars that France had fought against England between 1689 and 1815, most with unsatisfactory results. From his mother, Charles absorbed more of the emotional pain of his country's bitter history. "My mother loved her country with an uncompromising passion equal to her piety.... Nothing ever moved me more than her story of France's past misfortunes."

Charles-André-Joseph-Marie de Gaulle was born on November 22, 1890, in the house of his maternal grandmother in Lille, a prosperous but gritty industrial centre in the *Nord* of France. Henri had married, at the age of thirty-eight, the delicate Jeanne Maillot, second cousin of his mother and daughter of a well-to-do tobacco importer. Charles was the second son in what would be a family of four boys and one girl — all of them tall, after their six-foot father. While the de Gaulles returned to Paris soon after Charles's birth, as a young man he would consider himself "a native of Lille living in Paris," an attitude entrenched by happy vacations spent at his grandmother's home.

His schooling was thoroughly Catholic — he first received tutelage from the Christian Brothers, then from the Jesuits of the Collège de l'Immaculée Conception; later, he studied at the Collège du Sacré-Couer in Belgium. His sojourn there came as the result of the decision in 1905 of the Third Republic, in a burst of anti-clericalism, to eject the Church from public education. After, it was back to Paris and the Collège Stanislas on rue Notre-Dame-des-Champs, where his father served as prefect of studies, to prepare for admission to Saint-Cyr, the École Speciale Militaire founded by Napoleon. Charles was a mediocre student during his early school years, outshone in grades by his brothers. Xavier, the eldest, and Jacques, the third son, would become engineers although Jacques would fall victim to sleeping sickness at the age of thirty and survive in and out of a coma for another twenty years. Pierre, the fourth son, would become a successful Paris politician. It was said that until Pierre's death in 1959, he was the only man to address de Gaulle as "Charles."

During de Gaulle's boyhood, Henri de Gaulle, perhaps looking to broaden the influences in his children's lives, made a fortuitous purchase: a beautiful fourteenth-century manor house in the Dordogne countryside, not far from Bordeaux, which he acquired for next to nothing. He called it La Ligerie, and the de Gaulle children spent happy summers there, tramping the grounds abundant with streams, meadows, and groves of walnut trees. Here, in a valley in the Périgord Vert, the de Gaulle children ran about with sailor hats on their heads that bore the names of French battleships. Charles insisted that he be the king when he and his brothers played with their tin soldiers.

In Jean Lacouture's magisterial three-volume French biography of Charles de Gaulle, the boy's "very attentive elder sister" Marie-Agnés describes Charles at this time as a "rather difficult child." She adds: "My father had a great deal of authority over him, but my mother, on the other hand, had none whatsoever. He never obeyed her at any time." She cites an instance of the seven-year-old being denied a pony ride because he had had one the day before. "'Then I'm going to be naughty,' [he protested]. And straight away he threw his toys on the ground, shouted, cried, stamped."

For all his childhood tantrums, de Gaulle seems never to have questioned the Catholic faith taught him by a devout mother and the instructors in the religious schools he attended. Attending mass, he would later remark, was his favourite diversion during his worldwide travels.

The de Gaulle family's life remained, however, focused on Paris. Henri enjoyed taking his children on excursions to the Arc de Triomphe or to see Napoleon's tomb at Les Invalides. Young Charles especially delighted in visits to scenes of his father's battles of 1870 in the nearby settlements of Le Bourget, or Stains.

The France in which Charles de Gaulle and his siblings grew up was one where economic wealth and political power was concentrated in the hands of a few hundred prominent bourgeois families. The bourgeoisie included the nation's largest bankers, industrialists, and property owners, often descendants of pre-revolutionary aristocracy. Many were stubbornly monarchist, and their innate conservatism led them to oppose the anti-clericalism of France's post-1870 governments. Except for the brief interregnum of the Popular Front (1936–38), the unwritten rules of the Third Republic dictated that the politicians could play their games as long as they did not challenge the privileges of the financial and industrial classes.

In later life, de Gaulle would despise these players. "I have never been bourgeois," he often said. "The bourgeoisie is wealth … my family and I have always been poor." It was not with the bourgeois that de Gaulle would ever make common cause: "You start out giving your hat, then you give your coat, then your shirt, then your skin and finally your soul."[4]

The bourgeosie were in support of the military only as long as this brought no undue taxes or any need to put their sons in uniform. Anti-Semitism was widespread in their ranks; most bitterly opposed the rehabilitation of Captain Alfred Dreyfus, the Jewish officer wrongly accused in 1894 of passing secrets to the Germans. Henri de Gaulle believed in Dreyfus's innocence, and doubtless passed this conviction on to Charles.

The bourgeoisie were equally adamant in their economic convictions. With much of their wealth rooted in the multitude of small manufacturing concerns scattered about the country, they resisted economic consolidation, preferring a fragmented economy of largely uncompetitive but independent businesses. Few family firms enjoyed more than a small share of each industry's output; even in the great textile industry, the five largest firms accounted for less than one-fifth of production. Education and family were their concern, not the state of the nation.[5]

Ambition was viewed with distaste; the cure was "a country life with long walks, hunting, light food, massage, warm baths, and varied but not tiring reading."[6] Like wealthy Americans of the early twentieth century who practised the conspicuous consumption condemned by economist Thorstein Veblen, the French *haute bourgeoisie* felt obliged to wear respectable dress in the performance of any commercial task, thereby proscribing all forms of physically demanding work. Custom forbade them to carry parcels (that was for women or servants), ride in third-class coaches, or dine in cheap restaurants. Before the First World War, the bourgeoisie, *haute* and *petite*, made up about a third of the French population of forty million, slightly more than the number still on the farm.* Campaigning for the presidency, de Gaulle would declare: "I have against me the bourgeois, the military and the diplomats, and for me, only the people who take the Metro."

✝

By his early teens, he had learned to channel his natural rebelliousness into a serious ambition for a military career. At fourteen, he set his heart on attending Saint-Cyr, the French military school southwest of Paris. It would be his first step toward becoming an officer. After a summer spent travelling about Germany, de Gaulle enrolled for a year of preparatory study at Collège Stanislas, and in 1909, he passed his examination for entry to the military school. He volunteered for a four-year enlistment in which he was required to spend the first year serving in the ranks. De Gaulle chose the 33rd Infantry Regiment based in Arras. He willingly accepted the discipline required of the military, but it was not long before this new boy (called a *"bazar"* at Saint-Cyr) was expressing contempt toward many of the institution's time-honoured procedures. He would tell a friend that he remembered "with little enthusiasm" his makeshift instructors. The main thing he had learned was that if he were to take "measures directly opposed to those he had been the victim of, reasonably satisfactory results might be counted upon." His strong sense of irony was already showing itself. Nevertheless, de Gaulle was promoted to corporal, not without his commanding officer, Captain de Tugny, suggesting the young cadet would never be satisfied short of the rank of constable — the title borne by the commander of the French army under the monarchy.

In October 1910, de Gaulle was admitted to Saint-Cyr as an officer-cadet. He seems not to have made any close friends during two years there, although he took part in the usual extra-curricular activities of staging plays (in one of which he was costumed as a village bridegroom) and

---

* By 1950, only 7.9 percent of the French, according to a poll, described themselves as bourgeois.

writing short stories and poems. His large nose and his height attracted attention — leading to such nicknames as "the great asparagus" and "turkey-cock" — as did his loud snoring at night. It is said no fellow cadet ever saw him entirely naked.[7]

His superiors provided him with favourable reports, his captain terming his conduct "faultless," his major declaring him "a thorough soldier, much attached to the service, very conscientious, calm and forceful in command." The officer commanding the school praised his "continual progress" and predicted: "Cannot fail to make an excellent officer."[8] On October 1, 1912, aged twenty-two, de Gaulle graduated thirteenth in his class of 211, and assumed the uniform of a second lieutenant. Meticulous in his personal appearance, he would never while in the army be seen in anything but the most crisply ironed uniform, complete with kepi, white gloves, and polished boots.

De Gaulle had his choice of regiments. Eschewing the more prestigious cavalry corps, he chose to return to the 33rd Infantry Regiment, possibly a reflection of his commitment to the *Nord* of his birth and upbringing. Another reason has been advanced for his choice: the commander of the regiment was Colonel Philippe Pétain, whose reputation for arrogance and his intellectual capacities was well-known — qualities de Gaulle would probably have found quite admirable. The young lieutenant sent in the expected letter announcing his call "to the honour of serving under your orders."[9] It is said that when de Gaulle went to Pétain's office he found him at the door, only to hear him announce, "The colonel is not receiving."

But Pétain took close note of the young officer, especially when he challenged the verities of military lore handed down from the past. When Pétain gave a lecture in which he asserted that the loser in the Siege of Arras had actually proven superior to the victor in his choice of tactics, de Gaulle challenged him. "But colonel, no!" he cried. "Surely the proof of tactical skill is in the eventual result."

Rather than put down his young officer, Pétain replied, "You have obviously studied the siege very thoroughly. I applaud your diligence. We must talk over the lessons of this battle again sometime."

Another time, Pétain ordered de Gaulle confined to barracks after the soldiers in his unit had broken formation during inspection. When Pétain lifted the penalty at the weekend, de Gaulle rushed to the railway station to catch a train for Paris. Stepping into a coach, he encountered Pétain. After the colonel expressed surprise at seeing him, de Gaulle replied, "The penalty was unjust, so I was sure you would lift it."

We can take it that the young lieutenant's audacity must have appealed to Pétain. Now fifty-six, Colonel Pétain was nearing retirement and felt frustrated by the insistence of army leadership on conventional thinking. Pétain believed artillery attacks the key to both offense and defence. "Let us first crush the enemy by artillery fire, and afterward we shall win our victory," he told his officers.

De Gaulle took a decidedly more assertive approach. "One must have the offensive spirit," he told conscript troops in a 1913 lecture. "One must in all places and at all times have one single idea, that of advancing." To this, he added, almost *en passant*, a prescient warning: "And who can tell whether this very year may not be decisive for the country's future? I do not have to tell you that the situation abroad looks more threatening than ever. Let us reflect that tomorrow's victory may depend on each one of us."

Colonel Pétain left Arras at the end of 1913 to take up command of a brigade. The long careers of both men would intersect at important junctures in their lives, but de Gaulle would provide a final judgment of the elder man's military capacity in his *Mémoires de guerre:* "My first colonel, Pétain, showed me the real value of the gift and the art of commanding."

It is possible Pétain also showed the young lieutenant some techniques in attracting female attention. A notorious womanizer, Pétain had demonstrated his sense of comradeship with de Gaulle by taking him on long walks, and he may have found de Gaulle's youthfulness a magnet for young women he himself wished to approach. In his biography of de Gaulle, Jean Lacouture has François Mauriac, the French author and Nobel Prize winner, suggesting the two men may have collaborated in their romantic pursuits. "De Gaulle's women?" Mauriac answered, "The same as Pétain's."

It may be more than coincidence that while recovering from wounds sustained early in the First World War, de Gaulle wrote a short story about a lieutenant who was the lover of his captain's wife. The captain, after entrusting the lieutenant with his pocketbook that he was to turn over to his wife in the event of his death, is killed in battle. The lieutenant is wounded and when the wife visits him in the hospital where he is recovering, he hands her the pocketbook, grasps her hands, and kisses them "with the tenderness of a farewell."

The "war to end all wars" came to France on August 3, 1914, barely more than a month after the heir to the throne of the Austro-Hungarian Empire, Archduke Franz Ferdinand, had been assassinated along with his wife in Sarajevo, Bosnia. The killing gave the empire an excuse to attack neighbouring Serbia, the homeland of the assassin, and through a complicated tangle of alliances nearly every country in Europe was soon in the conflict. When Germany declared war on France, Lieutenant de Gaulle wrote in his notebook: "Goodbye, my rooms, my books, my familiar objects."

The 33rd Infantry Regiment, with de Gaulle in command of the 11th Company, was on its way to Belgium. Two weeks later, on the outskirts of the Belgian town of Dinant, de Gaulle led his company in a bayonet charge aimed at stopping German soldiers from crossing a bridge on the Meuse River. "I raced forward, knowing that our only chance of success was acting very fast," he later wrote of the incident. As he dashed through a final gap, "something struck my knee like a whip-lash." He fell with his sergeant, who had been killed outright, on top of him. De Gaulle dragged himself to the bridge. "There was an appalling hail of bullets all around me. I could hear the muffled sound of them hitting the dead and wounded scattered over the ground."

De Gaulle was taken by cart to a house in the town and later moved to Paris, where he was operated on at St. Joseph Hospital. He would have heard by then how the first German offensive of the war had come perilously close to capturing Paris. German troops advanced to within fifty kilometres of the capital before being turned back, in some cases by troops carried to the front in taxis. The government, as it would do in the Second World War, had fled to Bordeaux.

After convalescence in Lyon, de Gaulle asked to return to his old regiment, and he caught up with it in Champagne in October. He spent a dismal Christmas "in the middle of very violent shelling." He ordered his men to make their trenches deeper, but they had to stop digging when they encountered bodies of their comrades buried in the muck. Early in 1915 de Gaulle received the *Croix de Guerre* for bravery and was promoted to the rank of captain (temporary). His new duties required him to stay forty metres from the front trenches, but the rule did not stop a shell splinter from piercing his left hand. Infected, it kept him out of action until June. As the war dragged through that year and losses mounted into the millions of men, de Gaulle became ever more exasperated with France's political leadership. He wrote to his mother, sounding more like a revolutionary than a faithful son:

> Parliament grows more and more odious and stupid. The ministers have literally all their time taken up by the sittings of the chamber, the reading of petitions or the most absurd injunctions uttered by any odd tradesman that politics has made a deputy. Even if they wanted to, they absolutely could not find the time to run their departments. We shall be the conquerors as soon as we have swept this riff-raff out of the way, and there is not a Frenchman who will not shout for joy, especially the soldiers…. I shall be very much surprised if this regime shall out-live the war.[10]

At daybreak on February 26, 1916, the 33rd Infantry Regiment entered Verdun, early in what was to become one of the greatest battles of the First World War. Leading the 10th Company on a reconnaissance mission, de Gaulle manoeuvred his men to within a few metres of the fort of Douaumont that the Germans had just occupied. Returning unscathed, he reported that enemy troops were setting up machine guns and artillery for a fresh attack. It came on the afternoon of March 2, after hours of heavy shelling. There was nothing to do but charge into the oncoming waves of German troops. Outnumbered, de Gaulle's company was soon surrounded. With ammunition exhausted, rifle butts and bayonets became the weapons of choice. De Gaulle was struck in the thigh by a bayonet and fell to the ground, unconscious. French commanders assumed he had been killed. General Pétain endorsed a recommendation that he receive the Légion d'Honneur. He wrote that de Gaulle had "led his men in a furious charge and a fierce hand-to-hand engagement, the only solution he thought compatible with military honour. Fell in the fighting. An incomparable officer in all respects."

De Gaulle of course had survived, taken prisoner by soldiers of the Prussian Guard. He was operated on by two captured French doctors, and sent to a recovery camp in Osnabrück, Germany. His capture probably saved his life. An officer as impulsive, reckless — and dedicated — as de Gaulle was very likely to get himself killed. De Gaulle wrote of the ordeal before Douaumont during his time as a prisoner. "I had hardly gone ten metres when I came on a group of Boches crouching in a shellhole. They saw me at the same moment, and one of them ran his bayonet into me. The thrust went through my mapcase and wounded me in the thigh. Another Boche shot my orderly dead. Seconds later a grenade exploded in front of my face and I lost consciousness."[11]

De Gaulle spent thirty-two months as a prisoner of war, failing in five attempts to escape, and was freed only after the Armistice of November 11, 1918. He had worked on his German, read Greek and Roman history, and given a series of lectures that he would use in his 1924 book, *La Discorde chez l'Ennemi (Discord Among the Enemy)*. A month after the Armistice, de Gaulle was relaxing at La Ligerie, the family retreat in the Périgord. His mother and father marvelled at the fact all four of their sons — captains Charles and Xavier, lieutenant Jacques, and officer-cadet Pierre — had played the game, served their country, and returned safely to the family hearth.

The end of the war brought a new impetus to Charles de Gaulle's military career. Sent on a refresher course for ex-prisoners at Saint-Maixent in western France, a village he described as a "dump," he itched to return to duty. His opportunity came with a call from the War Ministry for volunteers to serve the newly restored government of Poland, now independent after having been divided among its conquering neighbours for over a century. De Gaulle was seconded to the Chasseurs Polonais with the rank of major, and sent to Warsaw, the Polish capital.

France's wartime army chief of staff, General Maxime Weygand, was in charge of the Allied mission sent to help Poland resist threats to its sovereignty. Historically an ally of Poland — the latter's aristocracy admired all things French and spoke the language with fluency — France welcomed the opportunity to help the Poles train a modern army. In the turmoil of postwar Europe, with new boundaries not yet fully accepted by the divided nations, de Gaulle watched the new Polish government, carried off by a dream of territorial expansion, send its army into the Ukraine in an attack that succeeded in capturing the capital, Kiev.

By a quirk of history, the Russian defence was led by Mikhail Tukhachevsky, a cavalry officer in the new Red Army who de Gaulle had gotten to know when they were in the same prisoner-of-war camp in Germany. Rallying his force, Tukhachevsky — with Josef Stalin at his side as his political commissar — pushed the Poles back to the Vistula River, on the outskirts of Warsaw. On August 5, 1920, de Gaulle noted in his journal, "noble Warsaw quite silent; the city felt the Russians at its gates." A Communist frontal attack might have succeeded, but Tukhachevsky divided his forces in an attempt to encircle the capital. The Poles, in a burst of patriotic zeal, fought off the Russians, and de Gaulle, a participant in the victory, watched the Red Army as it "broke and fled in every direction." An armistice was signed in October and Poland was assured, if only temporarily, of the sanctity of its borders.*

In the weeks between the relief of Warsaw in August and de Gaulle's going on leave to Paris in October, he enjoyed the pleasures of being a respected officer in a city that revered the French. His duties on the personal staff of General Henri Niessel, head of the French military mission, were light. He lived in a comfortable apartment on Nowy-Swiat, a fashionable thoroughfare, enjoyed pastries at the Blikie Café, and was seen often at society soirées. One companion among many was Countess Czetwertynska, a beauteous aristocrat "as tiny as de Gaulle was large."[12]

De Gaulle's bachelorhood was not to last long, however. While on leave in Paris he met a proper young lady, Yvonne Vendroux, the daughter

---

*Stalin and Tukhachevsky blamed each other for the failure in Poland. Although Tukhachevsky became head of the Red Army, he was executed on Stalin's orders in the 1937 purge of the Russian military.

of a well-off Calais bourgeosie. He owned a biscuit factory, had a palatial home in the Channel coast city, and rented an apartment in Paris. It was said that every Parisian family needed an infusion of provincial money at sometime or other, and perhaps that is what the de Gaulles received as a result of this romance.

Introduced at a party organized by friends of de Gaulle's parents, the pair took to each other immediately. Their courtship was rapid, but was conducted in a carefully correct way. A few days after the party, de Gaulle sent a joint invitation to Yvonne and her brother Jacques to join him at a Saint-Cyr ball in the Hôtel des Réservoirs in Versailles. Later, de Gaulle was invited to the Vendroux home in Calais, but it would not do for him to stay under the same roof as Yvonne. He had to take a room at a local hotel.

With his leave about to run out, de Gaulle proposed marriage. Their engagement was announced on the second anniversary of the Armistice, November 11, 1920. He returned briefly to Warsaw, but at the end of January was back in Paris as an assistant professor of history at Saint-Cyr Military Academy. Charles and Yvonne were married in a civil ceremony on April 6, 1921. De Gaulle's left hand had been so badly injured in the war that Yvonne had to place his wedding ring on the third finger of his right hand. The more meaningful ceremony for both families was conducted according to Catholic rites the following day in the church of Notre-Dame-de-Calais.

The newlyweds set up house in a three-room flat on boulevard de Grenelle in Paris, and on December 28, 1921, Yvonne was delivered of a baby boy, christened Philippe. Did de Gaulle name his first-born after his old comrade and commander Philippe Pétain, now a marshall of France? Possibly, but it is more likely that the name, a familiar one in the family trees of both de Gaulle and Yvonne, honoured some relative.

At Saint-Cyr, Captain de Gaulle (returned now to his normal rank) made an impressive appearance with his immaculate uniform, black boots, white gloves, and sword at his side. At the dozen or so lectures he delivered, he would unbuckle his sword, place it on his desk beside his kepi, and, still wearing his gloves, begin to speak. His dramatic flourishes came easily, foreshadowing the strength of speech that would distinguish his public appearances in later life.

In 1922, de Gaulle was admitted to the prestigious École Supérieure de la Guerre on the Champs de Mars on the Left Bank. It was an institution rife with conventional wisdom, which in the 1920s held that France, having recovered its lost territories in the east, had no military need other than to provide for its defence. De Gaulle argued often with the professors. Colonel Moyrand, professor of tactics, wrote that de Gaulle was "intelligent, cultured and serious-minded," qualities that were put at risk by "his excessive self-confidence, his severity toward the opinions of others and his attitude of a king in exile."[13] The publication of his book *La Discorde chez l'Ennemi*, at a time when he was still a relatively junior officer, did not endear him to his colleagues.

Passing out of the École Supérieure de la Guerre with less-than-distinguished marks, de Gaulle was assigned to the French Army of Occupation at Mainz in the German Rhineland. He was infuriated by the poor rating he had been given — a simple "good," the lowest passing grade — and bellowed in rage: "I will come back to this dirty hole only when I am commandant of it."

His rescue came when Marshall Pétain, his own dream of becoming commander-in-chief of the French army as yet unfilled, brought him back to Paris to work at the Counseil Supérieur de la Guerre where Pétain was vice-president. He also asked de Gaulle to help him write a historical portrait of the French soldier: *Le Soldat*. "It is agreed, is it not," Pétain wrote to de Gaulle, "that you do not tell anyone of this work, which is to remain between ourselves alone."

Along with de Gaulle's "ghosting" of the first chapters of the book, he was tasked by Pétain to give a series of three lectures to the staff and student body of the École. The marshall stood beside de Gaulle to introduce him in the great amphitheatre that served as the professor's room. "I ask you to listen attentively to the ideas that Captain de Gaulle is going to speak to you about!" By demonstrating his confidence in de Gaulle, Pétain was kicking back at the school's professors for the poor grading they had given his protegé. The lectures were forceful and incisive and most of those present had to admit they contained both wisdom and fact. His listeners could relate strongly to his more daring pronouncements.

"Our days are not very favourable for the education of military leaders," de Gaulle declared. "In times of peace, mechanically formed minds triumph over those that possess feeling and outstanding gifts. The recruitment of really able leaders becomes difficult when peace lasts a long time."[14]

The collaboration between de Gaulle and the marshall was not to last much longer. Troubled with his lowly role of ghostwriter, de Gaulle wrote to Pétain from Germany, where he was filling out a short-term assignment, to ask that his part in preparing *Le Soldat* be acknowledged in a preface. De Gaulle had touched a nerve: vanity, indifference, jealousy — all showed up in the marshall's future attitude toward him. Despite sending de Gaulle a placatory response, the partnership was at an end. Pétain put *Le Soldat* into a bottom drawer, never to retrieve it. Yet when de Gaulle published his second book, *Le Fil de l'Épée (The Edge of the Sword)* in 1932, he had a first copy printed on special paper and sent to Pétain with the handwritten inscription: "Homage from C. de Gaulle in deepest respect and devotion."*

De Gaulle's family life, enlivened by the birth of daughter Elisabeth in 1924, took on a sombre tone with the arrival of Anne on New Year's Day, 1928. De Gaulle was in command of the 19th Battalion at Triers, Germany, at last a full major, and had settled his family in a pleasant villa on the banks of the Moselle River. De Gaulle and his wife recognized from the beginning that Anne was not normal, and the diagnosis of Down's syndrome (its victims were then referred to as "mongoloids,") was accepted with a stoic determination to love her all the more.

That winter, influenza swept through the garrison, causing more than thirty deaths. An official inquiry absolved de Gaulle of any blame and when the occupation army was disbanded, de Gaulle requested a tour of duty in the French colony of Lebanon. Before leaving, he wrote a prophetic letter to an old friend, Colonel Lucien Nachin, that accurately fore-

---

* Pétain is said to have had the book with him when he died, at ninety-five, a prisoner on the Ile d'Yeu in 1951.

told the coming crisis in Europe. First would come the *Anschluss* (union) of Germany and Austria and then Germany's recovery "by fair means or foul, of what was taken from her for the benefit of Poland." After that, de Gaulle added, "we shall be asked to return Alsace. To me this seems written in the heavens."

In Lebanon, de Gaulle settled his family in the Druze district of Beirut, the capital, and took up duties with the General Staff in charge of the military administration of Lebanon and Syria. His tour of duty in this exotic locale passed without significant upset and in November 1931 de Gaulle was back in Paris, where he was taken on the staff of the secretariat of the Conseil de la Défense Nationale, nerve centre of the French army.

The next year stood out for two events: the death of de Gaulle's father, Henri, at the age of eighty-three, and de Gaulle's promotion to lieutenant-colonel. By now, with the children in school, Mme de Gaulle set about running a typical French household at 101 boulevard Raspail. One Saturday every month the de Gaulles were hosts to a small dinner party — "black tie," the invitations read. Biographer Jean Lacouture deftly assessed the milieu in which the de Gaulle family found itself:

> Strict hierarchy, the use of *vous* to one's parents, a nineteenth-century attitude towards marriage, extreme reticence about money, prudishness about morals, and a stubborn bigotry with regard to anything that concerned the rites: the de Gaulles seemed to have emerged from a novel by their grandmother Josephine Maillot. But if one can discover one field in this gently anachronistic society that brings them closer to the ordinary run of mortals, one may mention the cooking. Charles was not the only one of the de Gaulles to like the "vulgar dishes" — ragouts, offal, sauces and stews — which bought them back to the level of the populace.

Despite his contempt for bourgeois ways — as demonstrated by his preference for everyday cooking — de Gaulle aspired to that most bourgeois of ambitions: a second home. Having spent some of his best boyhood days in the country, he became interested in securing a calm summer residence for his family, especially in view of Anne's need for constant care. She had been treated with ultra-violet rays, to no effect.

The search for a quiet sanctuary led de Gaulle east, to the village of Colombey-les-Deux-Églises in the Haute-Marne department, on the high terraces above the Champagne vineyards. Its four hundred inhabitants were typical of French country people: quiet, unassuming, not entirely trustful of strangers. The village had inherited its name from two churches erected in the eleventh century, but only one now remained. In 1936 de Gaulle heard of an old estate that might be for sale. It was called La Brasserie, for the hops once grown on its grounds. De Gaulle approached the widow who lived there, Mme Bombal, who asked 50,000 francs (about $3,500), more than he could afford. A deal was struck: he would pay 28,000 francs down and an annuity of 2,000 francs a year as long as she lived. Two years later Mme Bombal died — drowned in her bath — and the old manor house was his. It was a noble but dour and drafty two-storey building, still reliant on oil lamps and lacking indoor plumbing. But it was surrounded by beautiful grounds and woods and de Gaulle fell in love with it the first time he saw it. Before long, he thought up a new name for it: *La Boisserie,* the wooded glade.[15] As with many things in de Gaulle's life, his choice of Colombey was prescient. In October 1937 he was given command of the 507th Tank Regiment in Metz, in eastern France. The posting put La Boisserie at the convenient halfway point between Paris and his new base.

All around de Gaulle, the tragedies of 1930s Europe were unfolding: the Great Depression, Hitler's accession to power in 1933, riots in Paris in 1934, Mussolini's attack on Abyssinia, the Spanish Civil War. France had just begun to recover from the terrible losses of the First World War — a death toll of 1.5 million men had left France without young workers and a generation of women without husbands — when the Depression sucked up what little remained of French financial fortitude. Promised war reparations from Germany never materialized. Successive governments refused to devalue the overpriced franc, crippling exports. As in other countries, falling government revenues led to slashes in public spending, causing further despair.

In their economic privation, the French people turned inward, content to accept the pronouncements of their leaders that the country was safe behind its great new defensive wall on the Rhine, the Maginot Line. When Premier Daladier returned from the Munich conference he told confidantes he expected to be shot. Instead, he was hailed as a hero. "Damn fools," he grumbled.

His warm reception should have been no surprise. A letter from Nobel Prize winner Roger Martin du Gard to a friend in September 1936 summed up the attitude of many of the French: "Anything rather than war. Anything ... even Fascism in France: Nothing, no trial, no servitude can be compared to war ... Anything, Hitler rather than war!"

Such thinking was beyond the pale for de Gaulle; he was convinced France must be capable of carrying war to the enemy if it was to defend itself. Most of his career in the military was spent challenging authority. He was not impressed with the lectures he'd heard at Saint-Cyr or at the École de Guerre, where the idea of the "fixed and continuous front" dictated strategies based not on attack, but on holding off the enemy. He had made his views clear that France must adapt to the new technological age of warfare. His third book, *Vers l'Armée de Metier (The Army of the Future)*, was a thin volume of forty-five thousand words and sold only 750 copies, but it served as the launch pad for his plan and his ideas when it was published in 1934. It leaned heavily on what de Gaulle had already written for Pétain's *Le Soldat*. Wrapped within a call for a professional army of one hundred thousand men, de Gaulle argued that France's geography doomed it to be invaded and that it could be saved only by mechanized tank and artillery divisions in the hands of experts. "No French protection is possible without a professional army," declared de Gaulle, arguing for a kind of organizational innovation generations before that concept would become embedded in modern business management. He foresaw soldiers as masters of technology who could "leap in one bound from peace into war," supported by air squadrons "capable of operating at a distance, endowed with astonishing speed, manoeuvring in the three dimensions and striking vertical blows."

The book was so critical of the prevailing static theories of war that General Gamelin responded by taking de Gaulle's name off the army's promotion list. It took the personal intervention of Paul Reynaud, then a senior cabinet minister, to secure his appointment as colonel. "I do not believe in Colonel de Gaulle's theories," Gamelin said. "They are unsound and unrealistic."

Marshall Pétain now thought de Gaulle "an arrogant man, an ingrate and surly."

"More a journalist than an officer," Weygand fumed. "His opinion of himself is blinding."

But de Gaulle managed to cultivate a supportive circle of military figures, journalists, and politicians — a considerable achievement for a man so reviled by his superiors. While the popular press largely ignored him, the conservative daily *l'Echo de Paris* took up de Gaulle's call with articles urging modernization of the army. He also found a welcome in the pages of smaller but influential papers such as *L'Ordre* and the *Journal des Débats*.

It was shortly after the release of *Vers l'armée de métier* that one of de Gaulle's contacts introduced him to Paul Reynaud. Reynaud was filled with questions for this tall, ramrod-straight, superbly self-assured man. His view of de Gaulle that emerged from this first meeting was considerably more favourable than that held by senior army officials. Reynaud would write in his memoirs of how he had found a man "imbued with an irresistibly evident truth." From his desk in the Chamber of Deputies, Reynaud argued for acceptance of de Gaulle's military theories. Within a year of their first meeting, he intervened in a conscription debate to propose the creation of an armoured corps of six divisions. Credit for the idea belonged, he said, to de Gaulle. After six months of recriminations, the amendment was rejected. The very idea went against all French principles, wrote a three-star general in a Paris newspaper: "France, peaceful and defensive, could only be 'anti-mechanized.'"

The game plans of Europe's leaders went into the waste bin on August 23, 1939, with the signing in Moscow, by Soviet foreign minister Vyacheslav Molotov and German foreign minister Joachim von Ribbentrop, of the Soviet-Nazi non-aggression treaty. Britain and France renewed their commitments to defend Poland. Two days later, Hitler called in the

French ambassador, Robert Coulondre, to tell him, "I have no hostility toward France. I shall not attack France, but if she starts a conflict, I shall go to the very end." As he spoke, the German army was massing on the Polish border. On September 1, the Führer sent his troops across the frontier and the Second World War was underway.

Simone de Beauvoir, not yet the doyenne of French writing she would someday become, heard of the German invasion from a waiter at her favourite café, the Dome on Boulevard Montparnasse. When Jean-Paul Sarte was called up a few days later, she spent her last hours with him at an outdoor table of the Café de Flore, bathed in the light of a full moon. Emergencies always found them, it seemed, at the favourite Left Bank hangouts of the city's artists and intellectuals.

Charles de Gaulle the rebel stood ready to do his duty. But he must have wondered, against the ominously looming autumn of 1939, how much comfort a nation could take in an army that still had not reconciled itself to the reality of mechanized warfare and was spending four times as much on fodder for its horses as on fuel for its armoured vehicles.[16]

CHAPTER 3
Into the Abyss

With vacations but a memory, shoppers filled the streets of Paris as September 1939 began, readying themselves for a new season of work and school. Premier Daladier called the nation's politicians back to the National Assembly, and on Saturday, September 2, the Chamber of Deputies and the Senate voted to spend 70 billion francs on war preparations. "Our duty is to finish with aggression and violence," Daladier asserted. But he insisted the vote was not a declaration of war, promising he would "come back" to the Assemby if this became necessary.* On the same day, de Gaulle was appointed to command of the tank regiments of the 5th Army — five battalions scattered behind the Maginot Line. Across the Channel, a worried British Parliament also was sitting. Nervous exchanges passed between the two foreign offices; London feared the French would drag their heels in following through with the consequences of their ultimatum to Berlin:

---

* Daladier's failure to do so furnished ammunition for Pierre Laval and others to claim that going to war without a specific vote of the National Assembly violated the constitution of the Third Republic.

Unless the German government are prepared to give the French government satisfactory assurances that the German government have suspended all aggressive action against Poland and are prepared to withdraw their forces from Polish territory, the French government will without hesitation fulfill their obligation to Poland.

On Sunday, with Adolf Hitler refusing to pull back the squadrons he had thrown into Poland, time ran out. The British ultimatum expired at 11 a.m. and the French one at 5 p.m. Premier Daladier signed the declaration of war on Germany a few hours after Prime Minister Neville Chamberlain, speaking for Great Britain, had sadly told the world "this country is at war with Germany." Britain and France had kept their promise to Poland to defend it from any enemy.

Neither country did much to immediately confront the German aggression; the French army made a feeble foray into the Saar before withdrawing, while British officials argued against air attacks on German cities lest the Luftwaffe retaliate in kind. General Gamelin, surveying the French forces at his command, gave himself to bizarre comments that led German war planners to conclude France had no real game plan to follow through on its threats. At first, he said the best service France could render Poland would be to mass its army on the German frontier, thereby forcing Hitler to keep divisions on the Rhine that could not be used against the Poles. To Pierre-Étienne Flandin, the one-time foreign minister who opposed the war and supported Marshall Pétain, Gamelin proposed to play a different card. "The Poles will hold out at least six months and we will come to their aid by way of Romania."[1] How French troops would get to that Black Sea country — unless via the Mediterranean and through the Dardanelles — was not explained.

Watching the drama unfold from his post with the 5th Army, Colonel de Gaulle struggled to build a tank force with the strength to launch offensive action. France did not have a single armoured division and de Gaulle's orders required him to disperse his tanks among various infantry divisions rather than, as he wished, assemble them together. On September 12, he led one battalion on a small raid on a German frontier post opposite the Maginot Line. President Lebrun told him on a visit, "I am acquainted with your ideas, but it does seem too late for the enemy to apply them."[2] In frustration, de Gaulle wrote his first wartime letter to Paul Reynaud, still minister of finance. "When the enemy thinks we are weary, confused and dissatisfied," de Gaulle wrote, he "will take the offensive against us."[3] Years later, he would observe in his *Mémoires de guerre* that it was "without astonishment" that he watched the French army "settle down into stagnation."[4]

Polish defences crumbled even before the Soviet Union, shielded by the non-aggression pact Josef Stalin had entered into with Hitler, joined the attack on September 17. Within five weeks, Poland had become a mere vassal state of the German Reich after being swallowed up by its two historic adversaries. The Daladier government did nothing to assist Poland, but it moved speedily to wage war on another front — against its domestic Communists. Decrees against the Communist Party, resulting in the arrest without charges of both deputies and party members, were yet another violation of the French constitution, crafted as the politicians connived to advance their own positions, rather than that of their country.

The French public, mindful of the immense losses of the First World War, resented the mobilization of men who might suffer similar slaughter. In this, public opinion was largely at one with the High Command. France had lost 1.5 million men between 1914 and 1918, with more than four million injured. Even the most intractable devotees of classical warfare were unwilling to throw another generation of men into the death traps their fathers had endured. It was partly this revulsion against the repetition of needless deaths that induced French commanders to put their faith in a policy of static defence, one symbolized by the fixed fortifications of the Maginot Line.

What the British called the phony war and the French termed the *drôle de guerre* dragged through the winter of 1939–40, immersing France in a cocoon of complacency. *"NOËL! NOËL!"* ran a headline on the front page of the popular daily *Le Petit Parisien* on Christmas Eve. *"PARIS optimiste et de bonne humeur."*[5] Colonel de Gaulle took leave from his command in Alsace to join Yvonne and Anne in Colombey-les-Deux-Églises. Philippe and Elizabeth came down from school in Paris. Yvonne cooked a Christmas Eve dinner and Charles poured hot water on their backyard birdbath to melt the ice. After, the family tramped a kilometre along a snowy road to attend midnight mass at the village church, Notre Dame de l'Assomption (Our Lady of Assumption).[6] During these few days of quiet respite, de Gaulle had time to ponder the direction of the war while reflecting on his own future.

Early in the New Year, de Gaulle received an invitation to a dinner in Paris. It came from his loyal supporter, Paul Reynaud, inviting him to Reynaud's flat in the rue de Rivoli. Their friendship had strengthened despite the failure of the politician to gain government backing for de Gaulle's military ideas. Léon Blum, premier during the Popular Front's time in government, was there that evening and he remembered de Gaulle's remarks as they walked back to the quai de Bourbon:

> I am playing my part in a horrible deception. The few dozen light tanks attached to my command are no more than trifles. I am afraid that the lesson of Poland, clear though it is, has been rejected as so much prejudice. Believe me, on our side everything is yet to be done. If we do not act in time we shall lose this war most wretchedly.[7]

The problems facing France, de Gaulle believed, lay more with the country's political leadership than with its military chiefs. The politicians might be good men individually, he would later write, "but the political game consumed them and paralyzed them."[8]

Fate also played tricks at the most inopportune times. In January, Premier Daladier, riding a horse in the forest of Rambouillet, traditional country home of French leaders, fell and broke his ankle. The pain he suffered from the mechanical therapy imposed by his doctors forced thoughts of the war from his mind.

In the same month, de Gaulle finished work on the latest of his carefully prepared critiques of France's military strategy. He titled it *L'avénement de la force mécanique (The Advent of Mechanized Forces)* and sent off copies, printed on a mimeograph machine, to Daladier and eighty members of the government and the High Command. It was yet another call for France to recognize the consequences of the revolution in military technology. Only if it did so would it be ready to deal with "breakthroughs and pursuits the scale of which will infinitely exceed those of the most lightning events of the past." De Gaulle's warning, as usual, went unheeded. "My memorandum produced no shock," he would remember.[9]

When the Soviet Union attacked neighbouring Finland in the "winter war" of 1939–40, a wave of sympathy built up in France and Britain for the courageous little nation fighting a Communist behemoth. Plans were hatched at a Paris meeting of the British-French Supreme War Council to bomb Russian oil fields and to send thirty thousand "volunteers" to Finland. It was too late. Finland capitulated in March. The flailing of the Daladier government finally exhausted the patience of the National Assembly. On March 21, Daladier and his Radical-Socialist Party were forced to resign and two days later Paul Reynaud was called on to become premier.

There was a peculiarly French dimension to the rivalry between these two men, but both were careful in their respect of public morality. Reynaud had taken a mistress, the Countess de Portes, only after separating from his wife. Daladier had acquired his mistress, the Marquise de Crussol, only after his wife had died. Both women were from wealthy bourgeois families. The marquise, like Mme de Portes, was the estranged wife of a notable man. Born Jeanne Beziers, daughter of a sardine tycoon, she was described by author André Maurois as "a graceful and beautiful woman, blonde and youthful … with a taste for power." The two women became bitter rivals as each sought to promote the careers of their paramours. According to André Géraud, who wrote under the pen name Pertinax, "From morning to night the two furies spied on and pursued each other. This quarrel became a public performance. If he went out with one, Reynaud had to fear the other would show up."

Reynaud had made a good deal of money in his law practice in the Basse-Alpes and he now sat in the National Assembly for the well-off Bourse district in Paris. His first speech as premier would have to summon both the Chamber and the country to a common purpose: to win the war. He called on de Gaulle to help write it. The speech was brief, but powerful. The new government had but one aim: "to arouse, reassemble, and direct all the sources of French energy to fight and to conquer."

De Gaulle watched from the gallery, but he found the scene "appalling." There was no appreciation of "the danger in which the country stood" and the deputies could speak only of "claims and complaints."[10] Most members of Reynaud's party, the Democratic Republican Alliance, abstained on the motion to confirm him as premier and it passed by only one vote. The president of the Chamber, Édouard Herriot told de Gaulle, "I'm not very sure it had that."

In order to preserve his slender hold on power, Reynaud had to accept Daladier as minister of defense, a move that for a time kept de Gaulle out of the Cabinet. "If de Gaulle comes here, I shall leave," Daladier had told a messenger from Reynaud. In the face of such opposition, de Gaulle felt he had no choice but to reject an invitation to become secretary of the War Cabinet.

A movement to undermine Reynaud began soon after. In a demonstration of the political gamesmanship that preoccupied Paris, thousands of copies of a four-page pamphlet were distributed carrying pictures of Marshall Pétain, hailing the old warrior: "Yesterday a great soldier. Today a great diplomat. Tomorrow?"

When German troops marched into Denmark and Norway on April 8, de Gaulle found himself the recipient of an invitation to a private meeting with General Gamelin. It took place at the commander-in-chief's headquarters in the massive Château de Vincennes in the eastern suburbs of Paris. The general had distanced himself from his senior staff at Château de Montry and the setting reminded de Gaulle of a convent with Gamelin immersed in an "ivory tower."[11] Others referred to the Vincennes command post as "a submarine without a periscope." There was not a single radio in the headquarters and when an officer suggested a teletype link be set up, he was told that "military orders cannot be compared to horse race results." De Gaulle may have reflected on how Premier Reynaud had learned of the Norway invasion not from the general but in a phone call from the Reuters news service. The premier had telephoned the commander-in-chief for confirmation. "I hope," he had said, "that you have prepared a thundering riposte."[12] But Gamelin knew nothing of the German action. He was not, however, entirely immune to the realities of mechanized warfare. When the novelist Jules Romains visited Gamelin in

December 1939, the general talked uninterruptedly for an hour about the direction of the war. It will be different than last time, he said. "Apparent immobility will lead suddenly to an operation in which total power will be used at once ... it will be very swift and very horrible."

In his meeting with Gamelin, de Gaulle learned he was to be put in charge of one of two new armoured divisions that the French army was at last setting up, bringing the total to four. The 4th Armoured Division would be formed from tank units detached from other divisions, and it was a signal honour for a man of the rank of colonel to be given the command. De Gaulle must have experienced a rush of pride at the news.

The long-awaited blow that de Gaulle had warned would come when France was "weary, confused, and dissatisfied" finally fell on May 10. Having subdued Denmark and Norway in barely more than a fortnight — despite the presence of expeditionary forces sent to the Norwegian coast by both the British and French — Hitler threw eighty divisions across the frontiers of Holland, Belgium, and Luxembourg. The Luftwaffe's Stuka dive bombers led the attack with raids on railways and road junctions, spreading confusion and fear among soldiers and civilians. By striking through neutral countries, German forces were able to outflank France's heavily fortified Maginot Line overlooking the Rhine River. The strategy defied all French expectations that the German army would never drive a wedge through the Ardennes Forest and into France; the High Command assumed that tanks and heavy equipment would be unable to navigate its narrow roads. A French pilot, flying reconnaissance the night the Germans drove into the Ardennes, reported seeing long convoys of military vehicles with their headlights blacked out. His report was met with "complete skepticism." Too late, it was realized the panzers would have been easy targets had the French chosen to hit them on those dusty trails.

In three days, ten armoured and six motorized divisions — the dreaded panzers — commanded by General der Panzertruppe Heinz Wilhelm Guderian, swept through the Belgian Ardennes, penetrated French territory, and crossed the Meuse River to capture the historic fortress town of Sedan. It fell after a massive aerial attack turned the Sedan valley into a smoking cauldron. German soldiers watching the attack from the north bank of the Meuse were as shocked as the French defenders caught in the devastation. When General Alphonse Georges, the French commander in the northeast region, received news of the town's fall he threw himself into a chair and burst into tears. "Our front has broken at Sedan … there has been a collapse." By May 15, when de Gaulle was put in command of the French 4th Armoured Division, German troops had swung north and were well on their way to the English Channel. Eight hundred thousand French and British troops were in retreat.

While preparing to take over his new command, de Gaulle found time to write to his wife in Colombey. Addressing Yvonne as "my dear little darling wife," he told her to "be very careful to take shelter by day if there is an alert and to turn out the lights at night." Later, he grew more worried and wrote again to advise her to move to her sister's place near Orléans. The owner of the village garage, M. Gadot, could drive her there, he said. In another letter, written "at the end of a long and hard fight which went very well for me," de Gaulle told Yvonne he had been promoted to brigadier general. He concluded: "If the general atmosphere is bad, it is excellent for your husband."[13]

Amid the turmoil, de Gaulle was anxious to see his son, Philippe. He'd had good reports of his studies at Collège Stanislas, the private Catholic school on Notre-Dame-des-Champs that de Gaulle had attended and where his father had been a teacher. Philippe, an eighteen-year-old with dreams of some day going to sea, would have been surprised when a car arrived at the school to take him to Château Montry, the French army headquarters.[14] It was actually a military vehicle and its driver was dressed in civilian clothes, a charade to make him look like a taxi driver. When Philippe entered the office where he was to meet his father, he found the maps on the wall had been carefully covered. He took it as a bad sign, thinking that if things were going well there would have been no need to cover up the army's movements. He stared at his father, later recalling his "severity and solemnity" as signs "of a man knowing he is not sure to see his son again for a long time." Philippe had always thought his father "had a different dimension" than others, not because of his "exceptional size, but due to his personality." At home, he learned at an early age that his father maintained his authority in a "quiet way" — it was enough for him to "send a little warning shot" from time to time.[15]

De Gaulle told Philippe that he and his sister should head for Orléans in order to meet up with their mother and Anne who were on their way from Colombey. "But," Philippe asked, "Elisabeth is about to sit for her *baccalauréat* [university entrance examination] — must we leave before she could do that?"

"Yes," de Gaulle nodded, whispering, "The situation is very serious. Be prepared to leave Paris without delay."

He gave Philippe two thousand francs which the boy saw as "a huge sum for me." The next morning de Gaulle left for the front.

De Gaulle's orders for the 4th Armoured Division were to gather up his forces and position them in the region of Laon, 120 kilometres northeast of Paris, and harass the flank of the German army driving to the English Channel. His small command would be reinforced, he was told, with units of the 6th Army that was being mustered in the east of France. When he got to Vesinet, the command post assigned him by General Georges, de Gaulle learned his new division existed only on paper; its scattered units had yet to be drawn together from other commands.

"Here you are, de Gaulle," General Georges proclaimed. "For you who have so long held the ideas which the enemy is putting into practice, here is the chance to act!"[16]

Act de Gaulle would, but first he had to organize the few tank units that were gathering south of Laon. He received a battalion of heavy Char B tanks and two battalions of light Renault tanks, but no infantry, no artillery, no air support, and no anti-aircraft cover. De Gaulle assessed the situation in Laon, already threatened by the flank of Guderian's panzers driving toward the Channel. He chose not to set up his headquarters within sight of the medieval, walled citadel that sat atop the narrow ridge that bisected the town — and held the historic Cathedral of Notre-Dame, begun in the 12th century — but in the village of Bruyères, on the open Picardy plain a few miles to the southeast. He toured his surroundings, noting the layout of the farm country that made it suitable for tank operations, and collected additional scattered units of artillery and cavalry.

At daybreak on May 17, still without major artillery or anti-aircraft guns, de Gaulle gathered up two hundred tanks and set off to attack the Germans holding Montcornet, where a Wehrmacht supply column was assembling fuel and food for the final assault on the Channel ports. De Gaulle was eager to carry out his mission; a successful counterattack would go a long way toward overcoming the spirit of defeat hanging over the French army.

By late afternoon, joined by two infantry regiments, de Gaulle's force was in the outskirts of the town and perilously close to seizing the headquarters of General Guderian. Several hundred Germans had been killed and 130 captured, with French casualties of "less than two hundred men."[17] Guderian would later write that "a few of his [de Gaulle's] tanks succeeded in penetrating to within a mile of my advanced headquarters in Holnon wood."

De Gaulle, under pressure from Stuka dive bombers and knowing his small force was vulnerable to a determined counterattack, withdrew before nightfall. "We were lost children," he would write of this engagement.[18]

That night, de Gaulle scrawled a note in pencil and handed it to his liaison officer, Captain Leton, with instructions to take it to General Robert Touchon at the headquarters of the 6th Army at Moussy. It was a request for reinforcements and Leton thought it had "an urgent tone, almost pleading."

When he delivered the note at midnight he found Touchon in his pajamas. The general called in a support officer who looked doubtfully at the message. "With what we have, we can't promise anything," he said.[19]

De Gaulle was on the move again the next morning, driving north from Laon with the support of additional artillery and tank regiments. After recapturing several towns and reaching the banks of the Serre River, the offensive bogged down in the face of a heavy German counterattack. General Georges ordered a withdrawal, and de Gaulle moved back south of Laon. A French radio crew interviewed de Gaulle and invited him to record his comments on the battle. He told listeners that France was caught up in mechanized warfare and while the enemy had gained an initial advantage, victory would come one day from "our armoured divisions and our attacks in the air." It was his first known radio broadcast and he used it to try to rally the country to fight on. He also understood the need to claim his own place in the victory that he was sure would one day belong to France: "The leader who speaks to you has the honour to command a French armoured division. This division has had a hard fight, and we can say very directly, very seriously — without any bragging — that we have dominated the battlefield from the first to the last hour of battle."[20]

For the next week the 4th Armoured Division careered about the countryside, finally receiving on May 26 the order to move west to Abbeville, the latest trophy to fall into General Guderian's hands. French journalist Jean-Raymond Tournoux recorded the impressions of one of de Gaulle's division officers. "He never tired, and you saw him everywhere — that leather jacket, his casque and the inevitable cigarette. He was not an easy man to be with, was aloof and serious…. He was tough, ruthless, inhuman, letting nothing and nobody count except the battle."[21]

In a night attack, de Gaulle moved on the German positions south of Abbeville, a Somme River port twenty-two kilometres from the English Channel. The first objective, Mont Caubet, was taken quickly. De Gaulle would recall how "an atmosphere of victory hung over the field. The wounded were smiling. The guns fired gaily. Before us, in a pitched battle, the Germans had retired."[22] Soon, however, reinforcements stiffened the German lines. De Gaulle lost nearly half his tanks, either to enemy fire or to the quagmire of nearby swamps. According to British historian Kenneth Macksey, de Gaulle's efforts caused "hardly a twitter of alarm on the German side." On May 25, Paris newspapers carried reports that Colonel de Gaulle was missing in action; and on May 30, the 4th Division was relieved by the newly arrived 51st Scottish Division. In subsequent fighting, most of that division was captured along with its commander, General Victor Fortune. Their defeat spelled the end of effective Allied resistance in France. But de Gaulle, by now growing accustomed to his new rank of brigadier general (a conditional appointment that would never be officially confirmed), had become the only French commander to force the Germans to retreat — fourteen kilometres in front of Abbeville — during the Battle of France.

It would later be established that contrary to popular belief, Allied and German forces were more or less evenly matched. General Gamelin estimated Allied strength at 144 divisions and the Germans at 140 divisions. However, much of the French army was tied down on the Maginot Line, rendering those units unavailable for offensive action. Even in tanks, the French were almost the equal in numbers — some 2,300 to around 2,600 for the Germans — and most were more heavily armed than the bulk of the German machines. Only in the air did the Germans have clear superiority.[23]

By the end of May, it became clear to de Gaulle that despite the approximate equality of forces "the battle was virtually lost." King Albert of Belgium had capitulated. Three hundred and fifty thousand troops of the British Expeditionary Force and the French 1st Army were encircled at Dunkirk. Most would be evacuated by a flotilla of navy vessels and small civilian boats after Hitler, fearing his forces were in danger of outrunning their supply lines, ordered a halt to their advance.

Despite this retreat, a ray of hope did emerge from Britain at this time. The country had a new prime minister, Winston Churchill, who was promising his countrymen "nothing but blood, toil, tears and sweat."

> We shall defend our island, whatever the cost may be, we shall fight on the beaches, we shall fight on the landing-grounds, we shall fight in the fields and in the streets, we shall never surrender, and even if … this Island were subjugated … then our Empire beyond the seas, armed and guarded by the British Fleet, would carry on the struggle, until, in God's good time, the New World, with all its power and might, steps forth to the rescue and liberation of the Old.[24]

This change seemed to guarantee that France would be able to count on British resolve in its fight. However, the present situation remained a very difficult one, and de Gaulle desperately wanted to ensure that all that could be done to save the country was being done.

In a letter to Premier Reynaud on June 1, de Gaulle let his frustration be known. The defeats suffered by France are due to "the enemy's application of ideas conceived by me and from our High Command's refusal to apply the same conceptions." If he could not serve in the Cabinet, at least he should be put in charge of "all the armoured corps" of the French army. "I alone am capable of commanding this corps." Further, de Gaulle argued, Reynaud must not abandon the country to "the men of former times." They are the ones who have brought France to "the edge of the abyss."[25]

Four days later, de Gaulle was handed a telegram from Paris. Premier Reynaud wanted him in the government. The commander of the 7th Army, General Aubert Frère, had heard of the order before it reached de Gaulle and hastened to offer his congratulations. "Rumour has it that you're to be Minister," he said. "It's certainly late in the day for a cure. Ah, at least let's save our honour!"[26]

De Gaulle hurried to Paris. He found the premier in a reflective mood but anxious to explain why he had brought back General Weygand and recruited Marshall Pétain. "It's better," he said, "to have him [Pétain] inside than out." De Gaulle insisted that if the Battle of France had been lost, the war could yet be won. France would fight on from its overseas possessions, but transport would be needed to evacuate men and equipment from Metropolitan France. Reynaud told de Gaulle to go to London and ask the help of Winston Churchill in supplying ships to move French forces to North Africa.

Before leaving for London, de Gaulle had one last visit with his son, over dinner in the ornate dining room of the Hôtel Lutetia on Boulevard Raspail. After telling Philippe of his promotion to the rank of brigadier general, de Gaulle repeated his instructions for him to go with his sister to the home of their aunt, Suzanne Rérolle, in Rebréchien, a village twenty kilometres from Orléans. By now, de Gaulle hoped, his wife would have found her way there with little Anne and her governess, Marguerite Potel. The next morning, Philippe tried to fight his way through the crowds clamouring for train tickets, first at the Gare d'Orsay and then at Gare d'Austerlitz. He found police blocking the doors to both stations. Hearing this, de Gaulle acted. He arranged for a "taxi" — probably the car and driver he'd used before — and had Philippe collect Elisabeth from her convent school, Notre-Dame-de-Sion in suburban Bondoufle. They drove south to Rebréchien, reaching there on Monday, the day before de Gaulle's arrival in Orléans. Philippe and Elisabeth found their mother already at their aunt's home.

They stayed in Rebréchien only a few hours. After releasing their driver, Philippe told his mother of the instructions his father had given him before leaving Paris. They were to return to the north, to the seacoast village of Carantec in Britanny, where de Gaulle had rented the upper two floors of a villa. No explanation for this trip is given in the memoirs of either Charles or Philippe de Gaulle. De Gaulle must have made up his mind to get his family to England as soon as possible. They set out for Britanny in Suzanne's husband's car, a small black Mathis barely large enough to hold the five adults, one disabled girl, and Suzanne's two children. Suzanne had no driver's licence and was not used to driving. In the absence of her husband, who was in the army, she had no choice but to take the wheel. Philippe, hunched up on the floor, decided to try his luck by train. He left the car at the railway station in Orléans and made his way north on local trains. A bus deposited him in Carantec on the night of June 13, where he found his family already installed at the villa.[27]

On Sunday, June 9, the morning after his dinner with Philippe, de Gaulle rose early and was taken by staff car to Le Bourget airport where he boarded an air force plane for his flight to London. With him was Premier Reynaud's *chef de cabinet*, Roland de Margerie who carried a letter of introduction to Winston Churchill, and de Gaulle's aide, Geoffroy de Courcel. The visit gave de Courcel — a blond-haired, apple-cheeked young man — the opportunity to demonstrate his impeccable English. That had been one of the reasons de Gaulle, who knew very little of the language, had taken him on.

To de Gaulle, the English capital was tranquil with "the streets and parks full of people peacefully out for a walk."[28] They lunched at the French Embassy and that afternoon de Gaulle saw Churchill at No. 10

Downing Street. This first meeting was a test for both men; they needed to measure each other's personality and gain an understanding of what was important to the other. Churchill bobbed up from his chair, paced the floor, and, cigar in hand, declaimed in high-school French that both countries must hang on; support from the British Dominions and the United States would eventually turn the tide.

De Gaulle had heard much of this energetic and unpredictable British figure. He knew Churchill was a friend of Reynaud, and he recalled the time the premier had told him that Churchill had flown to Paris in 1938 to urge him to remain in the French Cabinet. Reynaud quit anyway, in disgust with the Munich pact. At this first meeting with Churchill, it is likely de Gaulle did not entirely trust the prime minister. Raised in an atmosphere of historic antipathy toward England and knowing little of the country in which he now found himself, de Gaulle would have seen Churchill as a representative of a race that many Frenchmen felt had let France down in the past. On a personal level, we can understand that he would have found it hard to forget that "a young lady who was almost his fiancée" had been killed by British shelling of Lille in 1917.[29]

Churchill, in contrast, knew France intimately and loved everything about the country across the Channel, a place that offered exciting diversions from the often stultifying life he lived at home. Here an Englishman could feel free to be himself in a way he never could among his own people. It was in France that Churchill likely cultivated his taste for cognac and champagne, but he had never forgotten his first visit as a nine-year-old in 1883. Firmly etched in his memory was the memorial he had been shown in the Place de la Concorde honouring France's lost provinces of Alsace and Lorraine, taken by Prussia in 1870. Churchill became caught up in the study of French history.

From his time as First Lord of the Admiralty in the First World War to his political isolation in the interwar years and his return to power in May 1940 — "Winnie is back!" flashed the Admiralty message system — he was often in France, whether at the trenches during the war or in private conversations with leaders such as Paul Reynaud. Churchill would remember being told of the writings of a young Colonel de Gaulle, a man much taken with "the offensive power of modern armed vehicles." He hadn't put much stock in de Gaulle's arguments, convinced as he was that France in the 1930s possessed "the finest, though not the largest, army in existence at the present time." By now, Churchill had thrown that opinion out the window. On June 5, the day de Gaulle had been called into Reynaud's Cabinet, Churchill had written to Mackenzie King, the prime minister of Canada, to warn: "I do not know whether it will be possible to keep France in the war."[30]

Now, Churchill and de Gaulle were meeting as the French army lay virtually prostrate on the field of battle. Churchill, beyond being shocked as de Gaulle would recall, was convinced that France no longer had the spirit and determination to carry on the war. The prime minister made it clear he saw no hope of launching a British counteroffensive in France. When de Gaulle asked Churchill to send the Royal Air Force to French bases south of the Loire, he refused. The last two fighter squadrons in France had flown back to Britain the night before, where they would be held to protect England. Churchill promised to dispatch the 1st Canadian Division, the only fully equipped force left in England, across the Channel to reinforce British troops still there. The pledge eased the tension in the room, but did nothing to resolve the unsettled matter of transport to North Africa.

De Gaulle departed knowing he had failed in his mission to bring more British air power into the skies over France. But he had to admit, grudgingly, that Churchill's decision to retain the RAF in England was the right one for the future of the war. "Great Britain, led by such a fighter, would certainly not flinch," he thought.[31] Before leaving London, de Gaulle met with Anthony Eden, the British secretary of war. He also saw Jean Monnet, an economist with the French Economic Mission who was in charge of coordinating British-French war purchases. Finally, his visits completed, De Gaulle flew back to France where he landed uneasily at Le Bourget airport in Paris. The plane touched down ony a few hours after a German air raid had left unexploded bombs on the runway.

Standing on the steps of the Préfecture in Orléans on Tuesday morning June 11, de Gaulle may have reflected that much had happened in the past two days to confirm his worst fears. He would have been interrupted in his thoughts by the arrival of a car to drive him north, along with two armoured vehicles assigned as escorts. The road was heavy with refugee traffic coming south, but few vehicles were going north and de Gaulle made good time, reaching Huntziger's command post at Arcis-sur-Aube by mid-morning. Crossing the Seine River at Troyes, a city familiar to de Gaulle as it was close to Colombey-les-Deux-Églises, he may have thought of how a determined guerilla band could hold out against the Germans in the *forêt d'orient* — the Eastern Forest — that lay between it and Colombey. But his mind was focused on his meeting with Huntziger and on the possibility that General Heinz Guderian, the panzer commander, might be storming south on this very road.

As history would later reveal, de Gaulle and Guderian followed parallel career paths in their commitment to the use of mechanized forces. Guderian's superiors criticized him for impulsive actions and he was sacked when he disobeyed orders to slow his advance into France. Hitler, not wanting to lose the services of a fervent Nazi who had earned the Führer's praise by his quick conquest of Poland, insisted on Guderian's return to duty. The source, however, of much of Guderian's military expertise came from the books of Charles de Gaulle that he had read, and by emulating the tactics de Gaulle and others had advocated. Even Adolf Hitler admitted he had "learned much" from having had de Gaulle's books — before they were translated into German — read to him.[32]

To his meeting with Huntziger, de Gaulle brought a straightforward message: "The government sees plainly that the Battle of France is virtually lost, but it means to continue the war by transporting itself to Africa with all the resources that can be got across. The present generalissimo [Weygand] is not the man to carry it out. Would you be the man?"[33]

De Gaulle always insisted that Huntziger's answer was "Yes." He then told Huntziger he would be receiving the government's instructions. Huntziger would later give a different version of the meeting, maintaining he laughed at the offer. In any event, de Gaulle hurriedly finished the meeting and set out to retrace his steps south. Refugees clogging the bridge across the Seine at the village of Mércy, scene of the second-to-last of Napoleon's great battles — a calamitous loss to the Austrians in 1814 — held up de Gaulle's "small suite" for an hour. All along the route through

Romilly and Sens, he encountered "units retreating southwards, mixed pell-mell with the refugees." They reminded him of a "shepherdless flock." Adding to the confusion, a strange fog which many took to be poison gas hung over the countryside.[34]

It was late afternoon by the time de Gaulle reached Briare, where he headed for the Château du Muguet, a residence of minor presence among the great châteaux of the Loire. Weather-worn and ill-maintained, the eighty-year-old stone and lobster-red brick mansion had been assigned to General Weygand and was to serve as the site for that day's conference with Winston Churchill. One of Churchill's advisors, General Edward Spears, noted its "ridiculous name" — which he translated as Lily of the Valley Castle — and thought it "a hideous house" to which he took "an instant dislike."[35] De Gaulle does not record his impression of the place, but had he been asked, he no doubt would have agreed with Spears. It was an aptly ugly location for an ugly business.

CHAPTER 4
The Collapse of the Third Republic

The bonds that linked Paris and London in their alliance against Adolf Hitler were frayed and tenuous by the time Charles de Gaulle arrived at the Château du Muguy, a few kilometres north of Briare. The driveway was crowded with military vehicles when his car drew up just after five o'clock. The rays of a late afternoon sun glanced off the château's sloping French provincial roofs, softening the harsh lines of the multi-turreted building. It was a strange structure, its central tower capped by a weirdly out-of-place, almost Byzantine, onion-like sphere, suggestive of a lily bulb. We can picture de Gaulle brushing road dust from his uniform as he stepped onto the terrace where he would have returned the salutes of waiting officers. He'd not been to bed for thirty-six hours, but his usual sallow complexion glowed pinkly, perhaps from the stress of a day that had seen him drive more than four hundred kilometres to the front lines and back to the Loire Valley.

Inside, a long, glassed-in hallway led to a large dining room where Premier Reynaud and a scattering of the French Cabinet awaited the arrival of the British prime minister. Men darted in and out of a side door to a butler's pantry where the château's only telephone hung on a wall. The pantry also gave access to a lavatory. A quick visit by de Gaulle would have revealed a confusion of voices and bodies, with much shouting on the phone as a caller struggled to make himself heard.

De Gaulle sought out the premier to tell him of his meeting with General Huntziger. Their brief exchange quickly convinced de Gaulle that Reynaud had other things on his mind than finding a new commander-in-chief. Turning away, de Gaulle caught sight of Marshall Pétain, stooped but steady, the burden of years and the gravity of the situation weighing on him. "You're a general!" the marshall told him. "I don't congratulate you. What good are ranks in defeat?" De Gaulle reminded Pétain that he had received his first star while the French army was in retreat in 1914, but later the tide had turned. "No comparison," Pétain grunted. De Gaulle had to agree with him.[1]

The conversation was cut short by a bustle at the front door. The British delegation was arriving. Winston Churchill, inevitable cigar in hand, was accompanied by his secretary for war, Anthony Eden, the chief of the Imperial General Staff, Sir John Dill, Churchill's chief military adviser, General "Pug" Ismay, and a clutch of other officials.

Among the British arrivals was Major General Sir Edward L. Spears, an old friend of Churchill's and his personal representative to the French government. Spears, the perfect example of the correct English military officer — square jaw, clipped mustache, crisp accent — had served with distinction in the First World War. Shrewd and fluently bilingual, his sense of humour and his tendency to use literary allusions — encouraged perhaps by his marriage to the American novelist Mary Borden — set him apart from the others. He was a Francophile, and the pro-French views he had often expressed as a Conservative MP in the British House of Commons had led him to be dubbed the "member for Paris." They all had flown from London in a bright yellow de Havilland Flamingo aircraft, escorted by twelve Hurricane fighter planes. The Briare Conference was about to enter into history.

By the time everyone had moved into the large dining room, a clock struck seven. Rain began to fall from the heavy clouds hanging over the château, adding a touch of dreariness to the subdued gathering. On the

French side, Reynaud and de Gaulle were joined by Weygand, Pétain, and the disgraced General Georges — a man in whom the British PM still had much confidence — there at Churchill's personal request. It was not long before the two sides were snapping at each other. Reynaud began by asking that a joint British-French air raid on Genoa planned for that night be cancelled. The Italians would only retaliate, causing many deaths in unprotected French cities like Marseille and Lyon.

Churchill broke into a cherubic, almost wicked smile. "This operation cannot be stopped," he said. "The planes left England a quarter of an hour ago."[2] The translator's words hung over the conference table. Churchill pressed on. He said he had come to France to face the reality of all that had happened. He urged the French to fight on for Paris, reminding them of their great First World War premier, Georges Clemenceau, who had said, "I will fight in front of Paris, in Paris, and behind Paris."

Turning to Pétain, Churchill spoke of the nights they had spent together after a disastrous British retreat in 1918, and how Pétain and his comrade, Marshall Foch, had set the situation right. "Yes, and I sent forty divisions to rescue you," Pétain replied. "Today it's we who are smashed to pieces. Where are your forty divisions?"

Churchill's announcement that the 1st Canadian Division was landing in France that night did nothing to lift the pessimism in the room. Weygand painted a gloomy picture of French soldiers coping with neither food nor rest. "The troops fight all day and fall back to new positions during the night. They collapse into sleep when halted and have to be shaken in the morning to open fire. I am helpless, for I have no reserves. *C'est la dislocation.*"

De Gaulle listened carefully to the conversation around him but said little. He was the junior of the group and he wanted time to assess the attitude of others. But he drew confidence from the fact he'd talked with Churchill only the day before yesterday and that he'd been able to meet Eden and the other British officials on his visit to London. As committed as de Gaulle was to fighting on in Brittany or in North Africa, it was becoming clear to him that the solidarity of England and France could no longer be relied on. The French army, the government, and the High Command were rapidly losing credibility. Looking at the men on either side of him, he thought each was "no longer behaving as a partner in a game played in common, but as a man who, from now on, takes his own course and plays his own game."[3] Yet his face remained imperturbable.

General Spears, taking notes of the meeting, thought de Gaulle the only Frenchman whose bearing matched the phlegm of the English. "A strange-looking man, enormously tall; sitting at the table he dominated everyone else by his height," Spears elaborated later. "Small mouth, a long, drooping, elephantine nose over a closely cut mustache ... a high, receding forehead and pointed head surmounted by sparse black hair lying flat and neatly parted. When he did speak, he moved his head slightly, like a pendulum, while searching for words." Then Spears remembered the nickname Pétain had once given de Gaulle: *"Le Connétable"* — the Constable, the ancient title borne by commanders of France's royal armies. It fit him well, Spears thought.[4]

The talk around the table dragged on for three hours before Premier Reynaud announced that dinner would be served in an adjoining room. It was a makeshift meal — an omelette and a white *vin ordinaire* — and de Gaulle found himself sitting next to Winston Churchill, while the premier took the chair on the other side of the British leader. By now, Churchill was firming up in his mind lists of the French who could be counted on and those who had lost the will to carry on. De Gaulle seemed the only one willing to wage guerilla warfare, if necessary, to stop the Nazis from a complete takeover. As well as being concerned about France's land forces, Churchill also worried about the French navy. He was relieved by Admiral Darlan's assurance that he would never surrender the fleet to the Germans; if necessary, he would send it to Canada.

After coffee, it was agreed discussions would resume in the morning. As Churchill was led off to a small suite near Reynaud's quarters, the others adjourned to the train of French president, Albert Lebrun, shunted onto a nearby rail spur. De Gaulle, worried about preparing a final redoubt against the Germans, was driven through pouring rain to the Château de Beauvais at Azay-sur-Cher. He received a warm welcome from the owner, M. Provost de Launay.

✝

A four-poster bed swathed in pink curtains awaited de Gaulle that night. He would have slept well, having acquired the soldier's skill at snatching rest whenever chance presented itself. He awoke at dawn to begin another long day of travel. The skies had cleared and the air felt cool and clean. De Gaulle's destination was Rennes, the capital of Brittany and memorable in military lore as the site of the second trial of Alfred Dreyfus in 1899. It is unclear whether he flew or drove, as he makes no mention in his memoirs of his ill-fated meeting there with General René Altmayer.

Altmayer's V Corps had taken a severe mauling in the German assault and had withdrawn south of Paris in hopes of forming a new defensive line. The two made plans to move the remaining French army units to Quimper, a rustic town in Brittany where supplies could be brought in from England. But all this went up in smoke when it became evident it would take at least three months to turn Quimper into a last-ditch outpost. It would be useful only for an evacuation to North Africa. Returning to Briare, de Gaulle drove that night to the Château de Chissay where Reynaud was staying. He found Reynaud presiding over a Cabinet meeting that was debating where next the government should seek refuge. De Gaulle urged Quimper, but most were for Bordeaux, a signal that the government no longer had any stomach for the war.

De Gaulle had missed the second round of the Briare Conference. It began about eight o'clock in the morning, after Churchill had shocked his French equerries by emerging from his room wearing white pyjamas and a red silk robe, demanding to know where he would find his bath. Churchill's impatience would have been understandable, because he had just learned from Reynaud that Pétain had written a paper insisting that France seek an armistice, but that he was too ashamed to hand it to him. Weygand opened the session by pointing out it was he who had read Armistice terms to the Germans in 1918. "You can imagine what I feel now."[5] Churchill brought up the issue of the previous night's air raids on Italian cities. He revealed that British planes based in France had been unable to join the attack because the French had moved trucks onto the airstrips to prevent their taking off. "We shall bomb the Italians if they bomb us," Weygand interjected. After an apology by Reynaud, the matter was dropped, but the French premier continued to insist on the need for additional Royal Air Force units to be based in France.

Churchill spoke of the need to defend Paris, arguing that the Germans could be held long enough to allow other French columns to regroup. He was told the Germans had fifty-five divisions ready for combat (a serious exaggeration) and would have no trouble keeping the upper hand. "It is not the intention to hold Paris," Weygand asserted. He had, after all, already declared it an open city.

According to General Spears, who acted as interpreter (a task he detested), Churchill responded in a solemn tone: "There is a matter the importance of which overshadows all others, and which I must put to you.... I must request you, before coming to a final decision which may govern French action in the second phase of the war ... let the British government know at once." Don't quit without letting us know first, he was saying. Reynaud agreed this would be the case, and the Briare Conference was over.[6]

Churchill's flight back to Britain was made without the protection of Hurricane escorts, the skies having clouded up again. From eight thousand feet, he watched the French port of Le Havre burn from German bomb attacks. His Flamingo suddenly went into a dive, levelling off a hundred feet above the water. It had successfully eluded two German aircraft engaged in attacks on French fishing boats. That night, Churchill met with his Cabinet and then dictated a letter to President Roosevelt:

> The practical point is what will happen when and if the French front breaks, Paris is taken, and General Weygand reports formally to his Government that France can no longer continue what he calls "coordinated war." The aged Marshall Pétain, who was none too good in April and July, 1918, is, I feel, ready to lend his name and prestige to a treaty of peace for France. Reynaud, on the other hand, is for fighting on, and he has a young General de Gaulle, who believes much can be done.[7]

When de Gaulle returned to Reynaud's headquarters at Château de Chissay the next morning, he found members of the premier's staff preparing to move on to Bordeaux. Before they left, he convinced Reynaud to direct Weygand to continue fighting. "Hold out as long as possible in the Massif Central and in Brittany," the premier's letter to Weygand read. If the time comes when resistance is no longer possible in Metropolitan France, Weygand, should "organize the struggle in the Empire, making use of the freedom of the seas."

Another visitor to Château de Chissay was General Spears. He would not forget the sight of Reynaud's mistress, Mme de Portes, standing on the steps of the château, clad in a dressing gown over red pyjamas, directing traffic as military cars came and went. He was even more amazed when a secret government telegram that had gone astray was found in Mme de Portes's bed. During a meeting of Reynaud and the British ambassador, Sir Ronald Campbell, she "popped her head round the door" several times, frowning at the visitor. "If I have ever seen hate in a woman's eyes, it was in her glances as they swept across us like the strokes of a scythe," Spears concluded. She would rush into Reynaud after his meetings, demanding to know what had been discussed. Why did Reynaud hesitate to stop the war, she was said to ask, when thousands of men were being killed? "Delay will only mean harsher German terms." Spears said everyone readily believed the story. "The lady's every action bore it out."[8]

Spears had joined French officials moving toward Tours, which was to have been the site of the government but now became just a way stop on the road to Bordeaux. Passing through Amboise, he was held up at the Loire River bridge, "jammed between refugee cars surmounted by dripping mattresses." Orders had gone out to stop the exodus to the South, but there was no way to prevent it. Townspeople estimated they supplied forty thousand meals to refugees before Italian aircraft bombed Amboise and destroyed the bridge over which Spears had passed hours before.

While Spears settled himself in Tours, de Gaulle returned to the Château de Beauvais. He was at work in his room when he received a hurried phone call from Reynaud's chief of cabinet, Roland de Margerie. De Gaulle was surprised to hear that Reynaud had secretly invited Winston Churchill to return to France for another meeting and that the British prime minister was now at the Préfecture in Tours. "A conference is about to start in a moment," de Margerie said. "Although you are not invited, I suggest you should come."[9]

Churchill's trip to Tours was so secretive that no one had been assigned to welcome him when his plane landed just before noon. With him were his foreign secretary, Lord Halifax, his minister of aircraft production, the Canadian-born press baron Lord Beaverbrook, and General Ismay. They managed to secure a ride into Tours where an unsatisfactory lunch was obtained at the Grand Hotel. By the time Churchill settled into a deep leather armchair in the first floor study of the Préfeture, he still hoped that Reynaud might find a way to buck up a Cabinet resigned to defeat. That hope was dashed when Churchill saw that Reynaud had brought with him only one man: his undersecretary of state, Paul Baudouin. *How could his presence help?* Churchill must have thought, when Baudouin had been a strong opponent of France going to war against Germany.

Reynaud's opening remarks served to explain Baudouin's presence. General Weygand had advised the Cabinet that the situation of the French army was growing more desperate by the hour. In view of everything that had happened, Reynaud said, the United States remained the only hope. He would telegraph President Roosevelt immediately with a fresh appeal for help.

Churchill agreed, but stressed that no matter what, Britain would fight on. "We must fight, we will fight, and that is why we must ask our friends to fight on. The war will continue, and can but end in our destruction or our victory."

An admirable sentiment, Reynaud replied. But what if France found itself in a position where it no longer had anything to contribute to the common cause? Would Great Britain not be willing, in that circumstance, to release her from their mutual agreement not to conclude a separate peace?

"*Je comprends,*" Churchill replied, indicating, he believed, only that he understood the question. The conversation turned to other issues. Shortly after, the British delegation took a break to walk in the sunny garden behind the Préfecture.

General Spears was bewildered by the conversation. "Weygand, Pétain and others wished at all costs to stop a game they had ceased to understand," he would write.

When the British trooped back into the *préfet*'s study, they were surprised to see de Gaulle had joined the meeting. Reynaud suggested the two sides could meet again after a reply had been received from President Roosevelt. It would be a meeting to discuss ways and means of continuing the war, Reynaud promised. At that, the session ended. It was 5:50 p.m.

Downstairs, de Gaulle called Spears aside to give him disturbing news. Paul Baudouin had told the journalists swarming around the Préfecture that Churchill had shown complete comprehension of France's situation and would understand it if she had to make peace with Germany.

Spears was astonished. He assured de Gaulle that Churchill had said no such thing. He had merely muttered "*Je comprends*," in the sense of understanding what he had been told.

"Baudouin is putting it about that France is now released from her agreement to England," de Gaulle countered.

Churchill's statement was being cleverly misconstrued, but he had no one but himself to blame. As Spears has written, Churchill disdained translation and preferred to speak his own "pidgin French." A proficient interpreter might have put "*Je le sais*" in Churchill's mouth, indicating nothing more than that Churchill knew of the French position.

By now the British delegation was streaming out. At the end of a crowded passageway Churchill slipped up to de Gaulle who was "standing stolid and expressionless at the doorway." Churchill wrung his hand and said, in a tone so low that no one else could hear, "*L'homme du destin*."[10]

Supportive messages were coming in from around the world, but they did little to ease the sense of defeat hanging over the French government. Prime Minister Mackenzie King cabled Canada's "complete support to the extreme limit of her forces and resources. The sacrifices and devotion of France are an example to free men the world over."[11] A telegram from President Roosevelt reached the chancelleries in both Paris and London later that night. It was not in response to Reynaud's latest message, but was a reply to an appeal Reynaud had sent on June 10: "The magnificent Resistance of the French and British armies has profoundly impressed the American people."

Roosevelt's message offered no concrete help, nor should the French have expected anything beyond moral support. Roosevelt still had not overcome the shock — or betrayal, as some put it — of the French army's disastrous and unexpected rout. He'd been to France as assistant secretary of the U.S. Navy Department in the First World War, had attended the Versailles peace conference, and spoke French. Now, he saw France falling away from the ranks of the great powers. Not only that, Roosevelt was bound by the strictures of his country's 1939 Neutrality Act and he had to contend with a strong isolationist movement in the run-up to the November presidential election. Most Americans, while sympathetic to the plight of France and Britain, had no desire for "foreign entanglements" that could lead to war.

As Roosevelt's telegram was being decoded, the Canadian 1st Infantry Brigade, the advance guard of Canada's 1st Division was unloading at the docks in Brest. They would board trains the next morning to take them to their staging area at Le Mans, two hundred kilometres southwest of Paris. Neither their commander, Major-General Andrew McNaughton, nor anyone in the British 2nd Expeditionary Force, of which the Canadians were a part, had any realization that this night was the last night of freedom Paris would know for the next four years.

At six o'clock on the morning of Friday, June 14, in the northern Paris suburb of Écouen, a Major Devouges settled himself at a table opposite his German counterpart, Major Hans Brink. Together, they signed the surrender of Paris. Devouges was acting on orders of forty-eight-year-old General Henri-Fernand Dentz, the Commander of the Paris Region. Dentz had done everything he could to avoid treating with the Germans, arguing by a radio link that he had no authority to hold discussions with the enemy. He relented in the face of a German warning that if he did not Paris would be subject to all-out air and artillery attack. By the time the sun was well up, troops of the German 9th Division were streaming unopposed into the city. General Franz Halder, Chief of the German General Staff, enthused in his diary: "A great day in the history of the German army!" Joe Alex Morris, the United Press correspondent in Paris, began his file with a dramatic flourish.

> PARIS: Adolf Hitler's victorious legions marched into
> Paris today and Germany attacked on every French front
> — including the Maginot line — to blitzkrieg France out
> of the war.[12]

That night, Winston Churchill received a telephone call from the senior British commander in France, General Ronald Brooke. Chrurchill agreed that it was time to withdraw the remaining 150,000 troops of the British Expeditionary Forces from France. By the next day, the Canadian 1st Infantry Division and its British counterpart, the 52nd Division, had abandoned the trains that were to take them to Le Mans and were returning hurriedly to the ports of Brest, St. Malo, and St. Nazaire. Their ships sailed back to England without many of the armoured vehicles that had been unloaded, but they did manage to save all seventy-two of their artillery pieces.

De Gaulle received word of the fall of Paris as he was preparing to say goodbye to his hosts, the Le Provost de Launays, at the Château de Beauvais. De Gaulle is silent in his memoirs as to his reaction, but he would have felt a severe stab of distress at the not unexpected news.

Ministers frantically sought out transport for themselves and their wives or mistresses. De Gaulle was soon on the road for Bordeaux along with several hundred other government officials. He reached Bordeaux in the late afternoon and went directly to the residence of the local military commander, the Quartier Général on rue Vital-Carles, where Premier Reynaud was to be accommodated. While waiting for Reynaud, de Gaulle was briefed by the mayor, M. Marquet and his deputy on measures they had taken to handle the influx. De Gaulle was not encouraged by Marquet's defeatist attitude. When the premier finally showed up, accompanied by Hélène de Portes, de Gaulle told him that he had no intention of submitting to an armistice and neither should the premier.

"You must get to Algiers as quickly as possible," de Gaulle urged. "Are you — yes or no — resolved on that?" When Reynaud answered *yes*, he told de Gaulle to go to London to arrange transport for French troops. "Where shall I rejoin you?" de Gaulle wanted to know.

"I'll see you in Algiers," Reynaud answered.

At that point, Mme de Portes spotted de Gaulle and was overheard to mutter, "What's that one doing here? Another one who wants to turn himself into a politician. Let him go and lead his tanks and prove himself on the battlefield."[13] That evening, Reynaud and Mme de Portes quarrelled bitterly at dinner in the presence of a government official, Lieutenant-Colonel Paul de Villelume. It ended with Reynaud throwing two glasses of water in her face.[14]

Strengthened by Reynaud's assurance that he would continue the war, de Gaulle told Geoffroy de Courcel to find a plane to take them to London. While they waited for word of an aircraft, de Gaulle and his aide went to the Hôtel Splendide, where many government officials were staying. They sat down to a quick supper, noticing that the formalities of the dining room — waiters in tuxedos and a maitre d'hotel who carefully guarded the entrance — were still in place. When Marshall Pétain arrived for his dinner, accompanied by aides, de Gaulle went to his table to pay his respects. The marshall shook de Gaulle's hand, but said not a word. It was the last time de Gaulle would ever see him. *Old age is a shipwreck*, de Gaulle thought. The passing years had gnawed at the marshall's character and now he considered the game was lost.[15]

Bordeaux that night was teeming with government officials, refugees, correspondents, and diplomats. The port in the Gironde estuary was filled with a collection of ships ranging from French navy vessels to tramp steamers, each an object of possible escape for trapped refugees. Swedish journalist Victor Vinde described the scene in the city that had doubled in population in a little more than a week:

> The administration, surviving the debris with the rest of the Chamber of Deputies, the Senate, and the general staff, had found a new home in the old and famous city of wine. One could barely endure the crowds in the streets. Members of the Paris police, who had followed the authorities south, had to assume control of the traffic; in their view the local police had become a little nonchalant. Bordeaux soon resembled a real capital. Cafés and restaurants were filled with the nobility of the day; the bankers, ambassadors, and also pretty women who

had been inconvenienced by their experiences during the journey. All these newcomers seemed confused and somewhat frightened, but none of the upscale restaurants were empty and the kitchens of Bordeaux turned out their usual excellent meals.[16]

Not long after de Gaulle's encounter with Pétain, it became clear there would be no plane to fly him to London. At Mérignac, site of the Bordeaux airport, there was no official willing to authorize such a flight. De Gaulle immediately made up his mind that he and de Courcel would drive to Brest, on the Brittany coast, and there look for a ship to carry them to Britain. Another long night on the road, with hardly a word exchanged between the two of them followed; the driver of the black Renault would cover more than eight hundred kilometres by daybreak. On Saturday morning, after a detour to Rennes to confer again with General Altmayer and his two deputies — "all three doing their best in their respective fields" — de Gaulle had the vehicle turned west to the tiny village of Paimpont for a quick visit with his ailing mother. Then it was north to the coastal town of Carantec.[17]

For a precious half hour that afternoon, de Gaulle was with his family — Yvonne and the children, Philippe, Elisabeth, and Anne. He kissed the children and led his wife aside to speak with her out of their hearing. "Things are very bad," he said. "I am on my way to London. Perhaps we are going to carry on the fight in Africa, but I think it more likely that everything is about to collapse. I am warning you so that you will be ready to leave at the first sign."[18] He told her he would arrange for them to be sent diplomatic passports, which should arrive any day. He gave instructions that the family silver, linens, furs, financial securities, and his private papers be turned over to a local woman for safekeeping. Moments later, the family gathered at the front door to watch de Gaulle's car drive off, leaving in its trail a small cloud of dust.[19]

The French destroyer *Milan* was loading evacuees when de Gaulle and de Courcel reached Brest, barely in time to go aboard. Their companions included a group of chemists carrying a supply of precious "heavy water" to safekeeping in England. The battleship *Richelieu* gave de Gaulle a salute as the *Milan* sailed into the English Channel, bound for Plymouth. A British military car awaited their arrival. De Gaulle was swiftly driven to London, where he checked into the Hyde Park Hotel, conveniently close to the French Embassy. Two visitors arrived while he was changing — the French ambassador Charles Corbin, and Jean Monnet.

The ambassador reviewed the situation in Bordeaux, noting the French government was awaiting Britain's response to its request for release from its commitment not to make a separate peace with Germany. "It has occurred to us," he added, "that some sensational stroke, by throwing a new factor into the situation, might be what is needed." The stroke Corbin and Monnet had in mind was a breathtaking one: a "Declaration of Union" making France and Britain one country — "a complete linking of their respective destinies." They had worked out the scheme with senior officials of the British Foreign Office. Churchill had been briefed, but formal approval of the British government was needed before it could be presented to the French. "You alone can obtain that from Mr. Churchill," Corbin said.[20]

De Gaulle was struck by the "grandeur of the thing," although he realized something of such historic consequence could not be quickly arranged. What was important about it, he thought, was that it would give Reynaud something to toughen the spines of his Cabinet. He said he would certainly take it up with Churchill.

De Gaulle did so, over lunch at a crowded Carleton Club filled with Sunday diners. Churchill thought the idea "an enormous mouthful," but de Gaulle stressed the effects the gesture might have on the French government. It was agreed the proposal would be put before the British Cabinet that afternoon.[21]

De Gaulle, waiting with Corbin, de Courcel, and Monnet in an office at 10 Downing Street for the Cabinet decision, phoned Reynaud to say that "something stupendous" was in the air — the establishment of a single Franco-British government. At five o'clock, Churchill emerged from the session and with a broad smile declared, "*Nous sommes d'accord.*"

De Gaulle phoned Reynaud to dictate the text of the brief document. A key passage declared that "France and Great Britain shall no longer be two nations but one Franco-British Union.… Every citizen of France will enjoy immediately citizenship of Great Britain; every British subject will become a citizen of France." There would be a single War Cabinet and all French and British forces would be placed under its direction. "And thus, we shall conquer."[22]

Reynaud sounded uplifted by the dramatic gesture. "It is very important," he told de Gaulle. He would present it at a Cabinet meeting that was to begin in a few minutes.

De Gaulle put Churchill on the line, who added his voice in support of the scheme. "Our proposal may have great consequences," he said. "You must hold out!"

Hanging up the phone, whisky in hand, Churchill was jubilant. "What do you think?" he asked de Gaulle.

"We have nothing to lose," de Gaulle answered.

"Bravo," came Churchill's reply. "You will be commander-in-chief of the French-British army!"

Before hearing back from Reynaud, de Gaulle accepted Churchill's offer of a plane to return him to Bordeaux. It was agreed he would keep the machine, a twin-wing Dragon Rapide of the Royal Air Force 24th Squadron based at Heston, as long as he needed it. The plane was in the air at 6:30. One of the RAF's finest pilots, Squadron Leader Edward Fielden, bearing the unlikely nickname of "Mouse," was at the controls. He had been the personal pilot to King Edward VIII.[23] Meanwhile, Churchill and several of his Cabinet ministers went to Waterloo Station. A special train was waiting to take them to Southampton, where they would board a ship for Concarneau and a promised further meeting with the French Cabinet the next day.

In Bordeaux a state of near pandemonium reigned at the British Consulate, where General Spears found assorted refugees "begging to be given the means of returning to England." Rejecting the offer of a château fifty kilometres outside the city, Spears had managed to get rooms at the Grand Hôtel Montré, overlooking the circular Place des Grands-Hommes a few hundred yards from where Reynaud was staying. Spears spent Sunday shuffling between the consulate, his hotel where he'd finally gotten to bed at 4 a.m., and Reynaud's headquarters. There was barely time for lunch at Chapon Fin across the street, crowded with chattering dignitaries. Telegrams flowing in from Washington and London caused much consternation in Reynaud's circle. Roosevelt's reply to the premier's June 13 appeal carried no promise of armed intervention. The London cable, in the name of the British Cabinet, demanded that the French fleet sail to British harbours in return for Britain's consent to France seeking terms of an armistice.

"What a very silly thing to ask," Reynaud remarked to Spears. *"Non, vraiment, c'est trop bête."*

Spears was mulling over that comment when Reynaud received the call from de Gaulle proffering the Declaration of Union. When Reynaud put the receiver down, he seemed to Spears to be "transfigured with joy."

Once the message had been explained to him, Spears insisted it be typed up immediately for presentation to the French Cabinet. In the room where secretaries were working, he encountered the inevitable Mme de Portes. She stood over Spears's shoulder as he handed the sheets over for typing, forcing him to hold back the pages to give her time to read them.

At four o'clock, the Cabinet assembled to hear what Reynaud had to tell them. Spears and the British ambassador took an early supper at Chapon Fin and then returned to the Hôtel Montré. They paced the floor in their rooms as they nervously awaited the French decision. By 6:30, they were worried. If the Cabinet was going to approve the Declaration of Union, it surely would have done so by now. At 7:30, word came for them to return to rue Vital-Carles.

Troops were holding back the crowd outside the Quartier Général. Inside, they found a dejected Reynaud. He'd read the declaration twice to the Cabinet, and each time it had evoked disdain and derision. It was clear many of the ministers knew about the proposal before it was read; they could only have heard of it from Mme de Portes.

"A marriage with a corpse," pronounced Marshall Pétain.

"Better be a Nazi province, at least we know what that means," asserted another.

"England will have her neck wrung like a chicken," someone — likely Weygand — added.

Only Georges Mandel, the minister of the interior, and Jewish, spoke in favour. The scheme for union was never put to a vote and Reynaud decided he had no choice but to resign. Ambassador Campbell wired Churchill: "Ministerial crisis … meeting arranged for tomorrow impossible."

Later that night, President Lebrun asked Marshall Pétain to form a new government. The old soldier drew a piece of paper from his pocket. On it he had written the names of those he wanted in his Cabinet; the list included Weygand for Defense, Admiral Darlan for the Navy, Pierre Laval for Foreign Affairs.[24]

✝

The Dragon Rapide carrying Charles de Gaulle put down at Mérignac at 9:30. The chief of his military staff, Colonel Humbert, was there to give him the news. With Reynaud's resignation, de Gaulle was no longer a member of the government. It meant, he knew, certain capitulation. "I understood the dice were cast." He needed no time to decide his next step: he would leave as soon as morning came. But there were certain things he had to do right away.

First, a visit to Reynaud, who de Gaulle found facing "a system collapsing all around him, the people in flight, the Allies withdrawing, and the most illustrious leaders failing." No longer premier, Reynaud remained adamant that he would stay in France. "In these conditions, you will allow me to try my own luck," de Gaulle told him. "I don't want to stay in Bordeaux with Pétain and Weygand."[25] Reynaud not only agreed, but offered 100,000 francs ($40,000) from government funds still at his disposal. De Gaulle then asked Reynaud's aide, Roland de Margerie, to secure passports for his wife and children.

"I'll have them sent up by motorcycle," he promised.

When de Gaulle shook hands with Reynaud, he found the ex-premier's hand "moist and weak." De Gaulle asked himself if he was doing "something crazy … jumping into the water without knowing where is the other bank?"[26]

When he left Reynaud's study on the first floor, de Gaulle encountered General Spears and Ambassador Campbell, who had come to see the former premier. Spears remembered de Gaulle standing in a shadow beside a large column. "I must speak to you," he recalled de Gaulle telling him. "I have very good reason to believe Weygand intends arresting me." When Spears returned from a short session with Reynaud — a man who de Gaulle thought had by now "slipped into a world of unreality" — de Gaulle was waiting for him. The two agreed to meet with Ambassador Campbell a little later at the Hôtel Montré.

Accounts of what transpired there differ. According to Spears, they discussed the possibility of de Gaulle spending the night on a British warship anchored in the Gironde, but de Gaulle makes no mention of this in his memoirs or in later interviews. Spears said he offered to let de Gaulle fly back to London with him in the Dragon Rapide; de Gaulle always maintained it was the other way around. Spears said they arranged to meet in the Hôtel Montré lobby the next morning at seven o'clock; de Gaulle insisted to his son Philippe that they met at the Hôtel Majestic. He told Philippe of having checked in to the Majestic at eleven o'clock Sunday night. Famished, he found the bar closed and that the cook had left with the keys. Someone managed to put together a sandwich for de Gaulle's last supper in France.[27]

Early Monday morning, de Gaulle phoned de Courcel in his room. "I am leaving for England in half an hour. Do you want to come with me?"

The young lieutenant had been thinking about returning to his posting in Syria, but without a second's hesitation answered "I do."

De Gaulle and de Coucel were waiting at the agreed meeting place — most likely the Majestic — when General Spears showed up around seven o'clock. De Gaulle's driver, Marcel Hutin, had driven up in the Peugeot assigned to the general. Jean Laurent arrived with a package containing the 100,000 francs promised by Reynaud, as well as the keys to a flat that Laurent had rented in London. He told de Gaulle he could use the flat at 8 Seymour Place (now Curzon Place) near Hyde Park for as long as he liked. De Gaulle had with him two trunks, one in which he'd stuffed spare pants and an extra uniform along with his metal tank helmet, and the other he'd filled with files and official documents. De Courcel also had two bags and Spears had brought one suitcase. They decided a second car would be needed for the luggage. That took a few minutes to arrange, but by eight o'clock the two vehicles were ready to move out — just as dark clouds gathered over Bordeaux and rain began to fall. On the way to the airport, de Gaulle had the car stop at rue Vital-Carles, perhaps to give the impression he was merely on a round of official meetings.[28]

The stay was a short one, and at Mérignac airport they found things even more chaotic that when de Gaulle had flown in the night before. Planes were parked in a jumble near the terminal and it took some time to find the Dragon Rapide. While searching for the plane, de Gaulle was recognized by several officers who stopped to salute him. When the plane was finally located, everyone was relieved to learn that Squadron Leader Fielden had it fuelled and ready for takeoff. He had slept in it overnight.

Fielden had not, however, counted on so much luggage and he was concerned it would shift during the flight, upsetting the crucial balance of the aircraft. De Courcel was dispatched to find some rope. He returned in a few minutes holding, miraculously, a ball of heavy twine. The luggage was quickly tethered and Fielden revved the plane's two motors for takeoff.

At this point, the accounts of de Gaulle and Spears again diverge. Spears wrote that the general was still fearful of arrest and that "he must have found the tension excruciating." According to Spears, it was not until the plane had started to taxi that de Gaulle, hanging back as if he was there merely to see someone off, suddenly made to leap aboard. "With hooked hands I hoisted de Gaulle aboard," Spears wrote. "De Courcel, more nimble, was in in a trice. The door slammed. I just had time to see the gaping face of the chauffeur and one or two more beside him."

De Gaulle chose not to dignify Spears's claims — plausible though they might be — with a denial. In his *Mémoires* he wrote simply that "There was nothing romantic or difficult about the departure."

Hugging the coast of France, Fielden flew north out of the gathering storm above Bordeaux. Over La Rochelle and Rochefort, de Gaulle saw smoke rising from ships set on fire by German aircraft. Above the harbour of St. Nazaire they could see a large ship on its side, floundering in the water. It was the *Lancastria*, a British liner carrying five thousand troops, of whom two thousand were lost.* "We passed over Paimpont, where my mother lay very ill. The forest was all smoking with the munitions dumps which were being destroyed there."[29] Fielden guided the plane across Brit-

---

* On being informed of the sinking, Churchill ordered all news of it suppressed, fearing its effect on British morale. "The newspapers have got quite enough disaster for today, at least," he said.

tany, potentially the most hazardous section of the trip, before gaining the English Channel and setting down on the Isle of Jersey for refuelling. The airport manager, Jack Herbert, invited the trio to lunch at the Hôtel St. Pierre, but the offer was declined. De Gaulle asked for a cup of coffee and after taking a sip of the weak concoction, declared it must be tea. "His martyrdom had begun," Spears would remember. Spears had time to buy a case of whisky for Winston Churchill. Shortly after de Gaulle's aircraft took off, Herbert was alarmed to see a German fighter scream over the island. Fortunately, it veered off and flew away.

In the cabin of the noisy Dragon Rapide, conversation was muted. What does one do or think at such a time? A tear. A clearing of the throat. A straightening up. We can imagine de Gaulle leaning forward to look out the small portside window, where he would have seen the Isle of Wight and the coast of England draw near.

Geoffroy de Courcel would remember de Gaulle speaking of his confidence that the United States would eventually enter the war, and that Hitler would turn on Russia. "The great mistake the French government and our generals are making is in thinking of this as a local war, instead of realizing that this is a world war and there is all the world to fight in," he told de Courcel.[30]

Fielden set the plane down at the RAF base in Heston in the bright sunshine of early afternoon. The drive into London took most of an hour. It was when they were unloading at Seymour Place that a sudden feeling of aloneness gripped de Gaulle. The realization of what he was doing, he would later admit, was "appalling" to him. He was, he thought, "like a man on the shore of an ocean, proposing to swim across."[31]

II

Days of Defiance: The Wild Card Is Drawn

France is not alone! She is not alone! She is not alone! This war is not limited to the unfortunate territory of our country. This war is not finished by the battle of France. This war is a worldwide war.... Whatever happens, the flame of the French Resistance must not be extinguished and will not be extinguished.

— Charles de Gaulle
London, June 18, 1940

CHAPTER 5
The Appeal of June 18

I turn the knob on the wireless set, which is tuned to London. By a pure fluke I find myself listening to a transmission in French. A voice announces an appeal to be made by a French general. I don't catch his name. In a delivery that is jerky and peremptory — not at all well-suited to the radio — the general urges all Frenchmen to rally round him, to carry on the struggle. I feel I have come back to life. A feeling I thought had died forever stirs again within me: hope. There is one man after all — one alone, perhaps — who understands what I feel in my heart: "It's not over yet."[1]

— Agnès Humbert
Musée de l'Homme, Paris

With Paris under German occupation and England preparing for invasion, the focus of the war shifted suddenly from distress over the defeat of France to fear that Britain would be the next to fall. In Washington, President Roosevelt worried that the British fleet might pass into the hands of the Nazis. If Hitler could obtain command of the world's largest navy, backed up by the impressive battlewagons of the French and German fleets, even the shores of North America would no longer be safe.

Canada, the senior of the Dominions in the British Commonwealth of Nations, found itself transformed into Britain's most powerful ally.[2] "I should not be surprised to see the British fleet come here and with the fleet the British Cabinet," Canadian prime minister Mackenzie King wrote in his diary on June 17.[3] If this were to happen, he thought, it could lead to the setting up of an Empire government in Ottawa.

In London that day, Charles de Gaulle turned the key to the door of the small fourth-floor flat in Seymour Place to which fate had now brought him. He would have welcomed the loan of this *pied-à-terre*, but only one thing counted for him: the fate of France. His sublime belief in the eventual rescue of Europe by the United States allowed him to think beyond the crisis of the day. Get on with the war, of course, and ensure the eventual reappearance of French forces on the battlefield. But if he was to restore the grandeur of his country, he would have to "climb to the heights and never come down."[4]

Not bothering to unpack, de Gaulle and Geoffroy de Courcel returned to General Spears's car for the short drive to the Royal Automobile Club in Pall Mall, where they took lunch. Then it was on to No. 10 Downing Street, where Spears and de Gaulle found Winston Churchill relaxing in the garden, enjoying the warmth of a sunny afternoon.

Churchill had begun the day with his usual glass of white wine and he had a warm greeting for his visitors. "I was sure you would be back," he told de Gaulle, smiling. When the general asked for time to speak on the BBC to rally resistance in France, Churchill agreed. "I can give you some time once Pétain asks for an armistice," he said.

By the time de Gaulle got back to Seymour Place, the news was out that France had given up the struggle. "It is with a heavy heart," Pétain said in a broadcast, "that I tell you today that it is necessary to stop the fighting."

Arrangements were made for de Gaulle to speak on the BBC at six o'clock the following night. Ever mindful of military protocol (or perhaps as a side bet in his bid to defy Pétain) de Gaulle dictated a telegram to Bordeaux asking if he should continue negotiations with the British government for war materials. The reply demanded his immediate return to Bordeaux.

Lieutenant de Courcel had stayed at Seymour Place to work the telephone. He talked to Jean Monnet at the French Economic Mission, and accepted an invitation for he and de Gaulle to go to Monnet's apartment for dinner. De Courcel also called an old childhood friend, Elisabeth de Miribel, who had been at working at the mission since January. He gave her news of her family, whom he had encountered in Tours during the government's flight to Bordeaux, and asked if she would come to Seymour Place tomorrow to "type something important."

She agreed and, anxious to make a good impression, went out and bought a new hat. "It was probably childish and stupid," she wrote, "but I did it."

A great-granddaughter of Marshall MacMahon, first president of the Third Republic (1873–79), and descendant of a line of de Miribels distinguished for their service to the French military, Mlle de Miribel was accustomed to mingling with high officials. That night, she dined with Lady Warwick, the sister of Anthony Eden and widow of the sixth Earl of Warwick.

De Gaulle and de Courcel arrived at the apartment of Jean Monnet and his wife, Sylvie, shortly before eight o'clock. Monnet had not yet returned home. Ushered into the parlour, they sat silently, the general apparently lost in thought. Silvie Monnet asked de Gaulle how long his mission in London would last. De Gaulle bristled. "Madame," he said, "I am not here on a mission. I have come to London to save the honour of France."[5]

Later, the atmosphere around the dining table became tense when de Gaulle referred to Pétain as a traitor. Monnet tried to make a joke of it. "Don't say that to my butler — he's a veteran of Verdun and would be very shocked."

The exchange convinced de Courcel that Monnet held very different views from de Gaulle, and that he was unlikely to become a supporter of the general.

Tuesday, June 18 dawned as yet another beautiful day. From the large, sunlit living room of Seymour Place, de Gaulle could see people strolling in Hyde Park. He was at work on his speech by eight o'clock, seated at a small table smoking one cigarette after another, while dipping his pen into an inkwell and casting aside page after page of his early drafts.

Elisabeth de Miribel arrived at noon, to be welcomed with an offer of tea that the general served from a trolley. To the twenty-five-year-old de Miribel, de Gaulle was a figure of immense size, made the larger by his uniform, boots, and leggings. Despite his courtesy, she felt intimated as she listened to him speak with "great calm" about the war and the future of France.[6]

De Gaulle and de Courcel left soon after to have lunch with Duff Cooper, the minister of information in the British War Cabinet. Over lunch, Cooper worried about whether he should say anything to de Gaulle of a disturbing turn of events. In Churchill's absence at Cabinet that morning — the prime minister was preparing for an important speech to the House in the afternoon — Cooper had presented the proposal for de Gaulle to speak on the BBC. The Cabinet flatly rejected it, feeling now was no time to push the Pétain government further into Hitler's arms. Cooper, who had immediately alerted General Spears, decided not to mention this to de Gaulle.

De Gaulle returned to Seymour Place about three o'clock, quite unaware of the opposition Cooper had encountered. He gave his speech a final reading, scrawling yet more changes to it.

De Courcel had set up Elisabeth de Miribel in the entrance hall of the apartment, where his portable typewriter rested on a small table. She found it very difficult to read the general's much worked-over draft and had to appeal to de Courcel for help.[7] As he dictated, she clumsily typed it out, using only two fingers. It was hot in the apartment, but by five o'clock they were satisfied they had a clean copy. De Courcel telephoned for a taxi. After dropping Elisabeth off at her building on Brompton Place in the tony South Kensington district, he and de Gaulle reversed direction to go to the Broadcasting House of the BBC in Portland Place, at the top of Regent Street.

Earlier that afternoon, Winston Churchill had made another of his stirring speeches to the British House of Commons. He'd risen to his feet, well-fortified with wine and whisky, and spoken dramatically of his island's intention to turn back the enemy that was now at its shores. Members had pounded their benches and cheered as Churchill hurled defiance at Hitler and his legions. He hurried back to No. 10 Downing, changed to his pyjamas, and went immediately to bed. General Spears found him sound asleep and awakened him to tell him of the crisis that had arisen over de Gaulle. Speak to every member of the Cabinet, Churchill told him, and see if you can change their minds. By five o'clock, his rounds completed, Spears had won over every minister. They all agreed de Gaulle's speech should go to air as planned.

✝

At around the time de Courcel put in his request for a taxi, Patrick Smith of the BBC's news department received an unusual telephone call at Broadcasting House. The Foreign Office was on the line to say that a French general would be arriving to make a broadcast and Smith would have to verify that the text did not contain any secret messages. Smith could find none in the two and one-half pages of typing that de Gaulle handed over as they waited in studio 4C for a French news broadcast to finish.[8] Smith was feeling a little clumsy about how awkwardly the BBC was welcoming this distinguished visitor. It had taken time to find the deputy director-general, Sir Stephen Tallents, to officially greet de Gaulle, and the general had meanwhile declined all offers of coffee. The buckle of de Gaulle's Sam Browne belt had twice gotten entangled on the buttons of Smith's vest as they squeezed through narrow doors on the way into the studio.

When de Gaulle sat down to give technicians a voice level — only the words "La France" were needed — the French newsreader Maurice Thierry, sitting opposite, jerked to his feet to salute him. Thierry, who had downed several cognacs during a sorrowful lunch, hit his head against the microphone that hung over the table. It rocked to and fro, but by now de Gaulle had begun to speak and he did not stop. The technicians struggled to adjust the sound volume to compensate for the fading of de Gaulle's voice each time the mike swung away. Despite the maladroitness of the BBC's crew, de Gaulle was fulfilling the first objective of his flight to England — to "hoist the colours" and serve notice that the war was not over for France. He spoke in steady, measured tones:

> The leaders who, for many years, have been at the head of the French armies have formed a government. This government, alleging the defeat of our armies, has made contact with the enemy in order to stop the fighting. It is true, we were, we are, overwhelmed by the mechanical,

ground, and air forces of the enemy. Infinitely more than their number, it is the tanks, the aeroplanes, the tactics of the Germans which are causing us to retreat. It was the tanks, the aeroplanes, the tactics of the Germans that surprised our leaders to the point of bringing them to where they are today.

But has the last word been said? Must hope disappear? Is defeat final? No!

Believe me, I who am speaking to you with full knowledge of the facts, and who tells you that nothing is lost for France. The same means that overcame us can bring us victory one day. For France is not alone! She is not alone! She is not alone! She has a vast Empire behind her. She can align with the British Empire that holds the sea and continues the fight. She can, like England, use without limit the immense industry of the United States.

This war is not limited to the unfortunate territory of our country. This war is not over as a result of the Battle of France. This war is a worldwide war. All the mistakes, all the delays, all the suffering, do not alter the fact that there are, in the world, all the means necessary to crush our enemies one day. Vanquished today by mechanical force, in the future we will be able to overcome by a superior mechanical force. The fate of the world depends on it.

I, General de Gaulle, currently in London, invite the officers and the French soldiers who are located in British territory or who might end up here, with their weapons or without their weapons, I invite the engineers and the specialized workers of the armament industries who are located in British territory or who might end up here, to put themselves in contact with me.

Whatever happens, the flame of French Resistance must not be extinguished and will not be extinguished. Tomorrow, as today, I will speak on the radio from London.[9]

As de Gaulle's words flew from the studio, Patrick Smith saw tears roll down the general's cheeks, which had by now taken on a puffy appearance. Smith thought the speech was memorable; the cry of a patriotic soldier-statesman furious at the defeats his country had suffered. General Spears, de Courcel, and Sir Stephen had listened in an adjoining room, de Courcel struggling to keep himself from choking up. When de Gaulle was finished, he circled the studio and shook hands with everyone. It was then Smith discovered that no recording of the speech had been made. He knew de Gaulle would be furious when he found that out. That evening, de Gaulle and de Courcel dined together at the Langham Hotel, a short distance from Broadcasting House. They exchanged hardly a word. Elisabeth de Miribel ate alone at home and did not hear the broadcast.

The four-minute speech that was to become known as "the Appeal of June 18" was a carefully constructed denial of the defeat to which the Pétain government had consigned France. This denial was combined with an insistence that the reversals suffered at home could yet be overcome. Churchill had cautioned de Gaulle against condemning Pétain as a traitor. The general attached no specific blame to any of the "leaders who ... have been at the head of the French armies" beyond observing they had been surprised at the ferocity of the German attack.

Within de Gaulle's appeal there rested an irresistible proposition: join me, so that the flame of French resistance would not be squelched. Implicit, however, in his call to French troops to contact him was the fact that the issuance of such a summons was tantamount to an act of treason. Finally, his notice that he would be speaking again the next day made it clear that this speech was no mere impulsive act of the moment; there must be a plan. In barely more than three hundred words, de Gaulle had spelled out an analysis of why the Battle of France had been lost, and how the war could yet be won. In de Gaulle's view, he needed to "bring back into the war not merely some Frenchmen, but France." To do this — and to win the support of foreign allies — he must become "the inflexible champion of the nation."

De Gaulle's speech did not have a large audience the night of its broadcast. Among those who heard it, many — but not all — were motivated to make for London or to find other ways of helping France continue the fight. Agnès Humbert, having taken refuge in the home of a relative in Vicq-sur-Breuilh, a village in the Limousin district midway between Orléans and Bordeaux, hurried onto the street to tell an army captain what she'd just heard.

He was not impressed. "That'll be de Gaulle, the general; he's a crackpot, that's for sure."

In the small town of Locminé in Brittany, a priest rushed into the town square to tell evening strollers of de Gaulle's speech. Encountering a young girl escorting a frail lady dressed in black, he blurted out that a French general in London had said "nothing has been lost, we must keep on fighting."

"C'est mon fils, Monsieur le Curé, c'est mon fils," the woman answered. It was Charles de Gaulle's mother, on the arm of his niece Geneviève, daughter of his brother Xavier.[10]

Newspapers the next day — including some in unoccupied France — carried brief accounts of the Appeal and over the next twenty-four hours the BBC reported the speech four times in its newscasts. But it received not nearly the attention of Churchill's stirring "finest hour" speech, another magnificent performance of grand eloquence and defiance. Churchill, declaring Britain "more than capable" of meeting any sea-borne invasion, had urged the British people to "bear ourselves that, if the British Empire and its Commonwealth last for a thousand years, men will still say, 'This was their finest hour.'"

A trickle of visitors to Seymour Place soon turned into a steady stream. Mlle de Miribel was back, to stay. René Pleven, Jean Monnet's assistant, declared for Free France, as did his aide Pierre Denis,[11] and René Cassin, a law professor who asked de Gaulle, "In what way can an old jurist like me be useful to you?" De Gaulle asked him to figure out how to write an agreement between a government (the United Kingdom) and one man (de Gaulle).[12] The former politician Maurice Schumann, now a journalist with the Havas News Agency, on hearing of the Appeal while in Bordeaux, found his way into Spain from where he made for London.

Gaston Palewski, an aide to Reynaud who had escaped to Africa with his squadron, put himself under de Gaulle's command after being summoned by telegram: "Come and join me at once."

Palewski wondered why more of the French in London were not rallying to de Gaulle. "The London French, my dear fellow," de Gaulle told him, "fall into two groups — those who are in the United States and those who are getting ready to leave."

There were also other points on the compass that beckoned. Ambassador Charles Corbin made for South America while the head of the Economic Mission, the writer Paul Morand, returned to France to become an ambassador of Vichy.

De Gaulle made a priority of contacting French commanders throughout the Empire, hoping to bring them around, if necessary by offering to serve under them. Telegrams to General Charles Noguès, French commander-in-chief in North Africa, went unanswered. Noguès made his sentiments clear when he ordered the arrest in Casablanca of former Cabinet minister Georges Mandel, who had opposed the Armistice (and would be eventually murdered by the Nazis).

What of the French military? There were thousands of French soldiers in Britain who had been evacuated from Dunkirk, along with some ten thousand sailors aboard ships that had escaped from channel ports. British authorities did little to help de Gaulle recruit them; some regarded those willing to join him as "rebels against their own government."[13] General Émile Béthouart, commander of the French Alpine Division that had fought in Norway, declined to join de Gaulle, but cleared the way for him to visit French troops camped at Trentham Park outside London. In an afternoon, de Gaulle won over nearly one thousand volunteers, including the head of a Foreign Legion unit Lieutenant-Colonel Magrin-Verneret and his number two, Captain Pierre Koenig. Other Norway veterans joining de Gaulle included captains Pierre Tissier and André Dewavrin (later to take the code name Passy after the Metro station near his home in Paris). Vice Admiral Émile Muselier arrived in London from Gibraltar after having led a small contingent of naval craft to the British outpost. De Gaulle made him commander of the Free French navy, to be assembled from former French fighting ships and castoffs from other navies. Muselier was fated to have a stormy relationship with de Gaulle, despite having brought to him the idea of adopting the double-barred Cross of Lorraine as the symbol of the Free French. Other recruits stepped forward: Captain Philippe de Haute-clocque, bandaged from wounds received in the Battle of France, turned up in London. Thierry d'Argenlieu, a Catholic priest who had become the captain of a French navy corvette only to be captured during the battle for Cherbourg, escaped from a German prisoner-of-war train and found his way to de Gaulle's side. De Gaulle could count some seven thousand able-bodied men in the service of Free France in the summer of 1940. There would be thirty-five thousand by the end of the year.[14]

✝

On the day that Charles de Gaulle issued his Appeal, Yvonne de Gaulle shepherded her family aboard a British tramp steamer in Brest. A motorcycle courier had arrived from Bordeaux the day before with their passports and Yvonne coaxed her sister Suzanne to drive them to the port. Their luggage carried only a bit of clothing, some jewellery, and family papers. The fuel depots in Brest had been bombed and smoke hung over the city. Arrangement had been made to travel on a Polish ship, but they narrowly missed its departure. Later, they heard it had been bombed and sunk. The five, including Anne's caregiver, Mlle Potel, slept head-to-toe in a small cabin.

They disembarked the next morning at Falmouth and Yvonne paid in advance for three rooms at the Landsworn Hotel. They took an English breakfast in a dining room furnished with small tables inlaid with mother-of-pearl. Paintings of Scottish and Welsh country scenes hung on the walls. Yvonne read an account in the *Times* of de Gaulle's speech. Philippe hurried through his meal and headed to the police station. In barely understandable English, he told the police that he was the son of the French general who had spoken on the BBC the night before. "They listened patiently but with an air of skepticism," Philippe remembered. He was asked to write down everything, including where he was staying. He returned to the hotel to find other members of the family asleep.

That night, while they awaited dinner, a policeman came to the dining room with a phone number for de Gaulle in London. Yvonne rushed to the office and asked the innkeeper to put in a call. When it went through, she heard the voice of her husband, sounding distant and almost chilly. "Ah! It's you. Join me at 6 Seymour Grove. I'll expect you tomorrow." With that, he hung up. His family's arrival was not news to the general; René Pleven had already alerted him of their safe arrival.[15]

An official of the Foreign Office, identified by the white gardenia in his lapel, met the family at a London train station. Later, looking around the apartment at Seymour Place, Yvonne would have soon determined that it was far too small. At her urging, de Gaulle took a first-floor suite at the Rubens Hotel. It was one of the more upscale hostelries in London and cost more than de Gaulle could afford. Within a week, Yvonne found something more economical; a mock-Tudor villa in suburban Pettswood for which de Gaulle signed a lease at fourteen pounds, one shilling and eight pence per month.* The general commuted by train, staying over occasionally at the Connaught Hotel in Carlos Place, in the heart of Mayfair. He also had use of a chauffeured Renault provided by Alfred-Étienne Bellenger, director of the London branch of Cartier, the jeweller. Philippe left to attend a naval cadet school.

The French Cabinet may have thought they could negotiate the terms of an armistice with Germany, but when Berlin responded to Marshall Pétain's overture, the dictates of Adolf Hitler left little room for discussion. At seven o'clock on the evening of June 22, in the same railway car at Compiègne used for Germany's surrender in 1918, a French delegation led by General Huntziger — the man de Gaulle had thought might rally the army in the defence of France — agreed to the "cessation of hostilities against the German Reich." German OKW Chief General Wilhelm Keitel had given little in negotiations. The terms required the disarming of French troops, the splitting of France into occupied and unoccupied regions, and required the French government to pay the costs of the German Occupation. French prisoners of war were to remain in German hands for the duration. Article 8 called for the French fleet to be "demobilized and disarmed." A similar armistice treaty would be signed a few days later with Italy.[16] The British government reacted angrily. The Armistice was a violation "of agreements solemnly concluded" between Britain and France, and by agreeing to it, the Bordeaux government had given up "any right to represent free French citizens."

---

* This is the equivalent of US $56.00, or $900.00 in 2014 currency.

General de Gaulle returned to the BBC airwaves that night. He was more strident this time and the speech marked his first use of the term "Free French." He spoke again two nights later: "One day, I promise you, the mechanized army, navy, and air force, together with our Allies, will give freedom back to the world and greatness back to our country."

By now, more Frenchmen were hearing de Gaulle's broadcasts. He had just reached an agreement for Churchill's government to discuss with his newly organized French National Committee "all matters connected with the prosecution of the war." It emboldened de Gaulle to declare he was taking under his command "all the French who are now living in British territory or who may arrive later." The deal also meant British funding for Free French operations, to be paid back later on terms to be decided.** De Gaulle and a growing staff moved into four rooms in St. Stephen's House, a dingy Victoria Embankment building where General Spears kept an office.

Winston Churchill's gravest concern was for the uncertain future of the French fleet. It was imperative it not be allowed to fall into Axis hands. Should the French ships, anchored in North African ports, be attacked and sunk? After several days of discussion the Cabinet agreed to leave the decision up to Churchill. In a midnight walk in the garden of No. 10 Downing, Churchill had one last talk with his minister of munitions, the Canadian Max Beaverbrook. With Beaverbrook's "Good night, Winnie" ringing in his ears, Churchill made up his mind.

The red-roofed, whitewashed buildings of the Algerian city of Oran and the docks of the nearby port of Mers-el-Kabir lay baked from the sun of a hot afternoon when Force H of the Royal Navy, made up of the battle cruiser HMS *Hood* and twenty-six other warships unleashed Operation Catapult. It was 5:54 p.m. on July 3, 1940, and after sixteen minutes of firing by both sides, the French fleet was sunk, disabled, or in flight to other North African ports. The battleship *Bretagne*, which had carried 1,820 cases of French gold to Halifax, Canada, in March, blew up when a shell hit her ammunition magazine. The French commander, Admiral Marcel Gensoul, had been offered the alternatives of having his ships join the Royal Navy, being interned in a British port, or sailing to North Amer-

---

** Britain's aid to Free France amounted to £30 million by 1943, after which the movement became self-sufficient. The advances were repaid early in 1945.

ica for decommissioning. He rejected them all. A total of 1,297 French sailors were killed.[17] Not having been notified of the attack by the British, de Gaulle heard of it only later that evening. The news plunged him into despair over both what had happened, and the way the British had boasted of it as a victory.

The next day, a disheartened de Gaulle told General Spears he was thinking of "withdrawing to Canada and living there as a private citizen." But he had to recognize there was logic behind the British attack: "England might well fear that the enemy would one day manage to gain control of our fleet."[18] It was better for French ships to have been sunk than to have been anchored to a German Iron Cross.

The Pétain regime was quick to claim the attack demonstrated that England, not Germany, was France's real enemy. "France has never had a more inveterate enemy than Britain," declared Pierre Laval. The pro-Vichy Le Petit Parisien headlined the news, L'INCON-CEVABLE AGGRESSION. French sailors in Britain reacted with anger and recruitment trickled to near zero for the next several weeks.[19] To de Gaulle, the whole experience was "a lamentable event."[20] But, he concluded, "the saving of France ranked above everything, even above the fate of her ships ... our duty was still to go on with the fight."[21]

CHAPTER 6
Surviving the Swastika

The tread of German boots was first heard in Paris in the leafy suburb of Auteuil, on the streets leading out of the Bois de Boulogne. On one of these, rue Molitor, Claire Fauteux was awakened at dawn on Friday, June 14, by the passage of two hundred fair-haired German cavalrymen bound for the Arc de Triomphe. They were among the elite of the Occupation force and had been chosen for a ceremonial role in the triumphant parade of the German 18th Army down the Champs-Éysées. Fauteux had gone to bed exhausted and had left the shutters of her ground–floor, bedroom window open to the cooling night air. Peering out, her artist's eye caught the tired look on the faces of the young soldiers. They bore little resemblance to a vaunted "master race," she thought. Those on horseback struggled to stay awake, their heads sagging forward as they nodded off. It had been one thing to know, as did practically everyone in Paris when they went to bed the night before, that the Germans were coming. To actually see them — and Fauteux was one of the first — transformed mere apprehension into ghastly reality. Life under the swastika had begun.[1]

When Claire Fauteux summoned the courage to go out, she was horrified by the sight of the flag flying from a tower of Notre Dame. Nazi banners — a black swastika in a white circle against a red background — were unfurled atop all main public buildings, including l'Hôtel de Ville and Luxembourg Palace, the home of the Senate, and the Palais Bourbon, the seat of the Chamber of Deputies. German officers, resplendent in their uniforms, acted more like tourists than conquerors as they struggled to strike up conversations with shopkeepers and pedestrians. Their behaviour was summed up by Jean-Paul Sartre, who was captured near the Maginot Line but got back to Paris in 1941 after escaping from his prisoner-of-war camp on the Luxembourg border:

> They did not force civilians to make way for them on the pavements. They would offer their seats to old ladies on the Metro. They showed great fondness for children and would pat them on the cheek. They had been told to behave correctly and, being well-disciplined, they tried shyly and conscientiously to do so. Some of them even displayed a naïve kindliness which could find no practical expression.[2]

During the early days of the Occupation, young French girls giggled at the efforts of apple-cheeked soldiers, French-German phrase books in hand, to flirt with them. Place de la Concorde swarmed with Nazi newsreel photographers while planes flew low over the rooftops. Clocks were advanced an hour to put the city on Berlin time and posters announced a nine o'clock curfew. Other notices warned Parisians that under pain of death, they were to declare the presence of any Britons or Canadians.[3]

Claire Fauteux was a Canadian born to the French language in Quebec, and she had come to Paris thirty years before to pursue her determination to paint. A job at the Canadian Embassy kept her in France, but no one had contacted her when Colonel Georges Vanier, the Canadian minister to France, ordered the staff to join the diplomatic exodus from Paris the previous weekend. When she got to work she found the embassy locked and deserted. The day the Germans moved in, they commandeered the school across the street from her apartment as a barracks, and she went there to identify herself. "Do not fear," a German officer told her. "We have not come to arrest you." He added, in an unhappy voice as a German love song blared from a loudspeaker, "Today we sing for tomorrow we die." Fauteux thought he was referring to the intended invasion of England. His orders were firm: she was not to travel outside the city. Of that she had no intention. A bigger problem — with her job at the embassy gone — would be how to feed herself, and without a job how would she survive? Her plight was one she would have to share with other Parisians, both those who remained in the city and those who would soon be straggling back.

For the thirty thousand Americans in Paris, their neutral status enabled them to move about freely. The American Library as well as the American Hospital in Neuilly, the comfortable suburb not far from the Bois de Boulogne, remained open. The hospital's chief surgeon, Dr. Thierry de Martel, a French citizen, wrote to Ambassador Bullitt to tell him that while he had promised not to leave Paris, "I did not say if I would remain in Paris alive or dead."[4] Despondent at the fate of the city in which he had been born, de Martel went to his apartment at 18 rue Weber, settled himself on a sofa, and injected himself with strychnine. His suicide was one of more than a dozen in Paris that day.

It rained that first day the Nazis were in Paris, an occurrence that matched the tears of the city's people. The restaurants La Tour d'Argent and La Lorraine were the first to print menus in German. The city's most expensive brothel, La Chabanais, posted a notice that it would open at three o'clock, and when it did so, there was no shortage of German-speaking clients. Private cars were ordered off the road. Some enterprising shopkeepers were quick to post NO JEWS notices on their doors, in French and German. General von Studnitz, the German military commander of "Grosse-Paris," settled himself into the Hôtel Crillon and then visited the outgoing French military commander for Paris, General Henri Dentz at Les Invalides. He demanded the return of the German flags captured in the First World War. The day after the arrival of the Germans, restaurants on the Left Bank were returning chairs to their terraces and the Pigalle cinema reopened its doors.

For Parisians, coming to terms with the Occupation meant relearning the routine of daily life — getting to work, feeding their families, and keeping a roof over their heads. The working poor — comprising most of those left behind in Paris — saw their ordeal as yet another example of the failure of the *patrons* to put country ahead of selfish interests. The heavy French reparations to pay for the Occupation took as much as 400 million francs a day out of the country's economy, depleting funds to pay for schools, public utilities, or municipal services.[5] Food shortages spread that summer as more of the produce brought to the sales stalls of Les Halles was commandeered for German troops or for shipment to Germany. Rationing grew more stringent as the Occupation progressed; barely a morsel of meat a day was going into Parisian mouths. The mortality rate rose 40 percent and deaths from tuberculosis doubled.

As desperate as the situation was in Paris, conditions in the countryside were little better. The day after the Occupation of Paris, General Heinz Guderian wrote to his wife, Gretel, from a point near the Swiss border: "The country is in a catastrophic condition. As a result of the enforced evacuations, there is an indescribable refugee misery and all the cattle are dying. Everywhere, places are plundered by refugees and French soldiers. Up till now we have come across only scanty civilian populations. The Middle Ages were humane compared with the present."[6]

The fact the German invaders were conducting themselves carefully in Paris did not prevent brutal retaliation against anyone who displeased the occupiers. On June 17, Mme Bourgeois paid the penalty for speaking insolently to the troops who had requisitioned her home. She was tied to a tree in her backyard and, as her daughter looked on, she was shot. The body was left for twenty-four hours before it was buried in a grave her daughter had been forced to dig. A youth was shot for cutting telephone lines — a clear act of sabotage in the eyes of the Germans.[7] The incidents set the stage for the visit of Adolf Hitler on June 23. He took only a few hours to visit the Eiffel Tower, cast eyes on Napoleon's tomb at Hôtel des Invalides, and drive by the Opera and Sacre Coeur — which he pronounced as ugly. Nevertheless, he declared that his triumphal tour fulfilled "the dream of my life."

Far south of Paris, the remnants of the French government found themselves scattered about the country. Returning to Paris was out of the question, and under the terms of the Armistice, Bordeaux was in the Occupied Zone. Running a hand across the map of France, one could see that the major cities of the so-called *zone libre* such as Lyon or Marseille — one under the thumb of its radical mayor, Édouard Herriott, and the other too likely a jumping-off spot for anyone wanting to get out of the country — were unsuitable. The new Cabinet settled on the old spa town of Vichy "where ladies with triple chins and gentlemen with cirrhotic livers came to take the waters." Its ample supply of hotel rooms, now empty of guests, would serve to accommodate politicians and civil servants.[8]

Paul Reynaud, exhausted from his stressful days as premier, pondered an invitation from Pétain to become ambassador to Spain. It was with this assignment in mind that he and Hélène de Portes set out by car from Bordeaux to cross the south of France. Their destination was a vacation house in Sainte-Maxime, a Mediterranean seaside town fifty kilometres east of the great French naval base of Toulon. Reynaud looked forward to a rest beside the sea and the countess anticipated spending pleasant evenings at the casinos of the Riviera. As well, Sainte-Maxime provided a convenient departure point for passage out of the country — just in case the need for quick escape might arise.[9]

Reynaud had sent his two Cabinet secretaries on ahead to arrange accommodation in Spain, but they had not counted on being caught up in the careful scrutiny of Spanish border guards. Alert officers found a fortune in gold and jewels hidden in their car. The gold, valued at 18 million francs, could only have come from the government's secret funds. The jewels had belonged to Mme de Portes. Worse was to come. As Reynaud and his mistress made their way through the Languedoc countryside on June 28, she suggested he take the wheel. A bit of driving might relax him. A few minutes later, Reynaud failed to navigate a turn outside Nimes; the car swerved off the road and into a tree. Suitcases from the rear seat flew forward, one striking the countess on the back of the neck. The impact of the crash threw both she and Reynaud against the dashboard, rendering them unconscious. When Reynaud came to, he was unable to revive his mistress. Mme de Portes had been killed instantly. Reynaud, cut and bruised, stopped a passing motorist who brought police and doctors to the scene.

✝

General de Gaulle's confidence that he could rally France to his cause grew as his BBC broadcasts reached more of his countrymen. A postcard sent July 19, showing a group of men and women grieving at the tomb of the Unknown Soldier, told him: "De Gaulle, we have heard you. Now we shall wait for you!"[10] He also received the occasional bit of mail and information brought out by volunteers. Together, these messages painted a sketchy picture of conditions in France. De Gaulle mistrusted information from civilian sources, however; he needed the assurance that informers were bound by military discipline before he would rely on them. The ideal observer was a French soldier who he could instruct personally and then send on a mission. He understood, though, the extreme risk facing anyone daring enough to return to Nazi-occupied France.

De Gaulle dispatched his first agent, one Jacques Mansion, to France disguised as a fishermen. Others followed, some with radio transmitters, although the Free French intelligence network would remain haphazard and poorly organized for many months to come. The general was brutally frank with anyone willing to put his life at risk. Standing in his office at St. Stephen's House, his back to a fireplace in which a small blaze helped ward off the chill of a wet summer's day, cigar in hand, de Gaulle told Gilbert Renault that he was sure to be caught.

"I hope not," Renault responded.

"But, yes," came de Gaulle's retort, with the flicker of a smile. "One always gets caught in that line of work."[11]

Those who returned knew they were headed into a vortex of intrigue and suspicion. Paris was overrun with *agents provocateurs* — French-speaking Germans trained to trap civilians into betraying themselves. More dangerous were French with pro-German sentiments, or the many only too ready to settle a personal score or take out their enmities against Jewish neighbours by betraying them to the Gestapo. "I have the honour to draw to your attention," one citizen wrote, "that an apartment at 17 bis Boulevard Rochechouart, belonging to the Jew Greisalmer, contains very fine furniture...."[12] Everyone was playing a game of bet, bluff, and betrayal, and there were no real winners.

✝

Members of the vast French bureaucracy, a machine now creaking from the chaos of defeat, struggled to carry on with their normal duties. De Gaulle recognized that mayors and prefects — the latter the uniquely French functionary who carried out the will of the central government in each department of the country — could be especially useful to Free France. But were any prepared to risk their freedom — or their lives — to act in this hour of their country's need?

In Chartres, the old cathedral city on the great plain of the Beauce eighty kilometres southwest of Paris, the prefect for the Eure-et-Loire department had gained renown as the youngest man ever appointed to that exalted position. Jean Moulin was unknown to de Gaulle when he took up his appointment in Chartres in January 1939. A one-hour train ride from Paris, it was a more appealing post than the ones Moulin had held as a *sous-préfet* or *chef du cabinet* of prefectures in the south of France. Moulin had grown up in the Languedoc wine region, the son of a high-school headmaster. His father's occupation cast Moulin in the anti-clerical mode of radical political thinking, an attitude he carried forward into a busy life of leftist activism. Between prefecture assignments, he'd played his own Paris game as chief aide to Pierre Cot, the left-wing minister for air under the Popular Front government of Socialist Leon Blum. Among other feats, he claimed to have engineered the illegal transfer of a dozen planes to the Spanish Republican government as it attempted to fight off the fascist forces of General Francisco Franco.

In Chartres, admired around the world for its nine-hundred-year-old cathedral, Notre-Dame de Chartres, Moulin gained a reputation for decisive handling of budgets and a deft distribution of government largesse to the towns of the Eure-et-Loire department. At forty, he carried himself with a disarming boyishness, flavoured with a strong dose of arrogance and even insolence. Darkly handsome, an amateur painter of considerable skill, and a collector of French art and attractive women, Moulin reacted quickly to the German incursion into France. He had posters printed and helped paste them onto lampposts all over the department urging resistance. "People of the Eure-et-Loire, your sons are fighting victoriously against the German onslaught. Don't listen to people who are spreading panic. They are going to be punished.... Share my confidence. We are going to win."[13]

When the German 8th Infantry Division bypassed Paris and stood on the outskirts of Chartres on June 10, Moulin made a hurried drive into the capital with his mistress, Antoinette Sachs. Their destination was the apartment at 26 rue des Plantes that Moulin kept as a Parisian pied-à-terre. He retrieved confidential files belonging to Pierre Cot from a cupboard and loaded them into the car. Reaching Chartres, he told Antoinette to keep going south. Moulin received orders to evacuate the Préfecture, but he had no intention of leaving. A wave of German planes bombed the city's railway terminal district, causing great damage to civilian housing. Refugees surging south had to be taken care of, and as they moved on, most of the population of Chartres, including the mayor, the town's bishop, and the police force moved with them. Retreating French soldiers stole Moulin's car, forcing him to use a bicycle to move around the town. He struggled to meet the needs of Chartres's few hundred remaining residents for food and water, but managed to keep the town bakery open and put people to work carrying water supplies. In his memoir, *Premier Combat*, Moulin describes how he was standing in the courtyard of the Préfecture on the morning of June 17, dressed in his blue prefect's uniform and flanked by a priest and the only remaining town councillor, when a German armoured car carrying several officers pulled up. Moulin surrendered the city "according to the rules of war." Before driving off, the officers told him he was responsible for maintaining law and order. "Tell your people that for them the war is over."[14]

That evening, two German officers returned to the Préfecture as Moulin was having dinner with a vanload of postmen evacuated from Paris. He was taken to the Hôtel de France, which had been requisitioned as German headquarters. There, he was told that retreating French soldiers, members of a black Senegalese detachment, had raped and murdered a number of women and children.[15] At a barn outside town, he was shown bodies of nine of the victims. It was obvious they had died in an air raid and that the allegation of rape had been contrived as a cover-up for their deaths. Moulin denied that the troops would have carried out such an atrocity and he refused to sign a statement the Germans had prepared which blamed the Senagalese soldiers.

"You know I cannot put my signature on something that dishonours the army of France," Moulin told his captors.

He was taken to a shed where a German threw him onto the body of a woman, claiming she also had been a victim of the black troops. When he stood up, a second German began to beat him.[16]

The beating went on until one a.m. It turned ferocious when Moulin insisted on smiling after each blow. Taken back to Chartres, he was locked in a room with a Senegalese soldier. "I had reached the limit of my resistance," he would remember. He knew that if the beating "started again I would finish by signing." Left lying on the floor, Moulin drifted in and out of consciousness. He thought about taking his own life. "I know that the only human being who can hold me accountable for such an act is my mother, who gave me life. She will forgive me when I do this so that our soldiers cannot be treated as criminals." Shortly before dawn, using a piece of glass that had fallen from a window broken in the bombing, Moulin cut his throat.[17]

> Once I've made up my mind, it is simple to do what I must to carry out my duty. The soldier is asleep, unaware of the drama playing out less than a metre from him. The clock strikes five. The blood runs slow and warm on my chest before it congeals in large clots on the mattress. If everything is finished when they return, they will find me inert, one who cannot sign anything.[18]

But everything was not finished when a guard came upon him. Taken to the Hôtel-Dieu hospital, it was four days before his temperature returned to normal and he could be released. Nothing more was said about signing the false declaration. It took three months for Moulin's scar to heal and during this time he wore a scarf around his neck, a habit he was to retain for the rest of his life. Had he really tried to kill himself? Moulin had cut his throat high on his neck, just below the jaw. He had failed to sever his jugular vein. Whether it was an attempt at suicide or a ruse, he had survived.

Moulin worked at the Préfecture until November when Vichy, upset over his refusal to carry out orders to get rid of left-wing mayors, dismissed him. Retired on a pension of half-pay, he went first to Paris, where he spent two weeks at his old apartment on rue des Plantes.

He spent time with former colleagues from Pierre Cot's Air Ministry, most of them Communists or at least with strong leftist leanings. Cot by now was in the United States after having repudiated the Soviet-German pact, but those who stayed behind stuck to the Communist line that the war was an imperialist plot. Moulin does not record what the members of *la bande de Cot* may have thought of his reckless refusal to implicate French colonial soldiers in an alleged atrocity. One day at La Coupole, one of Moulin's favourite Montparnasse brasseries, he encountered his ex-wife, Marguerite Cerutty. He ended up spending the night with her at her mother's apartment on rue Littré.

In December, Moulin travelled to the Vichy zone on an *Ausweis*, a pass furnished by the German major now in command at Chartres. He visited his mother and sister Laure in Montpelier and settled on the sharing of their father's estate. She took title to the family farm at St. Andiol and he took his father's savings, which gave him the cash he needed to move about the countryside.[19] His status as a retired prefect, amateur painter, and art collector was genuine enough, but Moulin did not stop there. He made a trip to Toulouse, where he tried to get an exit permit through his former *sous-préfet* in Chartres. His old subordinate turned him down and reported his application to Vichy.[20] Moulin also travelled to Marseille, probably with Antoinette Sachs, staying at the Hôtel Moderne on rue Canebiere, the long street that ran down to the old port. He met with his old flatmate Louis Dolivet, who was working with the American diplomat Noel Field — who also happened to be a Soviet agent — on organizing escape routes for comrades trapped in Vichy France. On a side trip to Grasse, a village near Nice, he tricked a clerk in the sub-prefecture into leaving him alone in the office. He used the man's absence to stamp a false identity card with an exit permit. It was in the name of Joseph Jean Mercier and he had prepared it before leaving Chartres. Although Moulin had been attempting to make contact with the Resistance, he had to ensure he had a way of getting out of the country if that became necessary. The web of relationships he was building was far too elaborate for a simple art collector, even one who talked of opening his own gallery. Jean Moulin had another game plan, but he spoke of it to only a trusted few.

The terms of the Armistice left the French government free to return to Paris "should it choose," but despite repeated appeals from Pierre Laval and Marshall Pétain, this would never occur. "Paris was fading away," Jean-Paul Sartre wrote nostalgically, "and yawned hungrily under the empty sky … it possessed no more than an abstract and symbolic existence."[21]

The new État *Français* erected by the National Assembly at Vichy in July 1940 held the right to civil administration of all France, but its effective control was limited to the Unoccupied Zone, where it existed as little more than a vassal of Nazi Germany. The Chamber of Deputies had voted 569 to 80 — with 17 abstentions — to throw aside the constitution of the Third Republic and to invest Marshall Pétain with complete authority. When the Vichy foreign minister, Paul Baudouin, asked permission for the government's return to Paris, Germany's foreign minister, Joachim von Ribbentrop, was unsympathetic. Treat it "in a dilatory fashion," he told the German authorities in Paris. Future requests would be heard no more favourably. When Marshall Pétain, through either bravado or hubris, announced later in the year that the Vichy government was returning to Versailles, Ribbentrop simply vetoed the idea.

Over this miasma of defeat and dejection, Philippe Pétain reigned as a father figure to the French people; in a single year, twelve million portraits of him were purchased by the French. The majority of citizens, Charles de Gaulle reasoned, "wanted to believe that Marshall Pétain was playing a deep game and that, when the day came, he would take up arms again."[22]

With Pétain at the helm, Vichy mustered support for the steps it was taking to fulfill its Armistice. The first to be targeted were the Jews, not so much by direct German orders but a result of the latent anti-Semitism in French society. It began with the Statute des Juifs of October 1940. The law affected all 350,000 French Jews, but was especially harsh toward the seventy-five thousand who were refugees from German invasion of their homelands and were without French citizenship. The statute barred Jews from teaching, medicine, the law, and holding public office. Other drastic actions — the forced wearing of the yellow Star of David and pre-dawn roundups by the Paris police — were to become commonplace.[23]

A Jewish officer in the French army, Raymond-Raoul Lambert, wrote in his diary on October 19, 1940, of the awful prospects facing his country: "… either Germany will be conquered by the Anglo-American forces, and humanity will be saved, or, if Germany wins, a century-long night will descend on Europe. Judaism will maintain itself, as it did during the Middle Ages. But how we shall suffer from undeservedly becoming second-class citizens, after all the freedoms we have enjoyed…."[24]

"I will be your shield," the marshall had promised the French people, but that obviously did not include the Jews, of which Paris held some 140,000, two-thirds of them born in France. Pétain told his friend Henri Lémery, senator for the island of Martinique: "I am building a raft — so that France may keep afloat and survive."[25]

It was to be a different kind of France, the product of a *Revolution nationale* that began with repudiation of the traditional French commitment to *Liberté, Égalité, Fraternité* and its replacement with a dedication to *Travail, Famille, Patrie.* The sins of the old order — permissive Paris nightlife, alcohol, and the promiscuity of birth control — were to be cast aside, along with secularism, liberal politics and socialist thinking.

But in the chaos of the France of 1940, were de Gaulle and Pétain really so far apart? The two sprang from similar backgrounds, and de Gaulle was known to hold conservative views, though his were not as reactionary as those of his former mentor. Perhaps there was a "double game" at play here, an unspoken understanding that Pétain would safeguard the French homeland until the day when de Gaulle, in concert with the victorious Allies, could return from abroad to assume the country's destiny.

It is known that Marshall Pétain went so far as to establish a seven-man directorate in 1943 tasked with arranging an ultimate transfer of power to de Gaulle. Adolf Hitler told Benito Mussolini, the Italian dictator, that he had long suspected a secret Pétain-de Gaulle deal might be in the cards. He was apparently dissuaded of this idea when he met with the marshall in the town of Montoire in central France on October 24, 1940. It was after this meeting that Pétain made his damning declaration of abject obeisance to the Nazi occupiers: "I enter into the way of collaboration," he said in a speech. It was enough to gain the permission of Otto Abetz, now German ambassador, for Pierre Laval to install himself at the Hôtel Matignon in Paris, with the Tricolour flying overhead.[26]

If only the Germans would ease the Occupation penalties, Laval told his masters, he could "bring the French people with him" to the "German side." Hitler never bought into this, and never viewed France as a prospective partner in his New Europe. The role he assigned to France was that of a passive source of plunder, and the Vichy regime proved powerless to prevent the looting of its economy. From automobiles to locomotives, Germany became the beneficiary of most French production, including vast amounts of food purchased with the Occupation money paid by France. The French, more than the people of any occupied country, laboured to sustain a Nazi war machine that in 1940 was eating up 44 percent of Germany's domestic product.

If there was any "double game" being played, it was by Vichy, which had emissaries in Madrid trying to make a deal with the British to allow merchant ships carrying goods to France to pass through Gibraltar. Vichy offered a commitment that if the Germans seized these supplies, the French government would transfer itself to North Africa and resume the war on the side of the Allies. Pétain's speech wiped Vichy's chips from the table of that poker session. There was certainly no "double game" as far as Charles de Gaulle was concerned. He saw the Montoire meeting as official confirmation of Vichy's collaboration with the enemy. As he would write in his *Mémoires de guerre*, "... obvious reasons ordained that I should deny to the Vichy rulers, once and for all, the right of legitimacy...." He would have to become the "trustee of the interests of France." It was time for his Free French movement to exercise "the attributes of a government."[27]

In the summer of 1940, however, Charles de Gaulle, far from exercising the powers of government, faced the wrath of a regime determined to exact retribution from a defeated government. He ignored the command to return to Bordeaux and instead wrote to General Weygand urging him to take charge of the resistance to Germany. Weygand would have, de Gaulle added, "my entire obedience if he did so."

The response, when it came, was a kiss-off: de Gaulle should follow proper channels if he wished to communicate with the government. The High Command, faced with implementing the demands of the Armistice, found time to cancel de Gaulle's temporary rank of brigadier general and order his "compulsory retirement."

An even more peremptory order reached de Gaulle on June 28. It was from Foreign Minister Paul Baudouin and it instructed him "to place himself in a state of arrest at the Saint-Michel Prison in Toulose within the next five days." He was to be judged by a military court for "the misdemeanour of inciting soldiers to disobedience."

De Gaulle sent his response via the French Embassy in London: "In my view, this communication is devoid of interest." The trial was carried out as scheduled and de Gaulle was found guilty. He was sentenced to four years imprisonment, a fine of one hundred francs, and cancellation of his citizenship.[28] This might have been the end of a defeated regime's preoccupation with an outcast rebel, but on the insistence of General Weygand charges of treason and desertion were laid against de Gaulle and a second trial was ordered.[29]

The officers who filed into the military courtroom in Clermont-Ferrand* in central France on August 1, 1940, could have been under no illusion as to what was expected of them. For none of them would de Gaulle's trial, held at the headquarters of the French Armistice Army's 13th Region, have been a welcome task. This would have been especially the case for the presiding officer, General Aubert Frère, a career soldier who headed the Saint-Cyr military academy between 1931 and 1935. Like de Gaulle, he was wounded in the First World War, and had been in charge of a tank instruction school in the 1920s. He'd been de Gaulle's senior

---

* A manufacturing town on a plateau fringing the Massif Central mountains, Clermont-Ferrand was the site of the Michelin tire works, devoted under the Occupation to production for the German war machine.

officer as commander of the 7th Army during the Battle of France and was the first man to congratulate him on his appointment to the Reynaud Cabinet. General Frère may have had reservations about the case against a former comrade-in-arms, but if he did, he could not allow them to affect his dignity. There would be no nervous mannerisms, no fingering of his well-manicured mustache, an ornament that some thought added a dash of gallantry to his otherwise stern military demeanour.[30]

There was a stillness in the courtroom when the name of "de Gaulle, Charles André Joseph Marie, now returned to the rank of colonel," was called to answer to the charges facing him. General Frère ordered that the charges be heard in absentia. The prosecutor, a Colonel Degacher, alleged that de Gaulle's radio broadcasts had "provoked hostile acts by England" and that he had "incited soldiers and sailors to enter the service of a foreign power." He asked for a prohibition on publication of the proceedings. The court agreed, "having regard to the threat to public order that reports of the trial would create." After secret deliberations, General Frère and his six fellow judges found de Gaulle guilty on five of six charges; only the charge of treason failed to stick. He was ordered stripped of his rank, sentenced to death, and his property confiscated. A paper bearing the verdict was affixed to the door of the Vichy Town Hall.

In the official record, the finding carried a marginal note from Marshall Pétain: "This sentence was necessitated by considerations of discipline … it is clear that as a sentence in absentia, it can be no more than an affirmation of principle. It was never in my mind to take any further action."[31] Pétain would always insist he would not have had de Gaulle shot. A terse three-paragraph report of the trial ran at the bottom of page two of the August 3 issue of *Le Temps* although the more popular evening daily, *Paris Soir,* gave it front page coverage.[32]

No reference to these occurrences appears in de Gaulle's *Mémoires de guerre*, although he does refer to Frère as an "excellent soldier."[33] De Gaulle also makes no mention of an event that would have affected him more deeply than the trial — the death of his mother on July 16 at Paimpont.

According to the general's niece Genevieve, who was with her aunt when she died, large crowds gathered for her funeral despite the refusal of the Germans to permit a public announcement of her death. "People came from far, far places, many thousands of them, to pay tribute to her. They brought flowers to put on the grave. They even took stones from it to keep as one might keep a holy relic."[34] General de Gaulle heard of his mother's death only after a young Breton fishermen crossed the English Channel in his fishing boat to carry a photograph of her gravesite showing it covered with flowers.[35]

In little more than two months, Charles de Gaulle, like many other Frenchmen, had gone through the upheaval of war and defeat and the loss of a loved one. He had issued a lonely Appeal to continue the battle, a message heard by few of his countrymen. Yet the demonstrations of affection taking place at his mother's grave suggested something else: that the determination to survive remained robust among the French people. The message of Charles de Gaulle was being taken to heart.

Less than three weeks after de Gaulle's trial, General Frère was appointed military governor of the Lyon district and named commander of the army's 14th Region. It has never been established if this came as a reward for his service at de Gaulle's court martial, but the possibility has not escaped those who studied the tactics of the Vichy government. In the months to come, he would watch the Gestapo tighten its security on unoccupied France. His feelings about de Gaulle's trial would deepen, shifting from the skepticism he must have felt at its start, to the revulsion that he later clearly demonstrated.

By 1942, General Frère was deeply enmeshed in a secret movement he had founded, the Organisation de Résistance de l'Armée (ORA). Officers under his command were assembling a clandestine cache of arms and supplies to be used in an eventual uprising. A cautious man, Frère was suspicious of overtures from other Resistance groups. When one of de Gaulle's envoys got in touch with him in 1943, he was received coolly and told "this was no time to launch into adventures." Later that year, however, ORA came to terms with the Gaullist Armée secrète (AS) and agreed on a unified underground army that would become the Forces françaises de l'Intérieur (FFI).

So highly thought of by de Gaulle that he was offered evacuation to London — which he refused — Frère became aware in the spring of 1943 that he had fallen under Gestapo surveillance; his mail was being intercepted and unidentified cars sometimes followed him through the streets of Lyon. His suspicions were well-founded. General Frère and his wife were arrested at their home on June 13, 1943. His name may have been on a list of Secret Army contacts discovered by the Vichy police when they arrested a Resistance courier. General Frère was sent to Fresnes Prison outside Paris. He would die exactly one year after his arrest — on June 13, 1944 — in a prison camp at Struthof, in Alsace, of diphtheria and dysentery brought on by exhaustion while being transported to Germany. Only the knowledge that the Allies had landed in Normandy proved a consolation to him as he lay dying. A priest imprisoned with Frère declared him a saint and said, "The only thing I could do for him was to kiss him."[36] In a cruel twist of history, the officer who led the military tribunal in its condemnation of Charles de Gaulle had himself become a victim of the Nazi swastika over France.

CHAPTER 7
Soldiers of the Empire

The third-floor corner office that General de Gaulle moved into at St. Stephen's House offered a splendid view of the Thames River and its embankment, but was otherwise austere and bleak, containing only a white-wood table, a telephone, and four chairs. His first act was to pin a map of France to the wall. Next to it he put a map of the world. Like maps adorning thousands of classrooms around the globe, it showed the vast expanse of the British Empire in red and the territories of the French Empire, the world's second largest, in purple. The French Empire stretched across the midriff of Africa from Dakar on the Atlantic to the Gulf of Aden, filled much of the eastern shore of the Mediterranean, and spilled into the exotic lands of the Indochinese peninsula in Southeast Asia. These fabled lands, along with islands scattered around the globe — from St. Pierre off the coast of Canada to Tahiti in the South Pacific — were rich in resources and soldiers for the Empire. Metropolitan France was gone, but de Gaulle saw the road to Paris as running through these territories. To him, they were an integral part of France and he intended to rally them to the Free French cause. The French army commanded by Vichy, reduced to a mere corporal's guard under the demobilization terms of the Armistice and with two million of its men in prisoner-of-war camps, no longer posed a threat to German supremacy. The French navy, anchored idly at Toulon, with Admiral François Darlan dithering on the question of where its loyalties lay, seemed more likely to become an agent of German intimidation than a shield against further aggression. In France, de Gaulle had as yet no great following and no solid reputation. It was in the distant lands of the Empire, he reasoned, that Vichy's sway could be most readily challenged. If he could rally the Empire, that would change the end game in his favour.

For all his ability to detect profound shifts in the military and economic positions of France and the other countries of Europe, doubts about the future of colonialism would have been incomprehensible to de Gaulle. He was as anchored as Winston Churchill to the belief that empires won by stealth and struggle were the rightful property of their masters. It was only natural that those masters were whites, comfortably ensconced in handsome buildings in Europe — at least in peacetime — guided by God's will, and certain that the destinies of distant lands were their proper province. It was for this reason he had insisted that Britain "guarantee the re-establishment of the frontiers of Metropolitan France and of the French Empire."[1]

Churchill agreed only to the "restoration of the independence and greatness of France." Coming from a man who would famously say he had not become prime minister to "preside over the dissolution of the British Empire," this was the least that could be expected of him.

De Gaulle put his ambition for the Empire before one of the first meetings of his French National Committee at St. Stephen's House on July 15, 1940. All the early converts and the key members of his staff were there: Lieutenant Geoffroy de Courcel, now de Gaulle's *chef du cabinet*; Elisabeth de Miribel, who worked from a small table set up in a hallway; Captain Tissier, who de Gaulle had just made chief of staff; the priest Thierry d'Argenlieu, soon to go with de Gaulle on hazardous overseas forays; Captain Philippe de Hauteclocque, now using the name *Leclerc* to protect his family back in France; the jurist René Cassin, in charge of legal affairs and justice; Jean Monnett's former aide René Pleven, who had taken charge of finances; Maurice Schumann, now making nightly broadcasts back to France; and André Dewavrin, who would never forget the icy reception he'd received from de Gaulle after he'd found his way to London.[2]

"Good day, I shall see you again soon," de Gaulle had said after a two-minute grilling that ended with Dewavrin's appointment as head of the Free French intelligence department. Dewavrin, or "Colonel Passy" as he would become known, was already sending agents into France. He recorded the general's remarks:

> If we wish to put France into the war, and if we wish tor represent our country's interest adequately both with regard to our Allies and to the French in France and abroad whose eyes are upon us, it is of the very first importance that the seat of the French government that is carrying on the struggle should be on French soil. That is why I have decided — and the information I have tells me it is possible — to go to Dakar and there set up the capital of the Empire at war.[3]

Before de Gaulle could put such an ambitious scheme into action, he would need the support of France's overseas administrators, mostly men of military background. They held office at the pleasure of the French government. The question was, where and what was now the French government? To men posted far from the precincts of Paris, the French government had to be that which had signed the Armistice with Germany and Italy and was now established at Vichy, under the leadership of Marshall Pétain. To de Gaulle, the État français that Pétain had erected was an illegitimate offspring of the Third Republic. The British agreed, declaring that France was no longer an independent country. De Gaulle sent out a stream of telegrams and letters to colonial administrators aimed at convincing them his Free French were the true heirs of the immortal France. "We are France itself," de Gaulle told René Cassin in their discussions about the legal framework they were attempting to create.[4]

Not everyone in the French colonial system was won over to this view. Some saw de Gaulle as a tool of the British, and from the beginning the French governors of Morocco, Algeria, and Tunisia resisted the blandishments of both him and the British, opting to stay with Vichy. One factor in their reasoning was the continued diplomatic recognition extended to Vichy by the Soviet Union, the United States, Canada, and the Vatican. President Roosevelt relied on the advice of long-time State Department functionary Robert Murphy in selecting an old friend, Admiral William Leahy, as successor to Ambassador Bullitt.

The shuffle of diplomatic cards included one dealt by Winston Churchill when he asked Canada to keep a *chargé d'affaires*, Pierre Dupuy, accredited to Vichy. He would become Churchill's "window upon a courtyard to which we had no other access." When Pétain told Dupuy that he might have to hand over the French fleet to the Germans — "if I am offered a satisfactory compensation" — the Canadian promptly reported this to Churchill, with the advice that the British should try to get de Gaulle to stop attacking the French who were faithful to Vichy. Churchill rejected the idea, telling Dupuy he "was not going to 'card' his friends and make them enemies in the hope of making them friends."[5]

A week after speaking of his scheme to set up an Empire capital at Dakar, de Gaulle moved the Free French from St. Stephen's House to larger and more comfortable premises at No. 4 Carlton Gardens, the one-time home of nineteenth-century British prime minister Lord Palmerston. The fact Palmerston had been a bitter enemy of France did not disturb the new occupants. De Gaulle took a main-floor corner office in the elegant four-storey house that filled a pleasant terrace overlooking St. James's Park.

It was here he received word that General Georges Catroux, the governor general of Indochina, fired by Vichy after refusing to bow to Japanese demands, was coming to London to join Free France. De Gaulle and Catroux had shared a German prisoner-of-war camp in the First World War and de Gaulle anxiously awaited his old comrade's arrival. As a four-star lieutenant general, Catroux was superior to de Gaulle, but, he said, his willingness to serve under him was "self-evident." Another governor who switched to Free France — but who, like Catroux, was unable to carry his colony with him — was General Paul Legentilhomme of French

Somaliland, in East Africa. More decisive results came from the Pacific where the New Hebrides, New Caledonia, and Tahiti quickly lined up on de Gaulle's side. Their commitment buoyed his spirits and would have played a part in his decision to issue a new appeal: this time to the Empire. It was addressed to the governors of the colonies, but it was actually aimed at the white colonists who were in a position to persuade recalcitrant officials to part from Vichy. "If necessary I shall call upon the people," de Gaulle declared, hinting broadly at revolutionary action.

The people he was speaking of did not include the native populations, yet it was from that source that most of the Empire's soldiers would be drawn. De Gaulle was too late to recruit the two thousand black soldiers on duty in the Ivory Coast colony; they had been sent next door to Britain's Gold Coast* where the commander of the British detachment so admired them that he integrated them into his own force.

The first big breakthrough had come from another black quarter: one Félix Eboué, a man highly trained in the French colonial system who had become the governor of the Central African colony of Chad.[6] He telegraphed de Gaulle from Fort Lamy to say he and his military advisors were rallying to Free France. By securing Chad, which shared a border with Italian-controlled Libya, de Gaulle now had a direct line of attack on the enemy.

The time was ripe to grab for other colonies, and on August 7 a Free French mission that included René Pleven and Major Philippe de Hauteclocque Leclerc flew out of London bound for Lagos, in the British colony of Nigeria. Of all the African territories, the neighbouring Cameroon, a former German territory, offered the most promising prospect; a final victory by Hitler would bring back much detested German laws abolished at the time of the French takeover in 1918. Lerclerc took twenty volunteers inland in a convoy of three canoes and reached the key outpost of Douala in a driving rain. There, with Leclerc appointing himself a colonel and governor of the colony, the Free French took over the garrison. Lerclerc posted a proclamation asserting that the Cameroon was "determined to continue the struggle together with the Allies, under the orders of General de Gaulle."[7] His takeover, coinciding with the shift of power in Chad and the rallying of neighbouring French Congo to the Free French cause,

---

*Now the Republic of Ghana.

would take on legendary status as part of the Three Glorious Days of August 26–28, 1940, when the Gaullists won their first African territories. It was time to take aim at Dakar, the capital of Senegal. Capture it, and Free France would not only possess a great city facing out on the Atlantic, but a capital worthy of the Empire.

Moving men about the Empire like pawns on a chessboard was easier for de Gaulle than meeting the social and political prerequisites of life in a wartime London teeming with diplomats, politicians, high-ranking military officers, and refugees from all over Europe. It should not surprise us that his reserved manner and resolute sense of self would have ill served him socially. Winston Churchill recognized that while de Gaulle had been accepted by the British public, his image needed further polishing — if for no other reason than to underscore the wise choice the prime minister had made. As a keen observer of the press, Churchill knew the value of cultivating public curiosity about someone of the stature of de Gaulle. He arranged for a five-hundred-pound fee to be paid to Richmond Temple, one of the United Kingdom's most skillful public relations men, to burnish the general's image. De Gaulle growled that "Churchill wants to promote me like a brand of soap."[8] He refused to have his children included in official photographs taken by Cecil Beaton, the photographer of the British royal family, but did accede to Temple's request to write a short description of his purpose and aims. Later published in a Cairo newspaper, it offers a revealing insight into de Gaulle's self-assessment of character:

> I am a free Frenchman. I believe in God and in the future of my country. I am no man's subordinate. I have one mission and one mission only, that of carrying on the struggle for my country's liberation. I solemnly declare that I am not attached to any political party, nor bound to any politicians whatsoever, either of the right, the centre or the left. I have only one aim: to set France free.[9]

Mary Borden, the novelist wife of General Spears, did not need a publicist to gain access to de Gaulle. She financed a hospital for the Free French in the English countryside and saw de Gaulle often. She wrote that he was "like a man who had been skinned alive ... the slightest contact with friendly, well-meaning people got him on the raw to such an extent that he wanted to bite, as a dog that has been run over will bite any would-be friend who comes to its rescue."[10]

Always the soldier, de Gaulle paid a good deal of attention to his military wardrobe. For years, he had patronized the tailor shop of S.C. Johnson, an English tailor in Paris. Discovering that Johnson had gotten safely back to London, de Gaulle promptly ordered a new uniform. Johnson had to purloin three yards of khaki from a bolt consigned to high-ranking British officers.[11]

By now, something of a gastronome, although a light imbiber of wines, de Gaulle ate well during his London days despite food rationing. After a busy morning at Carleton Gardens, he would be driven to the Connaught Hotel where lunch was usually laid on for three or four guests. It was at these lunches that de Gaulle found relaxation. He commented jovially on the latest war developments and often digressed into the history of French food, jokingly asking how one could govern a country that made two hundred and forty-six different kinds of cheese. By three o'clock, cigars smoked and coffee finished, he'd walk the mile back to the office via Berkeley Square and Piccadilly. On other occasions, there was a meal with good company at the Royal Automobile Club, or perhaps the Savoy or Ritz hotels or the Cavalry Club. Weekends were often spent at Chequers, the country home of Prime Minister Churchill, where the entertainment sometimes consisted of fireworks displays using military rockets. One misfired and unleashed a twenty-three pound projectile that exploded within a few feet of General de Gaulle. Churchill promptly increased the budget to perfect the device.[12]

The summer of 1940 would be remembered for the Battle of Britain and the Luftwaffe's intensive bombing of London. The first great air battle took place over the English Channel on July 10 and by September the Royal Air Force had vanquished the German attackers. If the air assault had been intended to destroy Britain's morale or its ability to resist invasion, it was a complete failure.

The de Gaulle family did not escape the consequences of the nightly bombings. Anne huddled in her bed, hands clapped over her ears, as bombs fell on the aerodrome near their Pettswood home. The scream of sirens, the barking of dogs, the shudders of exploding bombs, and the smell of smoke from a burning cottage at the end of the street terrified the little girl. She was twelve, but her mother knew she could not count her age in years. Yvonne de Gaulle insisted the family move to a safer location, and when she found a place for rent near the convent of the Sisters of Zion, where Elisabeth was attending school, she eagerly packed everyone up for the long haul almost to the Welsh border. Their new home consisted of three rude brick cottages, lacking indoor sanitation or electricity, known as Gadlas Hall in the village of Ellesmere, halfway between Birmingham and Liverpool. But it was quiet and safe, although the fact it was eight hours' from London by train meant de Gaulle could visit no more than once a month. He took a small apartment at 15 Grosvenor Square. It was one of the choice locations in Mayfair and he continued to eat most of his meals at the Connaught Hotel. General and Lady Spears had de Gaulle to their home that Christmas. She later wrote that he so charmed their young son that the boy wanted to volunteer to fight by the general's side.[13]

The Free French successes in Africa set off alarms in Vichy and sent warning signals to Dakar. The Vichy loyalist Pierre Boisson, who had been governor of Equatorial Africa, was moved to Dakar to organize its defences. Boisson found a city protected by several aircraft squadrons and a naval flotilla that included the battleship *Richelieu*, recently escaped from France. De Gaulle knew Dakar would not be an easy target. He planned to land an invasion force some distance away and march on the city, gaining recruits as he moved forward. When he talked over the plan with Winston Churchill in the Cabinet room in Downing Street, the prime minister made it clear he thought the scheme far too cautious. Churchill "paced up and down, talking with animation." He had a more daring idea, and imagined for de Gaulle a drowsy Dakar awakened at dawn by the sight of an immense fleet gathered in its harbour: A small ship bearing de Gaulle envoys would be sent to parley with the governor. He might "for honour's sake" fire a few shots while British and Free French planes flew over the town dropping leaflets. "But he will not go further. And that evening he will dine with you and drink to the final victory." It was an eloquent appeal, and de Gaulle bought into it on one condition: that the general go there himself to lead the assault.[14]

Operation Menace began August 31 with the sailing from Liverpool of a dozen vessels, including the British aircraft carrier *Ark Royal* and two old battleships. De Gaulle, General Spears, and Commander Thierry d'Argenlieu were on board the *Westernland*, a Dutch transport now flying the French Tricolour. Miraculously, the Vichy French had no inkling of the operation, despite almost non-existent security. De Gaulle himself had shopped in Simpson's in Piccadilly for tropical outfits "for a trip to West Africa" and a British officer had wandered into a London map shop requesting a map of Dakar. British intelligence was hardly more effective. A squadron of Vichy ships from Toulon slipped through the Straits of Gibraltar without being challenged and succeeded in reaching Dakar.[15]

When the Anglo-French force anchored off Dakar on September 23, the scenario was hardly as Churchill had forecast. An unseasonable fog made the fleet invisible from shore; there would be no intimidating sight confronting Dakar's defenders. At six o'clock, de Gaulle addressed the city by radio, declaring his "friendly intentions." French planes sent aloft from the *Ark Royal* to drop leaflets attracted unexpected fire from the ground. Despite this, de Gaulle sent a launch bearing d'Argenlieu and several other officers to shore with a letter for Governor Boisson. When the port officer on duty told them he had orders to arrest them, they returned hurriedly to the launch. Before they had gone more than a few metres, they were raked by machine-gun fire. It caught d'Argenlieu in the leg, and he and the others were hauled back aboard the *Western-land*, bleeding and in shock. An attempt was made that afternoon to send a landing party ashore, but it was beaten off with heavy casualties. De Gaulle passed the night "on tenterhooks."[16] In the morning, a telegram from Churchill was filled with "astonishment and irritation" that the attack had not gone forward. De Gaulle sent a fresh demand for surrender which was turned down. Vichy shore batteries, joined by the

Richelieu, opened fire with deadly accuracy. By the end of the day, the Anglo-French flotilla was in serious trouble. The battleship *Resolution* was severely damaged and had to be taken in tow. Four aircraft had been lost and a destroyer and two submarines sunk. The force retreated to the British colony of Freetown, its mission to take Dakar a failure.

The days that followed were among the cruelest in de Gaulle's life. "I went through what a man must feel when an earthquake shakes his house brutally and he receives on his head the rain of tiles falling from the roof." To make things worse, from London he heard "a tempest of anger" and from Washington, "a hurricane of sarcasms."[17] The fiasco squelched any hope of healing the breach that had developed with the United States. President Roosevelt looked on Vichy as the rightful government of the defeated country, and he now saw de Gaulle as an ineffective bumbler, a mere pretender for power. Geoffroy de Courcel saw a man "deeply disturbed."[18]

De Gaulle told General Spears he would reflect on his future overnight. He would either continue to work with the British, or in view of the catastrophic failure at Dakar, retire to Canada as a private citizen.[19] He also, according to one authority, considered "blowing out my brains."[20] The night was long, de Gaulle's narrow cabin was stiflingly hot, and he got little sleep in a bunk that was too short for his long legs. By daybreak he had reached his decision. He was convinced he still had the support of the Free French and that everyone had been "hardened by the hostile attitude of Vichy."[21] His choice was clear: "The game continues ... we shall see how it turns out."[22]

De Gaulle stayed with the convoy only as far as Duala, the port capital of the Cameroon. After being acclaimed by an aroused crowd of settlers and natives, he set out for Fort Lamy, the capital of Chad, where he luckily escaped injury in the crash landing of his airplane. He had a meeting with Felix Éboué and at last met General Catroux, who had come from Hanoi to put himself at de Gaulle's disposal. Then it was on to Brazzaville in the French Congo, where de Gaulle set up the Council for the Defense of the Empire. The soldiers of Free France were on the march; the Empire would live again. Somewhere on that trip, de Gaulle contracted malaria, a recurrent illness for which his doctor would prescribe a diet of soft boiled eggs.

In a letter to his wife, de Gaulle put the best face he could on things. He admitted Dakar "was not a success" and explained that he did not want to fight a "pitched battle" between Frenchmen. "I withdrew my forces in time to prevent it. For the moment everything is upside down. But my faithful followers remain faithful and I have great hopes for the future."[23]

✝

On his return to London in mid-November, de Gaulle faced a discouraging mess. Recruitment had fallen off again, and the British press, normally friendly to de Gaulle's efforts, was in full cry. One of London's shrillest papers, the *Daily Mirror*, wrote of "gross miscalculation, muddled dash, hasty withdrawal, wishful thinking and half-measures." Winston Churchill delivered a carefully rehearsed speech in French over the BBC, reminding Frenchmen that Hitler's goal was "nothing less than the complete wiping out of the French nation and the disintegration of its whole life and future." Yet he now had his own doubts about de Gaulle. Churchill told General Catroux during a stopover in London that "the Free French movement needs to be led, and I believe you ought to assume its leadership."

The complicated game of leading a cause that was not yet a government was becoming bogged down in intrigue and strife between three factions — those who had chosen to stick with Vichy, those who had declared for de Gaulle, and a critically important element that refused to align with either side. In this group were such figures as the celebrated author André Maurois, and economic policy maker Jean Monnet. "You are wrong," Monnet wrote to de Gaulle, "to set up an organization which might appear in France as though created under the protection of England."[24]

More often, the biggest damage stemmed from conspiracies within the Free French camp, caused by petty jealousies and rival ambitions. Then came the first row between de Gaulle and Churchill, over the arrest by the British of Admiral Muselier, accused of having betrayed the Dakar mission by leaking details to Vichy. De Gaulle was convinced it was a frame-up and was ready to cut off relations with Britain if the admiral was not released. Before he could do that, the British realized they had acted on forged documents (presumably prepared by the admiral's enemies at Carleton

Gardens), and Muselier was freed. Churchill apologized to de Gaulle the next day, but it was not something that could be easily forgotten. De Gaulle continued to accept invitations for weekends at Chequers, however, and he was there when Churchill awakened him at dawn on March 9, 1941, "literally dancing with joy," to tell him the Americans had passed a Lend-Lease Act that would speed the delivery of war material to Britain.[25]

By now, it was clear to Charles de Gaulle that his Free French did not figure highly in President Roosevelt's calculations about the future course of the war. Roosevelt was well-acquainted with French culture and spoke the language passably well, but he had lost faith in France's ability to survive as a world power. Still committed to keeping America out of the war, he saw the Vichy government as the legitimate inheritor of French authority and believed the United States would be best served by restraining Marshall Pétain from falling further into Hitler's clutches. All his advisors, from Ambassador Bullitt to his new ambassador to Vichy, Admiral Leahy, and Robert Murphy, the other chief American diplomat to the French, agreed that de Gaulle was a minor figure of dictatorial ambition, backed by only a ragtag rabble with little or no support in France. Sumner Welles, the American assistant secretary of state, would put it this way: "De Gaulle's authority is based upon a small group of followers who sometimes fight each other, and on some territories overseas.... Eighty-five percent of the Frenchmen living in the United States are not for de Gaulle."[26] Roosevelt's entrenched anti-colonialism gave him another reason to disdain de Gaulle's attempts to wield the French Empire as a weapon against Vichy. In Washington, the new Vichy ambassador Gaston Henry-Haye, a member of the French Senate and the mayor of Versailles, was warmly received in the capital's diplomatic circles. He waged a well-financed anti-Gaullist campaign, drawing liberally on funds from a $250 million stock of gold that France had deposited in the United States before the war. His staff tracked the activities of pro-Gaullist French and sent reports back to Vichy that led to the cancellation of citizenship and seizure of property of those not toeing the Vichy line.

De Gaulle couldn't understand why the United States was inclined to favour "the apostles of defeat" over those who continued to fight the Nazis. His response was to launch a counter-offensive. In May 1941, while overseeing meetings of the Empire Defense Council in Brazzaville, de

Gaulle sent a telegram to René Pleven in London instructing him to lead a special mission to Washington: "In view of the almost belligerent attitude of the United States toward the collaboration between Vichy and Germany which is becoming more apparent each day, and the special economic conditions of our colonies in Africa and the Pacific, the moment has arrived for us to establish relations with the United States."

Pleven tried to enlist the former French ambassador to Washington, Alexis Léger, but Léger refused to serve "a general, however heroic, who had not received a mandate from the people."[27] Jean Monnet offered the same excuse. Pleven managed to scratch together "five French patriots of varying backgrounds, tradition, training, and political conviction who would join forces to help their country in a time of national disaster." Among them was Jacques de Sieyès, manager of the New York branch of Patou Perfumes and already de Gaulle's personal delegate to the United States. Their efforts to gain economic and financial support met with only limited success.

A similar effort was underway in Canada, led by Elisabeth de Miribel, who had gone there at de Gaulle's behest in August 1940. She was supporting herself with a part-time job as a translator at McGill University in Montreal. Mlle de Miribel was distressed to learn that opinion in the French Canadian population of Quebec strongly supported Marshall Pétain, although the Canadian prime minister, Mackenzie King, would become a staunch admirer of de Gaulle. Mlle de Miribel found French Catholics still clinging to traditions harkening back to the time of New France before the British conquest of 1763. They looked to Vichy to "remove the slightest trace" of the French Revolution and the Republic. "We regret that he (de Gaulle) is surrounded by leftists and Jews who will try to take over the country," she was told.[28]

The attitude of English Canadians was quite different, and Mlle de Miribel encountered a warm response in Ottawa where she set up a Free French Information office.[29] For a time, she was joined by Commander d'Argenlieu, the Carmelite priest turned naval officer and survivor of the attack on his motor launch at Dakar. De Gaulle had told de Miribel by telegram that d'Argenlieu wanted to be received as a Free French naval officer, not as a *religieux*.[30] On d'Argenlieu's return to London, he telegraphed de Gaulle in Brazzaville: "Canadian mission happily completed. Perfect relations established."[31]

For Elisabeth de Miribel, the best part of the assignment was the time it allowed her to spend with the former Canadian minister to France, Georges Vanier, and his wife, Pauline. Elisabeth had met Pauline when they'd worked at the same hospital as Red Cross volunteers. Colonel Vanier was now in charge of the Quebec military district. Elisabeth's friendship with the Vaniers became so warm it seemed as if they had adopted her. "They loved the same France as myself and served the same cause."

Charles de Gaulle was in another corner of the French Empire — the protectorate of Syria — when he received word in Damascus on June 22, 1941, that Adolf Hitler had flung his troops into the Soviet Union, thereby extending the war to two fronts. It came as no surprise to de Gaulle. He had told Maurice Schumann a year earlier that "Hitler is thinking of the Ukraine.... He will not resist against his longing to deal with Russia and that will be the beginning of the end for him."[32] Here was a chance for Free France to garner another ally, and de Gaulle sent René Cassin to see the Soviet ambassador in London, Ivan Maisky. As a result, the Russians withdrew their ambassador from Vichy and assigned him to the Free French, and formally recognized de Gaulle as "Leader of all the Free French."

De Gaulle now had a new card to play and he would not hesitate to use it when the time came to offset Roosevelt's refusal to treat the Free French as full-fledged Allies. Even the Japanese attack on Pearl Harbor on December 7, 1941, failed to change this. But it filled de Gaulle with confidence that the war was as good as won. He heard the news at Rodinghead House in Berkhamstead, after a walk in the woods with the Free French spy chief, André Dewavrin, "Colonel Passy," a weekend guest of the de Gaulles. This was a more comfortable home than Gadlas Hall, and much closer to London, allowing de Gaulle to be with Yvonne and Anne more often. Listening to the excited voices on the radio tell of the Japanese attack, de Gaulle declared, "The war is finished since the outcome is known from now on."

Yvonne rushed to the kitchen, leaving the men alone. She began to pray. "If Charles is right, then please God spare my son and all our family." And what about after the war? "He's always been a soldier, if he wants to stay as a leader he'll have to become a politician. Something he's always hated."[33]

Just as de Gaulle feared, America's entry into the war did little to move President Roosevelt to a more favourable view of the Free French. They were allowed to benefit from Lend-Lease arrangements, but when the United Nations (as the Allies had become known) proclaimed its Declaration vowing "complete victory," France was not among the twenty-six nations invited to sign it. Neither had France been a signatory to the Atlantic Charter of the previous August, signed by Churchill and Roosevelt aboard a ship anchored in Placentia Bay off the coast of Newfoundland.

Something that did change as a result of the Japanese attack was the further expansion of the Japanese influence through Southeast Asia. Hong Kong, defended by unprepared and ill-equipped Canadian detachments of the Royal Rifles and Winnipeg Grenediers, fell on Christmas Day. By spring, the Japanese held the Phillipines and were threatening Australia. French Indochina had been lost even before Pearl Harbor, when Vichy had given in to Japanese demands in the fall of 1941.

One tiny corner of the French Empire that remained in dispute was the archipelago of St. Pierre and Miquelon, some four thousand kilometres from France but just twenty kilometres off the coast of Newfoundland. The islands were under the control of Vichy, and the British feared the Germans might seize its powerful radio station and use it to alert their U-Boats to the movement of Atlantic convoys. The United States, more concerned about keeping European powers from encroaching on the Western Hemisphere, had signed an accord with Vichy to maintain the status quo of the islands. General de Gaulle sided with the British and decided "to act at the first opportunity."[34] That came when Admiral Muselier sailed with a flotilla of corvettes to Halifax to inspect the Free French submarine, *Surcouf*. De Gaulle intended, if he could get the approval of Winston Churchill, to send Muselier on a secret mission to seize the islands. "We would see no objection; indeed we would prefer it," back came the answer. Churchill deplored Vichy's use of the St. Pierre radio to spread "lies and poison."

Muselier, a stickler for protocol, thought he should discuss the scheme with the Canadians first, and after docking in Halifax, he took the train to Ottawa. The Canadians referred the issue to Washington and when President Roosevelt heard about it, he exploded. The American Secretary of State, Cordell Hull, was livid. Such an action, he would write, "might seriously interfere with our relations with Marshall Pétain's government."[35] The British Foreign office duly took notice and asked de Gaulle to call off the operation.

The tangled web of inter-state communications, never humming smoothly at best, broke down at this point — either accidentally or by intention. De Gaulle insisted in his *Mémoires de guerre* that he ordered Muselier to take possession of St. Pierre only after having learned that Canada was preparing to seize the island's radio station. "He (Muselier) did so on Christmas Eve, in the midst of the greatest enthusiasm from the inhabitants, without a shot having to be fired. A plebiscite gave Free France a crushing majority."[36] De Gaulle could never understand why this "small operation," involving only three hundred sailors, could stir such a fuss. Cordell Hull, filled with spite, fired off a communiqué deploring the "arbitrary action" taken by the "*so-called*" Free French force. The turn of phrase caused howls of laughter in the American press and Hull was inundated with letters addressed to the *so-called* Secretary of State.

The fact Churchill was visiting Washington at Christmas gave him a chance to try to heal the breach. "You take care of Vichy, we'll take care of de Gaulle," he joked to Roosevelt. In a speech to the Canadian Parliament, Churchill castigated "the men of Vichy ... prostrate at the foot of the conqueror," for their prediction that "England will have her neck wrung like a chicken." His response: "Some chicken; some neck." The members of the House of Commons roared with laughter. Churchill went on to laud de Gaulle's Free French. "They have been condemned to death, but their names are being held in increasing respect by nine Frenchmen out of every ten throughout the once happy, smiling land of France."[37]

Listening to the speech, Prime Minister Mackenzie King, by now a strong advocate of de Gaulle and the Free French, thought it was not as good as the one Churchill had made in Washington. Like de Gaulle, it was important to King that he not show himself too much under the influence of England; Canadians no longer regarded their country as a colony. King had stood up to the British when they demanded he let them have the $400 million in gold that the French had shipped to Canada. That would be a "betrayal of trust" to which he would not agree, he had told the Treasury official making the demand, Sir Frederick Phillips. Agitated with his visitor, King wrote in his diary that Sir Frederick "himself looks like a thug."[38]

When Admiral Muselier returned to London, he was hailed by both the British and the Free French as a hero, but he was no longer a satisfied follower of de Gaulle. He unleashed ferocious verbal assaults on the general, hoping to set the stage for a *coup d'état*. De Gaulle ordered him to take a thirty-day rest. Muselier resigned from the French National Committee, intending to stay on as commander-in-chief of the Free French Navy. The tactic failed to gain him support, and although the British protested Muselier's leaving, within a month he was out as head of the navy and no longer a player.

Muselier's defection was seen by the officers who had remained loyal to the Vichy government as reinforcement for their view that it was they, and not de Gaulle, who were upholding the principles of France. They chose to obey the orders of their government, rather than opt for what they saw as desertion. They thought, as General Dwight D. Eisenhower would later write of them in *Crusade in Europe*, "If de Gaulle were a loyal Frenchman, they had to regard themselves as cowards."[39]

Although North Africa still remained out of de Gaulle's grasp, the rallying to Free France of other colonies throughout the Empire enabled him to fulfill his first aim: to bring French forces back to the battlefield. Given his certainty of an ultimate Allied victory, de Gaulle now had to face the question of what France's role would be in the rest of the war. There was also the question of what its authority would be after the war. One thing was clear: from now on, he told himself, he would have to "play a cautious game."[40]

CHAPTER 8
Wild Cards in Play

General de Gaulle's success in rallying much of the Empire led to his becoming "obsessed" — his own word — with "vast schemes" to rouse resistance in France. But the questions of What to do? How? With what? reverberated in de Gaulle's mind. He knew there was "nothing in Metropolitan France" for his Free French to seize hold of and that any actions there "would have to be drawn out of the void." De Gaulle's *Deuxième bureau,* named for the old French military intelligence, was up and running in London under Major André Dewavrin, now calling himself Colonel Passy. Its future as an effective force under the name of the BCRA — Bureau central de renseignements et d'action — offered but hazy and uncertain prospects. The British, meanwhile, were organizing a Special Operations Executive (SOE) of saboteurs and spies, spurred by instructions from Winston Churchill to "set Europe alight."[1]

The first, mostly spontaneous protest against the German Occupation occurred in Paris on November 11, 1940, in commemoration of another armistice — that which ended the First World War with the surrender of

Germany. In response to an underground tract calling on the "Étudiants de France" to honour the day, some six thousand marched down the Champs Élysées to Place de l'Étoile and the Tomb of the Unknown Soldier. German troops used rifle and machine-gun fire to break up the demonstration, killing many and arresting hundreds. These were wild cards playing against enormous odds; journalist Emmanuel d'Astier de la Vigerie, who would emerge as one of the early Resistance leaders, thought "one could be a resister only if one was maladjusted."[2]

With de Gaulle detecting few signs that the French public was ready to take action — "the great majority wanted to believe that Pétain was playing a deep game" — he decided to ask for a demonstration of passive resistance on New Year's Day, 1941. Stay home, empty the streets and squares between three and four o'clock, he asked, and pass a simple "hour of hope." Thousands of people all over France responded by hurrying indoors at the appointed hour.[3]

Agnès Humbert, who had heard de Gaulle's June 18 appeal while on the run in the Limousin along with a million other evacuees from Paris, was back at her job as an art historian at the Musée national des Arts et traditions Populaires, an affiliate of the Musée de l'Homme. She was forty-four years old, divorced, and the mother of two sons. Her friends thought her "impulsive, impetuous, pugnacious and irreverent, with an indomitable sense of humour." Her father had been a senator and her mother an English author. She was writing faithfully every day in her diary, describing Marshall Pétain as "that ridiculous old fool" and recording her disgust at German soldiers being allowed free admission to the museum:[4]

> The atmosphere of the museum has become absolutely stifling. I have been relieved of virtually every single one of my former responsibilities. My duties are now carried out by "volunteers" conjured up out of thin air: ladies of considerable charm, elegance and wealth … all boast of being at the very least "close to someone close to the Marshall."[5]

Agnès Humbert had to do something, anything, and she leaped at the opportunity to join an unlikely mix of would-be *résistants* in what would become known as the Musée de l'Homme group, the first hint of a virus that would eventually infect and demoralize the German occupier. "I feel I will go mad, literally, if I don't do something," she wrote. She eagerly joined the group's prime movers, Russian émigrés Boris Vildé and Anatole Levitsky, and with other recruits was soon engaged as "runner, coordinator, ferreter, and — of course — typist for the group."

They disguised themselves as a literary society and their first mimeographed sheet of protest came out in September followed by the first issue of their paper, *Resistance*, on December 15. "Resist!" it beseeched Parisians. "This is the cry coming from all your hearts amid the distress caused by your country's disaster.... To resist is to keep your heart and head. But above all, it means acting — doing something that will bring about positive results; rational and useful acts."

Within months, the identity of the group became known to the Gestapo, names and addresses having been leaked by a Vichy sympathizer. So the great paradox of resistance and betrayal was established, a pattern that would persist until the liberation. After producing only five issues of its paper, the Musée de l'Homme group was rounded up in April 1941 and its eight key members, including Mme Humbert, were sentenced to death. She escaped execution by being sent to a women's prison. She was later transferred to a forced-labour camp in Germany, but she survived the war. Seven fellow conspirators died in front of a German firing squad at Mont Valérian, a military fortress overlooking the Bois de Boulogne. One is said to have shouted at the moment of execution: "Imbeciles, it's for you, too, that I die."[6]

The efforts of the Musée de l'Homme group were largely ineffectual, but they demonstrated one type of resistance that would be widely practised — the spreading of subversion through underground newspapers and pamphlets that instilled in French minds the idea that the fight was not yet over. More overt forms of resistance — helping downed British flyers to escape, hiding Jews, acts of sabotage, or gathering military intelligence to be passed on to the Allies — had to await the formation of more organized groups. They were not long in coming. The German invasion of the Soviet Union on June 22, 1941, freed up loyal followers of the French Communist Party to join the struggle. They began a cycle of violence offering a strategy of à *chacun son Boche* (to each his German), knowing this would lead to deadly reprisals of a dozen or fifty, or a hundred French victims for every German killed. A Communist action unit that would become known as Francs Tireurs et Partisans (French Irregulars and Partisans) made the first move.

That original act of defiance was triggered by a young Spanish Civil War veteran, Pierre Georges, the son of a baker and a graduate of the International Brigade that had fought for the Republican side against General Francisco Franco. At a little before eight o'clock on the morning of August 21, 1941, Georges placed himself on the platform of the Barbés-Rocheouart Metro station in the Montmartre district of Paris. Spotting a uniformed German emerging from a carriage, he fired two shots before escaping with three companions into the rush-hour crowd.[7] The German, one Alphonse Moser, was a young naval subaltern. He fell back into the carriage, dead, his feet sticking out the door. He was the first German to die by act of the French Resistance.

Georges, a thin, undernourished, twenty-two-year-old, would go on to gain fame as Colonel Fabien, after whom a Paris Metro station is named. The killing of Moser opened a vicious new phase in the Occupation; by the end of the year, there had been sixty-eight attacks on individual German soldiers. In total, there were not more than a few hundred German soldiers assassinated in France during the war, but their deaths were avenged by the execution of some forty thousand French hostages. After the war, the Communist Party would anoint itself *"le parti des fusillés"* (party of the shot, or martyred), claiming to have lost seventy-five thousand members. The figure was clearly an exaggeration of the actual number, but the act of citing it became a powerful political tool.

General de Gaulle would have heard of the attacks on German soldiers with a mix of pride and concern. He mourned the "victims of German vengeance" and saw their loss as "equivalent to the sacrifice of the soldiers on the battlefield." These emotions did not blind him, however, from the fact that sporadic harassment of occupying troops could achieve little and would bring only further massive retaliation. The national uprising he yearned for would have to be timed for the arrival of armies of liberation, still many years off. Any earlier action could lead to disaster, perhaps the creation of another Paris Commune. In a BBC broadcast on October 22, de Gaulle took up the issue of killing Germans:

> It is absolutely natural and absolutely right that Germans should be killed by Frenchmen. If the Germans did not wish to receive death at our hands, they had only to stay at home.... Since they have not succeeded in bringing the world to its knees, they are certain to become, each one of them, a corpse or a prisoner.... For the moment, my orders to those in occupied territory are not to kill Germans there openly. This for one reason only: that it is, at present, too easy for the enemy to retaliate by massacring our fighters, now, for the time being, disarmed. On the other hand, as soon as we are in a position to move to the attack, the orders for which you are waiting will be given.[8]

The "easy" killings by the Germans were already epidemic. The day before de Gaulle's BBC talk, forty-seven hostages had been shot at Châteaubriant near Nantes and fifty at a camp near Bordeaux. De Gaulle's warning, however, was not well-received by the Resistance, now taking shape in the form of several organized groups in both the Occupied Zone and in Vichy France. A leader of Francs Tireurs et Partisans, Charles Tillon, rejected de Gaulle's "lofty order" and declared that "duty required one to disobey the general."[9]

By now, other Resistance groups were playing their wild cards. Surveillance was less rigid in Vichy France, and it was there, especially in Lyon and in the bruising port city of Marseille, where the first Resistance battalions became active.

Resistance leaders came from across the political spectrum. Emmanuel d'Astier de la Vigerie, the journalist who had diagnosed fellow Resisters as "maladjusted," came from a family with right-wing views. He attended the Naval Academy after the First World War but resigned from the navy in 1923. D'Astier wrote for the monarchist journal *Action Française,* but turned to the left during the Spanish Civil War. He re-enlisted in the French navy in 1939 and quickly became head of naval intelligence before being dumped by Vichy for his political views. In Lyon in July 1941, he joined a noted Communist couple, Raymond and Lucie Aubrac, in forming their "Libération" Resistance movement, which was also known as Libération-Sud. They launched the underground newspaper *Libération.* Lucie, after sharing the dangers of their task, became d'Astier's mistress.

It was at this time that Captain Henri Frenay formed a grassroots movement to support Marshall Pétain and his ideas for "national liberation." Born Henri Frenay Sandoval, he had escaped from a German prisoner-of-war camp in Alsace and made his way to Marseille in 1940. "We are passionately attached to the work of Marshall Pétain," he declared. "We subscribe to the great reforms which have been undertaken."[10] His views changed as the Vichy government's pro-Nazi, anti-Jewish policies came to the fore. Frenay quit to launch the Resistance movement "Combat." The movement would put out an underground newspaper, edited by a young Albert Camus, and would eventually become known by another name, Libération national. In Marseille, three Catholic law professors led by François de Menthon, organized the Resistance movement "Liberté" and published a paper with the same name.

In Paris, a notable socialist figure, Christian Pineau, launched Libération-Nord and later linked up with the d'Astier outfit. Pineau had been head of a bank workers' union and enjoyed the support of the civil servants' union. He knew something of government, having worked for his stepfather, the playwright Jean Giraudoux, who was minister of information in the French Cabinet before the war. The few thousand adherents of these secret organizations in the two zones, along with the Communist FTP and its political arm, le Front nationale, would carry the burden of organized resistance to the Germans and their Vichy vassals. In time, they would be joined by localized groups like la Voix du Nord in Flanders, and by the armed combatants of the Maquis, rural guerilla bands that would rise in the hills of the Massif Central, and in rural Britanny and the Alpine regions of southeast France.

General de Gaulle faced fierce opposition from the Communists and his support was far from firm in other branches of the Resistance. Too many saw him as enjoying a comfortable refuge in London where he had become, they thought, little more than a tool of the British. Most thought of him as either too pro-monarchist, too rightist, or with an eye cast on becoming dictator of France. De Gaulle was aware of these prejudices and did his best to counteract them. His painstaking defence of French honour and his readiness to snap back at the slightest rebuke from his British allies were calculated, in large part, to appease his critics. De Gaulle saw himself, as the head of Free France, the champion of all free Frenchmen. It was he who would give the orders and he who would shape the government that would be installed in Paris after the liberation. However, these hopes rested on finding someone who could organize the Resistance so as to demonstrate that de Gaulle's support was as strong in Metropolitan France as throughout the Empire. Fate would entrust one man, Jean Moulin, with carrying out that task.

By staying in small, out-of-the-way hotels and riding night trains where there was less likelihood of being questioned by police, Jean Moulin moved freely throughout the Vichy zone in 1941. He had two main purposes: to secure introductions to leaders of embryonic Resistance movements, and to obtain documents that would allow him, when the time came, to get out of France. He sometimes stopped at what was now his sister's farm near St. Andiol, but he also made frequent visits to Marseille, Lyon, Toulose, and other cities. As Jean Moulin, he remained part art collector, part retired prefect. Using his alias of Joseph Jean Mercier, and the false identity card, false passport, and false exit permit issued in that name, he made application for Portuguese and Spanish transit visas. He also extracted, in his own name, an American entry visa by convincing Hugh Fullerton, the U.S. vice-consul in Marseille, that he could provide the State Department with information vital to the defence of the United

States. In March, he received a bank draft for U.S. $3,000 from Pierre Cot, while Cot's wife, Néna, paid a steamship company for Moulin's passage from Lisbon to New York. But for all Moulin's success in opening doors in the United States, he made no effort to pass through them.

In April, Moulin undertook a risky return to Paris that involved his illegal crossing of the demarcation line between north and south. He did it with the help of Joseph Paul-Boncour, a former premier of France who owned property spanning either side of the Loir-et-Cher River at Saint Agnan. The river served as the border at that point. Moulin crossed it by rowboat at night, while a guide awaited his arrival on the north bank. He returned by the same route, but not before meeting again with his old Cot confreres and letting it be known among art sellers that he was interested in pieces for a gallery he planned to open in Nice.

Back in Marseille — probably carrying paintings he'd picked up in Paris — Moulin checked into his favourite hangout, the Hôtel Moderne, using his own name. He often received mail there and he found a summons awaiting him to appear as a witness at the treason trial of Pierre Cot, about to start in Riom. He had no hesitation in testifying that Cot's "patriotism was beyond question." After picking up 140 francs for expenses, he returned to Marseille where Antoinette Sachs awaited him. His erratic travel pattern continued, often leaving the hotel for several days at a time while Antoinette would go to his room each night and muss the bed so as to make it look like it had been slept in. Unknown to her, he made visits to Aix-en-Provence where he had a new romantic interest in Jane Boullen, a nurse he'd met in Amiens who was now working at French air headquarters.[11]

Howard Lee Brooks, a minister of the Unitarian Church, arrived in Marseille from the United States that summer. He carried a list of introductions that included Moulin's name. We cannot be sure, but he had probably gotten it from Pierre Cot. Brooks made contact with Moulin, and it was through Brooks that Moulin met Henri Frenay, the head of Combat. The meeting took place at the home of Dr. Michel Recordier in Marseille in late July. According to Moulin biographer Patrick Marnham, Frenay was not impressed with Moulin's knowledge of the Resistance: "He knew nothing about it."[12] Moulin's apparent ignorance, however, was likely largely feigned. He had learned that Resistance activities were enveloped in a cone of silence and that identities and operations plans were closely guarded secrets that must be concealed from potential informers.

As Moulin learned more of the operations of Resistance groups — including the Communists — he was acquiring a deeper understanding of the makeup and tactics of the underground throughout France. All the groups were engaged, to varying degrees, in the stockpiling of arms, carrying out acts of sabotage, and collection of information on German military movements. What was lacking was a common commitment to a unified command, one that would declare its solidarity with General de Gaulle and the Free French. When Moulin finally got his Spanish and Portuguese travel permits in the name of Joseph Jean Mercier in Marseille in August, he was at last in a position to act. He boarded a Barcelona-bound train on September 9 and three days later checked into a cheap *pension* in Lisbon. De Gaulle's Lisbon delegate had been arrested shortly before, and Moulin found no Free French presence in the Portuguese capital.

Moulin decided to visit the British embassy where he secured an interview with Major L.H. Mortimore of the Special Operations Executive. Moulin told Mortimore he was the emissary of three French underground movements — a statement not entirely accurate — and that he was in need of transportation to London. "His patriotism shone out of him, his personality compelled you to notice and admire him," Mortimore wrote later to Moulin's sister. The combination of British red tape and poor communications left Moulin lounging about Lisbon for six weeks. Between being robbed of his toiletries and an alarm clock and having to move to another *pension*, Moulin typed up a lengthy report that described the activities and needs of the Resistance. Mortimore had it translated and sent to the Foreign Office in London. The British studied it carefully, but declined to turn it over to the Free French.

When Moulin, still travelling as Joseph Jean Mercier, arrived by seaplane at Bournemouth, England, on October 20, he was the first important Resistance figure to come out of France. The British handled him with care, but put him through four days of questioning at the Royal Patriotic School. His interrogator was Captain F. Eric Piquet-Wicks, head of the SOE section assigned to collaborate with the Free French. After satisfying himself that Moulin was who and what he claimed to be, Piquet-Wicks took him to the De Vere Hotel in Kensington High Street, where he was met by the Free French intelligence chief, Colonel Passy. Moulin gave him a carbon copy of the report he had presented to Major Mortimore in Lisbon, as well as a coded message to be broadcast on the BBC confirming his safe arrival in England: *"Henri Delacour se porte bien."*

A few days later — the precise date is unknown due to the disappearance of de Gaulle's appointment books — Moulin founding himself standing in the general's office at Carleton Gardens, ready to pledge the loyalty of the Resistance movement to Free France. De Gaulle would have towered over Moulin, but the two men met almost as equals; in fact, Moulin's position as a prefect was the equivalent of a major general, which meant he technically outranked de Gaulle. Their conversation went unrecorded, but if this first meeting was like many others, de Gaulle would have risen to his feet, positioned himself over Moulin, and extended his hand. "Tell me about France," he might have said, as he did to Christian Pineau when the leader of Liberation-Nord reached London some time later.

Moulin was not entirely convinced that de Gaulle was the leader France would wish to follow in peacetime; he had doubts about the general's democratic principles but asserted, in a conversation with one Resistance leader: "For the moment one should support de Gaulle, later we will see."[13] None of those doubts would have been on display at this meeting. Each man had what the other needed. Moulin's access to Resistance leadership in France matched de Gaulle's ability to fund and equip their activities, making them natural partners.

De Gaulle respected Moulin as a product of the French administrative class and realized he had before him the most credible figure to have come out of France since his own departure from Bordeaux. He admired the "firmness and dignity" Moulin had shown during his mistreatment by the Nazis in Chartres. Moulin, de Gaulle thought, had been "kneaded from the same dough as the best of my companions."[14] During the meeting, Moulin was so overcome by emotion that without realizing it, he found himself speaking in a barely remembered southern accent.

The report Moulin had brought to London described three movements — Liberté, Libération Nationale, and Libération — "born spontaneously and independently of the initiative of a few French patriots who had a place in the old political groups and parties."[15] He said they had entrusted him with reporting on their operations. The claim was somewhat self-serving; Patrick Marnham says Moulin had met only two leaders, Henri Frenay of Libération Nationale and François de Mentheon of Liberté, and that "neither had appointed him their delegate." Moulin identified the various newspapers being published by the *résistants* and described each group's work in counter-espionage, sabotage, military activities, and in "meting-out of justice." His most emotional section was an appeal for help: "This ardent mass of Frenchmen, which has remained under the yoke, is champing at the bit and is only awaiting the opportunity to shake off this yoke. It would be mad and criminal not to make use of these soldiers.... Without aid in all spheres of activity, the influence of the movements will be in vain."[16]

De Gaulle met with Moulin several times before appointing him as his representative to the Resistance in the Unoccupied Zone. His directions to Moulin were to meld the three groups into a single organization, one willing to accept the instructions of Free France. If they did so, they would be financed and supplied from London.

Moulin was in London, having another meeting with de Gaulle, when news came of the Japanese attack on Pearl Harbor on December 7. Like de Gaulle, he was heartened by the arrival of the Americans in the war following the attack, and he immediately redoubled his preparations for his return to France. Throughout December he took parachute training near Manchester. Colonel Passy, anxious to brush up his own jumping techniques, accompanied him. After rigorous physical training and two parachute jumps with Passy, Moulin was considered ready. At 3:30 in the morning, January 2, 1942, a Royal Air Force Whitley twin-engine bomber parachuted Jean Moulin and two other agents onto the south slope of the Alpille mountains whose jagged peaks bisect Provence from west to east. He was unaware that the Vichy Intelligence Service knew of his coming — the result of the arrest of an SOE agent weeks earlier in France.

Moulin had asked that he and his operations officer, Captain Raymond Fassin, and his radio operator, Hervé Montjarret, be dropped near an old stone farmhouse, La Leque, on the olive plains adjacent to the perched village of Egalières. Moulin had bought the property, a *bastidon* in Provençal patois, in 1941 in the belief he might someday need it as a safe refuge. The farm lay near of the family home in St. Andiol and close to the ruins of a medieval castle called Romanin, whose grounds Moulin had roamed as a boy. He later adopted its name as a pseudonym for his drawings and paintings. Their RAF Whitley had run into heavy flak over the French coast, but by the time they reached the target zone they were well beyond reach of the German coastal guns. The moon was full, the temperature in the aircraft was dropping, and Moulin, huddled in a blanket, wrapped a scarf around his head as he nibbled on a sandwich and sipped tea. Montjarret would remember that the getup reminded him of "someone suffering from a toothache." Moulin told him, "I never liked the dentist's office, either."

When the Whitley encountered difficulties with its navigation system, the green light to jump came on as the plane flew over the south side of the Alpilles rather than the north. Moulin went first, followed by Fassin and Montjarret. A fourth parachute carried a radio transmitter. All four chutes came down in a boggy marsh in the scrubland between Fontvielle and Mourié, some twenty kilometres off target. It took an hour for Moulin and Fassin to hook up with Montjarret, who made his presence known in the dark by whistling the tune of a popular song: "There's a nest in the pear tree, I hear the magpie sing." By now, it was raining hard, the Mistral — the bitter wind off the Rhone Valley — was blowing, and they faced a difficult hike along a lonely road through a pass in the mountains. The rain first turned to sleet, then to snow. Moulin had lost a bag of sandwiches when he landed, and by daybreak — alternately walking and running to keep warm — they reached the village of Aureille where they could smell coffee being brewed. Fearful of being found out, they resisted the temptation to seek breakfast. Nearing the next village Egalières, they encountered two policemen who showed up on bicycles. Montjarret convinced them he was a student from the University of Montpelier on a winter holiday with his professors. The gendarmes departed, "more confused than convinced" by the agent's explanation.[17]

The trio reached La Leque early in the afternoon. Moulin retrieved a key from under a stone and, after resting, they split up.[18] Montjarret found his way to a neighbouring village where he caught a bus, eventually reaching Marseille. Fassin set out for Lyon and a rendezvous with the Resistance organization Combat. After dark, Moulin walked into St. Andiol where his arrival was met with astonishment.[19] The next morning, he collected ration coupons from the *mairie* and set off by train to Megève in the French Alps. There, incredibly, he spent ten days skiing with yet another young woman in whom he had a romantic interest, Colette Pons.

The next months were a blur of intrigue and dissension as Moulin held meetings with Resistance leaders and began to impose controls on their operations. He checked up on their radio contact with London and how they spent the funds that were being received via air drops. By now, it was becoming difficult to separate his Resistance role as "Max," the code name under which he was now operating, and his role of a retired prefect, which he continued to carry on as Jean Moulin.

In May, he was summoned in his own name to Vichy, where Pierre Laval, back as premier after a brief period out of favour with Marshall Pétain, invited him to return to the ranks of government prefects. Moulin discreetly declined. At the time Laval met with Moulin, the report in the hands of the Vichy intelligence service identifying Moulin as a Resistance agent had not reached him. It had disappeared somewhere into the files, not to be seen until after the war.

While Jean Moulin was building his Resistance network, Free French forces were finally able to fulfill Charles de Gaulle's insistence on the "reappearance of our armies on the battlefields." For the first time since the Battle of France, French troops were in combat against German forces. The 1st Division of Fighting French (the term de Gaulle was now using for his Free French) came to the support of the British 8th Army by fighting a stubborn defensive battle against General Erwin Rommel — the "Desert Fox" — at the remote Libyan oasis of Bir Hakeim. General Pierre Koenig's 3,700 men — including several Foreign Legionnaire detachments of refugees from Nazi-conquered lands — held off German and Italian attacks from May 27 to June 11. Their stubborn defence of the old Turkish fort, which they abandoned only when water and food supplies ran out, gave British General Bernard Montgomery time to regroup his forces for a successful defence of Cairo and an ultimate counter-push across the North African desert.[20]

The achievement — de Gaulle thought his troops had "covered themselves with glory" — not only led to the Free French becoming the Fighting French (La France Combattante), but also to a jubilant meeting with Winston Churchill. De Gaulle used the occasion to speak of "dangers to our alliance" caused by recent disagreements between the two. He was referring to problems in Syria and Madagascar, French territories where common aims of the Allies had been lost in a cloud of mutual suspicion.

Responding to de Gaulle's criticisms, Churchill jumped to his feet, protesting "I am the friend of France!"

This was true, de Gaulle admitted. He added: "You even had the merit, after Vichy's Armistice, of continuing to play the card of France. That card is called de Gaulle. Don't lose it now!" It was a thinly veiled warning, but it worked. The meeting ended with nutual assurances that they would be together one day in France.

Churchill followed de Gaulle out of No. 10 Downing and onto the sidewalk. "I shan't desert you," the prime minister promised. "You can count on me."[21]

That night, according to biographer Jonathan Fenby, de Gaulle encountered two French prostitutes on a London street while walking with his aide Maurice Schumann. One recognized de Gaulle and took a photo of him from her bag and asked him to sign it. When de Gaulle asked her name he found out that she and her companion were both married to Englishmen. He good-humouredly signed the photo by noting she had "worked for the *entente cordiale*."[22]

The card of de Gaulle might by now have been having some effect on the course of the war in Africa, but it meant little to the thousands of French Jews who suffered harsh oppression in the Occupied Zone. On July 16 and 17, Paris police, operating under orders of the Gestapo and with the concurrence of René Bousquet, secretary-general of the Gendarmerie nationale, conducted two lighting raids. The first, begun at four o'clock on the morning of the 16th, swept 27,361 foreign Jews — refugees from Germany and Nazi-occupied lands — from their homes throughout the city. They were lodged in Drancy Prison, in suburban Paris, and held for shipment to German death camps. The next day, police targeted French Jews. Émile Hennequin, the Paris prefect of police, instructed his 4,500 men to act with "maximum speed, without pointless speaking and without comment." By afternoon, they had rounded up 12,984 Jews — including 4,051 children — and detained them in the Vélodrome d'Hiver cycling stadium (commonly known as the "Vel d'Hiv"), where they would await transfer to Germany.[23]

The raids, carried out under the code name Operation Spring Freeze, had been carefully planned in meetings at the Nazi SS office on avenue Foch. Adolf Eichmann had been among those in attendance. The Germans knew who to pick up because the Gestapo had their names from a list of the 150,000 Jews in Paris and its suburbs who had registered to obtain the yellow stars all Jews were being forced to wear. Raymond-Raoul Lambert, the former French army officer (and Jew) who had been recording the descent of his brothers and sisters into hell, noted in his diary a letter from a young female social worker assigned to the round-up:

> Fifteen thousand Jews have been "parked" in the Vel d'Hiv. It is horrible, demonic, something that grabs you around the throat so that you can't cry out. When you come in, you can hardly breathe at first on account of the stench. Then you come into the big velodrome, which is black with people piled up against one another, some with bundles already dirty and grey, others with nothing at all.… The handful of toilets are stopped up, there is no one to fix them. Everyone is forced to go to the toilet along the walls.…
>
> The state of mind of these people … is indescribable: hysterical screaming, cries of "Let us out!," suicide attempts. Some women try to jump from the top of the bleachers. People throw themselves at us. "Kill us!" —

"Don't leave us here!" — "An injection so we can die!"
… There are three doctors for fifteen thousand people,
and not enough nurses. Our medical unit doesn't know
which way to turn. Not a single German here — they're
right, they would be torn to pieces. What cowards they
are to make the French people do their dirty work…. If
those who are guilty of these things don't pay for them
one day, there is no justice.[24]

Of the estimated 350,000 Jews living in France at the outbreak of
the Second World War, some seventy-six thousand would be deported
to Germany. Only around 2,500 would survive. It would take fifty-three
years for the French government to acknowledge collective responsibility
for the roundups.[25]

✝

Another set of wild cards — those French who collaborated eagerly with
the Germans — dominated art, culture, and business in Paris during the
Occupation. Motion pictures continued to be made and nightclubs rede-
signed their shows to appeal to German troops. The Comédie Française
and the Paris Opera barely skipped a performance, and only the Louvre,
its most famous paintings having been sent for safekeeping to the Château
Chambord in the Loire Valley, suspended normal operations.

Otto Abetz, now the German ambassador to France, organized a
Groupe Collaboration that attracted forty-two thousand members by early
1944. Its tentacles reached into every aspect of French cultural life and
the economy.[26] Industrialists were bought off with large orders from Germany. Christian Dior and Coco Chanel, purveyors of *haute couture*, were
among the many who profited from the Nazi presence. Chanel, the *grande
dame* of French fashion and the perfume industry, had benefited from the
influence of officials in high places before the war and she continued to
enjoy their protection after the fall of Paris. She moved into the Ritz Hotel
with a German intelligence officer and laid claim to Parfums Chanel, the
company manufacturing her Chanel No. 5, citing it as "property of the

Jews," which had been "abandoned" by its owners.[27] Christian Dior found success in dressing the wives of Nazi officers while in the employ of couturier Lucien Lelong. His sister Catherine worked for the Resistance, was captured and sent to the Ravensbrück concentration camp in Germany. Dior would go on after the war to establish his own house and give the world the New Look in 1947.

Actors and singers faced difficult decisions, confronted with the choice of accepting roles that required German approval, or leaving their chosen fields. Their reputations rested on the degree of enthusiasm they brought to their new engagements at the more than one hundred nightclubs that flourished in Paris. Maurice Chevalier returned to the Casino de Paris in September 1941 in a revue called *Toujours Paris*. The Germans took advantage of him having gone to Germany to sing for French prisoners of war, publicizing his presence in Berlin without mentioning the reason for his trip. For this and other indiscretions, Chevalier found himself under sentence of death in 1944 by a Free French court sitting in Algiers. He would later be exonerated.

Josephine Baker, the American black singer who held dual U.S. and French citizenship, described Chevalier as "one of those Frenchmen who believed that the Germans had won the war and that it was time things returned to normal — on German terms." Ms. Baker, meanwhile, helped her French lover, a captain in the military intelligence, feed information to the Allies via Lisbon. She spent much of the war in North Africa and performed from Casablanca to Beirut, always as a supporter of Free France. In contrast, Edith Piaf and the equally legendary Mistinguett — born Jeanne Bourgeois — performed regularly in France during the war.[28]

More than entertainers, it was authors and journalists — from the young Albert Camus, who wrote for *Combat,* to Robert Brasillach, editor of the most reviled of the collaborationist press, *Je suis partout* — who most sharply etched the divisions between collaboration and resistance. Brasillach, one of the more vicious of the French fascists during the 1930s, served briefly in the French army before returning to Paris after ten months as a prisoner of war. The French government had closed his newspaper in May 1940 over its anti-war editorials. Relaunched under German auspices in 1941, *Je suis partout* under Brasillach was quick to applaud Nazi anti-Semitism. After the German roundup of Jews in the Vél' d'Hiv episode in July 1942, he wrote, "We must remove the Jews in a block, and not keep the young ones." Brasillach was fired in 1943 after a dispute with the owner, and was succeeded by Pierre-Antoine Cousteau, elder brother of the explorer Jacques-Yves Cousteau.[29]

Respected Paris newspapers such as Pierre Brisson's *Le Figaro* shifted operations to the Vichy zone and others simply stopped publishing, but some adjusted to the new reality and embraced the occupier. The prominent French rightist Maurice Bunau-Varilla was proprietor of the Paris daily *Le Matin*. He prided himself on possession of one of the finest wine cellars in France. With his brother Philippe, he had made a fortune with a mouthwash and all-round tonic, Synthol, packaged in a black box that adorned the shelves of thousands of French stores. Maurice Bunau-Varilla believed with many other French rightists that Germany was better positioned to resist Communism than the Third Republic, which he saw as having been dragged down by leftist influences and "decadent" cultural practices. Before the war, *Le Matin* had flaunted its pro-appeasement sentiments with its headline hailing the Munich pact: "LA VICTOIRE DE LA PAIX." Bunau-Varilla welcomed the German Occupation with the headline: "LA VIE CONTINUE" (Life goes on). Seeking to justify its stand, the paper published an editorial that declared: "The duty of a newspaper is to inform public opinion, and search for truth."

French literature needed a place to recover and revive, and it found it in Quebec. Between 1941 and 1945, more than twenty new French language publishers sprang up in Montreal. Catering to a global market — especially the United States and Latin America — they published French classics as well as new works by such writers as Jacques Maritain, Antoine de Saint-Exupery, and Jean Wahl, who had taken refuge in the United States. These writers and their new Quebec publishers pursued what they thought to be an exalted mission: to keep the flame of French thought and literature alight throughout the world.[30]

CHAPTER 9
Warriors at Odds

The weather was worsening in the North Atlantic when Task Force H of the Royal Navy, led by the battleship HMS *Duke of York*, turned southward off the coast of Ireland and set course for Gibraltar and the beaches of North Africa.[1] The ship was at the head of a pack of battle cruisers and destroyers guarding a convoy of five hundred and fifty troop carriers. Such a vast armada had not been seen since the days of sail, when the Spanish Armada circumnavigated the British Isles in King Phillip II's ill-fated attempt to conquer England. The *Duke of York*'s commander, Sir Neville Syfret, knew his men were accustomed to harsh conditions; they'd come through a frigid three days in pursuit of the German battleship *Tirpitz*, unable to sink it but successful in forcing it to break off its Atlantic convoy-hunting and retreat to its Norwegian lair. While Task Force H dodged enemy U-boats and patrol planes through the calmer waters of the Bay of Biscay, a second convoy of one hundred ships sailed from a U.S. East Coast port. Following a route that paralleled the horse latitudes across the Atlantic, it made for the beaches of French Morocco. Together, the two armadas were ferrying more than seventy thousand British and American infantry troops, commanded by such colourful figures as General George S. Patton, the irascible head of the U.S. 2nd Armoured Division.

The target was Vichy-controlled French North Africa, where months of intrigue, plotting, and counter-plotting by American agents would, it was hoped, pay off with little or no opposition to the Anglo-American landings. Late on the night of Saturday, November 7, 1942, all ships were at their stations, and by dawn, landings had commenced on the Atlantic coast of Morocco and on Mediterranean beaches near Oran and Algiers in Algeria. General Dwight Eisenhower, in overall command of Operation Torch, felt tension rising in him as he "paced away among Gibraltar's caverns" while the first great offensive of the Western Allies got underway.[2]

General de Gaulle spent Saturday evening at the Soviet Embassy in London's Kensington district, where Ambassador Ivan Maisky was hosting a party celebrating the twenty-fourth anniversary of the October Revolution (by the Russian calendar). De Gaulle had heard talk of a possible Allied attack on North Africa for months, but he left the party early, apparently oblivious to rumours that the landings might be only hours away. U.S. military radio beaming into Africa was broadcasting a cryptic message: "Hello Robert, Franklin is coming."[3] If it was intended as code, it was incredibly naïve, considering that President Roosevelt's minister in Algiers was Robert Murphy. Colonel Billotte, de Gaulle's military chief of staff, took a telephone call shortly after midnight from Lord Ismay, the head of Winston Churchill's office. He was told the landings were to start in three hours. Billotte waited until six o'clock to awaken de Gaulle at his villa in Hampstead in north London, fully aware of the rage he would encounter. Pulling a dressing gown over his white pyjamas, de Gaulle roared "I hope the Vichy people will fling them into the sea! You don't get France by burglary!"[4]

Winston Churchill had wanted to alert de Gaulle of the landings, worried about "the gravity of the affront which he would have to suffer by being deliberately excluded."[5]

President Roosevelt, suspicious of the ability of the Fighting French to maintain security, would have none of it. "Inadvisable for you to give de Gaulle any information," the president wired back, demanding "complete secrecy as a necessary safety precaution." Roosevelt still hadn't gotten over the collapse of France or the failure of de Gaulle's mission to Dakar, where ships and soldiers loyal to Vichy lay ready to repel him. The president had, however, agreed to Churchill's handing over the French island colony of Madagascar, occupied by the British, to de Gaulle's control. "It should be sufficient at the present time to maintain his prestige with his followers."

Much more than security was involved in Roosevelt's insistence that de Gaulle and the Fighting French be kept out of Operation Torch. Morocco, Algeria, and neighbouring Tunisia made up the heart of France's colonial Empire, and de Gaulle had been unable to win them from Vichy. Roosevelt was still angling to lure Marshall Pétain to the Allied side and the first draft of his message to him following the landings had been addressed to "My dear old friend." Roosevelt agreed to drop the phrase when Churchill protested it "seems to me too kind … his stock must be very low now."[6] Robert Murphy, the American diplomat sent to Algiers as Roosevelt's personal emissary, had been charged with winning over Vichy's representatives. His efforts failed to forestall stiff French resistance. Coastal batteries attacked General Patton's forces on the beaches of Morocco, and a naval battle broke out at Casablanca involving a sortie by French destroyers and cruisers. At Oran, French batteries exchanged gunfire with the invasion fleet.

By the time de Gaulle reached No. 10 Downing Street at noon, he had regained his composure. Once in Churchill's presence, however, he was confronted with fresh surprises. First he was given startling news about General Henri Giraud, the war hero who had been captured in the Ardennes forest during the Battle of France but had escaped from his German prisoner-of-war camp with the help of Britain's SOE and had made his way back to Vichy France. Giraud, Churchill said, had been taken to Gibraltar in a British submarine and General Eisenhower had invited him to assume command of French troops in North Africa. At first Giraud refused, insisting on being put in command of the entire operation. That morning, with the landings underway, he relented and undertook to rally Vichy troops to the Allied side. Next, Churchill loosed an even more devastating thunderbolt. "Did you know," Churchill asked de Gaulle, "that Darlan is in Algiers?"[7] Of all the names associated with Vichy, none drew such contempt from de Gaulle as that of François Darlan, admiral of the French navy, deputy to Marshall Pétain, and Vichy's commander of the French Armed Forces. It was all a coincidence, Churchill maintained, as Darlan had gone to Algiers to see his son, who was seriously ill with poliomyelitis.

De Gaulle struggled to contain his frustration. The invasion, he conceded, was a "highly satisfactory development." General Giraud was a "great soldier." It was too bad the initial landings had not included the German base of Bizerte in Tunisia, because the Nazis were sure to "rush in" before the battle was over. But as for co-operating with Darlan? Never. De Gaulle had not forgotten the events of June 1940, and his distress at Darlan's readiness to collaborate with the Germans. He would have no dealings with the traitor under any circumstance. That evening, de Gaulle spoke on the BBC to the French in North Africa. "Rise up, help our Allies, join them without reservations. Don't worry about names or formulas — rise up! Now is the great moment."

It took only a few days for British and American troops — with some help from Admiral Darlan — to put an end to the resistance of 125,000 Vichy French troops. In one of the stranger episodes of the exercise, just past noon on the day of the invasion a gang of French partisans under the direction of Algiers chief of police, Henri d'Astier de la Vigerie — brother of two famous Resistance leaders — swung into action. They occupied key posts in Algiers and arrested Admiral Darlan and French general Alphonse Juin, Vichy commander in North Africa. Robert Murphy was unable to persuade either to join the Allies and they were soon freed by local gendarmerie. The partisans managed to put themselves under the protection of the British invasion force. With U.S. troops ashore in Algiers, General Juin surrendered the city late that afternoon. When other French officers ignored General Giraud's appeal to stop the fighting — his ill-suited code name, "Kingpin," lent an ironic twist to the débacle — Eisenhower had little choice but to turn to Admiral Darlan.

Darlan, speaking with the authority of Vichy behind him, commanded the French Armée d'Afrique to lay down arms. His order brought about a ceasefire on November 10. "I assume authority over North Africa in the name of the Marshall," he declared.[8] In return, General Eisenhower agreed to name Darlan high commissioner for French North Africa. Darlan set up an Imperial Council, announced he would exercise the functions of head of state, and imposed rigid enforcement of anti-Semitic laws (cheerfully supported by Algeria's Muslim population) while Fighting French *résistants* were hunted down and jailed. "I shall extract from everybody the strictest obedience and most perfect discipline."[9] The day after Darlan's grasp for power — November 11 — German troops invaded the Unoccupied Zone and in defiance of the terms of the French-German Armistice, took full control, with their Italian allies, of all of Metropolitan France. Coincidentally, Marshall Pétain stripped Darlan of the last of his Vichy authority.

While Roosevelt had succeeded in sidestepping de Gaulle, the deal with Admiral Darlan caused great political blowback. It was seen as a betrayal of the Fighting French, leading to public indignation in Britain, Canada, and the United States. The influential American newspaperman Walter Lippmann warned that "Darlan has joined the Allies only to maintain Vichy's authority in France's overseas territories."[10] Columnist Raymond Clapper wrote: "There is some wonder as to how it is we denounce the Vichy regime as a puppet of Hitler and yet at the same time set up Vichy men, like Admiral Darlan, to run North Africa for us."[11]

Churchill thought Admiral Darlan could have been "a de Gaulle raised to the tenth power" if he had chosen in 1940 to fight on against Nazi Germany.[12] Now, he believed, "Darlan ought to be shot." He went along with the arrangement to maintain harmony with the United States, but not before warning Roosevelt that "Darlan has an odious record." The president saw Darlan in a different light: a "temporary expedient," as he told a press conference in Washington. He explained to Churchill how he had quoted an old Orthodox Church proverb: "My children, it is permitted you in time of grave danger to walk with the devil until you have crossed the bridge."[13]

The honeymoon that Charles de Gaulle had enjoyed with Churchill in the summer of 1940 was not, in fact, to last very long. By 1941, when de Gaulle found himself frozen out of the Atlantic Charter, his resentment simmered to the surface in an angry interview with *Chicago Daily News* correspondent George Weller. It took place in Brazzaville in Equatorial Africa where de Gaulle was visiting the Fighting French outpost. Asked by Weller why Britain had not "closed the door" on Vichy by recognizing the Free French as a government, de Gaulle said Britain was afraid of the French fleet and "is carrying on a wartime deal with Hitler in which Vichy serves as go-between."[14]

It was an outrageous statement, and de Gaulle regretted making it, especially as it had come on the heels of serious difficulties with Britain over the French protectorate of Syria and Lebanon. On de Gaulle's return from Africa, Churchill ordered that no British official have any contact with him. When he finally called de Gaulle to Downing Street, the atmosphere was cool. Two interpreters had to be dismissed when they failed to convey what Churchill thought was the true sense of what he was trying to say. Left alone, the two men talked for an hour, their differences eventually evaporating amid Churchill's cigar smoke and de Gaulle's cigarette fumes. Churchill told de Gaulle it was time to form a French national committee; such a body would put to rest the charge that de Gaulle was authoritarian. De Gaulle agreed. He thought the meeting "ended well after a bad beginning."[15]

Despite provocations on both sides, the two men never lost their respect or affection for each other. When one of Churchill's aides suggested de Gaulle was a great man notwithstanding all the problems he caused, the prime minister responded: "A great man? Why, he's selfish, he's arrogant, he thinks he's the centre of the universe.... You're right, he's a great man!"[16]

De Gaulle never had the opportunity to build a personal relationship with President Roosevelt. The president thought de Gaulle had a Joan of Arc complex and that he saw himself as the reincarnation of France's greatest heroine. He accused him of being a dictator in the making. By trusting the faulty intelligence that Admiral Leahy and Robert Murphy passed on to him, Roosevelt mistakenly concluded that de Gaulle had no real following in France. The president favoured putting a military government in place in France, "run by British and American generals."[17] It might be all right to make de Gaulle governor of Madagascar, he told Churchill.

Realizing that Roosevelt held him in poor repute, de Gaulle tried in October 1942 to explain himself. In a long letter to the president, he stressed that his Fighting French movement saw itself as only a provisional authority that would disappear when a free election could be held. He explained he had broken with Pétain in 1940 in order "to bring France back into the fight side by side with the Allied nations while at the same time watching over the country's sensitivities and its unity." The letter was delivered by two emissaries who got a meeting with the president, but little else. Roosevelt made clear the hand he was playing: in his view, he told them, there no longer was a France. He was already training a group of American political and military specialists who would govern France "until democracy is re-established." De Gaulle simply had no way to overcome the fact, as biographer Jean Lacouture would write, that in 1940 "the president had decided against de Gaulle and in favour of a Pétain who had considerable authority and a certain amount of room for manoeuvring." De Gaulle's letter went unanswered.[18]

The impasse over Operation Torch revealed how uneasy was the partnership between Churchill, Roosevelt, and de Gaulle. They were now warriors at odds with each other. Churchill's sole objective was to win the war. Roosevelt's goals went beyond that, to include postwar reconstruction, democratic self-determination, and the end of colonialism. De Gaulle, lacking the forces to significantly tip the balance of the battle and convinced that with the United States and the Soviet Union in the conflict the Allies were assured of winning the war, was locked onto an entirely different goal: to shape the future of France and his role in it. He was determined to win recognition for France and secure for his country and himself a full measure of influence in the postwar world.

While Admiral Darlan settled himself into the Palais d'Été (Summer Palace), events unfolded much as de Gaulle had forecast. It rained steadily in Tunisia, but that did not stop the Germans from rushing troops into the colony. Ahead lay six months of fierce fighting against General Rommel's combined German and Italian forces. With General Leclerc's Fighting French units fighting on the British left flank, UK troops occupied Tunis while American regiments took Bizerte. In Algiers, Darlan enjoyed the full support of General Eisenhower — so instructed by President Roosevelt — despite growing apprehension in both British and American quarters over the admiral's Vichy-like behaviour. Police chief Henri d'Astier, by now a member of Darlan's Cabinet, was compelled to organize round-ups of anti-Vichy figures, who were sent to vermin-ridden camps in the desert. The Algerian press was filled with anti-Semitic tirades. De Gaulle issued an official statement that there would be no Fighting French co-operation with Darlan. In London, an emissary arrived from France with a proclamation recognizing General de Gaulle as "the uncontested leader of the Resistance movement."

On November 11, de Gaulle gave a stirring speech at Albert Hall in London. "The cement of French unity," he declared, "is the blood of the Frenchmen who have never recognized the Armistice, of those who have died for France...."[19] A lone heckler — a retired French general who had taken refuge in London — was dragged from his seat in the balcony when he shouted that de Gaulle should submit to the orders of General Giraud.

As de Gaulle spoke, German forces were moving south toward the great French naval base of Toulon, once commanded by Admiral Darlan. They occupied the heights overlooking the harbour. Not wishing to allow the Germans to take the base, on November 27 the French commander, Admiral de Laborde, ordered the scuttling of the fleet. Three battleships, eight cruisers, and more than one hundred other vessels went to the bottom. The act deprived the Germans of the glittering naval prize they had sought since 1940. To de Gaulle, it was "the most pitiful and sterile suicide imaginable."[20]

The unease the British felt over Admiral Darlan became more pronounced as President Roosevelt began to shift responsibility for American policy from himself to General Eisenhower. Roosevelt told a press conference that he had accepted Eisenhower's "political arrangements" as a "temporary expedient" in order to save lives.[21] On November 16, Churchill told de Gaulle that "Darlan has no future" and assured him, "yours is the true path, you alone will remain."[22]

Some people were in favour of drastic action. Sir Alexander Cadogan, the British undersecretary for foreign affairs, noted in his diary: "We shall do no good until we have killed Darlan." W.H.B. Mack, head of the British political section in Algiers, signalled London that "Darlan must be got rid of; the question is when." Another British officer noted in his diary, "It is difficult to lay on an efficient assassination."[23]

The young French partisans who had been welcomed by the British army after their brief uprising took easily to the loose military discipline that prevailed in Algiers throughout November and December.[24] They enjoyed their training in the use of firearms and some looked for opportunities to design new adventures. On the night of November 20, in a barn on Cape Matifou outside Algiers, four of them reached a fateful decision. Philippe Ragueneau, their twenty-five-year-old leader, handed out straws. It was agreed that the one who drew the short straw would assassinate Admiral Darlan. It would all be carefully arranged — they surely had support for this action — and the man who did the act could be assured of a safe escape. One after another, Fernand Bonnier de la Chapelle, Bernard Pauphilet, and Mario Faivre took their turns, followed by Ragueneau. The youngest, Bonnier, a mere twenty, drew the short straw. Ragueneau, more experienced and tougher, offered to take his place. Bonnier, not one to admit to lacking courage, insisted he would do the deed.[25]

A few days later, Bonnier, who was known to have Royalist sentiments, was taken to the shooting range at Le Club des Pins where he was instructed in the use of a .38 Webley pistol. After receiving encouragement from his confessor Abbé Cordier (a lieutenant of the reserve), it was decided to replace the Webley with a more effective killing machine. A Colt .45 was tried out but discarded as too bulky and clumsy. Better to use a 7.65 pistol, Cordier decided, as it was a neat and accurate weapon. Bonnier is known to have met over the next month with a number of important figures: police head Henri d'Astier de la Vigerie, the banker Alfred Pose, and possibly an emissary of the Comte de Paris, Henri d'Orléans, the pretender to the French throne.

Christmas Eve dawned sunny and cold. Admiral Darlan spent the morning with Robert Murphy in discussing such questions as what to do about political prisoners and the Jews. Henri d'Astier's brother, General François d'Astier, caught a plane out of Algiers that morning to return to London. He had been sent to Algiers by General de Gaulle with the approval of General Eisenhower, ostensibly to see if the Fighting French could reach an accommodation with Admiral Darlan. D'Astier had met with Darlan, but no agreement was forthcoming.

Fernand Bonnier began the day by taking confession with Abbé Cordier. Sometime around noon he got into a black Peugeot and was driven by Mario Faivre to the Summer Palace. Along with his gun, he carried a pass in the name of Morand. At the Palace, he was told that Darlan had gone out but would be back in the afternoon. When Bonnier returned a little before three o'clock, he was recognized by the orderly and taken to a waiting room where he was asked to fill out a form. Admiral Darlan would not be long, he was told. Bonnier would be able to see him after the admiral finished meeting with another visitor.

A warm spell enveloped London in mid-December, but by Christmas Eve the weather had turned misty and cold. On the morning of December 24, General de Gaulle boarded a plane for an unexpected — and never explained — flight to Greenock, Scotland, a heavily bombed River Clyde port that was home to the Fighting French Navy. In contrast to the careful planning de Gaulle normally demanded for his travels, Greenock had been given only twenty-fours notice of his coming. When his motorcade climbed the hill above the town to visit Knockderry Castle, converted into a convalescent home for wounded French sailors, Dr. A.B. Walker had to apologize for the absence of welcoming officials. There had been no time to bring in the Secretary of State for Scotland. De Gaulle affected to be unconcerned at the lack of protocol.[26] He charmed the nurses, insisting on being introduced to each of the thirteen on duty. Schoolgirl Joan Baird, wearing the maroon tunic and white blouse mandatory at Greenock Academy, was on her way home from school when she saw de Gaulle emerge from a building that flew the French Tricolour. She was struck by the sight of "this very tall man in a strange uniform."[27] De Gaulle had lunch with Provost Morrison and the Greenock council members and inspected a French warship moored in the harbour. By four o'clock he was at the French Canteen in Martyrs' Church Hall where an orchestra struck up "La Marseillaise" as he entered the room. De Gaulle decorated a Christmas tree and accepted a bouquet of roses, white heather, and daffodils from six-year-old Françoise Langlais, daughter of the French naval commander. He presented gifts of cigarettes, candies, and socks to the French sailors, chatting easily with them. The occasion called for a speech and the general, clearly in an optimistic mood, spoke of his confidence that France "will rise again and become [once more] a great nation."[28]

De Gaulle returned to the Martyrs' Hall that evening for a dance; the *Greenock Telegraph* called it "a bright affair." He was chatting with a group of sailors when he was told he was wanted on the telephone. The caller was Michel Saint-Denis, otherwise known as "Jacques Duchesne" (after a popular character of the French Revolution) who was in charge of Fighting French broadcasts on the BBC. He was on the line from London, excited to be conveying *"Ça pour une nouvelle, c'est une nouvelle."*[29] His news was that Admiral Darlan had been assassinated; a young royalist by the name of Fernand Bonnier de la Chapelle had barged into the Summer Palace and fired two shots, hitting Darlan in the stomach. The admiral died a couple of hours later. Guards jumped Bonnier and he was being held by the Algiers police.

De Gaulle reacted calmly to the news. His *Mémoires de guerre* would record how "this young man, this child overwhelmed by the spectacle of odious events, thought his action would be a service to his lacerated country." No man, de Gaulle conceded, "has the right to kill save on the field of battle." Yet, "the very fact that he (Darlan) was forced from the stage seemed to be in accord with the harsh logic of events."[30] Digesting the news, de Gaulle realized there was no good reason to rush back that night to London where the British Foreign Office might wish some answers from him.

Did the elimination of Darlan have anything to do with this inexplicable trip? It seemed so trivial in comparison to everything else on de Gaulle's schedule — including a visit to the White House for which he was supposed to depart from London the day after Christmas. Why would a man so committed to his family and to the religious significance of Christmas steal these precious few days from home and hearth?

At this time, the de Gaulles were living in Hampstead, in a handsome house at 65 Frognal. This location allowed the general to come home most nights. Elisabeth visited often, and Anne felt comfortable in this quiet neighbourhood. The de Gaulles worshipped every Sunday at the Church of St. Mary, Holly Place, and it is there they would have gone for Christmas Eve mass had de Gaulle been home. As it was, Yvonne de Gaulle awoke without her husband on Christmas morning. She noticed the garden was white; it had snowed all night. When she tuned the radio to the BBC, she heard an announcer read the news: "Good morning — and a very happy Christmas to you all. Last night Admiral Darlan was assassinated." The killer, Fernand Bonnier, was to be shot the next day at dawn. President Roosevelt said "the cowardly assassination of Darlan is an unforgivable crime."[31]

De Gaulle arrived home late on Christmas Day. The next day, Saturday — before much was stirring at Whitehall — he was on his way to the airport to fly to Washington via Ireland and Newfoundland. A radio call came through telling him that President Roosevelt had cancelled his visit. De Gaulle returned home and on Sunday, Yvonne and Charles found themselves in the small Church of St. Mary. "She felt her husband by her side, buried in his thoughts. He too was alone with his God."[32]

Was the assassination of Admiral Darlan a British plot in which the Fighting French were complicit? Or was it a Fighting French conspiracy carried out with or without the clandestine support of the British? General de Gaulle's absence from London — a suspicious coincidence freeing him from the need to answer embarrassing questions — fits either scenario. Years later, according to CBS Paris correspondent David Schoenbrun, de Gaulle would blame Robert Murphy and the Americans for Darlan's death. "Murphy arranged the assassination of Darlan and the hasty execution of Bonnier de la Chapelle," Schoenbrun quoted de Gaulle. "Darlan had become an embarrassment to American policy and had to be disposed of."[33]

The claim seems implausible, in light of consistent United States sympathy toward Vichy personalities, including Darlan, General Giraud, and others. Immediately after Bonnier's execution, Murphy pressured the Imperial Council into appointing General Giraud as Darlan's successor. General Giraud blamed police chief Henri d'Astier de la Vigerie for Darlan's murder and launched a crackdown on Fighting French sympathizers. D'Astier, warned that his own police had orders to shoot him on sight, went into hiding. He was later arrested, to be released only after de Gaulle gained control of Algeria.

General Giraud may have been correct in his presumption that Henri d'Astier had a connection to Darlan's murder. D'Astier's position as head of the police as well as being the brother of General de Gaulle's Algiers emissary, General François d'Astier, would have facilitated his involvement. It is known that Bonnier was in possession of $2,000 when he was arrested, apparently given to him by Henri d'Astier. The money had presumably been drawn from the $38,000 that François d'Astier had brought with him to fund Fighting French activities. Bonnier was also found to be carrying a business card of Henri d'Astier, on the back of which he had written a few last words. In view of the prominent Resistance roles of both of Henri d'Astier's brothers — and his own later work with the Resistance in France in preparation for D-Day — it is difficult to cast Henri d'Astier in any other light than as an active supporter. More central to the question may be who had the most to gain from the death of Admiral Darlan? Darlan's demise left one less player at the table. It is difficult to escape the conclusion that the leader of the Free French would have had some involvement in Darlan's death. Whatever else may be said, Darlan's removal was hugely beneficial to Charles de Gaulle as he played out his "cautious game."

Despite his frequent recriminations with the Americans, de Gaulle was allowed to use the facilities of the United States Embassy in London to cable General Giraud in Algiers on December 27. "The assassination at Algiers is an indication and a warning," de Gaulle wrote. It was an indication of the exasperation the French were feeling and a warning about the consequences of the lack of "a national authority in the midst of the greatest national crisis of our history." De Gaulle proposed a meeting "as soon as possible ... in order to study the means of grouping under a provisional central authority all French forces inside and outside the country...."[34] Giraud, now firmly ensconced as head of the Imperial Council, ignored de Gaulle's appeal.

Churchill was vexed at the standoff and put the question of de Gaulle versus Giraud on the agenda for a conference he was to have with President Roosevelt in Casablanca. Winston Churchill landed there on January 13 and joined Roosevelt at a group of luxurious villas in the Casablanca suburb of Anfa. Roosevelt's attitude hardly helped to settle matters. He referred to Giraud as "the bridegroom" and offered up as "the bride the temperamental lady de Gaulle." All that was needed was to bring the two together in a "shotgun marriage."[35] Giraud arrived at Anfa on schedule, but de Gaulle, resentful of these foreign powers meeting on French soil without so much as a by your leave, resisted. He agreed to come only after Churchill warned him that his absence could lead to him "being replaced by someone else as the head of the French Liberation Committee in London."[36]

When de Gaulle finally arrived, he had an inconclusive lunch meeting with General Giraud and later met with Winston Churchill for "a very stony interview." Surprisingly, at a later meeting with President Roosevelt, the two got on "unexpectedly well."[37] Two days later, the president brought forth a proposal to set up a triumvirate to carry France forward in the war. It would be presided over by General Giraud, who would exercise military powers under General Eisenhower, assisted by de Gaulle and by Churchill's friend, General Georges, who bore much of the blame for the French defeat of 1940.[38] A draft communiqué noted that "the French commander-in-chief [Giraud] whose headquarters are at Algiers, has the right and the duty to act as director of the French military, economic and financial interests...." De Gaulle refused to have any part of it. He did allow — at Roosevelt's request — a photograph to be taken of him shaking hands with General Giraud.

By refusing to accede to the demands of Roosevelt and Churchill, de Gaulle won, in the opinion of Robert Murphy, an "unproclaimed victory" at Casablanca. "The miscalculation which all of us at Casablanca made about de Gaulle was belief that winning the war had top priority with him, as it did with us. His thoughts were two jumps ahead of everybody else's."[39] The outcome also hardened Roosevelt's objections to de Gaulle. He let it be known that the postwar map of Europe would look different. There would be room for a new state, to be called Wallonia, consisting of the Walloon (French) part of Belgium plus Luxembourg and parts of northern France, including Alsace-Lorraine.

Churchill, meanwhile, grew more apprehensive of de Gaulle's intransigent attitude. He told the official at the Foreign Office in charge of relations with the Fighting French to keep de Gaulle in England. "I hold you responsible that the Monster of Hampstead does not escape!"[40]

While Charles de Gaulle struggled to improve his position in North Africa, his delegate to the French Resistance, Jean Moulin, grappled with rivalries — sometimes bitter — among the underground leaders whose groups he was supposed to unite. Moulin argued for abolition of the distinction between northern and southern zones in order that he be accepted as leader of the unified Resistance in all of France. Others, especially the left-wing journalist Pierre Brossolette, who had run a bookstore in Paris as a cover for Resistance intelligence, sought to maintain their independence.[41] In an effort to settle these differences, Jean Moulin was picked up by a Royal Air Force Lysander on February 13, 1943, and flown to London, along with General Charles Delestraint, commander of the Armée secrète, for meetings with General de Gaulle.

Few of de Gaulle's wartime associates were ever invited to the general's home. De Gaulle made an exception for Jean Moulin and in a ceremony at Frognal House he decorated his Resistance chief with the Order of the Liberation. It was the highest honour of the Fighting French. Those who were there saw tears roll down Moulin's cheeks as de Gaulle, addressing him in his code name of Joseph Mercier, recognized him as "our companion in honour and victory for the liberation of France." De Gaulle found it "a most moving ceremony," and gave Moulin fresh orders. The distinction between the two zones would remain, but Moulin would be in charge of both. More important, he was to set up a national council — the Conseil national de la Résistance (CNR) — with himself as its head. Moulin's new mission, far from settling differences in France, brought on fresh friction. Emannuel d'Astier accused him of abuse of power and of treating Resistance leaders as a colonial officer would treat "native chieftains."[42]

Before departing for London, Moulin had achieved his "cover goal" of becoming the proprietor of an art gallery. He'd worked hard at finding a location in Nice, settling on an abandoned bookstore at 22 rue de France that he outfitted for the display of works by such artists as Picasso, Utrillo,

Dufy, and Matisse. He no longer had Antoinette Sachs at his side; unable to cope with police harassment, she'd fled to Switzerland to spend the rest of the war with her sister. Colette Pons, the girlfriend he'd taken skiing when he'd first arrived back in France, agreed to become the manager of Galerie Romanin.[43]

After his return from London, Moulin found himself under increasing pressure from the Gestapo. Betrayals and leaks had led to the arrest of many members of the underground. Moulin went to Paris at the end of March, taking Colette Pons with him. On April 1, he met with Colonel Passy and Pierre Brossolette in a clearing in the Bois de Boulogne, and the next day in an apartment in the avenue des Ternes. Everyone was feeling tense when Brossolette enraged Moulin by accusing him of "personal ambition." Moulin turned his back on Brossolette and lowered his trousers, yelling "Now, you can see my opinion of you!"[44] Less turbulent meetings followed, at which Moulin explained the need to unify the Resistance. He was finally able to send word to de Gaulle on May 15 confirming that the new body about to take form would recognize the general as "the sole leader of the French Resistance."[45]

The new Conseil was secretly launched at a meeting in a first-floor apartment overlooking the courtyard of 47 rue du Four on May 27. In was in a neighbourhood familiar to Moulin, not many metres from the intersection of rue de Rennes and boulevard Saint-Germain. Seventeen men took part, representing Resistance movements, political parties, and trade unions. Moulin chaired the meeting and after clearing away the preliminaries he called on Georges Bidault, representative of the Christian Democrats, to read a declaration of support for General de Gaulle "as the sole leader of French Resistance whatever the result of the negotiation" with General Giraud.[46] There could be no stronger assertion that the French were ready to fall in behind General de Gaulle. Neither a Communist *coup d'état* nor an American military government would be allowed to trump France's determination to shape its own destiny.

At the next meeting, held at the home of Dr. Frédéric Dugoujon in the Lyon suburb of Caluire on the afternoon of Monday, June 21, Moulin arrived wearing his habitual dark glasses, brown trilby, and a scarf that covered the scar on his neck, to which he added a grey suit that gave him an exceptionally well-turned-out appearance. It was a simple stone house overlooking Place Castellane, serving as both a home and an office for the doctor's practice. Seven other well-known leaders of the Resistance were to join Moulin that day. They included Henri Aubry and René Hardy of the right-wing Combat movement, Colonel Albert Lacaze of the independent France d'Abord, André Lassagne, a member of the pro-Communist Libération and a friend of Dr. Dugoujon, and Bruno Larat, who organized parachute drops for the Resistance. The men sat in a first-floor room — one up from the ground floor — waiting for Moulin. Forty-five minutes after the meeting was to have started, Moulin arrived with Raymond Aubrac of Libération and Lieutenant-Colonel Raymond Schwartzfield, also of France d'Abord.

Rather than being taken upstairs, they were shown into the ground-floor waiting room. Moulin — or Max — must have realized they were in the wrong room, but before he was able to straighten out the mix-up, a sudden loud banging was heard on the front door, followed by a crash. A half-dozen men armed with pistols, including the head of the Lyon Gestapo, Klaus Barbie, burst into the house. The Sonderkommando, a special anti-Resistance police unit, had arrived to break up the meeting. All seven men as well as Dr. Dugoujon were arrested. As they were being loaded into police cars, René Hardy broke loose from his captors and ran across the square and into some trees. Several shots were fired, one wounding Hardy, but the police made no real attempt to capture him.

Moulin and the others were questioned at the Gestapo headquarters in the École de Santé Militaire and then transferred to the central prison at Fort Montluc. For the next several days, Moulin was viciously interrogated, undergoing what is known today as waterboarding. He was seen being dragged back to his cell, heavily bandaged. Christian Pineau, the co-founder of Libération-Nord, was being held at the prison and had become the prison barber. He identified the man he had been told to shave as Jean Moulin. All Moulin could do was open his eyes and ask for water.

Klaus Barbie suspected the man he was torturing was Moulin, but he was not sure until he gave him a piece of paper and a pencil. Moulin drew a cruel caricature of Barbie and handed it back. Barbie or one of his accomplices wrote the name "Jean Moulins" on the sheet and returned it to him.[47] Moulin, unable to hear and barely able to see, crossed out the "s."[48] According to Barbie, Moulin used the last of his strength to repeatedly throw himself headfirst against the wall of his cell. He was determined not to survive questioning. There would be no betrayal of fellow *résistants*, but again he had failed to kill himself. On July 4, Moulin was driven to Paris by Barbie and turned over to Gestapo officers at 84 avenue Foch. Prisoners there testified he was heavily bandaged and looked as if he had been drugged. Sometime later, he was put on a train for Germany. The Germans would eventually issue a death certificate attesting that Moulin had died en route, at Metz, near the German border, at 2:00 a.m. on July 8.[49]

Moulin's arrest came at a time when the Gestapo was enjoying remarkable success against the Resistance. Between June 9 and 21, seven networks across France were cracked. General Delastraint, the top military figure in the Resistance, had been arrested in Paris on June 9 as he arrived for a rendezvous with René Hardy, who never showed up. Hardy thus lived to be present, and escape, from the Caluire meeting. Another victim was Pierre Brossolette, betrayed while making his way back to Paris from Brittany after the small boat he had been travelling in to England capsized during a storm. The Gestapo successes came mainly from betrayals.[50]

The arrest of Jean Moulin was another example of the horrendous deceptions that plagued the Resistence. Hardy was captured not long after Moulin's arrest but managed to escape and reach Algeria in 1944. After the war, he was charged with treason and tried twice in connection with Moulin's death, but was acquitted in both trials. If Hardy did not betray Moulin, who did? Was it a rival Resistance leader determined to get even for Moulin's seizure of power? Was it the Communists? Or perhaps it was someone from a right-wing group who suspected that Moulin, a known radical, was actually a Communist? Or did the Caluire raid result from a lucky break by the Gestapo, perhaps a chance overheard remark of the upcoming meeting? An unlikely possibility. Whatever the cause of Moulin's death, his loss deprived France of a man who might have some day challenged Charles de Gaulle for the leadership of the République.[51]

The death of Jean Moulin was but one indication of the fact the German Occupation became more brutal in response to the targeting of Gestapo leaders and important officers in the German army by the Resistance. After the assassination in Paris on September 28, 1943, of SS Colonel Julius Ritter, the Nazis unleashed a fierce search for his assailants. The shooting of Ritter, head of the hated Service du travail obligatoire (STO), which shipped thousands of French workers to Germany between 1941 and 1944, was the work of a group of Communist members of Francs Tireurs et Partisans, who came to be known as the Manouchian Group after their leader, Missak Manouchian. Within two months, probably aided by informers, the Gestapo was able to arrest twenty-three of its members. After torture, all twenty-three men (twenty of them foreigners, eleven Jews) were shot at Fort Mont Valerian in the Paris suburb of Suresnes on February 21, 1944. Due to a French law preventing the shooting of women, the sole woman in the group, Olga Bancic, was sent to Germany where she was decapitated with an axe.[52]

In Algeria, the rivalry between General Giraud and General de Gaulle became as bitter, in its own way, as the struggle of the Resistance against the Germans. Giraud soon came to realize he would have to accommodate de Gaulle, but it was de Gaulle's old London adversary, Jean Monnet, who cleared the way for a solution. Monnet drafted a set of proposals for a new National Committee to which the military would be accountable. The breakthrough came when Giraud conceded he would no longer insist on his "preponderance" and invited de Gaulle to come to Algiers "at once" to join him in a new central power. Yet to be overcome were the usual roadblocks: President Roosevelt and Winston Churchill.

The prime minister was becoming exhausted with the constant hectoring he was receiving from the president over their French ally. "Not a day passed that the President did not mention the subject to me."[53] En route to America aboard the *Queen Elizabeth*, Churchill drafted a message to his War Cabinet on May 22: "I must ask my colleagues to consider urgently whether we should not now eliminate de Gaulle as a political force and face Parliament and France upon the issues."[54] His colleagues unanimously rejected this abortive *coup de main*.

De Gaulle reached Algiers on May 30, and on June 4, he and General Giraud agreed to the proposal of the Monnet group to form the Comité français de Libération nationale (CFLN) with he and General Giraud as rotating co-presidents. It was at this point that Giraud's role began its steady decline into irrelevance. He was a man, in the words of General Eisenhower, whose "complete lack of interest in political matters … disqualified him for any political post."[55] At a meeting of de Gaulle and Giraud with Eisenhower on June 19, de Gaulle arrived late and spoke first, declaring, "I am here in my capacity as President of the French Government."[56] To Yvonne in England he wrote, "Here, as expected, I find myself in front of America and alone." [57] On October 2, the committee named de Gaulle to the new position of head of government, with Giraud, outmanoeuvred and outwitted, relegated to commissariat of defense. Giraud, who the Americans had hoped would fill the vacuum left by the death of Admiral Darlan, was no longer a factor.[58]

De Gaulle had moved his family to Algiers in July, setting up house in a large Moorish villa called Les Oliviers. Yvonne appreciated the spontaneity and warmth of the people she dealt with: the *fleuriste* from whom she bought big bouquets of pale blue jacarandas; the *pharmacien* in rue d'Isly who mixed potions of citronelle to ward off mosquitoes; the cloth merchants of rue Bab Azoun who sold her their best wool. In the heat of Algiers, she continued to dress as a conservative northern French woman in severe black dresses and a black hat. They flew in powdered milk for Anne, whose condition was deteriorating, and Elisabeth arrived to take up work in the foreign press office. With his family about him, de Gaulle now held all the cards. He was the undisputed leader of all the French forces opposed to Vichy and the German Occupation.[59]

While France is caught in political turmoil, a crowd watches children sail boats in a pond near the Eiffel Tower, 1936.

Robert W. Moore, National Geographic Creative / Bridgeman Art Library

Archives de Gaulle, Paris, France / Giraudon / Bridgeman Art Library

Charles de Gaulle (gun over shoulder) shooting rabbits near the Castle of Septfontaines at the place known as "La cote aux sapins," 1938.

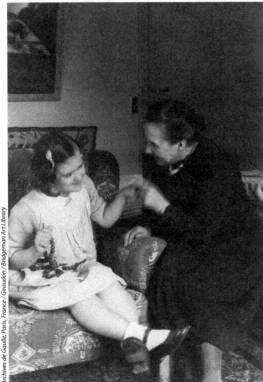

Archives de Gaulle, Paris, France / Giraudon / Bridgeman Art Library

Rare picture shows Anne de Gaulle and her governess, Marguerite Potel. The photo was taken either at the Villa "Les Oliviers" in Algiers, or in England, in 1943.

British troops slog through the mud evacuating Dunkirk in May 1940. Hitler held back his army while awaiting fresh supplies.

U.S. National Archives 242-EB-735

OCCUPATION OF FRANCE
1940 - 44

The Armistice of June 22, 1940 divides France into German Occupied Territory and Vichy France (the so-called "Free Zone"). No movement was permitted in or out of coastal areas. After the Anglo-American invasion of North Africa on November 8, 1942, Germany occupied all of France except for the area of Italian occupation.

Adolf Hitler visits a conquered Paris on June 23, 1940.

U.S. National Archives 242-HLB-3-20

U.S. National Archives 208-MFI-5H-1

A Frenchman weeps as Nazi troops march down a Paris street in June 1940.

U.S. National Archives 111-SC-196741

A French civilian is the victim of German firing squad.

Sur le " Massilia "
les parlementaires ont été
menés en bateau
C'est bien leur tour !

Paris-soir

Numéro 44

37, rue du Louvre, Paris (2)

DIMANCHE
4
AOUT
1940

ABONNEMENTS

SIXIEME
ÉDITION

50 cent.

LE GENERAL DE GAULLE
condamné à mort
par un nouveau tribunal militaire

Les congratulations des Gamelinards

VICHY, 3 Août.

Inculpé de trahison, d'agression à la sûreté extérieure de l'État pour une puissance étrangère en temps de guerre, le général de Gaulle a été condamné par contumace à la peine de mort, à la dégradation militaire et à la confiscation de ses biens.

La condamnation a été prononcée par le tribunal militaire de la 13e région, siégeant à Clermont-Ferrand.

Le général de Gaulle a été condamné en vertu des articles 71 et 79 du Code pénal et de l'article 195 du Code de justice militaire.

Heidelberg bombardé par l'aviation anglaise

Le Conseil des ministres a pris une décision concernant la loi sur le chômage

GENÈVE, 3 Août.

Un pétrolier anglais touché à mort.

De l'essence pour un mois

AVIS aux parents des prisonniers de guerre

Attention aux fausses nouvelles

500 grammes de sucre par personne pour le mois d'août

Sur les boulevards, la « petite reine » règne à son tour.

Le Japon refuse énergiquement toute intervention anglaise

« MARGOT » a été assassinée ainsi que sa fille

PASSIF

Communiqué allemand

BERLIN, 3 Août.

LA DÉMOBILISATION française

VICHY, 3 Août.

Le recensement des étrangers âgés de plus de 15 ans aura lieu le 6 août

La reprise du Sport cycliste

Ginette Leclerc donnera ce matin le départ des « Trophées de Longchamp »

Communiqué italien

ROME, 3 Août.

Dernière minute

BERLIN

HARLEM

K.X.X.

Archives de Gaulle, Paris, France / Bridgeman Art Library

Front page of *Paris-Soir*, August 4, 1940. The newspaper reports that General Charles de Gaulle had been condemned to death by a Vichy military tribunal.

McCord Museum, Montreal

Canadian painter Claire Fauteux lived through the Nazi occupation of Paris and joined Resistance fighters on the barricades when the city was liberated.

Archives Charmet / Bridgeman Art Library

Jean Moulin was delegated by Charles de Gaulle to head a united French Resistance movement. His murder by the Gestapo deprived France of an important postwar leader.

Archives de Gaulle, Paris, France / Giraudon / Bridgeman Art Library

Elisabeth de Miribel, shown in 1945, was secretary to General Charles de Gaulle. She typed de Gaulle's Appeal of June 18, 1940. She later spent time as a nun before joining the French diplomatic service.

III

Days of Might: The Bet Is Called

People of Western Europe! A landing was made this morning on the coast of France by troops of the Allied Expeditionary Force.... Citizens of France! I am proud to have again under my command the gallant forces of France. Fighting beside their Allies, they will play a worthy role in the liberation of their homeland.

— General Dwight D. Eisenhower
Supreme Commander, Allied Forces
June 6, 1944

CHAPTER 10
Débarquement at Dawn

The supreme battle has begun. It is the battle in France
and it is the battle of France. France is going to fight this
battle furiously. The clear, the sacred duty of the sons of
France, wherever they are and whoever they are, is to
fight the enemy with all the means at their disposal.

— Charles de Gaulle
BBC broadcast, June 6, 1944

Faces blackened with burnt cork, the sixteen men of the Fighting
French 2nd Chasseurs Parachute Regiment clambered aboard the two
Halifax bombers readying for takeoff from the Royal Air Force base at
Fairfield in western England. Their red berets and badges bearing the Cross
of Lorraine set them apart from the British airmen who had toasted them
with tots of whisky and sent them off with cheers and much hand-shaking.[1]
By eleven o'clock, they were over the Brittany countryside of northwestern

France. The signal lights in each plane's fuselage — first red, then green — came on and the men jumped. The two units — an officer and seven men in each — were the vanguard of the D-Day invasion. Their instructions were to engage with local Resistance and set in motion the sabotage and harassment that would delay any German attempt to move reinforcements into neighbouring Normandy, where the main landings would take place at dawn.

The unit commanded by Lieutenant Marienne, regrouping after the drop, began a stealthy walk toward its first objective. They had gone only a little way when they heard voices in a foreign language. Was it German? No, decided a paratrooper who claimed to know the language. Were they talking Breton? Corporal Émile Bouetard, a twenty-eight-year-old ex-sailor from Britanny's Côte du Nord district, thought not. Perhaps the strange voices were German after all because whoever they were, they opened fire. The shots were returned and the paratroopers dispersed. Only later, after the two groups had reassembled, did Lieutenant Marienne learn that Corporal Bouetard had been killed in the skirmish.

A farm lad who dreamed of adventure, Corporal Bouetard had run away to become a ship's boy at thirteen. He served in the French navy up to the Armistice and after demobilization made his way to Marseille where he shipped out on a vessel bound for the west coast of North America, ending up in Vancouver. From there, he'd made his way back to England, joined the Fighting French, and now, on this dark night in the familiar Breton countryside, he'd become the first man to die in the Allied invasion of Europe.

The dropping of the 2nd Chasseurs Parachute Regiment into Brittany might have been a minor diversionary tactic or a symbolic demonstration of French involvement in the D-Day operations. In any case, it was quickly overshadowed by the immensity of events occurring further eastward, where on the morning of June 6 the first of 155,000 men of the American, British and Canadian armies taking part in Operation Overlord — thirty-five divisions in all — were disembarking from four thousand ships onto the beaches of Normandy. By day's end, ten thousand aircraft would be flying sorties over the landing beaches.

News of the landings travelled quickly. Outside of the battle zones, the French first heard of the invasion on the German radio, which tried to play down its significance. Captain Raymond Dronne, whose name would become attached with the first elements of the Fighting French to enter Paris, recorded the reaction:

> The event that had been awaited for so long was welcomed with joy mixed with anxiety. With joy, because the French were sure that liberation was near. With concern and even skepticism, because of the fear of failure. Would the Allies be thrown back into the sea? The people could not help but remember what had happened in August 1942. Anglo-Canadian forces had landed one morning at Dieppe…. The Canadians had succeeded in reaching the centre of the city…. When the population of Paris learned via the radio of the attack, they thought the Second Front had been opened. They imagined that the tanks would arrive the next day in Paris. Dieppe is not so far away and the tanks could move so fast! That evening, the hope and enthusiasm was transformed: the German radio was singing of victory, the attempt had failed, the Anglo-Canadians had been thrown back into the sea with heavy losses.[2]

At the moment the men of the 2nd Parachute Regiment were dropping onto the moors of Brittany, Charles de Gaulle was finishing dinner with his son, Philippe, in the apartment in Seymour Place that he had kept since reaching London in 1940. De Gaulle had arrived from Algiers on Sunday morning June 4, in response to an invitation from Winston Churchill for what the general knew would be a briefing on the forthcoming invasion of Europe.

His dinner with Philippe brought de Gaulle a welcome respite from the difficult meetings he'd had with Churchill and General Eisenhower. An English valet available to everyone in the building served them "a very English dinner" of soup, boiled beef, and cabbage sprinkled with beer, followed by a cream dessert. De Gaulle cautioned Philippe the man was "without doubt an agent of the intelligence service." They talked mostly of family, of Philippe's mother and sisters in Algiers, and his uncles, Xavier and Jacques de Gaulle, who had managed to reach Switzerland with their younger children. More uncertain was the fate of General de Gaulle's sister,

Marie-Agnès, or her husband, Alfred Cailliau, or of Pierre de Gaulle and Philippe's cousin Geneviève, all of whom had been arrested and deported.

Philippe gave an account of his days at an infantry officers' training school in Worcestershire and spoke of his posting to the Fighting French 2nd Armoured Division. He was surprised at how long the dinner went on, as his father was normally not one to linger at the table. Philippe was about to leave when de Gaulle's face took on a serious look. After a glance at a clock on the wall that showed eleven, de Gaulle whispered in a hoarse voice, "That's it!"

"What's it?" Philippe asked. "The *debarquement!*" de Gaulle answered. "At this moment, our 2nd regiment of paratroopers is in the air! In addition to our thousands of Maquis fighting underground, these French are the first of the invasion force to land in France. The British and Americans are about to go into Normandy, taking with them our marine commandos." After swearing Philippe to secrecy until six o'clock next morning, de Gaulle told him he was living a day that had been four years in the making. Philippe asked if he believed the landing would be successful. "Of course, I trust in its success. If it is not, there will be a second, and if necessary a third, until the Reich finally falls."[3]

De Gaulle had flown to London in a Royal Air Force four-engine York troop transport loaned to him by the prime minister. The aircraft had been converted into a flying conference room and given the nickname *Ascalon*. De Gaulle was welcomed at Heston airport by an RAF honour guard and a band that played "La Marseillaise."[4] It was an occasion far different than the almost anonymous debut he'd made on June 17, 1940, and, de Gaulle would have reflected, one that suited his new position as president of the Provisional Government of France. The French National Committee had bestowed the title on him only the day before in Algiers. Thus, de Gaulle could congratulate himself on what he'd achieved since leaving France four years before as little more than a fugitive from a defeated country. He was at the top of his game. Yet he was perturbed on this overcast and storm-threatened morning by the further discourtesies of the Allies toward the Fighting French. The latest insult had been the ban on the transmission of coded French messages through the Allied communications system. De Gaulle had been forced to resort to courier packages to send instructions from Algiers to General Koenig, his military chief in London and the man in charge of the French Forces of the Interior — les Forces françaises de l'intérieur.

As de Gaulle would write in his *Mémoires de guerre*, France's sword might still be short but the Fighting French had marshalled 230,000 men in combat readiness. Four divisions of the Corps Expéditionaire Français under General Alphonse Juin were fighting their way alongside American and Canadian armies up the boot of Italy. Word would come this day of the fall of Rome. General Philippe Leclerc's 2nd Armoured Division, encamped in English bases after having helped conquer German and Italian armies in North Africa, was impatiently waiting to play its role in the coming liberation of the continent.

As de Gaulle completed his inspection of the honour guard, he was handed a letter from Winston Churchill. It was an invitation to lunch on the prime minister's train, parked on a siding near General Eisenhower's headquarters outside the English Channel port of Portsmouth. The letter promised details of "momentous and imminent events."[5] The 140 members of de Gaulle's staff had scattered throughout London while he travelled down to the coast with his ambassador to Britain, Pierre Viénot. They found Churchill waiting on the tracks outside his railway car, spreading his arms wide in welcome. In the party was the prime minister of South Africa, Marshall Jan Christian Smuts, who had earlier rubbed de Gaulle the wrong way by suggesting that as France was no longer a great power, it should join the Commonwealth. De Gaulle found Churchill in a buoyant mood as he vividly described the "enormous military enterprise" that would unfold in the next days.[6] The fact de Gaulle was being told of the invasion only at the last minute came as no surprise; he had known for months that President Roosevelt was insistent on exclusion of the Fighting French from D-Day planning.

During lunch, talk turned to post-invasion arrangements. Churchill suggested the two work out a plan for civilian administration in liberated territory, and that de Gaulle take it to Washington for Roosevelt's approval. The president would be sure to "recognize your administration in one form or another."

De Gaulle, having nursed for months his resentment at the president's scheme to impose an Anglo-American military government on France, exploded. "Why do you seem to think that I need to submit my candidacy for the authority in France to Roosevelt? The French government exists. I have nothing to ask, in this sphere, of the United States of America or of Great Britain." Thoroughly worked up, he had no intention of surrendering either autonomy or authority. De Gaulle went on to complain about monetary arrangements the Allies had undertaken for post-liberation France. The scheme to issue "so-called French currency ... [which] will have compulsory circulation on French territory" was especially maddening.[7]

Even the British press was onto this questionable exercise to put into circulation five billion of "unbacked" francs, headed "Emis en France," but bearing no mention of the French Republic or other authority. A *Daily Mail* journalist, Alastair Forbes, was writing that "issuance of Allied paper francs completely unbacked by anybody is as inept a piece of unintelligence as the Allies have been guilty of in this war."[8]

These Yankee francs looked very much like U.S. dollars and de Gaulle thought they would be "easy to counterfeit."

De Gaulle told Churchill he would not be surprised to hear Eisenhower proclaim he is taking France under his own authority, with approval of the prime minister and the president.

"And you!" Churchill retorted. "How do you expect that Britain should take a position separate from that of the United States? Each time I must choose between you and Roosevelt, I shall choose Roosevelt."

This was more than a mere personality clash. At the root of the disagreement was President Roosevelt's determination to ensure that the French people after the war would have the opportunity to choose a government other than that of Charles de Gaulle. Distrustful of de Gaulle's faithfulness to democracy and doubtful of the degree of support the general enjoyed in France, Roosevelt fought against letting the Fighting French establish civilian control in liberated areas.

A "School of Military Government" had been set up at the University of Virginia in 1942 to train officers to manage civil affairs in former enemy-occupied lands. Out of this came the Allied Military Government for Occupied Territories (AMGOT) that by early 1944 was in operation in Italy. Agreements were reached with governments in exile of Norway, Holland, and Belgium for American civil affairs officers to work alongside local personnel, but no such agreement had been made for France. How Americans who had no knowledge of the French language or culture could be trained in two months to act as prefects in French cities, with responsibility for utilities, railroads, the post office, and policing was a stunning question to which no one had an answer. These "sixty-day marvels," as they came to be known, would face insurmountable tasks without the support of French administrators. Military government, the French feared, would lead to precisely the anarchy in which communism thrives, and which the Provisional Government was determined to prevent.[9]

To de Gaulle, "the president's intentions seemed ... on the same order as Alice's adventures in Wonderland."[10] France, in the war more than two years before the United States, had no intention of changing one form of oppression for another.

Despite the president's opposition to de Gaulle, the tide was beginning to shift in the general's favour among senior Allied officers. General Eisenhower had promised de Gaulle in December 1943 that he would "recognize no French power in France other than your own."[11]

De Gaulle, speaking to him in English, replied: "You are a man."

Eisenhower may have been basing his judgment on military intelligence as well as his own experience with de Gaulle, both of which were more favourable to the Fighting French than anything coming from Washington.

In January 1944, the U.S. Military Intelligence Service produced a report affirming that the French Committee of National Liberation "enjoys extremely large popular support in Metropolitan France, among all classes of society." It added:

> Vichy has lost all vestiges of popular support except among the small but powerful pro-German group. Pétain is regarded as a senile figure without any real

power, hated by most, pitied by a few. Laval is considered a clever intriguer and unscrupulous opportunist and is thoroughly despised.... All evidence confirms that tremendous changes have taken place in French morale and that in the last year there has been a veritable national revival, animated by lofty ideals of patriotism and by a mysticism akin to the crusading spirit. Gaullism has a tremendous psychological appeal to the French.

The Resistance groups form a powerful and united force although they suffer from lack of arms and from constant attempts on the part of Vichy and the German police to break them up.... The acceptance by the Resistance movements in France of the leadership of General de Gaulle and the French National Committee is confirmed by the statement made by General de Lattre de Tassigny on 9 November 1943, to Admiral Stark, that the "Resistance movement naturally and inevitably accepted the leadership of de Gaulle as the present political head of the French national revival."

Inasmuch as the principal Resistance groups in Metropolitan France consider themselves a part of the French forces of National Liberation represented in Algiers by the French Committee, there appears to be little possibility of effective liaison through any other agency.[12]

The good sense of this stunningly well-reasoned analysis was reflected in two letters written by the American assistant secretary of war, John J. McCloy, to Henry L. Stimson, the secretary of war, on January 13 and 20. The first noted that U.S. relations with the French Committee "have not been good" and argued that the time had come to "deal with the Comité as the organization responsible for civil affairs in liberated areas of France." The Committee has declared, McCloy added, "its intention to restore free democratic government in France and has proposed a specific plan to accomplish this end." To this, McCloy added an ominous warning: "It would be 'dynamite' to intervene in the internal affairs of France as we used to do in small central American states." In his follow-up letter, McCloy set out to demolish arguments that American support for de Gaulle could "prejudice the eventual establishment of a French government based on the free and untrammelled selection by the French people." Deciding what group to support in each region would be to take sides "in French politics just as much." It was important to "lose no time" in obtaining authority to consult with the Committee on "basic plans for the administration of civil affairs" in France.[13]

In the face of such admonitions, President Roosevelt bent only slightly. He continued to rely on the advice of Admiral William Leahy, his former ambassador to Vichy, who now was head of the U.S. Joint Chiefs of Staff. "When Allied troops enter France," Leahy advised the president in February, "the most reliable person to whom we could look for help in rallying the French [is] Pétain."[14]

A month later, Roosevelt telegraphed General Eisenhower advising him that "you may consult with the FCNL, and may authorize them in your discretion to select and install the personnel necessary for such administration." He was not, however, limited to dealing with only the committee. He was further cautioned that "such dealings shall not constitute recognition."

Despite the rancorous exchange between Churchill and de Gaulle at lunch, the two men ended by toasting each other, with Churchill raising his glass "to de Gaulle who never accepted defeat."

Feeling well-fed, the party, led by the prime minister, who was dressed in a blue Royal Air Force uniform that fitted him somewhat snugly, set out for General Eisenhower's headquarters in the nearby New Forest. Eisenhower had been up most of the night weighing the weather forecasts of his meteorologists. On their advice, he had ordered a twenty-four-hour postponement in the invasion; any further delay would force the whole operation to be put off at least two weeks before there would be another favourable conjunction of the moon and the tides.

Eisenhower, perhaps more concerned with being considerate than in actual need of counsel, asked de Gaulle what he thought of the gamble on the weather. "I will only tell you," de Gaulle said, "that in your place I should not delay."[15]

These pleasantries soon vanished as talk got around to the radio broadcast Eisenhower would make after the landings. The discussion began with Eisenhower, displaying what de Gaulle detected as "evident embarrassment," handing over a copy of his talk.[16] De Gaulle reacted with distaste as he read it. He didn't like the part asserting that the French would be required to carry out Eisenhower's orders and that civil officials should "carry on in the exercise of their functions" until "the French themselves should choose their representatives and their government."

Especially objectionable was the lack of recognition of the French authority that for years had been arousing opposition to the Germans, and had now assembled a substantial army it had willingly put under Eisenhower's command. Clearly, the statement — written by officials in the State Department — was designed to reinforce the Rooseveltian strategy to blunt and deter any assumption of power by de Gaulle's provisional government: "I, Gen. Dwight Eisenhower ... call on all Frenchmen to obey the laws that I ... promulgate." It made it sound as if Eisenhower would be taking control of the country — a "summons to obey a foreign general." De Gaulle explained his objections. Eisenhower sounded accommodating. "It's only a draft I am ready to change according to your remarks," the American general told him.[17]

De Gaulle reworked the draft at his headquarters at Carlton Gardens later that day, and on Monday morning sent a revised text to Eisenhower. Word came back that it was too late to make any changes, which was about what de Gaulle had expected. For once, Eisenhower had been less than truthful, but there were other issues today to occupy everyone's mind. With all of southern England a vast military camp, the concentration of forces in the Channel ports had reached a point where the invasion fleet either had to go, or be retired for an indefinite period.

At 3:30 that morning, General Eisenhower had awoken in his trailer, dressed, and was driven through driving rain to naval headquarters. The meteorologists presented him with the "astonishing declaration" that "by the following morning a period of relatively good weather, heretofore completely unexpected, would ensue, lasting probably thirty-six hours."

The choice was clear: "OK, let's go." The invasion would take place at dawn Tuesday, June 6.[18]

The dispute between Eisenhower and de Gaulle renewed itself in more ugly fashion later in the day when Charles Peake, the U.K. Foreign Office delegate to the Fighting French, arrived at Carleton Gardens to discuss the radio broadcasts to be made after the landing. First the rulers of Norway, the Netherlands, and Luxembourg would speak, followed by the prime minister of Belgium, then Eisenhower, and finally, de Gaulle. This scenario would not "play," de Gaulle told Peake; if he spoke right after Eisenhower, he would appear to be sanctioning what he had said. Worse, it would mean accepting "a place in the succession unsuitable to the dignity of France." If de Gaulle were to speak, "it could only be at a different hour and distinct from the series."[19]

The reverberations of de Gaulle's declaration rocked Whitehall when Peake reported his refusal. Churchill, in a late afternoon Cabinet meeting at No. 10 Downing Street, flew into a tirade. Reinforced by several whiskies, he launched into a long, emotional diatribe against de Gaulle, concluding by calling him an "obstructionist saboteur." At a point where his anger seemed about to get the better of him, Churchill received word of a second Gaullist insult: the general was refusing to allow French liaison officers to embark with the invasion force. It had been intended they would work with British and American officers in restoring public services in liberated communities. It was all too much for the prime minister — a betrayal of loyalties and an act of "monstrous ingratitude" that could not be condoned.

Charles de Gaulle may have suspected the depth of the ruckus now enveloping the upper echelon of the Allied command, but if so he kept it from his son during their dinner at Seymour Place. At about ten o'clock, Anthony Eden, now foreign secretary in the Churchill government, summoned Pierre Viénot, de Gaulle's ambassador to London, to the Foreign Office. Viénot was at pains to deny that de Gaulle would not speak, only that it would have to be at a time of his choosing. As for the liaison officers, yes they had been withdrawn; "Fighting France could not associate itself with an 'occupation' of the national territory."

For the rest of the night, Viénot moved back and forth between the two camps. At two o'clock in the Connaught Hotel, he told de Gaulle of

Churchill's diatribe against him. "They wanted to trick me, I will not be tricked," de Gaulle declared. "I deny their right to know whether I shall speak to France." Then de Gaulle turned on his messenger and Viénot was forced to endure what he called "the worst dressing down of my life."[20]

When the ambassador returned to the Foreign Office to confirm that de Gaulle would speak but that the liaison officers would not leave, he found Churchill sitting in Eden's office. Another furious argument ensued. Churchill accused de Gaulle of "treason at the height of battle."[21] He then strode across to No. 10 and roused his officials with instructions to tell the American military to "put de Gaulle in a plane and send him back to Algiers — in chains, if necessary. He must not be allowed to re-enter France."[22] He dictated a letter to de Gaulle ordering him out of the country and told an aide, Desmond Morton, to deliver it in person. Instead, Morton took it to Eden, who phoned Churchill and somehow convinced him to back off. Eden burned the letter. By the time Viénot got back to de Gaulle, he found the general had resumed his usual "icy calm."

The longest night before the longest day was almost over. By dawn, more than twenty thousand airborne troops had landed in France; they were followed by seventy thousand British and Canadian troops and nearly sixty thousand American soldiers who disembarked from landing craft at beaches designated as Utah, Omaha, Gold, Juno, and Sword. A man attentive to every possibility, General Eisenhower had prepared two statements. The first was to be issued if the landings were successful, the second only if Allied forces failed to gain a foothold. In it, Eisenhower had written that he would bear full responsibility for the devastating turn of events.

General Eisenhower found the first reports "most encouraging" and by mid-morning it was "apparent that the landing was going fairly well."[23] He would not have to release the statement he had prepared in case of failure. Casualties, while substantial, were not more than expected: seven thousand by the time the invasion force had breached the first bastions of Hitler's Atlantic Wall that day.

De Gaulle spoke on the BBC at six o'clock. After his stirring pronounce-ment of the "supreme battle," he made it clear that his provisional French government would be in charge of areas liberated by the Allied armies:

> The orders given by the French government and by the
> French leaders it has named for that purpose [must be]
> obeyed exactly. The actions we carry out in the enemy's rear
> [must be] coordinated as closely as possible with those car-
> ried out at the same time by the Allied and French armies.
> Let none of those capable of action, either by arms, or by
> destruction, or by giving intelligence, or by refusing to do
> work useful to the enemy, allow themselves to be made
> prisoner; let them remove themselves beforehand from
> being seized and from being deported. The battle of France
> has begun. In the nation, the Empire and the armies there
> is no longer anything but one single hope, the same for all.
> Behind the terrible heavy cloud of our blood and our tears
> here is the sun of our grandeur shining out once again.[24]

There was no mention of the struggle for control over liberated ter-ritory, or of other frictions that had marred the relationship between de Gaulle and his Allies. His speech was a clear, inspiring call to renewal of the French fact in France. Listening to it in his office at No. 10, Churchill was caught up in the emotion of the moment. As Lord Ismay, his chief military advisor, looked on with astonishment, tears began to roll down Churchill's cheeks. The prime minister looked up with a jerk, uttering words "Pug" Ismay could hardly believe he had heard: "You tub of lard, have you no sensitivity?"[25]

In the days following the invasion, de Gaulle consolidated his posi-tion. In the first hours of D-Day, Resistance units — General Koenig's French Forces of the Interior — destroyed nearly one thousand targets, including railway lines, bridges, and telecommunications facilities. The 2nd Armoured Division awaited impatiently in North Africa for orders to sail to England, while the Fighting French expeditionary force in Italy was helping clean out the last German defensive positions in Italy.

A week after the landings, Allied forces had penetrated to a depth of thirty kilometres on a front 160 kilometres wide. Field Marshal Rommel, who had been visiting Hitler in Berchtesgarden when the invasion began, puzzled over where the next Allied push might come. He still expected a large-scale landing on the Channel coast east of Normandy, and consequently dispersed his forces rather than concentrate them for a decisive counterattack. In all, Rommel had command of twenty-eight infantry and eleven panzer divisions, but they would not be enough to hold back the Allied forces. Within a month, twenty-five divisions — almost one million men — had landed and the Allies had won command of the air after wiping out nearly all the German radar stations and landing fields.

In Vichy, collaboration gave way to consternation. "German and Anglo-Saxon armies are at war with each other on our soil," Marshall Pétain lamented. "We are not in the war. Your duty is to maintain a strict neutrality."[26]

Frenchmen did not really feel that way, as correspondents with the invasion forces soon found out. "All the French people with whom I have talked in the countryside, in the villages and in the townships of the liberated areas," wrote British United Press correspondent Richard D. McMillan, "are surprised at the idea there is any difference of opinion among the French on support of General Charles de Gaulle. 'We are solidly behind our leader de Gaulle,' they all said."[27]

In contrast to the favourable news from France, "the diplomatic firmament cleared only very slowly," de Gaulle would write of this period.[28] He was in no mood to negotiate away civil administration in France and the discussions, begun in a sense of accord, ended in stalemate. On June 10, the general went public to attack the *fausse monnaie* being circulated in France and to stress he had no intention of allowing his administrative officers to fall under command of the British and Americans. The Fighting French were not going to "contribute to the usurpation" of their authority. De Gaulle had other plans for resolving the issue of civil administration in France.

By now, de Gaulle was anxious to return to France. Winston Churchill had made a brief visit to the landing zone on June 12. He was met on the beach by Field Marshall Bernard Montgomery as he scrambled out of a landing craft while waves lapped the beach. Churchill lunched in a tent with his field commander, caught glimpses of the front line five kilometres distant, and reported he "slept soundly" on the four-hour return voyage to Portsmouth.[29]

The prime minister was not, however, as sanguine about permitting the leader of the Fighting French to step foot on his native soil. When he grudgingly gave in to de Gaulle's insistence that the general go ashore for a visit to the town of Bayeux, it was as if he were setting out instructions for a night out by a teenaged daughter: "It would not be possible for de Gaulle to hold a public meeting there, or gather crowds in the streets," Churchill wrote to Anthony Eden. "He would no doubt like to have a demonstration to show that he is the future president of the French Republic. I suggest that he should drive slowly through the town, shake hands with a few people, and then return...."[30]

Charles de Gaulle had a different approach in mind. He would go to France to do more than simply affirm the strength of support he had there. He would use the visit to put an end to President Roosevelt's scheme to establish a government of military occupation in France.

CHAPTER 11
Return of the Fighting French

The French destroyer *La Combattante* was anchored off the King's Stairs of Portsmouth harbour on the quiet evening of Tuesday, June 13. A deceptive air of tranquility belied the hectic history of a vessel that in the past week had made countless crossings of the English Channel, escorting ships carrying men of the 3rd Canadian Division to Juno Beach, the eight-kilometre stretch of sand and bluffs where they had been landing since before eight o'clock on D-Day. The destroyer had hung back, three thousand metres off the beach, to shell German positions while the Canadians went ashore in landing-craft assault boats. On that "longest day," the Canadians had fought their way the deepest into France of all the Allied armies, with the North Nova Scotia Highlanders only five kilometres from the strategic target of Caen. Tonight, André Patou, the captain of *La Combattante*, had taken special care to lay on food and drink for a reception in the ship's wardroom. Expected aboard shortly were twelve men, led by General Charles de Gaulle, about to step on French soil for the first time in four years. Their arrival would mark the return of the Fighting French to their tortured homeland.

We might have expected to see the general in a buoyant mood, but he was not. He was still upset about the counterfeit francs the Allies were circulating in France. He worried about the reaction to the audacious — and perhaps rash — action he'd taken in the past twenty-four hours to circumvent Allied military control over French civil administration.[1] By appointing his former ADC, Major François Coulet as commissioner for the Republic for the liberated part of Normandy, and Colonel Pierre de Chevigné as military authority in the area, he intended to demonstrate it would be the Provisional Government that would be in charge, not some "sixty-day wonders" seconded by Supreme Headquarters of the Allied Expeditionary Force (SHAEF).[2]

Among the containers piled onto the ship's deck was a trunk carrying 25 million francs in banknotes, intended to finance the operations of the general's delegates. Both of de Gaulle's new appointees were with him that night, along with stalwarts who had stood by him, most since the early days in London: Ambassador Viénot; Geoffroy de Courcel, now an infantry captain; Captain Pierre Billotte, who had been de Gaulle's chief of staff but was now attached to the 2nd Armoured Dvision; Commandant Pierre Larocque, a key Resistance figure from Combat; Gaston Palewski, de Gaulle's *chef de cabinet*; generals Pierre Koenig of the French Forces of the Interior and Émile Béthouart, de Gaulle's Defense chief-of-staff; Admiral Thierry d'Argenlieu, who had fought with de Gaulle at Dakar; and, finally, Colonel Claude de Boislambert, who had been captured at Dakar but later escaped to return to London. De Gaulle exchanged pleasantries at the reception but his heart wasn't in it. He went to his cabin right after dinner but did not sleep well, although the sea was calm.

De Gaulle was up early the next morning. He took a hurried cup of coffee and went up to the bridge where he first sighted the shoreline of France — beachfront that lay between the cantons of Graye-sur-mer and Courseulles. Wearing a heavy pilot coat against the morning chill, picking out landmarks through the binoculars that hung from his neck, he smoked cigarette after cigarette. Between drags, enveloped in silence, he "filled his lungs with the fresh air of France."[3] One could only imagine the emotion coursing through him. The morning passed slowly, and it was not until two o'clock that *La Combattante* stood a few hundred yards off the beach at Courseulles. More troops of the Canadian 3rd Division were coming ashore and de Gaulle's landing craft picked its way to a beach filled with the detritus of battle: burnt-out tanks, armoured cars with wheels sunk up to their hubcaps, and the ever-present anti-tank barriers that stabbed the sand between the beach and its grassy knolls. De Gaulle had taken only a few steps when Colonel Boislambert reminded him that it was four years to the day since the Germans had occupied Paris. *"Eh bien,"* de Gaulle answered laconically, "They made a mistake!"[4]

A Canadian major and a British naval commander arrived to welcome de Gaulle and invite him to inspect a guard of honour. Then it was into the major's Jeep, thoughtfully adorned with the French Tricolour, for the drive to General Montgomery's headquarters at Creuillet, six kilometres inland from Gold Beach. Montgomery had set himself up in a trailer on the grounds of a Louis XIII–style château that boasted six chimneys and a manorial garden. On the way, de Gaulle's Jeep stopped before a group of old people, the women dressed mostly in black. They wondered who these men were in their unfamiliar uniforms. General Béthouart told them the car contained General de Gaulle.

"Is it you who are *le general*?" a man asked.

Béthouart pointed to de Gaulle: "That is he, there in front of me."

Amazed, the man gazed at de Gaulle's face, transfixed with the appearance of the figure he considered his liberator.

Before the Jeep could start again, a horse galloped onto the road and its rider, a priest, leaped to the ground.[5] He announced he was the local curé and said he had heard de Gaulle's appeal of June 18, 1940. "I have sheltered parachutists, I have been in touch with the Maquis, and you have passed through my village without even shaking my hand," he told de Gaulle.

De Gaulle got out of the Jeep and put his arms around the priest. "Monsieur le Curé, I do not shake your hand, I embrace you."[6]

De Gaulle's meeting with Montgomery, the irascible British general in command of all Allied ground forces in France, was kept as short as politeness permitted. De Gaulle made a few remarks but declined an invitation to lunch. "Having expressed my confidence in him, I left Montgomery to his affairs and went to mine, in Bayeux."[7] His final word to "Monty" was a casual mention that he would be leaving Major Coulet behind to "look after the population." By telling Montgomery of Coulet's posting, de Gaulle could argue that he had kept the Allies informed of his moves. In fact, the two new commissioners of the Provisional Government were already taking charge in Bayeux and Admiral d'Argenlieu, General Koenig, and Colonel Boislambert were at that moment on their way there.

✝

General de Gaulle had chosen well in selecting Bayeux as the place to make his stand on the issue of who would govern France. The British 50th Infantry Division had liberated the town on D-Day+1 when the Germans withdrew without a fight. Their decision to concentrate on the defence of Caen allowed Bayeux, with its medieval cathedral and Bayeux Tapestry dating back to William the Conqueror, to come through the invasion unscathed.

When de Gaulle set out on the coast road from Courseulles, his Jeep took him west to the village of Saint-Côme-de-Fresne, then swung southwest ten kilometres to Bayeux. On the way, they met two gendarmes bicycling toward Bayeux. Both dropped their bicycles when they were told who was in the Jeep. Being part of a national police force subject to military discipline, they immediately stood to attention and saluted de Gaulle.

"My friends," de Gaulle asked, "do me a kindness. I am on my way to Bayeux. We will wait here fifteen minutes if you will tell them I am coming. That will prevent anyone being caught unawares." By now, de Gaulle found himself enraptured by the enthusiasm of the moment. Turning to his companions, he announced, perhaps smugly, "Gentlemen, the reconnaissance has been carried out."[8]

The mayor of Bayeux, M. Dodeman, and members of his council met de Gaulle's party at the gates of the town. Together they crossed the River Aure and headed toward the Préfecture de police. De Gaulle had gotten out of the Jeep by now and was on foot. As word spread that he was in the streets, people rushed from their homes.

They stood "in a kind of daze," de Gaulle would remember, "then burst into bravos or else into tears."[9]

Children surrounded him, women smiled and sobbed, and the men shook his hand. "We walked on together, all overwhelmed by comradeship, feeling national joy, pride, and hope, rise again from the depths of the abyss." He made short work of the meeting with Major Coulet at the Préfecture, declined an offer of champagne, and headed for the Place du Château where a large crowd was gathering in the grassy square.

Bareheaded in the afternoon sunshine, de Gaulle mounted an improvised platform. French, British, and American flags had been draped on it and the flag of the Cross of Lorraine hung from the branch of a large tree. Then he began to speak:

> We are all moved to find ourselves together again in one of the first French towns to be liberated; but it is no moment to talk of emotion. What the country expects of you, here behind the front, is to continue the fight today as you have never ceased from fighting since the beginning of the war, and since June 1940. Our cry now, as always, is a war cry, because the path of war is also the road to liberty and honour. This is the voice of the Mother Country. I promise you that we shall continue to fight till sovereignty is re-established over every inch of our soil. No one shall prevent our doing that. We shall fight beside the Allies, with the Allies, as an ally. And the victory we shall win will be the victory of liberty and the victory of France.[10]

With this short, almost perfunctory speech in one northern French town, Charles de Gaulle set in motion the national myth that would enable France to regain its self-respect and prepare itself for its future. Many of the good *citoyens* of this *ville* had done far less than fight "since the beginning of the war." The mayor was an appointee of Vichy. No matter — it was necessary they be encouraged to believe what must be believed in the interests of national reconciliation. As de Gaulle stood on the platform absorbing the the ecstasy of the crowd, he began to lift his arms, then to swing them out and down, as if signalling his listeners to genuflect before him. A band played "La Marseillaise" and de Gaulle, in a husky voice, led the singing of the anthem.

Leaving Bayeux, he stopped at the village of Isigny, which had been badly damaged in the fighting. De Gaulle would note that "corpses were still being carried out of the debris."[11] He spoke at the town's Great War memorial and, driving back to Courseulles, exchanged words with Allied troops and members of the Resistance along the road. By 6:30, tired and emotionally strained by the tumult of the day, he was glad to be back on the beach and boarding the *La Combattante*. As events would prove, this was a day when Charles de Gaulle had never held a stronger hand.

✝

In London, Anthony Eden was keeping a close watch on the events unfolding in Normandy. Ambassador Viénot was able to report to de Gaulle that in a meeting with the British foreign secretary he had achieved "90 percent success" in his efforts toward an agreement to recognize the Provisional Government.[12]

De Gaulle and Churchill exchanged mutually complementary letters, with the general pouring praise on "the power of the British nation" and the "indissoluble affection" between Britain and France.

Churchill, still bruised from their D-Day confrontations, merely reminded de Gaulle that he had been "a sincere friend of France since 1907."

It took more than a week for AMGOT officers from the U.S. Army to show up in Bayeux. They found Major Coulet, who had been relieved to discover that the town treasury held an ample reserve of francs, "well and truly settled."[13] When the "spurious currency" of American-made francs was put into circulation, cautious Normans tried to use them to pay their back taxes; Coulet refused to accept them.

Coulet dismissed both the Vichy-appointed *sub-prefet* and the mayor. He appointed his own administrators and oversaw the start-up of a newspaper. When foreign journalists questioned whether he had the authorization of the Allies, Coulet asked why the Provisional Government would need such approval to govern in France. At a testy meeting with the head of the British civil affairs detachment, Brigadier General R.M.H. Lewis, Coulet pounded his fist on his desk. He angrily told the Briton: "I have received from the GPRF the mission to administer the liberated territories of Normandy. I will renounce this position only on its orders."[14]

Coulet wrung from Lewis the admission that his authority would be accepted "provisionally," pending instructions from London. After that, according to Coulet's memoirs, his relationship with Allied officers was "perfectly euphoric."

De Gaulle's new commissioner was unaware — as he would later learn from General Walter Bedell Smith, Eisenhower's chief of staff — that there had been a plan to seize him and return him to Britain. What would have been a monumental gaffe was put aside, apparently on orders from Eisenhower, who observed that de Gaulle's commissioners were working well with Allied authorities. The pattern that had been set would find a fit in every liberated area of France.

Malcolm Muggeridge, the British author and satirist who served as a liaison to the Fighting French in North Africa, wrote of this time: "The brigadiers who had assembled at embarkation ports, putative gauleiters … briefed in the Code Napoleon and other lore for taking over their allotted districts, stole silently away, unwanted."[15] The threat of an American military government had been deftly turned aside.

General de Gaulle lifted his ban on co-operation by his liaison officers, and during June he won official recognition of his provisional government from six exile governments and several Latin American countries — but not yet Great Britain or the United States. By the time de Gaulle returned to Algiers on June 16, President Roosevelt's vision of a France benevolently ruled — even for a short while — by American and British army officers had vanished into the unreality from whence it had emerged. De Gaulle's determination to assert French authority had not alone circumvented it. The realization by General Eisenhower and others that the president's scheme was unrealistic and unworkable had proven an equally powerful factor.

De Gaulle's much-postponed visit to Washington finally came about on July 6, when he arrived aboard a United States transport plane from Algiers. The time had come for building diplomatic bridges. De Gaulle had just made a visit to Italy, where he'd had an audience with the Pope, and his North American trip would include stops in New York and Ottawa, Canada.

In his *Mémoires de guerre*, de Gaulle would write that Roosevelt greeted him "at the door of the White House, all smiles and cordiality."[16] De Gaulle was walking into a game where, he would have to admit if pressed, he was facing a player even more skilled than he in the acts of subtle flattery, obstinacy, and downright cussedness. The president still thought of de Gaulle as "a narrow-minded French zealot with too much ambition for his own good."[17] Shortly before the general's arrival, he went so far as to declare, "He's a nut."

The two met several times, but nothing substantive in matters of policy was achieved. De Gaulle must have decided it was time for a charm offensive. Leavening his deep military knowledge and resourceful political instinct with Gallic flair, he proceeded to impress the members of Roosevelt's inner circle. Admiral Leahy, still an advocate for Vichy, found de Gaulle "more agreeable in manner and appearance than I had expected."[18] Cordell Hull wrote that the general "went out of his way to make himself agreeable ... and to assure us emphatically and repeatedly that he had no intention of forcing himself or his committee upon France as her future government."[19] De Gaulle was filmed sitting in a wicker chair in the White House rose garden, thanking American troops — in very good English — for what they were doing to liberate his country.

Observing Roosevelt, de Gaulle concluded that "as he was only human, his will to power cloaked itself in idealism."[20] He listened as Roosevelt outlined a postwar world in which the United States, having given up isolationism, would enter onto "a permanent system of intervention."[21] The Brave New World would be run by four powers: the United States, Britain, Russia, and China. No mention was made of a place for France, nor of any arrangement for France to participate in the postwar occupation of Germany. Of even greater concern to de Gaulle was the fact that, in his view, Roosevelt's plan "risked endangering the Western world." Eastern Europe would have to be sacrificed to gain Stalin's approval to this new global arrangement, and there was no assurance that China would remain "what she was now."

De Gaulle wound up his visit to Washington more convinced than ever that France, as he told President Roosevelt, "must count only on herself." The general could not forget that, from the beginning, Roosevelt — for all his undisputed command of world affairs, his humanitarianism, and his unflagging leadership of the Western Alliance — had misread the situation in France. The president had confidently expected that the French army would contain the German onslaught in 1940; he believed it important to support Marshall Pétain's Vichy regime as an alternative to Hitler's seizure of even more French resources and materials of war; he was adamant in telling Churchill in 1943 of his wish for an Allied military government in France after liberation; he approved the creation of schools to train U.S. officers to run an AMGOT-style regime; he spoke jauntily of partially dismembering the country; he insisted de Gaulle be kept out of any military planning affecting France; he derided any prospect of France playing a meaningful role in the postwar world; he failed to recognize the support Charles de Gaulle enjoyed inside France; and, at least until the fall of 1944, well after the liberation of Paris, he expressed continued and implacable opposition to him.[22]

Perhaps Franklin Roosevelt recognized that a man so foolhardy or courageous as de Gaulle, who had defied his own government when it surrendered to Germany, would never be a willing supplicant of American hegemony in the postwar world. It is also possible that the president's health, which was not good during most of the war, left him with neither the energy nor the strength to seriously reevaluate his attitude toward de Gaulle.

Ironically, Roosevelt seemed not to be aware that in many respects, de Gaulle's political ideas were not that distant from his own. Only a few months before D-Day, de Gaulle told his Consultative Assembly in Algiers of his vision for French democracy. "It must be a social democracy, that is ensuring each man the organic right and liberty to work." He added that "France expects private interest to yield to the common good ... and [that] each of her sons and daughters be able to live, work, and raise their children in security and dignity."[23] Roosevelt had spoken of a future no less daunting when he struggled to arouse the American people from the despair of the Hungry Thirties. The president's promise of a government that would "apply social values more noble than mere monetary profit" was not dissimilar in principle from de Gaulle's commitment to "an economic system designed to develop national resources, and not to benefit private interests."[24]

In the case of France, de Gaulle was offering an alternative to fascism and communism, as Roosevelt had offered an alternative to laissez faire capitalism. De Gaulle's opposition to an Allied AMGOT was also driven by his realization that French Communists would find in this new form of occupation — even if it was only temporary — a pretext for the fomenting of a Marxist revolution. His success in restoring a fully legitimate government to France went far toward lifting the threat of communism not only from his own country, but from all of Western Europe. This profound understanding of France's needs and aspirations would inspire a generation of French men and women. Among them was François Mauriac, author and journalist, member of the Académie française, and future Nobel Prize winner. Measuring the achievements of de Gaulle, he would write: "My admiration for the game de Gaulle has played since 1940 continues unabated, a game that satisfies me all the more because his means are so limited and his adversaries so powerful."[25]

Leaving Washington, de Gaulle spent an exhilarating day in New York, where he toured the city with Mayor Fiorello LaGuardia and visited former colleagues at *France Forever*. In Ottawa, his old friends Georges Vanier and Prime Minister King were on hand to greet him. De Gaulle felt "inundated by a tide of French pride mingled with an inconsolable affection, both sentiments flowing from history's backwaters."[26] He admired Canada's war effort and felt privileged to be "secretly informed" of the "apocalyptic work" going on in Canada in connection with development of the atomic bomb. In Montreal, where anti-conscription feelings were running high among French-speaking Quebeckers opposed to sending their sons overseas, de Gaulle's welcome was more reserved.

He was relieved when he received word that President Roosevelt — detecting shifts in the wind as he began his campaign for another term in the White House — had told a news conference that the United States was finally prepared to recognize the French Committee of National Liberation as "qualified to exercise the administration of France." A formal agreement was soon worked out, although without full recognition. "We returned to France bearing independence, Empire, and a sword."

By the time de Gaulle arrived in Algiers on July 13, the Allied armies had broken through in Normandy and Brittany, capturing the deepwater port of Cherbourg, St. Malo in Brittany, and other German redoubts. The fighting was hard and difficult, none harder than the prolonged effort of British and Canadian troops to capture the historic Norman town of Caen, which fell July 20 but left the city virtually devastated. The breakthrough opened the way for the U.S. 3rd Army under General Patton to punch into the midsection of France, aiming at Orléans and Le Mans. French paratroopers joined Allied forces in clearing Germans out of Brittany, while members of the French Forces of the Interior, including those of the Maquis, fought engagements with eight German divisions. Now, much more than during the German invasion four years earlier, French cities were suffering heavy damage. Civilian casualties from street fighting, artillery shelling, and aerial bombardment were mounting. Between fifty and seventy thousand French civilians — no one was sure of the exact number — would die from these causes by the end of the war.

American soldiers who found themselves free of fighting were reading a seventy-two-page *Pocket Guide to France* that told them why they were there, gave a history of the country, and offered tips on how to get along with the people. It was written in a way any GI could understand: "You are about to play a personal part in pushing the Germans out of France." American soldiers could expect "a big welcome from the French," because their arrival "means freedom, food, and a second chance to fight Hitler." is successThe *Pocket Guide* paid tribute to Frenchmen "who were able to escape from France and rally to the Tricolor [*sic*], and the fighting record they made for themselves in the Tunisian campaign and in Italy." Of the "heroic struggle put up by the Fighting French at Bir Hakeim, in the Lybian campaign," the *Pocket Guide* declared that it "will live long in the annals of military enterprise."[27]

For General Philippe Leclerc — actually Vicomte Philippe-François de Hautecloque, born to a proud line of rural French nobility — the long journey was nearing its end. Wounded, captured, and twice escaped from German prison camps, he had reached London in June 1940 via Spain and Portugal, leaving behind a wife and six children. He joined the Free French and asked for an immediate battle posting. De Gaulle sent him to Africa, where he rallied the central African colonies to the cause. In 1941, he led a march across the Libyan desert and seized the oasis of Kufra, creating the legend of the Regiment of Tchad. It was a gloriously cosmopolitan mix of Foreign Legionaires, black tribesmen from Morocco, and white officers from Metropolitan France. They grew into the French 2nd Armoured Division — la Deuxième DB — in time to fight in Tunisia. In March 1944, the division was shipped to England, to await the invasion of Europe.

The 2nd Armoured crossed the English Channel on August 1 to enter battle under the command of General Patton. "The hour of our great revenge has come," General de Gaulle declared in a radio address from Algiers.[28] In the next two weeks, Leclerc, lean, tough, craggy-faced, forty-two years old, led his division as it helped encircle one hundred thousand German troops caught in the Falaise Gap — a pocket where the Allies irrevocably drew the string in one of the deadliest battles of the invasion. German dead were bulldozed into pits and buried en masse.

At the height of the battle, the Fighting French Air Force (Forces aériennes françaises libre — FAFL) joined British and American bombers in devastating German strong points. The French air arm had come into being when around one hundred French airmen, responding to General de Gaulle's call of June 18, made their way to England in the days following his broadcast. Thirteen of those pilots served with the Royal Air Force in the crucial Battle of Britain that raged in the skies over England in September and October of 1940. By D-Day, they had grown, under British auspices, into a sort of RAF "Foreign Legion." On the night of August 4–5, 1944, planes of the FAFL 342 Squadron were in the air over the Falaise Gap.

Aboard a Douglas Boston bomber, serving as an aerial gunner, was Sergeant Louis Ricardo, a veteran of the real French Foreign Legion who had joined the Free French in London on June 29, 1940. Ricardo, then thirty years old, had been a member of the French Expeditionary Force that fought in Norway and he had received a personal welcome from Charles de Gaulle when he turned up in London. De Gaulle warned him, as he did other volunteers, that he must prepare himself "patiently for a long and hard struggle." Ricardo took part in the ill-fated assault on Dakar and was badly wounded in later fighting in Syria, losing one leg at the thigh. He then volunteered for the Free French Air Force and appealed to de Gaulle to be allowed to serve as a pilot. De Gaulle sent him to General Martial Valin, head of the FAFL, who convinced the British to let him try out for air crew. Ricardo, despite his prosthetic leg, showed he could climb nimbly into the turret of a bomber. He was accepted, and was promoted to Sergeant Gunner in March 1944. The flight over the Falaise Gap marked Ricardo's thirty-third mission. Before each mission, Ricardo would take off his false leg and ask a mechanic to look after it until he returned. As his plane reached the target area near the Eraines Mountains in Normandy, it was hit by flak and crashed in the woods outside the town of Perrières. Two members of the four-man crew survived, but Ricardo and one other died. His death was but one of thousands of Frenchmen who fought and died with the Allies on the road to Paris, whether by land, air, or sea.[29]

The whole of what had been Vichy France was soon to come under the flag of the Fighting French. On August 15, the French 1st Army landed on the Mediterranean coast. Paratroopers of the American 1st Airborne Task Force were already on the ground, and the U.S. 6th Corps had also joined the assault. The south of France became one of the fastest moving battlefronts of the war. The 1st Army of General Jean de Lattre de Tassigny occupied the naval base of Toulon on August 21 and prepared to drive north, through Provence and the the great midriff of the country south and east of Paris.

"I left for Paris," General de Gaulle would write laconically in his *Mémoires de guerre*, of the day he flew out of Algiers for Normandy. The journey was not an easy one. Rather than take the Flying Fortress that the U.S. Air Force had wanted him to use, de Gaulle chose to fly in his own, unarmed Lockheed Lodestar. After stopovers in Casablanca and Gibraltar, de Gaulle was told it would be inadvisable for him to proceed in his own aircraft. He set off anyway at dawn on Sunday, August 20. Approaching Normandy, his pilot, Colonel de Marmier, became disoriented while flying through heavy weather. A short while later, he found himself over England. De Gaulle refused de Marmier permission to land, and with a map on his lap, peered through the clouds until he spotted a familiar landscape. *"La-bas,"* he signalled, pointing to the ground. The plane's fuel gauge read empty when the Lodestar came down on the landing strip at Maupertuis near Cherbourg, at the tip of the Contentin Peninsula. It was just after eight o'clock. General Koenig and de Gaulle's commissioner for

Normandy, François Coulet, were there to meet him, along with an officer from General Eisenhower's headquarters.[30]

Events were moving at a rapid pace. The Germans had arrested both Marshall Pétain and his premier, Pierre Laval, and taken them to Germany. Laval had played his last hand, and lost, when he pulled the former president of the National Assembly, Édouard Herriot, out of a mental institute near Nancy and took him to Paris. Laval had intended to reconvene the National Assembly and set up a new "national government." Despite these attempts by the Germans to maintain control, the death rattle of the Nazi regime was being heard everywhere in Europe and German generals in France were rapidly coming to the realization that the war was lost.

If the war was slowly drawing to a close, peace was still nowhere near at hand, and news of another momentous development awaited de Gaulle on this sultry August morning in Normandy. After receiving the salutes of the three men awaiting him, de Gaulle listened carefully to the blunt message conveyed to him in an urgent voice by General Koenig: "There has been an uprising in Paris. We need to move quickly."[31]

CHAPTER 12
To the Barricades!

The Île de la Cité had not seen such strife since the crushing of the Paris Commune in 1871. Here, in the spiritual heart of Paris, on the island where some of its greatest monuments had been erected over the ages, two thousand striking policemen milled about in the square between the Préfecture de police and Notre Dame Cathedral. Some, surly and snappish, argued among themselves while others kicked the paving stones, perhaps trading guesses as to what the day might bring. The French Tricolour flew above the Préfecture, put there at dawn to replace the Nazi banner that had desecrated its flagpole the past four years. Orders had gone out the night before from the Gaullist Honneur de la Police, one of three police Resistance organizations, to take possession of the Préfecture at first light. Charles de Gaulle would write of this time that Paris, for so long "asleep, captive and stupefied," was to suddenly "reappear among us," no longer "the remorse of the free world."[1]

At the Préfecture, a young blond policeman, dressed in civilian clothes like his comrades, climbed atop a car parked by the large iron gates that barred entry from the Boulevard du Palais. Yves Bayet was an intelligence officer with a history of opposition to the collaborationists who had given the Paris police such an unsavoury reputation. "In the name of the Republic and General de Gaulle," he shouted, "I take possession of the Préfecture de police!"[2] It was Saturday morning, August 19, and the start of a tumultuous weekend that would send Parisians into the streets to build barricades, harass enemy strong points, and take aim at German soldiers, using stolen rifles, hand guns, and homemade bombs, to prepare the way for the liberating armies now approaching the city.

First there had been walkouts by railwaymen, the postal and telegraph workers, and by the conductors and drivers of the Metro. Then, at midweek, all but a handful of the city's fifteen thousand policemen obeyed their leaders' calls to stay off the job. "The hour of liberation has come," the strike order declared. "Today it is the duty of the whole body of the police ... to do nothing further to maintain order for the enemy.... [Y]ou will refuse to arrest patriots.... March with the people of Paris to the final battle."[3] The police action came as an angry rebuttal to the Germans for having disarmed police detachments in two Paris suburbs.

The city ground to a halt, food was running short, and at the Hôtel Meurice on rue de Rivoli, headquarters of the German command, General Dietrich von Choltitz pondered the seriousness of the uprising. Adolf Hitler had personally given him command of the Paris Military District only two weeks before, at a bizarre meeting in the "Wolf's Lair" at Rastenburg, East Prussia. Hitler was still recovering from injuries received in the July 20 bomb attempt on his life. Von Choltitz had found the Fuhrer "filled with rage," demanding that Paris be made into "a frontline city."[4]

In picking von Choltitz, Hitler had chosen a man with a record of devastation behind him, having led the attacks that all but wiped out Rotterdam and Sevastopol during the first great German offensives of the war. Heavy set, the very image of the stern Prussian officer, von Choltitz, just turning fifty, was also a realist. He knew he had no real chance of defending Paris against the Allied armies. He was more concerned about how to achieve a largely peaceful withdrawal of his remaining twenty-two thousand troops and the several thousand German civilian workers still in the city.

Policeman Bayet's call from atop the police car outside the Préfecture was met by applause and the singing of "La Marseillaise." This was followed by a surge of men through the gates and into the vast courtyard around which the building had been erected. Among the policemen were workers who would keep the building functioning, and by mid-morning a measure of deliberate organization had settled over it. In the lull, Yves Bayet headed out to a destination that had been given him the day before: the café Les Deux Magots on boulevard Saint-Germain, just across the Seine. There, he found Charles Luizet, a bespectacled man formally dressed in a suit, vest, and tie, taking coffee on the terrace. "Monsieur le Préfet, your office and your men await you," Bayet told him. He hustled Luizet into a black Citroen and escorted by two other vehicles, had him driven to the Préfecture.[5]

Charles Luizet was one of General de Gaulle's most trusted lieutenants. A graduate of Saint-Cyr and a former student of de Gaulle's, he had put in a decade of army service in Algeria before being appointed the French administrator of the international zone of Tangier. It was there, on hearing of de Gaulle's Appeal of June 18, that he wired London to volunteer with the Free French. De Gaulle told him to stay put but to send him intelligence. He was appointed prefect for Corsica after the island's liberation, and in July was called to London where he was told he would be the prefect of police in a liberated Paris. Luizet parachuted into the Vaucluse district of Provence just in time to make his way to Paris. It is unclear how deeply he was involved in planning the occupation of the Préfecture, but there is no doubt the bold move gave the Gaullist wing of the Resistance an upper hand in deciding the fate of Paris.

Luizet was still feeling his way around his new office when the man who was technically in charge of Resistance forces in Paris, Henri Georges René Tanguy — better known by his pseudonym, Colonel Rol-Tanguy — arrived at the Préfecture. As head of the French Forces of the Interior (FFI), this devout Communist and wounded veteran of the Spanish Civil War, thirty-six years old, a metalworker and trade union organizer, was one of the most powerful of Resistance leaders. Yet he had known nothing of the Préfecture takeover, and when he arrived on his bicycle and tried to gain entrance, he was blocked at the door. He retreated to a nearby garage that served as a safe house, put on his old Spanish Civil War uniform, and, returning to the Préfecture, managed to gain entrance. Rol-Tanguy and Luizet would have eyed each other warily, but they agreed to travel together to an important meeting that was about to begin in a Left Bank apartment on rue de Grenelle, just beyond Saint-Germain des Prés.

Accompanied by Yves Bayet, the men sat down to hear reports of fighting breaking out all over Paris. There was talk of the latest German atrocity: thirty-five young prisoners of the Gestapo had been taken to the Bois de Boulogne, shot, and their bodies dumped in a grove of oak trees. Representatives of all the main Resistance groups were in the room. This session of the Comité National de la Resistance faced a monumental decision: whether to accede to the demands of the Communist-led Paris Liberation Committee for an all-out uprising. Although German forces vastly outnumbered the Resistance in both men and firepower, the Communists were determined on immediate rebellion.

The head of the CNR, Georges Bidault, a school teacher who had joined the Resistance at the behest of Jean Moulin, counselled caution. As he spoke, a burst of rifle fire could be heard from the street. As the sound of shooting died out, Bidault was joined by Alexandre Parodi, who as de Gaulle's delegate-general in France was the highest-ranking Gaullist in the room. A senior civil servant in pre-war France, fired by Vichy for "wrongful thinking," Parodi was playing a perilous game. He had ordered the taking of the Préfecture as a means of asserting Gaullist leadership of the police; now he was struggling to prevent the Communists from riding roughshod over the CNR. He had just begun to speak when André Tollet, the head of the Paris Liberation Committee, interrupted him. Tollet accused Parodi of having started the insurrection prematurely by ordering the action at the Préfecture. Colonel Rol-Tanguy leaped in, shouting "Paris is worth two hundred thousand dead!"[6] The meeting had to be interrupted while tempers cooled. Rol-Tanguy was in an argumentative mood. Not only was he upset over not being told about the seizure of the Préfecture, but the night before he had written an inflammatory call to arms that ended with the injunction: *Chacun* à *son Boche* ("Everyone Kill his Hun").[7] Across Paris that morning, in accordance with a carefully orchestrated plan Rol-Tanguy had drawn up, assaults were being made on eighty public buildings. The targets included the *mairies* (town halls) of the city's twenty arrondissements, the post offices, the slaughterhouse, and even the Comédie Française.

Alexandre Parodi realized that an uprising engineered by Communists alone carried the risk that de Gaulle could be faced with a *coup d'état* on his arrival in Paris. It was for this reason that he made the wrenching choice, with the backing of Charles Luizet, to extend Gaullist support to the insurrection. The decision brought Parodi into conflict with Charles de Gaulle's military delegate in France, General Jacques Chaban-Delmas. Later that day, Chaban (his Resistance name) demanded of Parodi: "Why did you ignore orders forbidding you to launch an insurrection?"[8] Parodi's answer was that it was necessary to maintain a united Resistance front.

The painful decision made, Parodi took it one step further. He ordered mobilization of all Resistance members between the ages of eighteen and fifty, and instructed they be enlisted in the French Forces of the Interior. That concession put them under the command of Colonel Rol-Tanguy. He hoped it was the right decision. "If I have made a mistake I shall have a lifetime to regret it in the ruins of Paris."[9] He did not want another Warsaw, where the Red Army idled outside the Polish capital while in the city the Armija Krajowa (Home Army) fought a hopeless battle against a well-armed and ruthless occupier.

The Préfecture now became the first test of the ability of the FFI to hold their ground. They did not have long to wait. As the Germans had done in the Paris suburb of Neuilly, where they sent tanks to shell the town hall after its takeover by the Resistance, heavy armour was brought into the Boulevard du Palais. Behind a parade of armoured cars came three German tanks led by a powerful Tiger I machine equipped with an 88 mm cannon. It was followed by two smaller, French-built Renault tanks from the 5th Sicherunregiment. It was 3:30. Police in the Préfecture answered their appearance with marksmen shooting from open windows. There was occasional firing from some old machine guns sheltered behind sandbag barriers. With bullets whizzing into the square across from the Préfecture, the Tiger unleashed two shells. One scored a direct hit on the iron gates of the Préfecture, blowing the left side of the great door off its hinges and opening the way into the building. The second made a hole in the Préfecture's outer wall. Inside, the impact lifted Edgar Pisani out of his chair at the Préfecture's switchboard. Regaining his feet, he pressed an alarm button signalling every Paris police station of the attack. As the smoke from the tank shells cleared in the courtyard, someone drove a bus into the open gateway, wedging it there as a barrier. Others panicked, and ran down a stairway to a special entrance to the Metro used only by the police. Armand Fournet, a police sergeant, leaped onto a handcart and threatened to shoot the first man who tried to get by him. "Our only chance of survival," he told them, "is to win!"[10] The rush to the Metro stopped.

In the basement of the Préfecture, a civilian was busy with two assistants, pulling corks from champagne bottles. Frédéric Joliot-Curie, son-in-law of Marie Curie, the co-discoverer of radium, refilled the bottles with gasoline and sulfuric acid. He was a committed Communist and had brought the deadly mix from the Curie laboratory. The bottles were wrapped in rags soaked in potassium chlorate and a team of runners carried these Molotov cocktails up to the roof. From there, police hurled the missiles onto the German cars and tanks. Several splattered on the pavement, but one fell into the open turret of a Renault tank, exploded, and sent a sheet of flame high into the air. Other German tanks and armoured vehicles began to make their way across the bridge from the Left Bank.

The police scored more direct hits with their Molotov cocktails, prisoners were taken, and ammunition and medical supplies in the armoured vehicles was confiscated. By five o'clock, twenty vehicles had been destroyed and fifty German soldiers killed. Whether it was due to the ferocity of the police counterattack or a lack of firm orders from the German command centre, the tanks remaining at the Préfecture, including the massive Tiger, backed up and drove off. The streets around the Préfecture fell silent. The police still held the building, but for how long?

A troubled observer of the day's events was Raoul Nordling, the Swedish consul in Paris. Born in France, married to a French woman, he was able, due to his status as a neutral diplomat, to act as a go-between with the German authorities. Late in the afternoon he received a call from Charles Luizet pleading for help. Nordling agreed to see General von Choltitz, with whom he had earlier arranged a prisoner swap that freed four thousand men from jails around Paris. He hoped to build on that success by bringing the fighting at the Préfecture to an end. When he went to see the German commander at the Hôtel Meurice, he heard a torrent of invective against the police. Von Choltitz told Nordling he was planning an aerial attack on the Préfecture in the morning. When Nordling warned him this would likely result in severe damage to Notre Dame and other nearby churches, von Choltitz replied, "I am a soldier. I get orders. I execute them."[11]

Nordling pressed the issue, urging von Cholltitz to consider a truce. He told him the struggle of the Resistance was mainly against Vichy, and the Germans were really only caught in the middle. There was no point in fighting over Paris, the diplomat reminded von Choltitz, because in the end he would have to withdraw anyway. These arguments made sense to the German general. He knew or cared little or nothing of French politics and was concerned only with the welfare of his men. If a truce would put a stop to their killing while he completed plans to evacuate the city, it could be a useful tool. Left unsaid was any reference to orders von Choltitz had received from Hitler to destroy Paris. By nine o'clock, the two had worked out the terms of a truce. The conditions came close to delivering victory to the Resistance: the Germans would recognize members of the FFI as regular soldiers, not as terrorists; they would not attack the Préfecture de police; and the Germans would make an orderly evacuation from Paris using outer boulevards of the city. The FFI, in turn, would have to agree not to attack German positions. Now, Nordling faced the task of winning Resistance agreement to this remarkable diplomatic achievement.

A wild thunderstorm drenched Paris early on Sunday, but that did not deter a group of French Garde Mobile who rushed into l'Hôtel de Ville, the Paris city hall, just before seven o'clock. Their leader, Léo Hamon, went to the prefect's office to announce that he was taking possession "in the name of the Paris Liberation Committee and on behalf of the Provisional Government of the French Republic." The first thing he did was demand that a bust of Marshall Pétain be removed. Hamon then ordered the arrest of the prefect, René Bouffet, and the entire municipal council including the mayor, Pierre Taittinger, on grounds of collaboration.[12]

Hundreds of little skirmishes were breaking out across the city, nearly every incident claiming lives. A German sound truck drove along the main streets blasting out word of the truce. The truce had not yet been ratified by the Resistance; this would have to wait for an eleven o'clock meeting of the Committee of National Resistance. Perhaps because of the turmoil, only six members showed up to vote on whether to accept the arrangement that Nordling had negotiated. After hearing Parodi and Chaban-Delmas make the argument for the truce, all but the lone Communist present, Pierre Villon, voted to accept it.

Two who voted "yes" at the meeting, Jacques Chaban-Delmas and Léo Hamon, were sent with one other man to the Swedish consulate where Nordling shuttled between rooms containing the French and German representatives. It did not take long to ratify the agreement, but the truce almost fell apart before it had time to take effect. Around three o'clock, the Gestapo stopped a car carrying Alexandre Parodi and two of his Gaullist colleagues. They found maps and plans of the uprising, and took the trio to a Gestapo office. They likely would have been shot, except that a German intelligence agent named Émile "Bobby" Bender convinced the Gestapo to phone General von Choltitz for instructions.[13] Von Choltitz ordered the three men, described as "members of the de Gaulle government," brought to him at the Hôtel Meurice. Then he called Nordling, who arrived quickly and identified the trio.

By the time Parodi was released, around 6:30, many Parisians were in the streets celebrating. They also assumed the curfew had been cancelled, but this was not the case, and German soldiers fired over the heads of crowds. An FFI radio station went on the air long enough to play the national anthem.

Colonel Rol-Tanguy, convinced that as long as the Germans were in the streets of Paris Frenchmen should fight them, announced he was not accepting the truce. Remembering the electrifying message, *Tous aux Barricades!*, that had summoned people into the streets of Paris on more than one occasion, Rol ordered the printing of posters bearing that slogan, directing people to erect barricades around the city. Before the week was out, four hundred such barriers would be thrown up. They were made of paving stones torn from the street, trees that had been cut down, furniture dragged out to create an obstacle, and anything else Parisians could get their hands on. *"Peuple de Paris,"* one poster exhorted, "the long-awaited day has arrived! French and Allied troops are at the gates of Paris. It is the sacred duty of all Parisians to do battle! The hour of national resurrection has sounded." The German occupiers of the City of Light might be prepared for a peaceful end to the Occupation, but the citizens of Paris were not.

✝

During a ninety-kilometre drive into Cherbourg and the headquarters of General Eisenhower, Charles de Gaulle reflected on what he'd heard of events in Paris. When he met Eisenhower, he was told the pace of the Allied advance was picking up all along the front. General Patton's 3rd Army would soon cross the River Seine south of Paris, while the American 1st Army under General Hodges would make the leap north of the city. Meanwhile, General Montgomery's British and Canadian forces were advancing toward Rouen on the east bank of the Seine. De Gaulle was surprised there had been no mention of entering Paris. "I don't see why you cross the Seine everywhere, yet at Paris and Paris alone you do not cross," he told Eisenhower.[14] This was de Gaulle's first meeting with Eisenhower since before D-Day.

Both men were feeling edgy and de Gaulle sensed he was embarrassing the supreme commander. It was all a matter of strategy, Eisenhower explained; he didn't want to risk the destruction of Paris and the heavy loss of civilian life that might come from a direct assault. It would be preferable to bypass the city, returning to it afterwards. Anyway, the Resistance had started too soon, Eisenhower added.

"Why too soon," de Gaulle asked, "since at this very moment your forces are at the Seine? The fate of Paris is of fundamental concern to the French government."[15]

Left unsaid, de Gaulle may have thought, was the matter of feeding Paris. Once liberated, the well-being of this hungry city would become a joint French and Allied responsibility; it would take four thousand tons of supplies a day to support the five million people in Paris and its suburbs.

Was it that the Allies had no wish to divert army supplies to satisfy the hunger of famished Parisians? De Gaulle added, ominously, that if necessary he would personally order General Leclerc's 2nd Armoured Division to move forward. Eisenhower, possessed of diplomatic skills rare among generals, made the decision to soothe de Gaulle's feelings. He told him it would not be long before he would give the order to march on Paris. General Leclerc and the 2nd Armoured Division would be the ones to get the call.

Settling for that assurance, de Gaulle and General Koenig steered for Rennes, passing through "demolished cities and burned-out villages" en route to the Breton capital. People gathered to greet him along the road and the streets of the towns were bedecked with flags and flowers. At each place he spoke briefly and led the townspeople in "La Marseillaise." That night, standing in the rain in Rennes, de Gaulle addressed a large crowd that included the mayor and his council and the general's own newly appointed commissioner. The next day, de Gaulle made it as far as Laval and delivered another of the impromptu speeches he would repeat hundreds of times all across France. He began work on a letter to General Eisenhower which he sent via General Koenig on August 22.

De Gaulle used the letter to renew his argument for an immediate drive on Paris:

> The information I have received from Paris today makes me think that in view of the almost complete disappearance of the police and of the German forces in Paris and the extreme shortage of food there, serious trouble is to be expected in the capital very shortly. I believe it necessary to have Paris occupied by the French and Allied forces as soon as possible even if it means a certain amount of fighting and a certain amount of damage within the city.[16]

To Eisenhower, the pressure to bow to de Gaulle had become irresistible. He scrawled a note across the top of the letter before sending it to his assistant, General Bedell Smith: "It looks now as if we'd be compelled to go into Paris. Bradley [American ground forces commander] and his G-2 [Intelligence] think we can and must walk in."[17]

✝

General von Choltitz held the telephone from his ear. It was the only way he could soften the berating he was receiving from the new commander of German forces in France, Field Marshall Walter Model. Model had skilfully extracted the remnants of German 7th Army from the trap of the Falaise Gap, and now it was up to him to oversee the defence of Paris. Hitler had told him to "hold the Paris bridgehead at any price ... regardless of the city's destruction."[18] It would take two hundred thousand men, he told Hitler, knowing that no such force could be assembled for such an unlikely task. Now, he was on the phone to von Choltitz. General Model accused the Paris commander of having lost control of the city. There were even rumours he was negotiating with terrorists. Von Choltitz denied the charges, but he couldn't put out of his mind the fact that the truce agreement he had made with the Resistance was not working very well. Barricades were going up in the streets and sharpshooters were picking off German troops. In the last twenty-four hours he'd lost another seventy-five men.

Von Choltitz had no sooner put down the phone than he was confronted by Otto Abetz, the truculent German ambassador who, it seemed, had his fingers in every intrigue of Nazi-occupied Paris. His years in France had brought him to an intimate familiarity with French culture (he was married to a beautiful French woman), but it was said of him that he "loved France rather as a peasant does the livestock he will one day eat."[19] Abetz, no doubt already having chosen the hour he would leave Paris, asked von Choltitz how he could be of use to him.

"My dear Ambassador," von Choltitz replied, "in what way could you be useful to me?"

Abetz had a ready answer: "I could send to Headquarters and to Ribbentrop [Nazi foreign minister] a signal condemning your brutal behaviour in Paris."

And so he did, thereby lifting from von Choltitz's head the threat of condemnation for any failure to enthusiastically execute the Führer's orders. These were growing more frantic by the hour. The latest demanded that Paris be "transformed into a heap of rubble." The last German defender must, if necessary, "be buried beneath it."

Among the members of the CNR, second thoughts about the truce spread on Monday and Tuesday. Colonel Rol-Tanguy, having rejected it outright, told the FFI to step up its attacks on such German strong points as the Palais du Luxembourg and the École Militaire. The latest FFI success was the occupation of the Hôtel Matignon, traditional home of the head of the French government. Alexandre Parodi established himself there and began issuing orders to his appointees throughout the city. By Tuesday afternoon, the 22nd, the truce no longer had widespread support. In the name of the Paris Liberation Committee, Parodi signed the order to renew the insurrection. He didn't bother to refer the proclamation to the CNR. His statement bristled with determination:

> The struggle continues. It must be prosecuted until the enemy is driven from the Paris region. More than ever now, all must take part in the fight. Respond to the general order of mobilization. Join the FFI. The population must use all means of preventing the movement of the enemy. Cut down trees, dig anti-tank ditches, erect barricades. It will be a victorious people who will welcome the Allies.[20]

Parodi's order added yet more confusion to a tumultuous situation where no one had a complete picture of what was happening. It was amid this disorder that a Paris doctor, Robert Monod, sent a letter to Colonel Rol-Tanguy proposing that a mission be sent through the German lines to tell the Americans of the urgent need of their intervention in Paris. When he got no answer, he began phoning contacts in the FFI, and at six o'clock Sunday evening, Rol-Tanguy's chief of staff, Major Roger Gallois, showed up at his apartment. The FFI had decided Monod's gambit was worth a try. They left in Monod's car at 5:30 Monday morning, carrying a Red Cross pass that allowed them into the front lines.

That evening they reached a sanatorium that Monad knew of at Saint Nom la Bretèche, thirty kilometres from Versailles. From there, a contact pointed Gallois to the American lines while Monod returned to Paris. Just before dark, Gallois slipped through a forest and found himself at an American forward base. It took him several hours to convince the soldiers to take him to the main American camp a few miles behind the front line. He eventually told his story to an intelligence officer who recognized the value of Gallois's information: the fact that an uprising was underway in Paris, barricades were being erected, and the German high command had accepted a truce — one that was already being violated. It was now Tuesday, August 22, and at 1:30 in the morning, Gallois found himself in front of a sleepy American general, George S. Patton. A lively discussion ended with Patton producing a bottle of champagne and offering a toast to victory.

Later in the day, Patton had Gallois flown to Le Mans, a city of fine museums and public gardens that had become the nerve centre of the American forward operation. Patton told General Omar Bradley, commander of all American ground forces, of what he'd learned from Gallois about the situation in Paris. Bradley himself flew to Le Mans, where General Jacques Leclerc was waiting at the airport with Gallois for Bradley's arrival. Over the noise of the still running engines, Leclerc was told, "You win. They've decided to send you straight to Paris." Standing on the Le Mans air strip, Bradley impressed on Gallois the seriousness of the steps they were taking: "A grave decision has been made and we three bear the responsibility for it: me, because I am giving the order to take Paris; General Leclerc, because he is the one who has to carry out this order; and you, because it is based on the information that you have brought that we have acted."[21]

The order from General Eisenhower had come just in time to prevent an irreparable split in the Allied front. General de Gaulle, irritated and frustrated by what he considered to be further stalling, had already given Leclerc the order to launch a reconnaissance column toward Paris. To lead it, Leclerc chose Major Jacques de Guillebon, a veteran of African fighting. He had commanded a regiment of black riflemen from Senegal, the West African colony, and had played a key part in the capture of Kufra in Libya. Twenty-four hours later, de Guillebon's column was well on its way to Rambouillet, the jumping off point for Paris. The road to the capital now was open to whoever dared take it; any opposition would come from German defenders, not from dissenting voices in the Allied High Command.

CHAPTER 13
The Road to Paris

The noise and smells of tanks and armoured cars grinding their gears and belching gas fumes filled the moist air hanging over the apple orchards and farm fields of Normandy. German troops were falling back toward Paris, their numbers drastically reduced by losses sustained in the Battle of the Falaise Gap. The fifty-six fully equipped divisions that awaited the Allied assault on D-Day had been reduced to forty that in some cases were mere skeleton forces. Some panzer divisions were down to fifteen tanks instead of 150, and the 2nd SS Division, which bore the brunt of the attack around Falaise, reported a strength of only 450 men, fifteen tanks, and six guns. Two hundred thousand Germans had been captured and fifty thousand had died in the battle. Yet the Wehrmacht remained a powerful force. The 7th and 5th panzer armies, backed up against the Seine, managed to move three hundred thousand men across the river between Paris and the English Channel. They accomplished the feat — almost a Dunkirk in reverse — by using twenty-three ferries and a pontoon bridge and crossing only on nights when bad weather kept Allied air forces grounded.[1]

Outside a tent near the village of Écouché, a few kilometres west of the devastated town of Argentan, which had been recently liberated by the American 5th Army Corps, General Philippe Leclerc waved his malacca cane and sputtered epithets. Within a few hours of receiving his *feu vert* (green light) to move on Paris, Leclerc had assembled his 2nd Armoured Division and was giving final instructions to three of his most trusted officers. Their detachments were to leave at dawn on August 23, a Wednesday, taking separate routes on the 240-kilometre track eastward to the capital. The first assault, meant to be only a feint, was to consist of a handful of regiments led by Major Morel-Deville. Its task was to work its way past Trappes and Saint-Cyr, aiming for Paris via the pont de Sèvres. A second thrust, directed by Lieutenant Colonel Paul de Langlade, would move cross-country through the valley of the River Chevreuse. The largest column, under Colonel Pierre Billotte, was to throw every ounce of its strength along an arc aiming at Fresnes, site of the infamous prison twenty kilometres from the capital. That would put Billotte in a position to slam into the city via Versailles and the Porte d'Orléans, the old southern gateway to Paris.

By now, the 2nd Armoured Division — the proud Deuxième Division Blindée — had become a highly effective war machine. It included sixteen thousand battle-hardened men, two hundred U.S. Sherman tanks, four thousand cars and armoured vehicles, and more than six hundred artillery pieces. General Leclerc had brought the division seamlessly into the Allied offensive after its August 1 landing, and by August 12 had secured its first major victory with the capture of Alençon, a town of fifteen thousand near the southern edge of Normandy.

Leclerc was somewhat bemused to find his division had been transferred to the command of General Leonard Gerow, chief of the American 5th Corps. He had no objection to serving alongside such celebrated outfits as the U.S. 29th Infantry Division or the even more illustrious 1st Infantry Division — the "Big Red One" — he just wanted to get on the move to Paris. It didn't matter now that Gerow was in a rage over the reconnaissance mission of Major de Guillebon. Upset though Gerow might be, the American commander's first priority was to coordinate the movements of the 2nd Armoured Division with his own 4th Infantry

Division. It too was bound for Paris with orders to hook around the city from the northwest, cross the Seine, and enter via the neighbourhoods of the Bois de Bologne.

In Paris, Colonel Rol-Tanguy directed the rebelling Forces françaises de l'intérieur from his bunker in the sewer below Place Denfert-Rochereau, a location code named Duroc. Far below the now idle Metro station, Rol-Tanguy monitored reports of the fighting throughout the city and sent instructions to FFI units to hold their hard-won positions.[2]

The Gare de l'Est fell to the Resistance, cutting off the last hope of German escape via rail. German tanks and motorized artillery attacked the Grand Palais at the bottom of the Champs-Élysées, setting one wing afire. The assault saw the use of a new weapon — a metre-long, remote controlled robot that looked like a small tank, dubbed a Goliath. It was exploded as it reached the building. The fact a Swedish circus owner blessed with exquisitely bad timing had rented the building for a week-long run was of no concern to the Germans. Animals — lions, tigers, and panthers — caught in the inferno roared with fright before dying in the flames. Horses that escaped were shot by German soldiers and later hacked up by Parisians desperate for meat. The Grand Palais also held a police station whose basement cells housed prostitutes arrested the night before. They were hurriedly released, but other prisoners died in the blazing building.

Around the main post office, recently occupied by an FFI cell, a fierce gunfight broke out. Barricades patched together from overturned vehicles and sandbags sprang up at key intersections. Grim portraits of Adolf Hitler and Marshall Pétain were thrown onto the rubble of a barricade on rue Saint-Jacques. Boulevard Saint-Michel, a main north-south artery, was blocked at both boulevard Montparnasse and boulevard Saint-Germain, denying German forces ready access to Resistance strong points. By mid-week, four hundred barricades would make the streets of Paris virtually impassable to heavy trucks or tanks. At each, young men — and some young women — clambered about, proudly displaying FFI armbands or bits of military uniforms picked up from dead Germans. To Jean-Paul Sartre, the uprising was "a symbolic rebellion in a symbolic city." Those who couldn't play in the Resistance "felt left out of the game."[3]

To the Germans, Paris still had great military significance as a funnel through which their forces could retreat toward the River Somme, where a new defensive line could be prepared. The Route nationale highway system radiating outward from the capital offered the Germans their last means of escape. In Paris, defended only by tired, aging soldiers of the 352nd Infantry Division supported by seventeen-year-old troops manning 88 mm guns, German officers were burning secret documents. The same acrid smell that had spread over the city in June 1940 filled the nostrils of people on the streets.

Adolf Hitler, in his final message to General Model on August 23, seemed to recognize the inevitable. "In history the loss of Paris ... always signified the loss of all of France," he conceded. But there could be no surrender. "Paris must not fall into enemy hands, or if it does, only as a field of rubble."[4] No longer able to control Paris by force, General von Choltitz now tried persuasion. A low-flying German plane dropped thousands of leaflets demanding obedience to the occupier:

> Paris is still in the hands of the Germans! It is possible it may not be evacuated at all! Under our protection it has known four years of relative peace.... But shooting continues in Paris. Criminal elements insist on terrorizing the city! Blood has been spilled, French blood as well as German!... It would be a simple matter to leave Paris after first blowing up all warehouses, all factories, bridges and railway stations, and to seal the suburbs hermetically off if the city should be encircled.... You may rely on our love for this marvellous centre of European culture, on our sympathy for all reasonable Frenchmen, for the women and children of Paris, but if all these things are not considered sacred by the populace itself, there would no longer be any reason for us to remain tolerant.
>
> FOR THE LAST TIME WE WARN THE CRIMINAL ELEMENTS!
>
> We demand the immediate and unconditional cessation of acts of violence against us and against citizens.... We demand that the citizens of Paris defend themselves

against the terrorists.… This, and this alone, can guarantee the life of the city, its victualment, and its salvation.[5]

Collaborators might have taken some comfort from these leaflets, but most looked for ways to disappear before a vengeful Resistance could exact revenge. The notorious anti-Semitic journalist Robert Brasillach hid in an attic after urging in *le Petit Parisien* that all members of the Resistance should face summary execution. He wrote in his diary, "Jews have been living in cupboards for four years, why not imitate them?" *Le Matin,* the strident anti-Semitic daily that had served France's German masters the past four years, published its last edition August 17. It reported heavy fighting between Chartres and Paris, but insisted that on the Eastern Front, a successful German counterattack had stopped the Russian advance. The paper's publisher, Maurice Bunau-Varilla, had died two weeks earlier, allowing him to escape the vengeance of the Resistance.

By now, Resistance radio stations were on the air and the underground press had come into the open. Printers who had gone on strike at collaborationist papers helped put out street editions of *Combat, Libération, L'Humanité,* and *Franc-Tireur,* all proudly signalling their Resistance origins. Albert Camus wrote in *Combat* of the city's fierce pride in itself: "This enormous Paris, hot and black, with its two storms, one in the sky and one in the streets, will become more than ever the luminous City of Light that is the envy of the world."[6] *Petit Parisien,* under new management, became *Le Parisien Libéré.* Thousands of free copies were distributed to Resistance bastions. In the cafés that dared open their doors, Parisians openly devoured their first uncensored news in four years.

Couriers from Paris who worked their way through the German lines brought Charles de Gaulle copies of the first editions. He devoured them, "pleased by the spirit of the struggle" reflected in their columns.[7] What he read strengthened his resolve that his authority to govern France must come from no other source than "the voice of the people."

On leaving Le Mans on Wednesday morning, de Gaulle received word that the truce in Paris had broken down and that the FFI was taking over whole neighbourhoods. He debated whether the German failure to respond more aggressively to the uprising stemmed from "fear of the future" in the shape of an all-out Allied assault, or from some conscious-stricken "desire to spare Paris." Growing more reflective, de Gaulle felt gripped by an inner tension unlike anything he'd yet experienced.

As he followed the route cleared by General Leclerc's forces, that feeling vanished, to be replaced by "a veritable flood of joy." He passed through crowds massed on both sides of the road, cheering and waving flags. At Chartres, de Gaulle paid homage to Jean Moulin and recalled the courage the prefect had shown in resisting the Germans. A message from Leclerc advised de Gaulle that Major de Guillebon's advance column had done battle with "a good many Germans." One officer, Brigadier André Brés, had been lost to a sharpshooter who had to be flushed out of a clump of trees on the edge of Rambouillet Forest. "I shall begin the operation at dawn tomorrow," Lerclerc wrote, signalling his final advance on Paris.

De Gaulle scrawled a quick reply: "I shall sleep in Rambouillet tonight. I would like to see you there. I embrace you."[8]

De Gaulle headed directly for Château Rambouillet, the old country estate of French presidents, fifty kilometres southwest of Paris. The 2nd Armoured Division liberated Rambouillet shortly before noon, finding the village abandoned by the Germans. The four-storey château, boasting imposing towers rising from its pentagonal footprint, had been the scene of spectacular soirees since the era of King Louis XVI. The German Occupation had left it relatively unscathed but without electricity. The head of de Gaulle's personal staff, Commandant Lignières, found a mobile generator in the cellar and by evening, lights were burning weakly throughout the château. When de Gaulle strode the terrace and viewed the gardens of the château and the small lake on which swans swam contentedly, he could be forgiven if the bucolic scene removed thoughts of the war from his mind.

Such thoughts were not long absent. Waiting to see de Gaulle was a delegation from Paris that had worked its way through the lines. They had travelled with two letters of safe passage, one signed by Alexandre

Parodi and the other by General von Choltitz. The mission was to have been led by Raoul Nordling, the Swedish consul, but he had suffered a heart attack and his place had been taken by his brother, Rolf. It included a prominent Parisian banker, Alexandre de Saint-Phalle; de Gaulle's private secretary from the days of the Reynaud government, Jean Laurent; the ever-present Major "Bobby" Bender; and a second German officer, Baron Poch-Pastor, who, unknown to von Choltitz, was actually an Allied agent. The delegation was playing a complicated game. Its purpose, as conceived by von Choltitz, was to convince de Gaulle to put a stop to the uprising. Parodi, one the other hand, wanted de Gaulle to know the importance of his entering Paris as soon as possible. De Gaulle was not prepared to call off the uprising and he was already urging his forces forward with all haste. Nor was he in agreement with Saint-Phalle's suggestion that he convene the "National Assembly" to put the stamp of legality on a de Gaulle government. He had no intention of seeking authority from politicians who had stayed spinelessly behind and who represented all that had been rotten in the pre-war parliamentary scene.[9]

While soldiers of General Leclerc's command camped among the rain-soaked bushes of Rambouillet, two of Charles de Gaulle's most senior officers, General Koenig and General Alphonse Juin, joined him at the château. They dined Wednesday evening on cold canned C rations in the ornate Salle des Fêtes. Dinner done, de Gaulle had Leclerc ushered into the room. Leclerc outlined his battle plans for the next day, pointing out the routes for each of his three columns. De Gaulle pondered the report of his young commander and, after a brief moment, nodded his assent. As to his own plans, de Gaulle explained he would go directly to the "centre" — his old office at the Ministry of War — and from there he would assume command in the name of the Provisional Government. The general stood up and held out his hand to Leclerc. They shook. "How lucky you are," de Gaulle said. Then he added, apparently with thoughts of the bloody aftermath of the Franco-Prussian War of 1870 in mind, "Go quickly. We cannot afford another Commune."[10]

That night, de Gaulle relaxed with a book from the château's library, Molière's *Le Bourgeois Gentilhomme*. His supply officer, Commander Lignières, had prepared the presidential bedroom for him, complete with silk sheets last slept on by Marshall Pétain. The bedroom was nestled under a cupola of the château and could be reached only by a narrow, winding stairway from the president's study. "Do you mean to say you have made ready for me the presidential bedroom? You don't really imagine, do you, that I'm going to sleep in the president of the Republic's bed?"[11] For all de Gaulle's swaggering arrogance, and notwithstanding his sense of himself as the saviour of France, this was too much, too soon. He would sleep that night in a lesser room.

With the French and American armies in pursuit of the Germans, another army was gathering at the rear of the Allied forces — an army of war correspondents. They included, at various times, Ernest Hemingway foraging the countryside with what almost amounted to his own private army; Larry LeSueur of the United Press who had landed on Utah Beach with the American 4th Division; Ross Munro, the scholarly reporter of the Canadian Press wire service; and star female correspondents Helen Kirkpatrick of the *Chicago Daily News* and Sonia Tamara of the *New York Herald Tribune*. There was one other woman of note accredited to Leclerc's division. Elisabeth de Miribel, who had typed Charles de Gaulle's Appeal of June 18 in the flat in Seymour Place four long summers ago, had caught up with Leclerc in an orchard outside Alençon on July 16. She found him sitting under an apple tree eating K rations.

After three years in Canada stirring up support for Free France, and a stay in Algiers where she was accredited to the French national committee, de Miribel coaxed her way into France with the personal endorsement of Charles de Gaulle. "It is my desire," he had written French officials in London, "that Mlle de Miribel should go to France without delay, as a war correspondent." The fact she had not been hired by any newspaper or news agency did not seem to matter. Reaching England, she asked General Leclerc to take her with him. "We'll make a bet," he told her. "If you can join me in France, I'll keep you." She crossed the channel two weeks later in the company of de Gaulle spokesman Maurice Schumann. True to his word, General Leclerc welcomed her to his command. He gave her a car and a driver and she followed the division to Rambouillet. "Slender, well fitted in his uniform, cane in hand, he speaks with force and dignity," she would write of Leclerc in her memoirs. "He does not know fear, he ignores compromise."[12] When her driver found the brakes on the car were no longer safe, she was given another vehicle — an Amilcar, a French-built sports car in which Elisabeth de Miribel would enter Paris.

At six o'clock Thursday morning, Leclerc's three columns were on the move along a front thirty kilometres wide. His Sherman tanks crunched along Route nationale 20 in a grey drizzle while African soldiers used to fighting in the Libyan sands followed in their trail, their puttees soaked from the dew on the grass. Others, veterans of the Spanish Civil War, downed shots of pastis offered by delirious townsfolk who had risen early to find a liberating army on their doorsteps. The advance slowed as the crowds grew larger through the day, leading General Bradley to complain the French were "dancing their way into Paris."

All that changed when heavy opposition on the outskirts of Trappes brought Major Morel-Deville's column to a halt twenty-five kilometres from Paris. The front had narrowed by now and on the column's right flank Colonel Louis Dio's regiments made for the pont de Sèvres, the original goal of Morel-Deauville's now-stalled column. They clashed with German defenders at the Bièvre River and the Villacoublay airfield, but shortly after sunset were able to force the bridge which still stood undamaged.

Colonel Pierre Billotte watched from his command car as his squad of Sherman tanks approached the grey stone walls of Fresnes Prison. He was the son of a French general who had cracked under the strain of the German blitzkrieg across northern France in 1940. After suffering a nervous breakdown, Bilotte's father had been killed in a car accident. Having fought his own tank battles during those dark days, Billottte *fils* knew he would have to sacrifice some of his machines if he was to overcome this last obstacle in his advance on Paris. A German 88 cannon at the mouth of the prison began firing at two French tanks when they moved up the avenue de la République. A direct hit on the lead tank lifted it off the ground and turned it on its side in a fiery ball. Its occupants tumbled out, one aflame, the other rolling on the ground, his legs shot off. The 88 itself blew up when a shot from a French tank hit an ammunition truck next to it. By the end of the battle, five French tanks lay burned out on the street and Billotte's advance was temporarily halted. There was blood aplenty on the road to Paris. Rather than risk more losses, Billotte ordered his men to bed down for the night.

At Château Rambouillet, de Gaulle received reports of the fighting as he paced the flagstone terrace with his aide, Geoffroy de Courcel, at his side. De Gaulle smoked one cigarette after another, saying little, reflective in his thoughts. He was occupied with more than the progress of his divisions. His son, Philippe, now a lieutenant seconded to Leclerc's 2nd Armoured, had driven out of Rambouillet that morning in a Marine tank destroyer. It was a machine that would be the first target of any German tank that sighted it. Later in the day, de Gaulle received a telegram from King George congratulating him on the liberation of Paris. The message was premature, as was the announcement broadcast shortly after on the BBC.

At a crossroads not far from Trappes, Captain Raymond Dronne was manoeuvring the tanks and armoured cars of the 9th Company of the Regiment de Tchad into a reserve position before settling down for the night. Dronne was distressed at the prospect of further delay in the drive on Paris. Born into a farm family, he'd been mobilized in 1939 after earning university degrees in law and journalism. He'd joined the Free French in the Cameroon, fought across North Africa, and been wounded when strafed by a German pilot in Tunisia. A big, red-haired man, he took pride in his appearance, and even in battle he made a point of keeping his beard trimmed and his hair groomed. It was a little after six o'clock when Dronne noticed General Leclerc pacing at the side of the road. It was obvious that Leclerc, slashing at the weeds with his cane, was in a foul mood. Dronne stopped his Jeep anyway.

"Dronne," Leclerc called out to him, "What the fuck are you doing here?" Dronne explained he'd been ordered to return to reserves.

"Never carry out an idiotic order," Leclerc answered. He told Dronne there was no serious resistance to the east of the Fresnes road and that the way to Paris was open to an advance party willing to make the foray. Dronne was delighted to hear it.

"Dronne, get on into Paris immediately," Leclerc ordered, pointing his cane toward the capital.

"Is my objective to be the heart of Paris?" Dronne asked.

"That's right, Paris. Tell Paris and the Resistance not to lose heart, that tomorrow morning the entire division will be there."[13]

Dronne thought Leclerc looked less tense now; he was smiling, at least. In less than an hour, Dronne was back in his Jeep, leading a column of three tanks and a dozen armoured cars toward the capital. Each bore on their sides the white Cross of Lorraine. Most of the men were veterans from Spain and they'd named their half-tracks after Civil War battles — Madrid, Guadalajara, Guernica. The tanks bore illustrious names from French military history — *Romilly*, the *Montmirail*, and the *Champaubert*. At first, the column moved slowly, the road congested with traffic. All around him, Dronne heard sounds of cannon fire, the shooting of automatic weapons, and the calls of wounded men for help.

Closer to Paris, Dronne found his column alone on the road. Dodging fallen trees and barricades, his force entered Paris through the Porte d'Italie and began a careful reconnoitre of the streets in front of them. It was a quarter to nine. Avenue d'Italie seemed empty, but Dronne directed his driver, Private Krikor Pirlian, to swing onto rue de la Vistule and work his way through a maze of side streets that would lead them to the boulevard de l'Hopital and the River Seine. The column was quickly engulfed by crowds blocking their way. *"Les Américains!"* someone shouted. *"Ce sont des Français,"* an even more excited voiced called out. A heavyset girl scrambled onto Dronne's Jeep, breaking the windshield. Draping herself over the hood, she announced herself as Jeanne Borchet, an "authentic Alsatian" from Strasbourg. She wore a traditional outfit of the district, a red skirt and black bodice. A young man aboard a small motorcycle, an Armenian named Lorenian Dikran, said he knew the way to the Hôtel de Ville and would lead the column there. Dronne thought they might have looked like performers from a carnival, but they had become part of a deadly serious drama.

German sharpshooters fired at the column as it passed the Gare d'Austerlitz, but Dronne moved his men on quickly, not bothering to return the shots. The pont d'Austerlitz was unguarded and undamaged despite the orders to von Choltitz to blow the bridges of the Seine. Once across the river, the column dipped down onto the quais along the right bank, rolling first up the quai des Célestins and then into the quai de l'Hôtel de Ville. The clock in the tower of l'Hôtel de Ville showed 9:22 Central European time — Berlin time — when Dronne led his tanks into the square in front of the building.

Dronne realized the building was in the hands of the Resistance when FFI men on duty rushed to welcome him. There was cheering when he and Private Pirlian made their way up the main staircase and into the Grand Salon, brightly lit and filled with Resistance leaders. Georges Bidault threw his arms around Dronne and began a speech. Overcome by emotion, he was unable to finish it. Word quickly went out by telephone — miraculously, the phones were still working — that the first of de Gaulle's forces had arrived and that tomorrow the general, along with the rest of Leclerc's division, would be in Paris.

One after another, the churches of Paris began to ring their bells, with the great fourteen-ton bell of Notre Dame Cathedral the last to join the chorus. Pierre Crenesse, a reporter for the Resistance radio, intercepted Private Pirlian. "I have before me a French soldier, a brave homegrown guy," Crenesse proclaimed on air. "Where are you from?"

Pirlian, who was not French but was a veteran of Spanish battles, told him: "Constantinople (Istanbul)."[14]

Back at the main radio studio on rue de Grenelle, Pierre Schaeffer cut into the broadcast to add, "Parisians, rejoice! We have come on the air to tell you of the rescue of Paris!" All over the city, people threw open their windows and called out to their neighbours. Others rushed into the streets, banging pots and pans and singing "La Marseillaise." Anticipating the uproar, Schaeffer cautioned his listeners to take care: "All is not finished … close your windows … do not get yourself killed unnecessarily."

Dronne thought the fuss a tad annoying, He instructed one of his signallers to radio General Leclerc to confirm their arrival, and left l'Hôtel de Ville to go to the Préfecture de police. The prefect, Charles Luizet, asked him if there was anything he needed. "A bath," Dronne replied.[15]

✝

The seventeen thousand German troops taking orders from the Grösse Paris Kommandateur had not yet been told to abandon Paris. In a dining room on the first floor of the Hôtel Meurice, von Choltitz shared a solemn dinner that Thursday evening with two aides and two faithful secretaries. He had dressed carefully in his finest uniform, the food as usual was good, and there was wine with the meal. After dinner, he stood with his staff before the windows overlooking the rue de Rivoli, contemplating what would likely be their last night in Paris.[16] Suddenly, the pealing of church bells sounded clearly in the room.

"Herr General, what does that mean?" a secretary asked.

"It means the Allies are making their entry into Paris," von Choltitz answered.

He reached for the telephone and called General Hans Speidel at Army Group B headquarters in eastern France. Von Choltitz held the phone to an open window so that Speidel could hear the bells. "There is nothing left to do but say goodbye," von Choltitz told him. They rang off without any discussion of Hitler's orders to destroy Paris. On that subject, von Choltitz and his commanding officers had played their own deadly game, each vowing fealty to their orders, but none taking the fateful step to see to their execution. When von Choltitz finally went to bed long after midnight, the bridges of Paris were still intact.[17]

The village of Rambouillet slept quietly on this last night before the liberation of Paris. General de Gaulle had gone to bed early after calling for a doctor to treat a touch of laryngitis brought on by all the speeches he'd made. He was awakened around two o'clock by a tapping on his bedroom door. Captain Alfred Touya, back from a scouting mission to check on the advance of Leclerc's division, entered the room with several maps under his arm. He noticed an open copy of Adolphe Thiers's *History of the French Revolution* on the night table beside the bed. Laying out his maps, he showed de Gaulle the positions of Leclerc's columns and advised him of Captain Dronne's arrival at l'Hôtel de Ville. Paris would be freed in the morning, he said. Comfortable in his favoured white pyjamas, de Gaulle allowed himself a moment of quiet repose. "You see, Captain, we have succeeded," he finally replied. "Now go and rest."[18]

IV

Days of Liberation: The Stakes Are Raised

Once more France rises, proud and ardent before her
destiny, ready to resume her mission, ready to make her
voice heard, the voice of a great and independent nation.

    — Poster of the Paris Liberation Committee
    August 1944

CHAPTER 14
Paris Liberated

Paris, the capital of worldly wisdom, used to everything, astonished by nothing, neither by disastrous failure, dazzling success, excessive abundance nor extreme privation; Paris which understands and loves life and knows that death is inevitable; Paris used to tempests and to the ashes from which it knows it will surely rise again.

— Alice Jahier
France Remembered, 1944

While Paris slept uneasily, forward units of General Jacques Leclerc's 2nd Armoured Division spent the night probing the outer ring of the German defences. Warnings had come from the Resistance of enemy troop concentrations, some supported by panzer units, at key locations: the École Militaire near the Eiffel Tower; the Palais Bourbon, home of the National Assembly, overlooking the Seine; the

Ministry of Foreign Affairs; Les Invalides; the Luxembourg Gardens (pre-war meeting place of the French Senate and now Luftwaffe headquarters); and the Prince Eugène barracks at the Place de la République. The fact Captain Dronne had been able to skirt these danger zones on his way to l'Hôtel de Ville did not mean the Germans would not fight ferociously to hold their ground. Shortly after midnight, a detachment of Colonel de Langlade's column that had secured the pont de Sevres stealthily made its way across the bridge. Once on the right bank of the Seine, a regiment moved cautiously down the avenue de Bellevue. It was pitch-dark. The battle of Paris was at hand.

As Commandant Jacques Massu led his men forward, they could hear sounds of Germans soldiers advancing toward them. A Moroccan infantryman caught sight of a large artillery piece pulled by a half-track — an armoured vehicle with wheels at the front and caterpillar tracks at the rear. When he cried out in alarm, German machine guns set up along the side of the road began firing aimlessly in the dark. During the next half hour, bitter hand-to-hand fighting punctuated by grenade blasts shattered the night calm. The half-track blew up when a grenade exploded its gas tank.[1] Massu, a veteran of the African campaigns who had commanded a colonial unit in the Tibesti Mountains of Chad, remembered the flames lighting up the area enough to allow the French troops to "adjust their fire and not kill each other." The hurried tossing of grenades down a staircase that connected the avenue with a lower street turned back a fresh attack. The Germans abandoned three armoured cars and three guns before retreating. Massu's men estimated they'd killed forty to fifty Germans and taken prisoner a dozen wounded. For the rest of the night, French patrols fanned out from the site of the battle, alert to any return of the enemy.[2]

At dawn on that never-to-be-forgotten Friday, August 25, Commandant Massu reassembled his men and began a march that would take them to the Place de l'Étoile by half past nine. On the way, they laid siege to the Hôtel Majestic, a secondary German headquaters located just off the Étoile. Massu, a brawler of a man almost as tall as de Gaulle, but much heavier, swept into a room filled with German officers. When he shouted "Heraus! Heraus!" (Out! Out!), the startled officers threw their hands into the air and surrendered. After securing the Majestic, Massu and his men raced to the Arc de Triomphe, where they paused to tear down the Nazi banner and run up the Tricolour. As Massu bowed his head in tribute to the Unknown Soldier buried at the Étoile,* a shell from a German tank in the Place de la Concorde whistled through the arch and fell on bare paving stones. Fortunately, there were no injuries. Massu's detachment next stormed down the Champs Élysées toward the Place de la Concorde where some of the fiercest fighting of the liberation was to take place.

Fighting French columns had streamed into Paris from early morning, welcomed by delirious citizens up at dawn to celebrate their liberation. The mist had lifted to reveal a sunny day. At six o'clock, Simone de Beauvoir ran along the boulevard Raspail to see "the Leclerc division parade on the avenue d'Orléans** and along the sidewalks, an immense crowd applauded … From time to time, a shot was fired; a sniper on the roofs, someone fell, was carried off, but no one seemed upset; enthusiasm stamped out fear."[3] On every route taken by the 2nd Division, people flooded into the streets with offerings of wine and food, while women covered the faces of the soldiers with so much lipstick some looked as if they had been bloodied. Church bells pealed continuously. Those of Leclerc's men who had never been in Paris — especially black colonial soldiers — felt themselves in a dream world, receiving offerings beyond anything they'd ever imagined. Many who had family in the city handed down notes from their tanks to people in the crowd asking them to phone their relatives to announce their return.

It was four years to the day since General Leclerc had joined the Free French in the Cameroon, and he began this day by following Colonel Billotte's column through the Porte de Gentilly at 7:45. Immaculate in an American-type uniform topped by a French kepi, Leclerc moved on to Gare Montparnasse where he established his headquarters. Colonel Billotte was on the Île de la Cité at 8:30, receiving the congratulations of policemen defending the Préfecture. Colonel Louis Dio's men had moved through the adjacent Porte d'Orléans and split into two groups, one headed for Les Invalides and the other for the Palais Bourbon and the Quai d'Orsay. The main body of Colonel de Langlade's column began

* Now Place Charles de Gaulle
** Now Avenue du Général Leclerc.

the day by taking the big Renault factory before entering through Porte de Saint-Cloud and making for the Étoile. The U.S. 4th Infantry Division, meanwhile, had come in through the Porte d'Italie opening that Dronne had used the night before. The American regiments turned eastward at the Place de la Bastille and made their way along the longest street in Paris, the avenue Daumesnil, leading to the Bois de Vincennes at the eastern edge of the city. Once there, they would regroup for the final push through eastern France toward the Rhine River.

Amid fighting between regiments of the 2nd Armoured Division and German defenders, random firing from rooftops and windows was killing French and Germans alike. Volunteers, mostly young and mostly men, who had joined FFI units, were picking off German troops from upper-floor windows. Wearing homemade Cross of Lorraine armbands, they used any weapon they could lay their hands on — First World War rifles, hunting guns, pistols, or weapons taken from captured Germans. At many points, German snipers killed civilians as they rushed to the aid of wounded Resistance members. Red Cross nurses ran to rescue the victims. In the Place de la Concorde, German troops lined up six young men and one woman against a wall and shot them. Other Germans fired aimlessly into any window flying a French flag. When the FFI surrounded the Prince Eugène barracks to prevent its twelve hundred German troops from breaking out, a steady barrage of shots from inside kept the Resistance at bay. Germans who tried to escape the barracks through the subway tunnels under the Place de la République found themselves trapped in bitter fighting, with exploding grenades and the flash of rifle fire the only light in the dark passageways. Germans who were taken prisoner were marched off, grim-faced and sullen, their hands on their heads, to be confined in buildings under control of the FFI.

On the streets, Parisians began to parade known collaborators who had been rousted from their homes. In a scene repeated throughout Paris, four women accused of having consorted with Germans — *collaboration horizontale* — were marched down boulevard Saint-Michel, their heads sheared "as bald as babies." The crowd jeered. "That woman," a bystander said pointing to one who glared defiantly at the crowd, "had a husband in Germany as a prisoner. He escaped and returned to her, but she betrayed him and he was shot."[4]

The barricades that had been hastily thrown up to block German tanks had by now become barriers to the liberating forces. At an intersection near the Trocadero, Claire Fauteux came upon a crowd busily demolishing a barricade to allow troops to move along rue Jean de la Fontaine. The Canadian painter, who had been stranded in Paris four years earlier, had endured a German prison camp and for the past two years had lived under Gestapo surveillance. She had spent the morning dodging bullets and crouching behind sandbags as she joined in the joyous welcome to the Fighting French. Her happiness helped blot out bitter memories of Nazi brutalities she'd witnessed since being put on a prison train that took her to Besançon in eastern France. She would not forget seeing the mother of a newborn baby who died after being dragged from her bed, or the Englishwoman beaten and kicked for stepping off the train before its departure from the Gare de l'Est. Her thoughts were diverted by the arrival of a Sherman tank that spurred the work of demolition. When Fauteux climbed up to shake the hand of the young French soldier who had poked his head out of its turret, she warned him about the snipers. "Do be careful," she said, "They are firing from the rooftops."[5] Some were Germans, others were members of the dreaded Milice, pro-German traitors doing the work of the Nazis. As the soldier lifted himself from the tank, Fauteux heard two shots and saw him stagger and fall over the side, blood pouring from his mouth. He died at her feet.

At Place Denfert-Rochereau, where Simone de Beauvoir had run to catch a glimpse of General Leclerc, Elisabeth de Miribel paused in her little sports car when Leclerc's column halted before a barricade at the Lion de Belfort, the huge statue dominating the square. *Résistants* had torn up the pavement to build the barricade, but Leclerc's tank rolled easily over the stones. Soldiers cried with joy as they were showered with kisses and flowers. While de Miribel waited for the rubble to be removed so she could drive on, a tall, beautiful woman approached her. "What can I do for you?" she asked. Elisabeth de Miribel gave her the phone number of her parents and asked her to let them know she had arrived safely in Paris. Later, she took lunch with a Resistance cell on rue Schoelcher before heading for Gare Montparnasse, where General Leclerc would await the arrival of General de Gaulle. The hundred-year-old, low, grey building, with its slanting wooden floors, unswept and dirty, held silent echoes of the footsteps of thousands of travellers who had trod its boards. She noticed that a wooden table and a few chairs had been set out on the departure platform in preparation for a momentous ceremony later in the day.[6]

Before that could happen, General von Choltitz would have to be induced to surrender without carrying out Hitler's orders to destroy the city. And the surrender had to be taken by the Fighting French, in order to fulfill General de Gaulle's orders that the Communist-led uprising be given no opportunity to take credit for freeing the city. General Von Choltitz, his monocle firmly in place, took his last meal in the Hôtel Meurice at noon, having rejected a demand from Colonel Billotte — conveyed through Consul General Nordling — that he lay down his arms.

"I don't accept ultimatums," he stuffily replied.[7]

While he ate, his orderly packed a suitcase of clothing for him, and after lunch von Chotitz told his officers to prepare for surrender, but only to Fighting French or U.S. soldiers, not to the Resistance. He had issued no order to destroy any buildings, bridges, or other landmarks.[8] Von Choltiz could clearly hear the fighting going on around the rue de Rivoli and Place de la Concorde, where a squadron of Billotte's tanks was engaged in battle with German defenders. One tank, the *Mort-Homme*, burned to bits on the rue Royale, and a second, the *Douaumont*, was abandoned in the Place de la Concorde, its dead left inside it.

The first soldiers of the 2nd Armoured Division reached the Hôtel Meurice around two o'clock. Lieutenant Henri Karcher, anxious to reconnect with his Parisian family, rushed the front door of the hotel with three of his men. Smashing it open, Karcher spotted a huge picture of Adolf Hitler hanging in the lobby. He turned his machine gun on it, ducked behind the reception desk, and threw a phosphorous grenade in the direction of an old German soldier firing at them from behind a pile of sandbags. Karcher saw the old man's helmet clatter to the floor as the German fell dead. A second Frenchman, Private Walter Herreman, aimed his flamethrower at the elevator cage.

As the lobby filled with smoke and flames, the remaining Germans threw their hands into the air. Karcher bounded up the stairs to the first floor where he confronted a German who quickly surrendered and agreed to take him to von Choltitz. Opening the door to where the general sat, Karcher saluted and announced: "Lieutenant Henri Karcher of the Army of General de Gaulle." He asked von Chotitz if he was ready to surrender. The German said he was.

More French soldiers were pouring into the room. One of them, Major Jean de la Horie, escorted von Choltitz to a waiting armoured car and stuffed him inside, barely escaping a mob of civilians screaming *"Le général boche, le général boche, tuez-le!"* (kill him). An FFI man knocked von Choltitz's valise from the hands of his orderly and as it fell open, people grabbed at the general's uniform that had dropped on the road.

Back in the Meurice, Karcher picked up a telephone, asked for Auteuil 04.21, and spoke to his stepfather, a retired general who did not think highly of de Gaulle. Karcher told him he had "just captured a German general, his staff, and his flag."[9]

It was shortly after three o'clock when Major de la Horie, with an escort of foot soldiers and an armoured car, delivered General von Choltitz to the Préfecture de police on Île de la Cité. Colonel Billotte and twenty policemen took von Choltitz through the courtyard and into the building. General Leclerc was waiting for the German in the billiard room, with sets of the surrender paper, typewritten and reproduced on a Gestetner machine, laid out on the table. With Leclerc was de Gaulle's military designate to the Resistance, General Chaban-Delmas. The préfect de police, Charles Luizet, and the commander of the U.S. 4th Infantry Division, Major General Raymond Barton, stood close by.

The surrender document was in the name of the Provisional Government of the French Republic and it consisted of six clauses. The German command was to order that all its units cease fire and fly a white flag, with arms to be collected and troops mustered in the open. No sooner had Leclerc and von Choltitz exchanged the formalities demanded by their positions, though, than Colonel Rol-Tanguy burst into the room with his deputy, Maurice Kriegel-Valrimont. Rol was furious that he had not been invited to the ceremony. There was no mention of the FFI in the surrender document and it failed to provide a place for Rol-Tanguy's signature. He argued volubly with Leclerc while von Choltitz, listening with his imperfect French, must have wondered what the dispute was about. General Barton, not wishing to be part of a French political argument, left the room. It was only after Charles Luizet argued in favour of Rol-Tanguy being allowed to sign the surrender that Leclerc gave in. With a German officer acting as interpreter, everyone around the table began a clause by clause review of the document. Von Choltitz asked for one minor change. It was made, and the surrender was duly signed.

Leclerc ordered that teams of French and German officers drive together throughout the city and make the surrender known to the public. He led the German general out of the Préfecture and into an armoured car for the drive to Gare Montparnasse, where they were to await General de Gaulle. Proceeding down boulevard Saint-Michel and along boulevard Montparnasse, Leclerc stood while von Choltiz sat behind. Rol-Tanguy's Communist deputy, Kriegel-Valrimont, drove the car.

The crowds cheered Leclerc and directed insults at von Choltitz. Arriving at Gare Montparnasse, von Choltitz clutched his chest. The stress of surrendering Paris may have brought on a heart attack. He was taken to the baggage master's office where he extracted a pill from his pocket and downed it with a drink of water. For a moment it was feared he had poisoned himself, but this was not the case. After resting, he asked for a sheet of paper. On it, General von Choltitz wrote out the cease-fire order: "Resistance in the military district and defense points is immediately to be stopped."[10]

Charles de Gaulle spent most of Friday as he had the day before, pacing the flagstone terrace of Château Rambouillet while receiving reports on the progress of the 2nd Armoured Division. He had put on a plain khaki uniform, adorned only with the insignia of the Cross of Lorraine and a patch that bore the symbol of FFI ground forces, a red sword between two blue wings. De Gaulle's mind was on the plans he had made for his return to the capital. All that he did, he had decided, would be aimed at fusing "all minds into a single national purpose" — and to demonstrate that "the authority of the state" was once more on display in France.[11] At about three o'clock, came the signal to move. The motorcade of three black sedans escorted by two Jeeps armed with machine guns swept out of the village and headed east, picking up Route national 20 as it neared Paris. De Gaulle and General Juin rode in the back seat of an open, black Hotchkiss. De Gaulle was ecstatic at the thought of returning to his beloved Paris. He felt both "gripped by emotion and filled with serenity."

By the time the convoy reached Longjumeau, a market town less than twenty kilometres south of Paris, cheering crowds formed a "jubilant tide," until, on reaching Porte d'Orleans, the mob became almost impassable. Instead of proceeding to l'Hôtel de Ville as the crowd had expected, de Gaulle branched onto an almost deserted avenue du Maine. He reached Gare Montparnasse shortly before four o'clock; there he was taken directly to Platform No. 3. General Leclerc, his red kepi tilted to one side and his uniform now sweat-stained and dusty, was the first to welcome him. De Gaulle hugged his old friend, delighted that Leclerc's troops had "brought off a complete victory without the city's suffering the demolitions or the population the losses that had been feared."[12] De Gaulle reacted with surprise as he was introduced to his military delegate, General Chaban-Delmas. The man was so young! "Well, I'll be damned," de Gaulle was heard to mutter. Next in line was the Communist, Colonel Rol-Tanguy. De Gaulle congratulated him for having "driven the enemy from our streets, decimated and demoralized."[13] Rol-Tanguy must have cursed silently to himself; the presence of the general meant there would be no new Paris Commune, after all.

Standing off to one side, the American, General Barton, was content to leave the spotlight to his French comrades. When de Gaulle took his seat, spectacles on his nose, he read the surrender document on which the ink had barely had time to dry. He stiffened when he saw Colonel Rol-Tanguy's signature on the paper, an indication that the Germans had surrendered to the Resistance as well as to the Provisional Government. "That is not exactly true," he told Leclerc. "You were the highest ranking officer, therefore the only person responsible."[14] Then de Gaulle read out the proclamation that had been issued that morning on behalf of "the French nation." He told

Leclerc he had no business allowing the Resistance to be a party to the surrender. Leclerc apologized for his error, and the two embraced again.

De Gaulle's next embrace was for his son, Philippe, who was present as an ensign in the 2nd Armoured Regiment of Naval Rifles. He kissed Philippe on both cheeks and wished him well as he sent him off with a German major to take the surrender of troops at the Palais-Bourbon.

The ceremony at Gare Montparnsse completed, de Gaulle returned to his car and made for his next point of call, the War Ministry on rue Saint-Dominique. As the four-car convoy rolled north, a burst of fire from nearby houses caused everyone in the cars but de Gaulle to duck for cover. The convoy veered off boulevard des Invalides and onto rue Vaneau and rue de Borgogne for the run to the War Ministry at 14 rue Saint-Dominique. Its long, low stoneworks loomed up before de Gaulle, giving, as it always had, the appearance of a structure formidable and dark. A unit of the Garde Républicaine waited in the courtyard to present arms. When de Gaulle reached his old office, he found everything just as it had been when he left on the night of June 10, 1940. "Not a piece of furniture, not a rug, not a curtain had been disturbed."[15] He had brief meetings with Charles Luizit, the prefect of police, and Alexandre Parodi, his delegate-general. Law and order and food supplies were of utmost priority, and it was on those matters that their brief discussions centred.

De Gaulle was urged to move onto l'Hôtel de Ville where leaders of the FFI and the Committee of National Resistance were awaiting him. "Let them wait," he declared. He had no intention of elevating the Resistance to the level of government. Instead, he would stop next at the Préfecture de police in order to demonstrate his appreciation for the support of the police. At seven o'clock, de Gaulle stood in the courtyard of the Préfecture, where he received the adulation of the assembled officers "now trembling with joy and pride." It was clear to de Gaulle that the police had at last "revenged themselves for a long humiliation." From the Préfecture, de Gaulle went on foot to l'Hôtel de Ville, pressing through the crowd along avenue Victoria to the square in front of the city hall. Another guard of honour, this time made up of FFI irregulars, many with tears in their eyes, saluted his entrance.[16]

A tumultuous roar filled the building as de Gaulle made his way to the foot of the grand staircase leading to the great salon on the first floor.

Waiting for him were Georges Bidault, president of the CNR, André Tollet, head of the Paris Liberation Committee, and Marcel Flouret, prefect of the Seine. As the crowd clustered around, de Gaulle felt surrounded by "combatants of the same battle, an incomparable link ... the excitement of the dangers risked and the cataclysms survived." Climbing the stairs to the great hall, he made a point of asking Flouret, "How is the purge coming along? The whole business must be finished within a few weeks."[17] He was signalling that collaborators must be dealt with speedily.

Once in the hall, the crowd surged around de Gaulle as cameras flashed and everyone began talking at once. Georges Bidault called the crowd to quiet and began to speak. "Here is the man who we have been waiting for four years ... it is splendid!" De Gaulle had not prepared a speech and he had no podium from which to address the throng. Had we been there to witness the momentous occasion, we would have seen a man towering over those who stood around him, calm and even aloof, surveying all about him with cool detachment. Bareheaded, driven by a determination summoned up from the struggle that had consumed his every moment for the past four years, his gesturing hands kept time with his words as he spoke:

> Let us not conceal the emotion we all feel, both men and women, who are now here and at home in a Paris that has been roused to liberate itself and has done so of its own volition. Paris! Paris outraged! Paris broken! Paris martyred! But Paris liberated! Liberated by itself, liberated by its people with the help of the French armies, with the support and the help of all France, of the France that fights, of the only France, of the real France, of the eternal France!
>
> Since the enemy which held Paris has capitulated into our hands, France returns to Paris, to her home. She returns bloody, but quite resolute. She returns there enlightened by the immense lesson, but more certain than ever of her duties and of her rights.
>
> I speak of her duties first, and I will sum them all up by saying that for now it is a matter of the duties of war.

The enemy is staggering, but he is not beaten yet. He remains on our soil.

It will not even be enough that we have, with the help of our dear and admirable Allies, chased him from our home for us to consider ourselves satisfied after what had happened. We want to enter his territory as is fitting, as victors.

This is why the French vanguard has entered Paris with guns blazing. This is why the great French army from Italy had landed in the south and is advancing rapidly up the Rhone valley. This is why our brave and dear forces of the interior are going to arm themselves with modern weapons. It is for this revenge, this vengeance and justice, that we will keep fighting until the last day, until the day of total and complete victory.

There was more, but the crowd was already entranced by the lyrical phrases that had enveloped the room. The task done, as film of the occasion would show, de Gaulle gulped nervously, inhaling deeply. Cries of "*Vive de Gaulle*" and "*Vive la France*" followed him as he strode into the office of the prefect.

Now would be the time, Georges Bidault thought, for de Gaulle to "proclaim the Republic before the people who have gathered here."[18] De Gaulle refused; the Republic had never ceased to exist — despite the actions of Vichy, now null and void — and as he was president of the government of the Republic, there was no need to proclaim it. Instead, de Gaulle stepped onto a small balcony outside the prefect's office. To the horror of those behind him, he leaned over the low railing to wave to the mass of people assembled below, oblivious to the danger of falling. A terrified Bidault grabbed de Gaulle by his belt and stiffened himself to hold on. In a moment, de Gaulle stepped back, smiling.

The echoes of another singing of "La Marseillaise" followed de Gaulle from l'Hôtel de Ville. Returning to the War Ministry, he found that Commandant de Lignières had done his work well. His only instructions had been: "De Gaulle will sleep tonight at the Ministry ... prepare a dinner for fifty people." It was by chance that de Lignières had been told of a master chef who was out of work. Summoned, the man shamefacedly admitted he had been in the service of the Vichy government and had been sent to Paris to wait for Marshall Pétain's return. He was pleased to serve the Provisional Government and with the supply of a dozen chickens, the menu that night featured coq au vin and foie gras, with vegetables, American rations, and French wine. The City of Light with its "symbols of our glories" that had meant so much to Charles de Gaulle as a young man was free now, and the soldier had come home.

CHAPTER 15
Paris Exultant

The celebration that was Paris went on long into the night of the city's liberation. Prized bottles of champagne hidden in secret places were brought out to be uncorked. Restaurants threw open their doors and poured free drinks for their liberators. Some cinemas resumed showings — the electricity supply, if not the food chain, was working efficiently — and hotel managers scurried to dispose of German signs and placemats imprinted with the swastika. In the rue de la Huchette, the FFI's discovery of a black-market cache of butter, tinned meat, and sugar made for sumptuous feasts at Resistance tables.[1] Paris Radio featured reports from exultant throngs on the streets, interspersed with repeated playing of "La Marseillaise."

Soldiers with families in Paris enjoyed happy homecomings, as did Elisabeth de Miribel when she chose to pass up de Gaulle's appearance at l'Hôtel de Ville in favour of "the joy of reunion" with her parents.[2] Lieutenant Henri Karcher was headed home too, but first he enjoyed the finest dinner the Hôtel Meurice could offer, a present for not "having caused too much damage" while capturing General von Choltitz.[3]

American correspondent Larry Lesueur of CBS haunted the French radio offices on rue de Grenelle until he was allowed to use its transmitter for the first broadcast to the outside world. Amorous company was abundant and free for French and American soldiers alike, whether in French homes, in hotel rooms, or in the U.S. 4th Division encampment in the Bois de Vincennes where at dawn, a tired GI and a sleepy-eyed girl could be seen emerging from almost every pup tent.

Ernest Hemingway had entered Paris with a collection of Maquis guerrillas who constituted a virtual private army. On a battered portable typewriter, he wrote of how "I had a funny choke in my throat and I had to clean my glasses because there now, below us, grey and always beautiful, was spread the city I love best in all the world."[4] Hemingway rushed to the apartment of Sylvia Beach at 12 rue de l'Odéon and, while his Maquis companions ousted a German sympathizer from an upper floor, he poured whisky for the woman who had befriended him at her Shakespeare and Company bookstore in the 1920s. Hemingway celebrated that night at the Ritz Hotel on Place Vendome, where he dined with eight American army officers on "food fit for the Gods." The group included the U.S. Army historian colonel S.L.A. Marshall, who had met up with Hemingway in Rambouillet. They all autographed a paper on which was written, "We think we took Paris." Hemingway's gang refused to pay the Vichy tax the waiter tried to collect, preferring instead to tip him $100.

Pablo Picasso, a privileged neutral due to his Spanish citizenship, was stunned when he opened his door on rue des Grands Augustines that day to find the beautiful Lee Miller, who had once posed for the great painter and was now a war correspondent for *Vogue* magazine, smiling broadly at him. Come evening, joined by Picasso's ex-lover Dora Maar, a surrealist photographer, they went around the corner and dined on a skinny roast chicken at a neighbourhood bistro. Among Picasso's callers the next day was his old friend Ernest Hemingway.[5]

On streets such as the Champs-Élysées and the boulevard Saint-Germain, the sweet smell of perfume worn by fashionably dressed women made it seem as if the Parisian penchant for elegance and chic had been little dulled by the German Occupation. Jean-Paul Sartre wrote of those who had this impression. "Upon arriving in Paris, many Englishmen and

Americans were surprised that we were not as thin as they had expected. They saw women wearing elegant dresses that appeared new and men in jackets that, from afar, still looked good." But it was all an illusion, Sartre insisted: "... they rarely encountered that facial pallor, that psychological misery that is usually proof of starvation." He pondered whether these foreign arrivals might have "wondered in the depth of their heart if the Occupation had been quite so terrible after all and if France shouldn't consider the defeat as a lucky break that would allow her to regain its place as a great power without having deserved it...."[6]

The French themselves had to be assured they had waged a virtuous war. At the War Ministry on the night of liberation, Charles de Gaulle was taking the first steps to implant this conviction in the national psyche. The battle lines of the political game were already being drawn, but de Gaulle was encouraged by what François Mauriac, the celebrated author and member of the Académie française, had written that day in the first edition of *Le Figaro* to be printed in Paris since June 1940. Mauriac recalled how Frenchmen had huddled in their cellars, their ears glued to their radios for the voice of Charles de Gaulle "while the steps of the German officer shook the ceiling overhead." It was de Gaulle who kept alive the French spirit "during those bitter winter nights." It didn't matter that he had been "slandered by a valet press" or sentenced to death by the Vichy regime. "At the peak of the Nazi triumph, everything that we see coming true today was announced by that prophetic voice..."[7]

For the moment, de Gaulle had to deal with more mundane matters. He gave Major Robert J. Levy, newly assigned as his American army liaison in Paris, the task of rounding up a supply of cigarettes, C rations, and Coleman lanterns that would keep the War Ministry functioning. Then he called in General Leclerc to receive his account of military operations in Paris. Leclerc estimated German dead in the day's fighting at around two thousand, with fifteen thousand Germans having been taken prisoner. The 2nd Armoured Division had lost more than six hundred officers and men in the fighting. Part of the German 47th Division had entrenched itself around

Le Bourget airport, eleven kilometres northeast of the city. Small units of German troops were attempting to work their way back into the Paris suburbs. General Gerow, the American commander under whose orders the 2nd Division was operating, had told Leclerc to repulse those forays.[8]

De Gaulle recognized the danger the Germans still posed, but he was determined to give Leclerc's force a different task. He wanted the 2nd Armoured Division as part of a daring — and dangerous — procession down the Champs Éysées from the Arch de Triomphe to Notre Dame Cathedral on Saturday afternoon. It would mark de Gaulle's "official entry" into Paris. Already, the radio was alerting Parisians to the event and de Gaulle hoped for a turnout of a million people. Printing presses were ordered to run through the night to turn out thousands of banners reading VIVE DE GAULLE. The presence of Leclerc's Deuxième Division Blindée in the parade would demonstrate the strength of the French armed forces, as well as provide security against any possible disturbance by the Milice or by any remaining Germans. As for the Germans at Le Bourget, Leclerc said he would send a tactical group to watch over them.

The streets leading into central Paris, the scene the day before of tumultuous celebrations, were quieter but no less crowded Saturday morning. From all parts of a city where no Metro trains were yet running, people came on foot to see Charles de Gaulle fulfill his "rendezvous with the people."[9] Around ten o'clock, de Gaulle was going over a checklist for the parade when General Leclerc brought him a worried visitor. It was Major Levy, his American liaison, who nervously presented an ultimatum General Gerow had sent to Leclerc. "Your command will not participate in any parade this afternoon," Gerow had declared in his note to Leclerc. To do so would be taken as a "formal breach of military discipline."[10] The note was one more irritant to the troubled American-French relationship.

De Gaulle looked at Major Levy with a mixture of sadness and contempt. "Naturally, I ignored this advice," he would write in his *Mémoires de guerre.*[11]

The crowds that had assembled along the Champs Éysées were ten and more deep when Charles de Gaulle appeared, shortly before three o'clock, at the tomb of France's Unknown Soldier. He laid a wreath of red gladiolas in the shape of a Cross of Lorraine on its stone slab, and, with bowed head, relit its eternal flame that had been smothered in 1940. He turned back to look down the long, descending avenue as the crowd roared its approval. De Gaulle knew he was making an enormous wager against the possibility that an assassin might show his hand. He was well aware that an enemy air raid would cause disastrous loss of life. Neither danger would deter him. A police car drove ahead to broadcast a reassuring message: "General de Gaulle entrusts his safety to the people of Paris. He asks them to see to the maintenance of order themselves and to help the police and the FFI in this duty, they being worn out with five days of fighting."[12]

Behind de Gaulle were lined up, row by row, the leading figures of Fighting France and the Resistance — generals Juin, Koenig, and Chaban-Delmas, Georges Bidault of the CNR, Alexandre Parodi, Admiral d'Argenlieu, and many others who had played a critical part in the events that had shaped this day. The Communist leaders, Colonel Rol-Tanguy and Maurice Kriegel-Valrimont, marched with General Juin, whose discomfort betrayed his uncertainty at having to walk beside these non-uniformed soldiers. Off to one side cavorted a gangly young man, cigarette in his mouth, who responded eagerly when de Gaulle motioned him to come forward: "There is no smoking during a procession," de Gaulle told him.[13]

At 3:18 p.m., the procession began with four tanks in the lead. It was not merely a wave that rolled down the Champs Éysées, but "rather the sea!" De Gaulle led it all the way, the soldiers of the 2nd Armoured Division marching proudly in his wake. Once, when Georges Bidault breasted him, de Gaulle calmly told him, "Monsieur, step back please." De Gaulle would remember this march for its "inexpressible exultation of the crowd." A "storm of voices" echoed his name, and as he advanced, "raising and lowering my arms to reply to the acclamations," de Gaulle tried to look every person in the eye. He was used to setting impossible tasks for himself! He thought perhaps two million people were along the route, "clinging to ladders, flagpoles, lampposts ... nothing but this living tide of humanity in the sunshine, beneath the Tricolour.... But that afternoon, I believed in the fortune of France."[14]

Leaving behind the chestnut trees of the great avenue, the procession reached the Place de la Concorde, and it was here that the spell was briefly broken. Shots rang out and most of the marchers dove for cover. Not de

Gaulle; hardly breaking his stride, he crossed the square and got into an open car to be driven to Notre Dame Cathedral. Safely across the bridge onto Île de la Cité, he headed into Notre Dame on foot when yet more shots were heard, this time coming from the towers of the cathedral.

Robert Reid, a BBC reporter who was taping the event, gave a dramatic description of the incident. "He went straight ahead without hesitation," Reid said of de Gaulle, "his shoulders flung back ... right down the centre aisle, even while the bullets were pouring around him." Shooting and shouting is clearly heard on Reid's recording. "It was the most extraordinary example of courage I have ever seen," Reid added.[15]

Several people — perhaps as many as one hundred — were wounded before four men in grey-flannel trousers were rousted from their hiding place. Some thought they looked like Germans, but there is no record of what became of them. De Gaulle says in his memoirs, "Despite all efforts to find out who was responsible, no one was arrested." It was his personal view that Communists were behind the disorder. He thought it their purpose not to kill him but to create a bogus need for "the maintenance of a revolutionary power" — meaning a Communist-controlled, armed Resistance that would have put itself in charge of the police and justice.[16]

By now, de Gaulle had calmly moved to his place of honour at the left of the transept. The archpriest, Monsignor Brot, went to de Gaulle to offer greetings from the archbishop of Paris, Cardinal Suhard, and also to present the cardinal's protest at having been told he was not welcome at the ceremony. The cardinal had seen fit to officiate at Marshall Pétain's final visit to Paris, an act that in de Gaulle's view made him unacceptable for today's ceremony.

General Koenig, disturbed at the continuing chatter of the crowd, rose and shouted, "Have you no pride? Stand up!"[17]

The music of *The Magnifcat* rose to quell the commotion in the seats, but at its conclusion the priest chose to abbreviate the ceremony. Everyone left Notre Dame without further incident. De Gaulle biographer Jean Lacouture would later write of the risk the general had taken that day: "The enormous wager had been accepted." De Gaulle stood unchallenged as the inheritor of the spirit of France.

That night, while de Gaulle worked on his papers in his office at the War Ministry, the sounds of war returned to Paris. A Luftwaffe flight soared over the city and bombed vital railway targets. The raid cut off the power to the Ministry and de Gaulle continued his work by the light of one of Major Levy's Coleman lamps. A survey of the damage the next day found that about five hundred houses had been destroyed and nearly one thousand people killed. When all the French losses from a week of uprising and the liberation itself were totalled up, it was found that 901 FFI and 582 civilians had been killed, against 2,788 Germans.*[18]

The destruction from the air raid was multiplied a thousand times, de Gaulle knew, by the devastation wrought in the two invasions that had brought Allied armies into Normandy and the south of France. Transport was at a standstill, food production had fallen almost to zero, and assembly lines in the factories were silent. When General Eisenhower arrived on Sunday for his first visit to Paris, the need for immediate shipments of food and other supplies was uppermost in de Gaulle's mind.

"I went to call on General de Gaulle promptly, and I did this very deliberately as a kind of de facto recognition of him as the provisional President of France," Eisenhower would write in *Crusade in Europe.* He found de Gaulle a grateful but worried man. He asked for "thousands of uniforms," as he intended to incorporate FFI and Maquis fighters into the regular French army. Eisenhower said he also asked — although de Gaulle denies this — for an American division to ensure order in the city.

Eisenhower's main interest was the pursuit of the Germans across France, and after reviewing a parade of American soldiers, he left to resume his battle command. Much heavy fighting remained to be done. The French 1st Army, its way often cleared by Maquis units who had subdued the Germans in large chunks of territory, moved northward steadily in company with the American 6th Corps. General Patton's forces, joined by Leclerc's 2nd Armoured Division, pushed east of Paris, and in the north, British and Canadian troops under General Montgomery cleared one Channel port after another in their drive toward Belgium and Holland. The narrow strip of France's Atlantic coast remained in German hands. Bordeaux, cut off from the newly liberated areas, became

---

* Plaques commemorating the deaths of FFI fighters and civilians have been erected at 1,200 sites throughout Paris.

the scene of frantic Communist activity where plans were being hatched to set up a "soviet of the South of France."

✝

The showdown with the Resistance came on August 28. "The iron was hot, I struck," de Gaulle would remember.[19] He summoned leaders of the Committee of National Resistance and the Paris Liberation Committee to the War Ministry, or *the centre*, as he thought of it. He warmly congratulated each of his visitors, jovially commenting on the Restistance practice of assigning military rank to its leaders. "There are a lot of colonels here!" He asked each man what his job had been. When he heard one had been a steel worker, another a teacher, he told both it was time for them to go back to their jobs. Then he read a decree abolishing the Resistance organizations. Public order would be maintained by the police and the *gendarmerie* and the Ministry of War would take direct charge of the FFI. Those who wished would be enrolled in General Billotte's 10th Infantry Division, henceforth known as the "Paris division," but others were to surrender their weapons. There was no longer any need for the Resistance. There were protests, both at the meeting and later in public, but there was no serious challenge to de Gaulle's dictates. Maurice Thorez, the French Communist Party leader, was still in Moscow, but he sent instructions to accept the general's edict. Thorez was acting, apparently, on orders of Marshall Stalin, who worried that French fear of a Communist takeover might rouse the Western Allies into a conflict with the Soviet Union.[20]

The Provisional Government would need a Cabinet, and de Gaulle would be its head, serving as president of the council — in effect, prime minister. He worked for a week putting names on a list and designating their duties, sometimes shifting one or dropping another. Those who had served in the Provisional Government in Algiers were called to Paris and the new Cabinet of twenty-one was presented to the public on September 9, the day of its first meeting at the Hôtel Matignon. De Gaulle's two most prominent choices were Georges Bidault, whom he made foreign minister, and Jules Jeanneney, the former president of the Senate, given the task as minister of state for reform of the government structure. General Catroux, loyal to de Gaulle from the beginning, was also named a minister of state. Bidault's appointment paid due respect to the Resistance, which received eight postings, but de Gaulle was careful to put the former CNR president into an area where he intended to be the main player. Recognizing the need for diversity, de Gaulle took two Communists into his Cabinet and rewarded Socialists and Radicals with several positions. Resistance hero Henri Frenay became minister of prisoners, deportees, and refugees. He was facing an enormous task, with a million French soldiers still in German prison camps and untold numbers of refugees living on the streets of French cities.

Three days later, at a rally of eight thousand people in the Palais de Chaillot, de Gaulle set forth the policies his government would follow. "We are at war!" he reminded his listeners. "In today's battle as in those to come, we intend to participate to the fullest extent." The French army was to go into Germany, and it would take part in the occupation of enemy territory. As for the postwar era, "We believe any determination of the political, economic, and moral conditions of the earth's inhabitants after the conflict to be a foolhardy one if that determination is reached without France." After all, one hundred million loyal men "live under our flag and any large-scale human edifice will be arbitrary and ephemeral if the seal of France is not affixed to it."[21]

There were, however, immense problems to be faced. In his *Mémoires de guerre,* de Gaulle lists, for example, the devastation to the French transport system: "The railroads were virtually paralyzed. Of our 12,000 locomotives, 2,800 were left. As for our roads, 3,000 bridges had been blown up; scarcely 300,000 vehicles, out of the three million we once had." Some may have thought that all the elements of a recovery would be quickly put in place, and as for de Gaulle, "that almost legendary character ... it was naturally assumed that he would be able to accomplish all these anticipated miracles by himself." To the contrary, "I laboured under no such illusion." He took stock of the cold houses and dark windows he saw in Paris, the empty shops, shut-down factories, forsaken railroad stations. "Action would have to be taken at every level."[22]

De Gaulle was also anxious to bring his family together. On August 29 he had written to Yvonne in Algiers. "I am at the Ministry of War. But it is a temporary arrangement. When you come, we will take a house with a garden next to the Bois de Boulogne, and I will have offices somewhere else."[23] True to his promise, he installed Yvonne and Anne in a fine house at Neuilly, on the edge of Paris. It was a place that Yvonne, with her preference for a simple way of life, found "a degree above what I would have liked."[24] On Sundays, de Gaulle was driven to a wood outside Paris where he took long, lonely walks that lasted several hours. He kept his official duties separate from his home life and when he chose to receive important people, he did so at the War Ministry.

François Mauriac, whose son Claude had become the head of de Gaulle's private office, came for lunch on September 1. Mauriac found himself overcome by emotion: he had to "lean against the wall in order not to stumble." The meeting gave Mauriac "a new sense of what true greatness and true glory were."[25]

Three days later, the poet Paul Valery, who had been on close terms with Marshall Pétain, found himself at the de Gaulle dinner table. He noted de Gaulle's "gaze fairly powerful and heavy." After dinner, they sat together on a sofa. Valery found it difficult to separate the man, the soldier, and the politician. "It seems to me, however, that he has the concentration of a man who is playing one of the most complicated games. He holds a lot of cards in the game being played at the moment."[26]

Charles de Gaulle's decision to bring people of all the political parties into his Cabinet was driven by the realization that the country needed unity, and this could only be achieved if all factions worked together in a common cause. His own authority, he knew, stemmed from the affection of the French people, and not from any base of political power. De Gaulle accepted Communists at the Cabinet table because of the party's strong following in many parts of the country; subsequent elections would prove it to be the most popular party in France. He welcomed Radicals, Socialists, and men bearing other political stripes for the same reason. As he would learn to his chagrin, however, the cynical manipulation and political squabbling that had beset the old Third Republic would also fatally infect the about-to-be-born Fourth Republic — the republic that François Mauriac had described as the "daughter of the martyrs" of the Resistance.

The exultation that had swept Paris at liberation slowly dissolved into grim acceptance of the realities facing France. It was time for de Gaulle to reach out to the provincial French, and he set out on a series of trips to examine conditions in every region of the country and to explain the sacrifices that the French would yet be called on to make. He had gone to Lyon on September 14, ten days after its liberation. Lyon occupied a special place in the heart of Resistance; it had been the headquarters of Free French revival during the Occupation. De Gaulle would have remembered that it was in Lyon that Jean Moulin, his closest *résistant* confidant, had been taken. All but two of the city's bridges over the Saône and Rhone rivers were in ruins, but de Gaulle left Lyon "convinced that the government … would here surmount all obstacles." In Marseille, de Gaulle found the atmosphere ominous. Large areas of the city had been demolished in the fighting and a local Communist leader had imposed a virtual dictatorship on the city. More problematical, de Gaulle's commissioner for the region, Raymond Aubrac, was regarded as a Communist sympathizer. It took the dispatch of a regiment of infantry from Algiers to ensure the compliance of FFI units with the directives of the Provisional Government.

At the big naval base of Toulon, site of the scuttling of much of the French fleet in 1942, de Gaulle boarded an escort vessel and reviewed forty vessels, from battleships to torpedo boats, as they passed down the line. In Toulouse, de Gaulle found "a city considerably disturbed" and on the verge of being taken over by a local soviet. His appointee as regional commissioner, Jean Cassou, had been gravely wounded in a firefight with retreating Germans. Since then, his deputy, Pierre Bertaux, had been struggling without help from Paris to restore public services and maintain law and order. Several thousand *résistants* were under the active control of a young French army lieutenant, Serge Asher, who had taken the Resistance name of "Colonel Ravenel." The picture was muddied by the presence of three thousand men who were refugees from the Spanish Civil War. They were all anxious to take advantage of the turmoil by mounting an attack on Barcelona in the hope of overthrowing Generalissimo Franco. A final complication was presented by a British agent of the Special Operations

Executive, a "Colonel Hilary," who had control of about seven hundred men. De Gaulle had Hilary packed into a plane and flown to England. The Spaniards were conscripted into the French army and "Colonel Ravenol" had no choice but to obey a written order from Paris to return to duty.

Bordeaux was a similar story, complicated by the fact that pockets of German troops were continuing to hold out on the Gironde estuary. The mayor, Adrien Marquet, and the chief of police, Maurice Papon, had reputations as collaborators and friends of Pierre Laval. De Gaulle gave the city's FFI units two choices — prison or the army. They took the army. We can imagine that de Gaulle would have felt some emotion at arriving back in the city where events had launched him onto "the shore of an ocean" with no assurance of ever returning to land. It was here, at the same Mérignac airport where de Gaulle had taken off with General Spears in Winston Churchill's personal airplane, that he arrived as liberator. Although not a sentimentalist, we can imagine de Gaulle would have thought of the close friendship he had enjoyed at the time with Spears. Their later falling-out over rival British and French policies in Syria and Lebanon had caused the two men to become bitterly estranged.

De Gaulle's travels took him through all of liberated France, but he returned to Paris with a troubled mind. "In several weeks, I had covered a great deal of the territory," he would write in his war memoirs. "What I had seen, beneath the speeches, the cheers and the flags, left me with the impression of enormous material damage and of a profound rift in the nation's political, administrative, social, and moral structure."[27]

Hoping to close that rift, de Gaulle set up a new Consultative Assembly and gave it the task of drawing up a constitution for a Fourth Republic. Former members of the Resistance were prominent among its 248 delegates.[28] Hard on its heels came, at last, recognition of de Gaulle's government by the major powers. On the afternoon of October 23, Great Britain, the Soviet Union, the United States, and Canada all announced their official recognition, long after most European governments had done so. Two days later, de Gaulle held his first major press conference for the international press. It was, as would be all de Gaulle press conferences, a highly orchestrated and formal affair. When asked for his response to his government's recognition, he observed, "The French government is pleased that it is to be called by its name."[29] There was perhaps a hint of hauteur rather than exultation in his voice.

De Gaulle had another, more important message he wished to deliver that day. Accustomed to being accused of wanting to be a dictator, de Gaulle in fact was wholly committed to re-establishing a democratic structure in France. "The French people wish to decide the form of their institutions for themselves," he told the press conference. "They are determined not to accept a dictatorship of any sort. France will step forth on the road of new democracy without any trouble, because it is the will of the people."[30]

The journey from exultation to reality was to be a hard one, but it was one well begun. There would be scores to be settled along the way, but civil war had been averted, the influence of Vichy had been obliterated, and most important of all, France again had a government of the French.

CHAPTER 16
Getting Even

Four days after the landing of Allied armies on the beaches of Normandy, a village 350 kilometres southwest of Paris was visited by the most terrible German atrocity of the war in France. Oradour-sur-Glane, in the old Limousin region noted for its beef cattle, oak forests, and fine Limoges chinaware, was slumbering in the quiet of early afternoon when soldiers of the 4th Grenadier Regiment of the 2nd SS Panzer Division (Das Reich) began their rampage through its narrow streets. The division had been moving north that day, June 10, 1944, toward Normandy when an informer reported the death at the hands of the Resistance of a German officer. A battalion commanded by Sturmbannfuhrer Adolf Diekmann, who may have picked the wrong village in which the killing was alleged to have occurred, descended on Oradour-sur-Glane a little after two o'clock.

Diekmann called for the mayor, Jean Desourteaux, a retired doctor, and told him the village would be searched for weapons and explosives. Women, some of them pushing baby carriages, were sent to the church along with the village children. They were told to sing as they walked. Once everyone was inside the church, German soldiers set off a gas bomb, intending to asphyxiate the occupants. When it misfired, they resorted to machine guns and grenades. Only one person, Mme Rouffanche, managed to escape alive — by jumping out a window. She was followed by a woman with an infant. Both were shot and killed by German soldiers.

The men, meanwhile, were herded into barns. The SS turned machine guns on them, piled wood and straw on the bodies, and set them alight. Some of the injured were hanged. Five men managed to escape. At the village school, seven-year-old Roger Godfrin jumped out a window when German soldiers arrived. He was shot at and fell, but he played dead when a soldier kicked him. Another soldier told him to run away. He hid in the cemetery. A street railway line connected the village with Limoges, twenty minutes away, and the last tram from the city arrived about six o'clock. The Germans shot the driver. No word had reached the outside world, as the village telephone operator was among those killed in the barns. By nightfall, the village had been burned out and 642 people were dead — 245 women, 207 children, and 190 men. The battalion commander, Adolf Diekman, later died fighting in Normandy.

The day before the Oradour-sur-Glane incident, at Tulle, one hundred kilometres further south, the same Waffen SS division had perpetrated a reprisal massacre in which 213 civilians were murdered. Earlier that year, on April 1, at Ascq in northern France, ninety-two men living in houses alongside a railway line were shot following the derailment of a train carrying the 12th SS Panzer Division (Hitlerjugend). It was just one of many acts of revenge for a spate of Resistance attacks on French railways, each intended to disrupt German troop movements. On the day that Paris was liberated, eighty Waffen-SS soldiers of the 17th Panzer Division (Götz von Berlichingen) entered Maillé, a town forty kilometres south of Tours, and shot, bludgeoned, and bayoneted to death 124 people. Four days later, members of the 3rd SS Panzer Division massacred eighty-six inhabitants of Robert-Espagne in northern France.

For none of these war crimes did the perpetrators ever suffer serious punishment. The few trials of German officers in France after the war resulted in light sentences, and within a short time, all the accused —

including some Alsatian French (so-called *malgré-nous*)* who participated in the Oradour-sur-Glane atrocity — were given their freedom. After the war, General de Gaulle ordered that the ruins of Oradour-sur-Glane be left intact as a memorial to the victims. The town was rebuilt on nearby ground.[1]

In eastern France, the Resistance took it into its own hands to extract revenge for German misdeeds. Germaine Manquet was a teenage *résistant* living in Annecy, a town in the foothills of the French Alps. Her father, a guard at the local prison who was secretly a member of the Resistance, awakened her one morning in August 1943 to say that forty of his prisoners had been taken to the nearby village of Sacconge. The Gestapo intended to shoot them. Germaine tried desperately to alert the Resistance but was unable to locate her contact. Later that day, she rode her bicycle to the killing field where she found the ground littered with blood-covered bodies. Many had their eyes still open. "I trembled and cried because I had been unable to save them," she would remember. That night, she had dreams of blood washing over her body.[2]

Sacconge would become the site of a retaliatory killing a year later, on August 28, 1944, following liberation of the district by the French 1st Army. Forty-four Germans were taken from a prisoner-of-war camp to a nearby airstrip and shot. Their deaths were in retaliation for the execution of 120 *résistants* held at the Montluc Prison in Lyon. According to a German survivor, the French commander, a Major Barrelet, told the POWs, "You all cried 'Heil Hitler' and now you will pay for it!"[3]

It has been suggested the executions were carried out with the approval of Yves Farge, later to be named by de Gaulle a commissioner of the Republic in Lyon.[4] He was a man de Gaulle later described as a "leader in a region distinguished for its action against the enemy."[5]

A mixture of impulses — fear and frustration on the part of German occupiers, pride and patriotism on the part of French *résistants* — drove the thinking behind these deadly games that recklessly exceeded the accepted bounds of legitimate warfare. The German army regarded the Resistance

---

*Alsatians pressed into the German army were said to have been conscripted "in spite of ourselves."

as made up of nothing but terrorists and felt justified in taking reprisal against civilians. As for the Resistance, historical records and personal accounts suggest that, for the most part, members of the FFI and the Maquis felt morally justified in killing the enemy — although how does one know how someone feels after killing another person, regardless of the circumstances?

In warning against indiscriminate assassinations, de Gaulle had signalled the futility of killing Germans when they had the power to retaliate in far greater measure against the civilian population. He judged such actions from a strategic perspective in which concern for the morality of taking enemy lives played little part. "No individual has the right to kill except on the field of battle," de Gaulle had observed.[6] The territory of Metropolitan France certainly encompassed the field of battle between 1939 and 1945.

There was little that the new French government installed after the liberation could do to prosecute perpetrators of German war crimes. There was, however, the question of how the people of France were to deal with the legacy of collaboration and betrayal left in the wake of four years of German occupation. Writing in *Combat* in the first heady months of regained freedom, Albert Camus declared that France was made up of either "men of the Resistance" or "men of betrayal and injustice." France could be saved only if [the men of betrayal] "still living in its midst were destroyed in order to save the nation's soul."[7] Charles de Gaulle expressed himself similarly: "The hour for settling accounts had come."[8] François Mauriac, on the other hand, felt that some things had to be overlooked in the interests of "national reconciliation."

So began the *Épuration* — a time of purification, of settling scores and getting even, and of holding to account thousands of people accused of consorting with the enemy. The accusations, triggered by the flood of emotions accompanying liberation, boiled up within hours whenever German troops were cleared from French territory. Often, the first to be accused were those least able to defend themselves — the twenty thousand or so women assailed for "horizontal collaboration." In punishment, their heads were shaved, then they were disrobed and paraded in humiliation before their neighbours.

De Gaulle wanted the purge to be done quickly and efficiently, so that the French could get on to rebuilding the nation. The crimes of the Occupation had been so great, however, that "resentment was beyond control." In his memoirs, de Gaulle recounts the tally of the years of occupation: sixty thousand executed, two hundred thousand deported of whom a bare fifty thousand survived, and the condemnation of another thirty-five thousand men and women by Vichy tribunals. "Justice must be rendered here," he wrote, "and it was."[9]

The wave of accusations against alleged collaborators was so great that it swept aside due process of law. Mobs attacked the homes of suspected collaborators, often killing the accused at once, or after a "trial" before their neighbours. This also was the time when the *attentistes* came into view — fence-sitters who had waited until the last minute to proclaim they had been *résistants* all along. The *Épuration* fractured French society, destroying friendships and splitting families, but it was something the country had to endure if it was ever to settle its internal accounts. De Gaulle calculated the number of those killed at the hands of the Resistance at 10,842, with about four thousand deaths occurring after liberation. Many of those brought to trial were convicted on the flimsiest of evidence.

Few voices were raised against these excesses. Preaching at Notre Dame on Palm Sunday, 1945, one Father Pancini deplored the "innumerable illegal arrests ... people imprisoned for indefensible reasons ... massacres without trial, tortures inflicted even on those condemned to death...; people [who] have been assassinated ... by wretches who invade their prisons to gratify their lust for vengeance."[10] The Ministry of Justice saw to it that Father Pancini gave no more Palm Sunday sermons.

The final balance sheet of legal trials would show that of 163,077 people detained on allegations of collaboration, 73,501, or 45 percent, were acquitted. Of those convicted at legally constituted trials, 7,037 were sentenced to death, but only 767 were actually executed, the balance representing convictions *in absentia* or commutations granted by General de Gaulle.[11]

The trials of Vichy collaborators, some before a high court created especially for the purpose, went on for four years. Some attracted more attention than others. Robert Brasillach, the Nazi-admiring editor of *Je suis partout*, gave himself up but was sentenced to death after a five-hour trial, a verdict that brought protests from writers and intellectuals. François Mauriac backed a petition for his commutation and met personally with de Gaulle to appeal for a pardon. Perhaps influenced by the fact Brasillach had allowed himself to be photographed in a Nazi uniform, de Gaulle refused, and Brasillach was shot. Joseph Darnand, head of the Milice, the paramilitary force of thirty-five thousand Frenchmen who worked with the Vichy regime and the Gestapo to hunt down Jews and *résistants*, also died before a firing squad. Marcel Déat, a former Socialist who became a right-wing politician and helped found the Légion des Volontaires Français that fought for the Germans, avoided the death penalty by escaping to Italy, where he later died. Charles Maurras, whose l'Action Française applauded the removal of Jews, was sentenced to both life imprisonment and degradation. The latter was a penalty for a new offence, *l'indignité nationale* — consisting of acts short of crimes but with the smell of collaboration. The penalties ranged from being deprived of the right to wear decorations to disbarment from teaching or practising law.

Admiral Jean Decoux, the governor general of French Indochina for the Vichy government, was one of the nearly half of all those accused of collaboration who were cleared of their charges. He was restored to his former rank following acquittal. Henri Béraud, a best-selling French novelist who published anti-British diatribes in the fascist weekly *Gringoire*, was saved from the firing squad when de Gaulle commuted his sentence to life imprisonment. None of these, nor similar trials of personalities such as Louis Renault, the car maker who died in prison, roused the French population as did the trials of the two leading political figures of the Vichy regime — Pierre Laval and Marshall Philippe Pétain.

After the collapse of his futile effort to set up a government that would make peace with the Allies, Laval fled to Spain. With the end of the war, the Spanish shipped him to Germany, where the American army took custody of him before handing him over to the French. Twice premier of France in the 1930s, the one-time Socialist had long since converted to right-wing views as a pillar of the Vichy regime. His business interests included newspapers and printing plants that he used to good effect to promote his opinions. He was in some respects the original collaborator, having been on close terms with the German ambassador, Otto Abetz, and having met with

Adolf Hitler and Hermann Goering in October 1940. His intense pro-Nazi position worried even the members of Pétain's Cabinet, and for a time he was forced from office. After surviving an assassination attempt, Laval was brought back in 1942. Once more premier, he vigorously pursued roundups of Jews and engineered the creation of the dreaded Milice.

Laval testified briefly at the trial of Marshall Pétain before going on trial himself in what could only be described as a burlesque of traditional court procedure. He appeared in court disheveled, overweight, and contemptuous of his prosecutors. He engaged in name-calling with the judges, refused to attend parts of his four-day trial, and tried to argue that his collaboration had saved France from worse treatment by Germany. A jury of twelve *résistants* and twelve parliamentarians found him guilty. On October 15, 1945, the day he was to be shot, he swallowed a cyanide tablet, but was revived. Doctors pronounced him fit for execution. As the firing squad performed its duty, Laval cried, *"Vive la France."*

Marshall Pétain's trial was closely watched by Charles de Gaulle, who devotes several pages in his memoirs to the fate of his old mentor. In the face of the advancing Allies, the marshall had been taken to Germany. Shortly after the liberation of Paris, Pétain had sent a message to de Gaulle in which he proposed formation of a new government that would "prevent civil war and reconcile all Frenchmen of good faith."

De Gaulle's response? "The only reply I could give him was my silence."[12]

Having been allowed by the Germans to go to Switzerland, Pétain returned voluntarily to France. His train was met at the border by General Koenig, who refused to shake hands with him. Pétain was held in a fort in the Paris suburb of Montrouge before going on trial on July 26, 1945.

De Gaulle would write of Pétain that during his trial he "shrouded himself in silence," and that "[g]iven his age, his exhaustion, and the fact that what he had shielded was indefensible, his attitude seemed to me to be one of discretion." De Gaulle was determined to "sign a reprieve whatever the result."[13] In Pétain's defence, his lawyer argued that the Armistice the marshall had signed contributed to the Allied cause by keeping Vichy as a bulwark against the Germans gaining control of the Mediterranean.

For most Frenchmen, the trial provided their first real understanding of the signing of the Armistice and the Vichy regime's collaboration with

Germany. The chaos that accompanied the fall of the Reynaud government in June 1940 — when people were fleeing Paris and the newspapers had stopped publishing — put a shroud on what was happening in Bordeaux. People were amazed to learn that Marshall Pétain had lurked about that city awaiting his turn at power, a list in his pocket of the collaborators he would take into his Cabinet. When Pétain's lawyer challenged the court as to whether anyone present knew the Armistice terms, the prosecutor jumped to his feet and began to reel off from memory the terms that empowered the Germans to occupy two-thirds of the country. "That's unfair," Pétain's lawyer screamed. "You've no right to begin with the worst part."

All of the old French political figures — Reynaud, Blum, Daladier, Herriot, Weygand — were there to testify, for or against. Pétain often nodded off during the examination of his former peers. "Deal with me according to your conscience," he said in his final statement, "mine brings me no reproach since during a life that is already long, and, having arrived at the threshold of death, I state that I have no ambition other than to serve France."[14]

By a vote of fourteen to thirteen, the judges found Pétain guilty but recommended he be spared the death penalty. De Gaulle had Pétain confined on the Île d'Yeu off the west coast of France, with the intention that after a couple of years "he would finish his days in retirement in his home near Antibes." Pétain died at Île d'Yeu on July 21, 1951, aged ninety-five. De Gaulle would remember him as "a leader once distinguished by the most exceptional powers, an old soldier in whom at the time of the catastrophe many Frenchmen had put their trust and for whom, in spite of everything, many still felt respect or pity."[15]

France tried to put its collaborationist past behind it with a general amnesty in 1953, but history could not be so easily dismissed. From the day of his return to Paris, de Gaulle had wished to focus French eyes on the heroic role of the Resistance and how it exemplified the nation's refusal to bow down to its Nazi occupiers. Most people were only too willing to accept this mythic portrayal of France's recent past. It continues to weave a central pattern in the long arc of the years from 1944 to the present day — typically in the way the anniversary of the liberation of Paris is still commemorated.*

---

*As noted in the Introduction to this book, remembrance of the Resistance plays a central role in these ceremonies.

As more evidence came to light of the collaborationist backgrounds of prominent French figures in the years between 1950 and 2000, however, public attitudes shifted. A possible turning point was the release in French theatres in 1972 of Marcel Ophuls's film made for West German television, *Le chagrin et la pitié (The Sorrow and the Pity)*. It helped the French realize that the choice between resistance and collaboration was not always simple or clear — one was not necessarily always good and the other always bad.

Two prominent figures of late twentieth-century Paris — Police Chief Maurice Papon and French president François Mitterrand — serve to illustrate the difficult reconciliation with history that the French have been called upon to make. First, consider the case of Papon, secretary-general of the police in Bordeaux under the Vichy regime.[16] He would become the tough but respected prefect of the Paris police under Charles de Gaulle, decorated with the Legion of Honour and elected to the National Assembly, yet would be finally convicted in 1998 of crimes against humanity for his involvement in the deportation of 1,600 Jews from Bordeaux.

Our second example, François Mitterrand, was a Socialist who would twice be elected president of France, serving from 1981 to 1995. His career was far too varied and complex to be dealt with here, but we know that his connections with the Vichy regime, which he served in minor capacities, and his links with right-wing movements generated much controversy during and after his time in office. He was heavily criticized for his long association with René Bousquet, secretary-general of the Vichy police under Marshall Pétain. Charles de Gaulle has been quoted as describing Mitterrand and Bousquet as "ghosts who come from the deepest depths of the collaboration."[17]

The frenzy over the trials of collaborators was not something that Charles de Gaulle could allow to command his full attention. There was still French territory to be liberated, and the matter of fixing France's role in the peace that would soon be upon Europe. "The German capitulation was no longer anything but a matter of formalities," de Gaulle would remember.[18]

Overtures from the enemy were rejected out of hand, none more abruptly than a memorandum from Heinrich Himmler, who had been an architect of the holocaust. "Agreed," Himmler's memo to de Gaulle began, "You have won." It went on: "Considering where you have started from, one bows low indeed to you, General de Gaulle.... But now what will you do? Rely on Americans and the British?

They will deal with you as a satellite, and you will lose all the honour you have won."[19]

Himmler's appeal to join Germany against the Soviet Union was less than meaningless. The issue of France's relationship with her two major allies, however, was one that could not be so easily dealt with. In de Gaulle's view, France had never been granted her "rightful place" in the Allied leadership. The Anglo-American command maintained tight control over military strategy. Even as the French armed forces grew to a force of one million men, de Gaulle worried about the reluctance of the United States to recognize France's contribution to the war. Always it was the Americans, and not the British, who were the primary cause of Gaullian apprehension. De Gaulle's overriding concern was to ensure that Germany would never again pose a threat to France. Three times the two countries had gone to war, in 1870, 1914, and 1939, and France now had no choice but to assume Germany might remain a threat in the future. De Gaulle saw the solution in abolition of a centralized Reich, to be succeeded by several smaller new states such as the Ruhr, the Rhineland, and the Saar, connected only through a loose federation.

De Gaulle knew he would need Churchill's support if he was to have any hope of persuading the Americans of such a bold plan. The visit of the British prime minister to help commemorate Armistice Day on November 11 offered the perfect occasion for a discussion of his idea. De Gaulle met the prime minister and Clementine Churchill at Orly airport the day before and drove with them to the Quai d'Orsay where they were billeted. The visitors got the full treatment, including use of a luxurious suite where Churchill enjoyed relaxing in a gold bathtub that had been installed for Hermann Goering. A great parade, rivalling that of August 26, brought a million cheering Parisians onto the Champs Élysée. After laying a wreath at the Tomb of the Unknown Soldier, de Gaulle and Churchill moved in an open car down the long avenue. Yvonne de Gaulle joined in the festivities, sitting with Clementine Churchill in the review stand. Churchill confessed to de Gaulle that the British Cabinet had hesitated to approve his trip, so fearful was it of disorder in Paris. In fact, Churchill found "everything in its normal order, the crowds respecting the barricades and quite capable of bursting into cheers … [with] splendid troops — yesterday's French Forces of the Interior — parading in perfect marching order." Churchill told de Gaulle he felt as if he "were watching a ressurection."[20]

De Gaulle tried to obtain Churchill's blessing for his plan to break up Germany, but he found the prime minister unwilling to consider anything specific as to Germany's future. Churchill did agree that France should have its own zone of occupation in Germany but was "evasive" as to what the zone would be. Churchill's proposal for a Franco-British alliance fell away when de Gaulle suggested such a deal would work only if both countries agreed to act independently of the United States.

The British, de Gaulle thought, "considered themselves participants in a game to which we ourselves were not admitted."[21]

Still, Churchill was insistent that France would be at the table in the future. "As for France," he told de Gaulle, "thanks to you, she is reappearing in the eyes of the world. Don't be impatient! Already, the doors are ajar. Soon they will be open to you."

For all the high stakes political games played after the liberation, the small triumphs of individuals' daily lives perhaps counted for more than some of the decisions reached in affairs of state. Early on a fall morning in 1944, the artist Claire Fauteux was building a fire in the small stove of her new apartment on rue de la Fontaine when she received an unexpected visitor. It was Pauline Vanier, wife of Georges Vanier, who had returned to Paris to take up his old duties as the Canadian minister to France. Neither could speak as they stared at each other, thinking about what the years since the occupation of Paris had wrought. Finally, Mme Vanier spoke: "You have not changed a bit — always the same."[22]

Later, the wife of the concierge of the building wondered querulously why Fauteux had received the wife of the Canadian ambassador. Claire concluded the woman was a "curious busybody" but noticed that she behaved more amiably toward her after the visit. She later sold Fauteux a lamb roast at "an exorbitant price." After it had been cooked and the table set for a meal, the concierge returned to demand it back. It had all been a mistake and it belonged to someone else, as the *agent de police* who accompanied her made haste to confirm. Soon after, a food parcel arrived from Mme Vanier: canned meat, fruit, marmalade, all delicacies she had not seen for many years and were nowhere to be found in Paris.

Late in November, Fauteux was flown to London and travelled by train to Greenock, Scotland, where she boarded the *Acquitania* for New York. Claire Fauteux never again lived in Paris, spending the rest of her life teaching and painting in Quebec, where she died in 1988 at the age of ninety-seven. She had lived through an era that saw Paris as the cultural and artistic capital of the world, and a magnet for writers, poets, and painters from around the world. For all the greatness that Paris might yet attain, the era that the City of Light had now left behind was one that would be long celebrated, but never replicated.

CHAPTER 17
From Rebel to Ruler

It is widely accepted that Charles de Gaulle, in one of his more revealing pronouncements early in the Second World War, said to Lord Halifax, the British foreign secretary, "I am France." There is an apocryphal overtone to such an extravagant claim — reminiscent of Louis XIV's *"l'État, c'est moi"* — but the words accurately register the general's sentiments. De Gaulle and the forces under his command did in fact constitute, with the support of the Resistance, all of the France engaged in the war against Germany from 1940 to 1944. In de Gaulle's view, there was no other France that counted. With his Provisional Government in office in Paris in the fall of 1944, de Gaulle was no longer the audacious rebel who had defied his superiors in Bordeaux, rejected the rule of the Pétain regime in Vichy, and played a high-stakes poker game to win recognition from his Allies in London and Washington. He now sat as the president of the council, or prime minister, of a French government facing a nation that he realized had been "ruined, decimated, torn apart."

There was never any doubt that Charles de Gaulle meant to rule, but the fear that he might become a dictator lingered for a very long time in the minds of many, especially those on the left. The transition from an occupied state to a self-ruling nation was achieved in de Gaulle's France over a period of less than three months, beginning with the general's naming of François Coulet as his first commissioner for the Republic at Bayeux on June 14. His appointment effectively made Bayeux the administrative capital of liberated France until the liberation of Paris. The establishment by decree of a "Government of National Unity" on September 5 completed the first phase of national restoration.

The Cabinet's composition reflected both the strength of the Resistance and the presence of party representatives who came from Communist, Socialist, and Republican ranks. Pierre Mendès France became economics minister and Georges Bidault, head of the now defunct Committee of National Liberation, took foreign affairs — which de Gaulle would closely control. The two Communists were in minor posts, de Gaulle having rejected their demands for the security ministry that would have given them control of the police and justice.

A week later, in an address to a meeting at the Palais de Chaillot organized by the National Council of the Resistance, de Gaulle set out his program to "renew the economy so that it serve[s] the collectivity before furnishing profits to private interests." This would involve the abolition of private monopolies that had "weighed so heavily on our human condition" and their replacement with publicly-owned industries and services that would permit French men and women to live, work and bring up their children in "security and dignity."[1] The speech set the direction of French public policy for the future — a liberal welfare state with a mixture of government ownership and private enterprise, but with core elements of the economy in public hands and all private business under close government scrutiny.

It was clear to everyone that drastic action was needed to deal with the country's economic problems. Fighting during August and September had disrupted the harvest in key regions, although the farmers de Gaulle spoke to on his tours "seemed resolved to keep their shirt sleeves rolled up."[2] Perhaps they did, but farms were short of both machinery and manpower, with over two million Frenchmen still in German camps or factories. When farmers were able to obtain space on the few freight trains still running, they often held back what supply they had to meet local needs. Food rationing was set at 1,200 calories a day, about half the level considered necessary to maintain health. Everyone resorted to the black market. Housewives had to make soup from a few slices of carrot and a potato, and the precious baguette had become a rarity for many. Paris and other cities lacked coal for heating, natural gas supplies were minimal, and the electricity was off more than it was on.

Janet Flanner, the American correspondent for the *New Yorker* magazine, summed up the mood:

> The brightest news here is the infinite resilience of the French as human beings. Parisians are politer and more patient in their troubles than they were in their prosperity. Though they have no soap that lathers, both men and women smell civilized when you encounter them in the Metro, which everybody rides in, there being no buses or taxis. Everything here is a substitute for something else. The women who are not neat, thin, and frayed look neat, thin, and chic clattering along in their platform shoes of wood — substitute for shoe leather — which sound like horses' hooves. Their broad-shouldered, slightly shabby coats of sheepskin — substitute for wool cloth, which the Nazis preferred for themselves — were bought on the black market three winters ago.[3]

It was French society, however, as much as the economy, that needed to recover from the war and from the struggles that had preceded it. It was de Gaulle's view that the class struggle that raged before the war had so consumed France that the economy had been left to stagnate and a weakened political regime — the "parties system" — had been unable to impose needed changes. To all that was added the German threat that forced a weakened economy to focus on rearmament. After four years of war, prices had risen 50 percent and national production was at 40 percent of pre-war levels. Failure to fix the economy, de Gaulle wrote in his memoirs, would have given the Communist Party "every likelihood of seizing control of the country." As well as being wary of the Communists, de Gaulle remained, as always, critical of the bourgeoisie, which he said had accepted Vichy rule "because it wanted no interruption in its dinner parties."

Ironically, it was these same bourgeoisie who came to the Provisional Government's rescue by enthusiastically supporting a "Liberation Loan" that raised 165 billion francs — an enormous sum today — through the sale of 3 percent government bonds. De Gaulle credited the success of this loan with staving off inflation, even though the government still faced a 50 percent budget deficit in 1945. The loan also came at a human cost. Finance minister André Lepercq died in an automobile accident while on tour promoting the loan.

Price controls were imposed in November 1944, but their most immediate effect was a boost for the black market. Nevertheless nearly two-thirds of the French public, according to an opinion poll, supported de Gaulle's initiatives.

No cleansing of French society could be complete without the purging of corrupt or collaborationist newspapers. The most egregious, such as *Le Matin*, simply disappeared, while de Gaulle suppressed other long-time fixtures of the fourth estate, such as the one-time semi-official *Le Temps*. To replace that disgraced journal, he ordered his minister of information, Pierre-Henri Teitgen, to see to the creation of *Le Monde,* to which he granted a newsprint licence that allowed it to become the new unofficial paper of record.[4]

De Gaulle had a poor opinion of journalists and an equally poor relationship with most of the press. He was disturbed to find evidence of corrupt practices in the pre-war press — some of which extended into the Fourth Republic — and once spoke of "envelopes from foreign embassies" directed to compliant journalists. In his *Mémoires de guerre*, de Gaulle is blunt about the control he exercised over the press at the end of the war. A government licence was needed to buy newsprint and de Gaulle intervened on behalf of new papers that he thought had enough backing to survive financially. He accorded them "the right to enter the market place" in the belief that the French press should be made up of "various formulations and styles."[5] Even so, the newsprint shortage was so severe that most papers came out in editions of two pages, and *Le Monde* had to switch to tabloid format, earning it the nickname of *Le Demi-Monde*.

In the turmoil of liberation, the Communists moved quickly to establish their organs, which would multiply to more than 120 throughout France. Their two Paris dailies, *L'Humanité* and *Ce Soir*, adopted a restrained attitude toward de Gaulle, reflecting Moscow's strategy to counteract fears of a possible Communist takeover. Mainstream newspapers *Le Figaro, L'Aurore, L'Epoque,* and *L'Ordre* that had quit publishing rather than submit to German or Vichy censorship, resumed printing in Paris. Despite Moscow's go-easy orders on de Gaulle, there was no lack of criticism of him by the Communist press. *L'Humanité* attacked de Gaulle's program of nationalization for putting only 51 percent of the big banks, coal mines, and manufacturers such as Renault in government hands, leaving the other 49 percent to private interests. If state ownership was Communist, these journals argued, then Louis XI was Communist for having established the French post office.

De Gaulle needed a stout gatekeeper to protect him from unwanted interruptions. He found it in Gaston Palewski, his old comrade whom he now installed as *chef du cabinet*, or chief of staff. Palewski made up de Gaulle's appointment calendar, checked the mail, screened telephone calls (when the phone was working), and generally controlled access to the general. He was smart, ambitious, and vain, and also a notorious womanizer, despite an unappealing face and mottled skin. His longest-running affair was with the English author Nancy Mitford of the notorious Mitford sisters, earning himself fictionalized portrayals in two of her novels.[6]

Palewski also had deep roots in the diplomatic colony and was a confidant of Duff Cooper, the British ambassador, who would check with him on the suitability of prospective dinner guests at the British Embassy. Cooper made personal use of Palewski's social contacts and took as his lover the beautiful writer Louise de Vilmorin, to whom he was introduced by Palewski at a Russian Embassy party. These extra-marital liaisons were not uncommon, but Mme de Gaulle, an admirer of Lady Diana Cooper, abhorred adultery and refused even to speak the name of a divorced woman friend. When the Coopers were invited to dine with the general, she refused to speak to the ambassador, despite being seated next to him. She was more tolerant toward the American ambassador, Jefferson Cafffery, who, though married, was a closet homosexual with a lover who was a member of his staff. Mme de Gaulle probably never learned of this interesting *ménage à trois*.

✝

If ever Charles de Gaulle found himself bogged down in the dreariness of domestic issues, there was always the more alluring foreign field — which he reserved almost entirely to himself — to offer ever-changing challenges. De Gaulle laid out his foreign policy in a speech to the Consultative Assembly on November 22. He outlined plans for a series of high-level meetings with foreign governments that would resolve France's status in the world. He left for Moscow two days later, on a trip that would last over three weeks and which he considered important enough to warrant twenty-four pages in his memoirs. Accompanied by Gaston Palewski, Georges Bidault, and General Juin, de Gaulle stopped en route in Cairo to meet with King Farouk, saw the shah of Iran in Teheran, and then flew to Baku and visited Stalingrad before proceeding to Moscow. He was met at the Moscow railway station by Vyacheslav Molotov, the foreign minister, and put up at the French Embassy. De Gaulle was disappointed to find it lacked heating against Moscow's sub-zero temperatures. The visit was at de Gaulle's request, and despite his aversion to Communists in France, he regarded the Soviet Union as an ace card he might play against his Western allies should he some time lose their support.

When de Gaulle met Stalin, he had the impression "of confronting the astute and implacable champion of a Russia exhausted by suffering and tyranny but afire with national ambition."[7] Of the fifteen or so hours he spent with the Russian leader, most involved eating and drinking. They had long talks about Poland, with de Gaulle drawing on his experiences there after the First World War. Stalin insisted the western border of Poland had to be pushed to the Oder River in Germany, but as for Germany's western borders, that should be left up to future four-power negotiations. De Gaulle agreed to the return of French Communist leader Maurice Thorez. As to the question of a Russian-French alliance, de Gaulle rejected the original Russian draft and a revised version incorporating French requests was produced only after an all-night binge. De Gaulle had absented himself following dinner, numerous vodka toasts, and the showing of an interminable Soviet war film.

"Thirty times," de Gaulle would record, "Stalin stood up to drink the health of those Russians present."

At dawn, de Gaulle was summoned back to the Kremlin where the final draft of the treaty was signed by Bidault and Molotov, with Stalin and de Gaulle looking on. Stalin congratulated de Gaulle, remarking, "You have played well. Well done! I like dealing with someone who knows what he wants, even if he doesn't share my views."

As de Gaulle took his leave he saw Stalin "sitting alone, at the table. He had started eating again."

The treaty never really amounted to much, but de Gaulle saw it as something that signalled "our return to the concert of great powers."[8]

By now, de Gaulle had a new foreign policy worry. The "Big Three" were planning to meet in Yalta in January 1945 to map out the rest of the war and begin the design of postwar Europe. France was not invited. Its exclusion convinced de Gaulle that Russia, Britain, and the United States were about to "conclude a series of bargains from which the rights of France, the liberty of peoples, and the equilibrium of Europe had everything to lose." In his view, this was exactly what happened. It was true that, largely at Churchill's insistence, France was given an occupation zone in Germany, made a member of the Allied Control Commission to be set up in Berlin, and would be one of the five powers to invite other states to a founding conference of the United Nations, thereby ensuring it a permanent seat on the Security Council. But despite a declaration asserting the rights of all peoples to free elections, it was clear that Communist-imposed governments were to hold power in Poland, Yugoslavia, and other countries now occupied by Soviet troops.

As troublesome as it was to see these trends emerge without France having the opportunity to influence them, de Gaulle was personally more disturbed by the invitation he received from President Roosevelt to meet him in Algiers. Thoroughly put out that FDR would presume to extend an invitation for a meeting with the French head of government on French soil, de Gaulle sent word "that it was impossible for me to come to Algiers at this time." But any time Roosevelt wanted to come to Paris — de Gaulle had invited him there for the November 11 ceremonies — he would be made welcome.[9]

De Gaulle's diplomatic affront represented the last contact he would have with the American president. When Roosevelt died on April 12, de Gaulle declared a week of national mourning. In a letter to the new president, Harry Truman, he spoke of his "immense emotion and profound sadness" at the loss of a man who "France admired and loved." As always, de Gaulle was generous in writing of an adversary after his death.

Le Monde marked FDR's passing by asking the nation to "weep for this man and hope that his wise and generous conception of the human communities remains like a light to brighten the path of all men of good will." Georges Bidault called Roosevelt "one of the most loved and venerated men in France."[10]

On April 1, 1945 — Easter Sunday — the 9th Colonial Division of General de Lattre de Tassigny's French 1st Army stood on the banks of the Rhine River, the historic borderline between Germany and France. Getting there had involved a long and arduous advance in combination with General Leclerc's 2nd Armoured Division. The French 1st Army's drive up the eastern flank of France had proven relentless. In fifteen days in November, the 1st Army killed ten thousand Germans and captured eighteen thousand prisoners, while five columns of the 2nd Armoured Division had burst into Strasbourg on the twenty-third of the month, liberating the capital of the Alsace region. It was almost like Paris all over again, considering that both Alsace and its neighbour, Lorraine, had been incorporated into Germany under the terms of the 1940 Armistice. De Gaulle described the capture of Strasbourg as "one of the most brilliant episodes of our military history." When he broke the news to the Consultative Assembly, its members forgot "any partisan consideration" and stood to cheer the announcement.[11]

The taking of Strasbourg proved to be easier than holding it. The German counter-offensive, known as the Battle of the Bulge, began on December 16 when Field Marshall von Rundstedt launched a ninety-minute artillery barrage across a 125-kilometre front. It was the very day that de Gaulle had arrived in Paris from Moscow, via Teheran, Cairo, and Tunis. As American troops fell back in the face of the fierce and unexpected attack, General Eisenhower ordered the transfer of all available forces to the Ardennes sector, where the Germans had punched a one-hundred-kilometre bulge in the Allied line. In order to shorten his lines, Eisenhower ordered French forces holding Strasbourg to withdraw. The order came on December 26, the day after de Gaulle had visited the city to congratulate General Leclerc and his troops. De Gaulle wrote to Eisenhower to tell him that the French government "obviously cannot let Strasbourg fall into enemy hands again." He also cabled Churchill and Roosevelt, pointing out that loss of the city would be demoralizing to France.[12]

De Gaulle ordered General de Lattre to "take matters into your own hands and to assure the defence of Strasbourg." He realized his order contradicted the instructions of the Allied Command, but he considered that to lose the city would amount to a "national disaster." In a meeting at Supreme Headquarters of the Allied Command in Versailles on January 3, de Gaulle explained to Eisenhower that "Alsace is sacred ground." If the Germans were to recapture it, they would take revenge against its citizens. "I have ordered the French 1st Army to defend the city. It will therefore do so, in any case."[13] Winston Churchill, who had come to the meeting in response to de Gaulle's cable, backed him up. At this point, the German offensive had ground to a halt and Eisenhower agreed the French should hold fast in Strasbourg. After two more weeks of heavy fighting, the Germans were pushed out of the area.

It was not by chance that the first French troops into Germany were colonial soldiers from north and central Africa. These men had formed the bulk of the 1st Army and had fought courageously from Marseille to the Rhine, often with inferior equipment, poorer clothing, and less-nourishing food than that supplied to other divisions of the French army. General Eisenhower, betraying the unconscious racist attitudes prevalent at the time, lamented the low efficiency of these troops, "who were unable to endure the cold and exposure incident to campaigning in a European winter." Writing in his *Crusade in Europe*, Eisenhower added: "In the spring of 1945, however, during the final operations of the war, the French army advanced gallantly and effectively to occupy great portions of southern Germany."[14]

As we shall see, the French army did perform nobly but not without causing further discord in the Allied High Command. General de Lattre, having secured Strasbourg and completed the crossing of the Rhine in small boats and light bridges built on the spot, took Karlsruhe and pressed on to Stuttgart, the capital of the German state of Württemberg. It fell on April 23. De Lattre should not have gone there: Stuttgart had been reserved for the taking by General Alexander Patch's U.S. 7th Army. General Eisenhower ordered de Lattre to withdraw; de Gaulle overruled de Lattre and told him to stay put. Eisenhower wrote to de Gaulle with a threat to stop using French forces. President Truman stepped in, threatening to cut off supplies to the French. De Gaulle backed down, and turned the French army southward as directed by Eisenhower's command. Another breach in Allied unity would arise in June, when de Gaulle sent army units into the Italian border area of Val d'Aosta against U.S. instructions. When de Gaulle's commander threatened to open fire on American troops, Truman told de Gaulle that such a threat was "almost unbelievable." Again General de Gaulle backed down, his latest ploy having clearly gone beyond the rules of the game.

The French fought a two-front war during this period, as German forces were still to be liquidated along the strip of the Atlantic coast they held from north of Bordeaux to Brittany. That task fell to seventy thousand former members of the Maquis, the French rural underground who were enlisted in the "Atlantic Army Detachment" under General Edgard de Larminat. After clearing fifteen thousand Germans out of the Gironde estuary at Bordeaux, another eighteen thousand of the enemy were subdued at La Rochelle. De Gaulle rushed to the city to congratulate his troops. By the time Germany surrendered, ninety thousand Germans had been taken prisoner and five thousand killed in the coastal regions.

Liberation, longer spring days, and warmer weather brought a flow of forced labourers and military prisoners back to France from Germany. In a single weekend in April, eight thousand men and nearly three hundred women returned from German camps. The men were flown home in

American transport planes while the women, held in the prison camp of Ravensbruck east of Berlin, arrived on trains at the Gare de Lyon. Janet Flanner wrote that the women brought "with them as very nearly their only baggage the proofs, on their faces and their bodies and in their weakly spoken reports, of the atrocities that had been their lot and that of hundreds of thousands of others in the numerous concentration camps our armies are liberating, almost too late." They were met by a reception committee that included General de Gaulle, "who wept." Flanner wrote of how the welcomers carried bouquets of lilac blossoms that they gave to the women. "As the lilacs fell from inert hands, the flowers made a purple carpet on the platform and the perfume of the trampled flowers mixed with the stench of illness and dirt."[15]

On Monday, May 7, at 2:41 a.m. Berlin time, in a schoolhouse at Rheims, France, General de Lattre signed on behalf of France the documents in which the German armed forces surrendered unconditionally to the Allies. A week earlier, Adolf Hitler had committed suicide and the leadership of Germany had passed to Grand Admiral Karl Doenitz. General Alfred Jodl, chief of staff at the Wehrmacht, signed for Germany while General Eisenhower, for reasons of protocol, waited in an adjoining room. Correspondents who had been invited to the ceremony were sworn to a thirty-six-hour embargo, in order to satisfy Russian insistence that announcement of the war's end be held until the next day to coincide with the capitulation of German forces in Berlin. Edward Kennedy, the correspondent of the Associated Press, broke the embargo when he heard the announcement on German radio a few hours later. The story he dictated to the AP bureau in London flashed out on the wires around the world.[16] People in Paris paid little attention until General de Gaulle went on the air at 3 p.m. the next day, May 8: "The war has been won! Victory is here! It is the victory of the United Nations and the victory of France. The French commander was present and took part in the signing of the surrender document."[17]

De Gaulle's speech was broadcast over loudspeakers on the streets and crowds soon began to gather to share the good news. At first, they milled around, filling the Champs Élysées from curb to curb. As more people poured into the Place de l'Étoile where a huge French flag flew beneath the Arch de Triomphe, the crowds began to form spontaneously into marching masses, and round and round they marched, singing snatches of the "Marseillaise" — "*Le jour de gloire est arrive … marchons, marchons.*" American Flying Fortresses buzzed the crowds. At the American Embassy overlooking the Place de la Concorde, a man in khaki appeared on a balcony and the crowd cheered lustily. They thought it was General Eisenhower, but it was actually the former American ambassador, William C. Bullitt. That evening, all the famous monuments of Paris were illuminated for the first time since 1939. Most restaurants were closed, wine and liquor was hard to obtain, electricity was unreliable, and the Metro stopped running at eleven o'clock. None of this lessened the joy of the crowds. They knew life in Paris would still be difficult, but at least it would be free.

By now, the Allies were dividing up Germany for occupation purposes. With the Soviet Union occupying all of the east of the country, including Berlin, the British took control of the northwest of Germany and the Americans settled in to govern southern Germany, including the vital state of Bavaria. France was initially left off the list of occupying powers. De Gaulle still wanted Germany split into smaller states, but he was equally concerned that France have its own zone of occupation. De Gaulle's protests led to the British and Americans each turning over parts of their zones, so France held two chunks of German territory, both fronting on the Rhine and touching only at a single point on the river. The final Big Three conference of the war, held at Potsdam in Germany in late July, again left France waiting outside the door. De Gaulle was sanguine about not being invited. All the crucial wartime decisions having already been made, he wrote later, "everything had been arranged — what could I have done at Potsdam?"[18]

The big event was Winston Churchill's departure in mid-conference. His government had been defeated in the general election of July 25 and the new prime minister, Labour leader Clement Attlee, took over Britain's seat. It was but a portent of other momentous changes to come in Europe after the war.

President Truman had been willing to visit Paris on his way home from Potsdam, but de Gaulle thought better of it. "I indicated to the President that because of the reactions of French public opinion, his arrival in Paris or mine in Washington should not immediately precede or follow" Potsdam. It was a shrewd calculation. The world's attention was next focused on the dropping of two atomic bombs on Japan that led to the country's surrender on August 14.

De Gaulle arrived in Washington a week later, and over three days spent a total of seven hours in talks with Truman. It was clear to de Gaulle that the problems of the old world did not in any way intimidate the new president. It would be a long time before Russia would be in a position to risk war, Truman said, and this was why the United States was rapidly withdrawing the bulk of its troops from Europe. The problems of peace would be largely economic, he added, making it essential to help Germany back on its feet. De Gaulle thought Truman didn't really understand the awful losses that had been suffered at the hands of the Germans in two wars of aggression. France must have guarantees, he said, "to prevent the German threat from ever reappearing." After touching on the situation in the Pacific — de Gaulle told the president he was not eager to see British troops replace the Japanese in French Indochina — the meeting ended. "We parted on good terms."[19]

In New York, de Gaulle received a rousing welcome and a ticker-tape "Victory Parade" down Fifth Avenue. Chicago was equally enthusiastic, and "Canada, in turn, gave us a warm welcome." He was received in Ottawa by the governor general, the Earl of Athlone, and his wife, and Prime Minister Mackenzie King. Over sandwiches and drinks of Scotch (Mackenzie King felt he could hardly stand up, not having tasted whisky for years), de Gaulle made it clear he felt "Churchill and the President had gone too far in what they had done for Russia at Potsdam." He seemed to feel, Mackenzie King wrote in his diary, that both the United States and Russia "were too conscious of their power and determined to manage everything."[20]

King and de Gaulle spent an hour together the next day. De Gaulle wrote in his memoirs of having told Mackenzie King that two world wars had shown France the value of co-operation with Canada. When the prime minister assured de Gaulle of continued Canadian support, the general replied: "What you have just said convinces me that France was quite right in coming here long ago and planting the seed of civilization."[21] In neither Mackenzie King's diary nor in de Gaulle's memoirs is there any mention that the French-speaking population of Canada strongly supported the Vichy government throughout the war.

☦

With the war brought to a sudden end by the awesome power of the atom bomb, Charles de Gaulle returned to Paris convinced that France would have to undergo "profound and rapid changes" if it was to achieve order in an era where "technology dominated the universe." His worry was whether the working class would be the "victim or the beneficiary of technical progress."[22]

De Gaulle went many times before the Consultative Assembly to outline his policies, all the while conscious of the fact that the old "party system" was making a comeback. As each group focused on its own self-interest, de Gaulle "saw the clouds gathering on the horizon" and worried about how he would cope in "an atmosphere heavy with criticism and objections."[23]

One of the acts for which de Gaulle was most criticized was the "solidarity tax" that he established by decree. The government needed money to bring home French prisoners and demobilize the troops at the same time as it was sending an expeditionary corps to Indochina. Politicians on the left cried for higher taxes on the rich; those on the right foresaw "incalculable damage" to business. In the end, the Assembly voted almost unanimously for the new levy.

It was the last time de Gaulle would have its support, a signal that the real test would come in a clash over the right of the legislature to challenge the power of the executive. Let the people decide, de Gaulle concluded. He called on French voters to go to the polls to elect members of a new Constituent Assembly* and to vote in a referendum on dumping the Third Republic. They would face two questions: Do you want a new constitution, and do you agree to limit the powers of the Assembly, with

---

* The Constituent Assembly was a temporary legislative body, created after the Second World War to write a new constitution for France. With the creation of the Fourth Republic, it was replaced by a bi-cameral legislature consisting of the National Assembly and the Council of the Republic.

it being required to produce a constitution for a Fourth Republic within seven months? De Gaulle demanded a double majority — he told Claude Mauriac, "the French must vote yes-yes. They must. Or I shall …"[24]

All the parties held big rallies and the turnout on October 21, 1945, was heavy, with women voting for the first time. As expected, the vote in favour of a new constitution was overwhelming — 96 percent of the 19.2 million (out of 25.7 million eligible) marked their ballots "yes." De Gaulle's victory on the second question was much narrower — the parties had urged a "no" vote — and only 66 percent voted "yes." The Communists under Maurice Thorez emerged as the largest party in the new 544-seat Assembly, winning 160 seats. The Mouvement républicain populaire (MRP) led by Maurice Schumann, de Gaulle's former spokesman, took 152, and the Socialists 142, the other 90 seats going to a mix of conservatives and Radicals. Leon Blum led the Socialists but did not himself stand for election. When the Assembly met, it chose as its president one of de Gaulle's veterans of Algiers, Felix Gouin. The election of de Gaulle as the head of the new government was unanimous: the 545 members also declared: "Charles de Gaulle had deserved well of his country." The results of the voting had led to the creation of an uneasy three-party coalition, and de Gaulle's selection of his new Cabinet reflected the divisions in the Assembly. He was forced to give posts to five Communists, but again denied them the major portfolios of defense and security they had demanded.

As de Gaulle saw it, the Assembly had become a "wasp's nest of intrigue" and he soon realized that his power was hanging "by a thread." He warned the members that they must be prepared to grant authority to the executive. Now exercising all the power of a ruler, de Gaulle set out to nationalize the coal industry and the distribution of electricity and gas (accomplished in an hour's debate), take over the Bank of France and the four leading private banks (a day of debate), set up Air France, and turn the Renault auto works into a public trust. He was driven by protest as much as by principle; workers in Marseille had seized fifteen large companies and were operating them as soviet-style enterprises. In an equally drastic move, the franc was devalued to the equivalent of four-fifths of a cent (compared to the twenty cents the franc would be worth with the introduction of the Euro in 1995).

Other Gaullist measures that won approval included establishment of an atomic energy authority, creation of a scientific research organization, and organization of the elite school for civil servants, the École Nationale d'Administration (ENA). De Gaulle's success, however, was only temporary. When the Assembly met to debate his government's new budget on January 1, 1946, the Socialists suddenly demanded a 20 percent slash in defence spending. De Gaulle rushed to the Palais Bourbon from his rue St-Dominique office to warn that if his budget was rejected "the government would not remain in office another hour." Warming to the subject, he painted a frightening picture of a France operating under the old party system that had brought the country such dissolution and decay:

> I repeat that I am speaking for the future. We have begun the reconstruction of the Republic. You will continue with the work. However you do it, I think I can tell you in all conscience — and it will no doubt be the last time that I shall speak here — that if you do it without taking into account the lessons of our political history over the last fifty years and in particular what took place in 1940, if you fail to take account of the absolute need for authority, dignity, and responsibility in Government, you will find yourselves in a situation in which you will bitterly regret taking the course that you will have taken.[25]

When the vote was called, the budget passed, but de Gaulle was reading the writing on the wall. There was one further bill he needed to have enacted. His one-time adversary, Jean Monnet, had agreed to develop an economic plan to guide France in the future. Monnet had created a breathtakingly bold design, almost as visionary as the scheme for Franco-British union he had put forward in London in 1940. The plan set targets for investment, construction, and production, all to be carried forward under the guiding hand of the state. The plan for "French Modernization and Investment" won the approval of the Assembly on January 3, thereby becoming the main tool in the re-engineering of the French economy.

De Gaulle had less success in the design of the constitution for the Fourth Republic. He'd been rudely rebuffed, told that as he was not an elected member of the Assembly he could have no say in its deliberations. Left to its own, it was intent on making the National Assembly all-powerful, with authority to elect the president, who would be restricted to the most ceremonial of duties. "It was apparent," he wrote in his memoirs, "that if de Gaulle tolerated this situation in order to remain in office, his prestige would decline, until one day the parties would either no longer tolerate him or else relegate him to some harmless and decorative function."* [26] Was it time to prepare for his departure? The ruler who had struggled to first obtain and then to manage power now found himself rebelling against the forces that would limit his exercise of the prize. Perhaps the game had been in vain. There was only one way to find out.

---

* De Gaulle often referred to himself in the third person.

CHAPTER 18
The Gamble for France

Man soon grows accustomed to his own miracles.

> — François Mauriac
> *Mémoires interieurs,* 1959

Cap d'Antibes is a hammerhead peninsula of hillocks, rocks, pine trees, and sandy beaches on the French Riviera, halfway between Cannes and Nice. On the western shoulder of the promontory lies the resort of Eden Roc, which Charles and Mme de Gaulle reached on Sunday, January 6, 1946, having enjoyed the comfort of the presidential car on the overnight train from Paris. The general's big Cadillac — a gift of the U.S. government — met them at the train station in Golfe Juan and took them to a commodious villa, *Sous le vent,* loaned by an anonymous friend for their week's vacation. Charles's youngest brother, Pierre, who looked so alike his elder brother that many mistook him for the general, was with them, along with Yvonne de Gaulle's brother, Jacques Vendroux.

De Gaulle was tired from the strain of getting legislation through the Constituent Assembly. He was fifty-five now, and this was the first time in seven years he had taken a few days' rest. He welcomed the respite that came with quiet walks along the beach and drives around the Cap, enveloped in the strong Turkish aroma of his Gauloise cigarettes. Charles and Yvonne may have stopped in Antibes to visit the museum in the historic Château Grimaldi, where Pablo Picasso would soon work on his paintings and lithographs while tending to a wounded owl.

Before leaving Paris, the de Gaulles had attended the wedding of their daughter Elisabeth to Major Alain de Boissieu, a comrade of General Leclerc. Yvonne would have been pleased that Elisabeth had married such an upstanding young man with a future as brilliant as his past. He had served valiantly in the Battle of France, having led one of the last cavalry charges in history, was with the Canadians at Dieppe, and had taken part in the liberation of Paris with the 2nd Armoured Division. The Boissieus were honeymooning in Morocco.

General de Gaulle tells us in his memoirs that when he went home to Neuilly on the evening of January 1, he had made up his mind to resign. "All that remained was to select the date, without making any concessions whatever."[1] His thinking was that the decision must not appear to have been taken impulsively; he needed a vacation and that would provide the opportunity for further reflection.

If his mind was made up, he apparently had not shared his intentions with either Pierre or with Jacques Vendroux, who represented Calais in the Constituent Assembly, having been elected on the MRP ticket. Between dodging photographers while touring the Cap — granting but one news conference for the local press — de Gaulle sat down for several heart-to-heart talks with the two men. On the train back to Paris on January 13, Pierre urged him to stay on and allow the Assembly to proceed with a new constitution. That would require a fresh election and the general could then decide whether to stay or go. Jacques Vendroux thought the general should resign right away. After the Assembly made a mess of things, the country would plead with him to return. Vendroux spoke with the knowledge of his own experience. As a member of the

Assembly, he'd watched with disgust the petty jealousies and intrigues of the parties. As they talked, Vendroux had the feeling that de Gaulle "had already decided, deep in himself, to go."[2]

Wishing to avoid the fuss that he knew his arrival at the Gare de Lyon would cause, de Gaulle left the presidential carriage at Maisons-Alfort, just south of the capital. He did not count on the persistence of the minister of public works and transport, Jules Moch. Faithful to the tradition that the head of the government should be welcomed back to Paris by the official in charge of transport, Moch rushed to the suburban station as soon as he got word of the change in plans. "Oh, kind of you to come," de Gaulle said on seeing him. He invited the minister to ride with him in his limousine. Moch recounts that once they got into the car, de Gaulle told him he had something important to tell him, but that it must be kept a secret. "I can't resign myself to enduring the criticisms of parties and irresponsible men, to seeing my decisions challenged, my ministers criticized, myself attacked, my prestige diminished. Since I cannot govern as I wish, that is to say fully, rather than see my power diminished, *I'm going!*"[3]

Moch was shaken by the disclosure, but not stunned into silence. "You have no right to leave," he told de Gaulle. "You joined the parliamentary game, you must go on playing it."[4]

De Gaulle thought otherwise. It was not as if his uneasy coalition was without accomplishments. In less than eighteen months, his provisional government had sent the French army across the Rhine, gained a zone of occupation in Germany, brought in a drastic plan to modernize the French economy, nationalized the banks and big industry, extended the vote to women, and begun the building of a welfare state. Paris was once again taking control of the far-flung French colonies with de Gaulle espousing the vague concept of a French Union in which all its members could realize their destinies. But to continue to put up with the asinine demands of the politicians? Especially under a new constitution that would reduce the president to the task of laying wreaths on memorials and presiding over ceremonial openings of the National Assembly? No!

In the week after his return, de Gaulle went only once to the National Assembly. He got into a terrible argument defending the Légion d'honneur given by General Giraud to combatants killed in defending Algeria against the Allied landing in November 1942. They were French soldiers who had died doing their duty as their orders had commanded. "I've had enough," de Gaulle told one of his ministers, Francis Gay. "Next Sunday I'll summon you all at midday to tell you I am going." When Gay protested, de Gaulle took on a condescending tone, replying: "Come now, before a week is up, they'll be sending a delegation asking me to come back. It shall be on my conditions."[5]

Members of de Gaulle's Cabinet, who were having dinner at home on the night of Saturday, January 19, were interrupted with the arrival of a special messenger at their doors. The promised summons had arrived. Those who gathered early in the Salles des Armures at rue Saint-Dominique in the bleakness of a wintry Sunday saw General de Gaulle arrive "stiff and drawn," according to Jules Moch. De Gaulle described the events that followed:

> I came in, shook hands all around and before anyone sat down, spoke these words: "The exclusive regime of parties has reappeared. I disapprove of it. But aside from establishing by force a dictatorship which I do not desire and which would certainly end in disaster, I have not the means of preventing this experiment. I must therefore withdraw. Today, in fact, I shall send the President of the National Assembly a letter informing him of the government's resignation. I sincerely thank each of you for the support you have given me and urge you to remain at your posts in order to assure the conduct of business until your successors are appointed."

No one said a word, and de Gaulle went home. Shortly after, he left his Neuilly villa, paid for by the state, and rented a government guest house, a modest and rather rundown Louis XIV hunting lodge, the Pavillon de Marly near Versailles. He stayed until the end of May while renovations were being completed to his country home, La Boisserie, which had been ransacked by the Germans. He gave up the Cadillac, bought a small French car, and turned over to the French air force the DC-4 Skymaster that had been a gift of President Truman. Yvonne de Gaulle learned to drive and Charles and she celebrated their silver wedding anniversary at Marly on April 7. A visit was made on May 12 to the tomb of First World War statesman Georges Clemenceau, in company with a handful of the old inner circle, including Gaston Palewski, Claude Mauriac, and Elizabeth de Miribel. In a solemn moment, de Gaulle spoke of how "there can be no security, no freedom, no efficiency, without the acceptance of great discipline, under the guidance of a strong State and with the enthusiastic support of a people rallied in unity."[6]

De Gaulle's departure had been met with indifference by a public worn down by conflict and tumult. A poll showed only 27 percent of the voters wanted him back. The press praised the general's achievements, with one editorial hailing him for having "retired with his dignity intact." Janet Flanner noted, "The general is still France's unknown soldier. No two people who have worked with him, and no two who have analyzed him from afar, seem to have come to the same conclusion."[7] Still, when he spoke out against the constitution devised by the Constituent Assembly, people heard him and voted it down. In new elections for the Assembly in June, the three-party coalition of the MRP, the Communists, and the Socialists was returned. Rumours of a Communist coup evaporated, but to de Gaulle, the time seemed favourable for a return to the public eye.

The general travelled to the scene of his first liberation triumph, Bayeux, on June 16, to commemorate his London Appeal of 1940. Wearing his uniform, he stood bareheaded in the pouring rain before fifty thousand people. It was a speech in which he set out the core principles of what would become Gaullism. "In our glorious and mutilated Normandy," he began, "Bayeux was witness to one of the greatest events of our history. It was here, four years after the initial disaster of France and the Allies, the final victory of the Allies and France began."[8] De Gaulle went on to renew his warning that France needed a strong government if it was to avoid the fate of previous Republics. Weak parliaments ended in dictatorship, but dictatorship was not a choice for France. The country needed a president with the power to choose prime ministers, dissolve the National Assembly, manage the government, make treaties and direct foreign affairs, and control the armed forces. "It is from the Head of State, placed above the parties ... that the executive power must come."

The speech described almost precisely the scenario de Gaulle would create a decade hence in formulating the Fifth Republic. But it had little immediate effect. A revised constitution was approved by referendum in October, new elections returned the Communists as the largest party, and on January 16, 1947, the Fourth Republic came into existence with Vincent Auriol as president and Paul Ramadier of the Socialist Party as prime minister.

Had de Gaulle's gamble — a game-changing roll of the dice — been a failure? Had he become so accustomed to pulling off miracles that he thought another would be easily achieved? François Mauriac would write that "he was gambling — but not wildly."[9] Mauriac considered that de Gaulle had "measured the risk. By remaining, he would have been bound, impotent. From outside, he could act. He was not mistaken; he acted. What this has cost us, we know. The Fourth Republic was an endless demonstration, a clinical lesson taught on the very body of France. And the surgeon was in the wings, ready to intervene at any moment, but the doctors acted as if they preferred their patient to die."

Today, Colombey-les-Deux-Églises is a small but busy village astride Route 619D three hours southeast of Paris. It caters to the many visitors to the Charles de Gaulle Memorial Museum who come also to see the huge Cross of Lorraine that dominates the hillside above La Boisserie.[10] When Charles de Gaulle returned here in May 1946, it was a typically quiet French country village where life centred around the church, the local épicerie, the garage, and the school. The de Gaulle family was welcomed back into the neighbourhood and the general fell into an easy routine. Jean Lacouture tells us de Gaulle arose around seven o'clock, breakfasted on tea and *biscottes*, walked three times a day through his well-treed property, played solitaire at his big Empire desk, and began work on his memoirs.

Labourers were a constant presence on the property as renovations went forward, including the addition of a three-storey tower. (Philippe de

Gaulle had been the first to see the old place when he reached La Boisserie in September 1944 during the eastward advance of the 2nd Armoured Division. He found it burned out, leaving "nothing but ruins, rubble, and garbage.")[11] Rather than carry a mortgage to pay for the renovations, de Gaulle obtained a loan from the Rothschild Bank in Paris where Georges Pompidou, a friend, was the manager. Central heating was added, easing the chill that spread throughout the house on the cold winter days for which the high country of the Haute Marne district was well-known.[12]

Mme de Gaulle, aided by two servants, reigned over the house. She saw to it that the occasional guest was given a "vulgar" dish such as *miroton* (beef hash with onions) washed down with *vin ordinaire*. Some meals were of rabbit or chicken raised on the grounds of La Boisserie. Yvonne de Gaulle was frugal in their finances, it being said that when de Gaulle noticed a particular piece of silver missing, she responded, "And what do you think we're living on, *mon ami*?"

De Gaulle preferred to drink beer with his lunch, followed by brandy and a cigar. He had the service of an aide-de-camp, Gaston de Bonneval, once a colonel in the Foreign Legion. Neighbours were respectful of the de Gaulles' privacy. Charles occasionally drove Yvonne into Chaumont, the nearest market town twenty kilometres to the east. Other forays were made toward the Champagne countryside to the north, stopping in such places as Cirey-sur-Blaise to admire the château where Voltaire spent fifteen years as the guest of a mistress, Gabrielle Emilie de Breteuil, the Marquise du Chatelet.

Not long after moving to Colombey-les-Deux-Églises, two sad occasions brought Charles de Gaulle close to despair. In November 1947, his great wartime friend, Jacques-Philippe Leclerc de Hauteclocque, was killed when a sandstorm threw his taxiing plane against a railway embankment in Algeria. De Gaulle confessed in a letter to Leclerc's widow, Thérèse, "I loved your husband; he was not only the companion of the worst and greatest days, but a dependable friend, incapable of any feeling, any action, any gesture, any word that betrayed the slightest mediocrity."[13] De Gaulle chose this time to give up smoking, "in one go," he claimed.

De Gaulle's sadness was lifted slightly by the marriage on December 30, 1947, of his son, Philippe, to Henriette de Montalembert Cers, a descendant of the family of the Marquis de Montalembert. However, still greater grief was to descend on the de Gaulles with the death of their beloved Anne, on February 6, 1948. The general wrote to his daughter Elisabeth to describe her sister's passing, which came when a doctor gave her an injection to release her from the suffering of bronchial pneumonia. "Anne grew weaker and weaker, finding it more and more difficult to breathe. She is a freed soul."[14] Anne was buried in the cemetery next to the church where they worshipped. "Now she is like the others," de Gaulle said to Yvonne as they left the churchyard. When royalties from de Gaulle's *Mémoires de guerre* began to flow in 1955, he passed them on to the Fondation Anne-de-Gaulle, a charity for handicapped children established in his daughter's memory.

These sad events in the first years after the war came as Charles de Gaulle was making his fateful decision to take up what he had always abhorred: the political life. It was the political gamesmanship of the party system that de Gaulle had blamed for France's unpreparedness for the Second World War. He kept in touch with his old comrades and when Claude Mauriac came to visit in February 1947, he gave the first hint of his plans: "I suffer deeply to see France in this situation. I'm going to try a *Rassemblement*. It's the only hope."[15]

De Gaulle had to first carefully prepare the ground. On March 30, 1947, he travelled to the Normandy coast for a reunion of Resistance fighters under the cliffs of the hamlet of Bruneval. It was here on the night of February 27, 1942, that the British Airborne Division, accompanied by members of the French Resistance, had raided the German radar station and escaped with key components.* Fifty thousand people gathered to hear whether de Gaulle was ready to declare himself for the leadership of France. He made no bones about not retiring gracefully from the field of battle. "The day will come," de Gaulle declared, "when rejecting the sterile games, and reforming the poorly constructed framework in which the nation is losing its way and the state is disqualifying itself, the great

---

* The raid revealed that German radar was far less sophisticated than that of the British.

mass of the French people will rally around France!"[16] He meant, of course, himself, as it was his conception that he was indistinguishable from France. The crowd was ecstatic, loosening volleys of *"De Gaulle au pouvoir!"*

The speech brought Paul Ramadier, the Socialist premier who was about to throw the Communists out of the tri-partite government, hurrying to Colombey the next night — just as de Gaulle was going to bed. Ramadier had come to inquire of the general's intentions; de Gaulle assured him he planned no *coup d'état*. "I serve only France," he said over coffee before showing the premier the door.

The official announcement of the launch of de Gaulle's Rassemblement du peuple français (Rally of the French People), the RPF, came on April 7 in Strasbourg, where he had travelled to honour the American soldiers who had died in liberating the city. He had thought up the name for the new party himself, but he had no intention of personally seeking a seat in the National Assembly. To do so would be to reduce himself to the rank of a party game-player, limited to becoming premier under a constitution that that was doomed to fail. He was not going to put his "little cap in the little cupboard in the cloakroom of the Palais Bourbon."

With the onset of the Cold War and the threat of a powerful Communist Party within France, the RPF was the only force that could protect the future. Speaking at the Hôtel de Ville, de Gaulle told a large and enthusiastic crowd that he had brought France "out of the tomb" and that it must now decide on renewal with "efficiency, concord and liberty," or face "impotence and dissolution as we see it disappear." It was time for a Rally of the French People so that "the great effort of common salvation and the profound reform of the State may be begun and triumph." A week later, André Malraux, the novelist and cultural critic, issued a statement in Paris officially launching the new party. Jacques Soustelle, de Gaulle's old minister of information and a former vice-director of the Musée de l'Homme, became secretary-general. De Gaulle commuted to RPF headquarters on the rue de Solférino from his home in Colombey.

When Cyrus Sulzberger, scion of the family owning the *New York Times* interviewed him, de Gaulle declared that his new movement would bring France back to "full productive capacity and power." It would try to make up for the fact "[t]he Germans deliberately killed all the best men and the Communists did the same in the underground movement."[17]

The Fourth Republic, barely out of the starting gate, stumbled when the first of its many governments fell that spring and forty-one members of the National Assembly formed themselves into a Gaullist bloc. The first public opinion poll after formation of the Rally showed it had the support of 40 percent of the voters, almost enough to give de Gaulle a majority. The general saw his first great opportunity in the municipal elections held throughout France on October 19. De Gaulle toured the provinces and the results surpassed even his fondest hopes. The RPF carried thirteen of France's twenty-five largest cities, including Paris, Marseille, and Bordeaux. In the contests for local councillors, 40 percent of French voters, just as the polls had predicted, had opted to back de Gaulle's followers.

This was surely a show of strength the government could not ignore. André Malraux declared that the general "will accept power only after a referendum and a formal mandate from the people even if the President of the Republic were to offer him power." De Gaulle called for dissolution of the National Assembly and a new electoral system. To expect both was assuming a lot. Even in the fevered atmosphere of postwar France, with a failure in the harvest, rising inflation, and a desperate unfilled need for foreign aid, the parties were not yet ready to throw in their cards.

A year later, in the November 1948 elections for Parliament's upper house, the Council of the Republic, the RPF claimed 123 of its 320 seats. The Rally may have looked like the party of the future, but its stresses were making themselves evident. Fifty-six of the new Council members ended up in a Gaullist rump called the Democratic and Social Action, the others having been drained off for choice positions requiring fealty to other parties. An extreme faction within the RPF began to look to revolution. A paramilitary force, the Service d'Ordre, commanded by a former Resistance chief, began to harass opponents at RPF rallies. A rally in Grenoble ended in a riot when members of the Order, many carrying guns, drove their Jeeps into the crowd. De Gaulle refused publicly to dismiss the possibility of a coup, and in June 1949, sixteen of the Order's members were arrested on allegations they were preparing to take over the government by force.

The big test for the RPF came on June 17, 1951, when the government of Henri Queuille, who would serve on three occasions as premier, called elections for the National Assembly under a new and highly convoluted voting system. The Rally actually emerged as the single largest party, winning 120 of the 627 seats with more than four million votes — but only 22 percent of all those cast. The general charged that the country had been swindled, but he was powerless against a clever system of alliances that put the old parties — organized now as a "Third Force" — back in command with 396 seats. Promises, votes, and perhaps other inducements were traded, and when the new government of Antoine Pinay was voted in, twenty-seven RPF delegates gave him their support. There were further disappointments in municipal elections. Jacques Soustelle called the RPF deputies "lost children" in the "terribly difficult game of parliamentary Gaullism."[18]

Soustelle split with de Gaulle over the Rally's future and on May 6, 1953, de Gaulle wrapped it up, freeing his deputies to do as they wished. "The efforts that I have put in since the war, surrounded by resolute Frenchmen, have not so far succeeded. What is the Rassemblement to do?… Not in Parliament will they take part, as a body and as such, in the series of combinations, deals, votes of confidence, investitures that are the games, poisons, and delights of the system.… The collapse of illusions is at hand. We must prepare the remedy."[19] That unstated remedy he did not spell out.

Just as Charles de Gaulle had a "certain idea" of France, his personality had a certain affect on the people of France. His call to grandeur echoed a larger sentiment present in the French soul, a conviction that the marriage of reason and emotion could lead the country to an exceptional destiny. For those exposed to the force of de Gaulle's character, the outcome was almost invariably intense loyalty or sudden aversion. François Mauriac's reaction on meeting him was wholly positive: De Gaulle gave him "a new sense of what constitutes true greatness and true glory."[20]

Elisabeth de Miribel's admiration for the general would always be "pure and wholehearted," as it had been since the day she arrived at Seymour Place to type his Appeal of June 18, finding him a man of "simplicity and courtesy." This impression was strengthened when she travelled with de Gaulle to North America in August 1945, and later served as his press secretary. She mourned, with her "adoptive mother," Pauline Vanier, wife of the Canadian ambassador, the death of de Gaulle's field commander — and Pauline Vanier's cousin — General Leclerc. But she disagreed with de Gaulle on the formation of his Rassemblement and never joined it, unhappy at its admission of former adherents of Vichy. She was also disappointed that de Gaulle "had stepped down into the arena, making of his movement a party competing with the others."[21]

Both de Miribel and de Gaulle had been raised in conventional Catholic families, but while the general became consumed with temporal matters, de Miribel found a reaffirmation of her childhood religion during her "lonely days" in Canada. "How does one explain the mystery of a [religious] vocation?" she asks in her memoir. "It is a deep and undeniable call which has taken possession of you."[22] Shortly after the war, she became disenchanted with the direction of French life. The "New Look," so dubbed by *Harper's Bazaar* fashion writer Carmel Snow when Christian Dior introduced his 1947 collection, no longer interested her. She would have approved of the fact brothels had been officially abolished, but would not have been so naïve as to think that would put an end to women selling their bodies. After a last visit by André Malraux to her apartment in the Place du Pantheon, when they argued about religion with Malraux maintaining his agnosticism, Elisabeth de Miribel made her decision. She would become a nun.

On a snowy February 2, 1949, the day of the Feast of the Candlemas, the attractive young woman so often seen smoking and enjoying a glass of wine at cocktail parties and diplomatic soirees was driven to the Carmelite convent of Christ the King at Nogent-sur-Marne, a suburb of Paris. She travelled in a convoy of three cars that included her parents, Canadian ambassador, Georges Vanier, and Pauline. Mlle De Miribel had informed the general of her intention when she had gone to Colombey-les-Deux-Églises for a lunch. "In leaving him, I am not losing him. I shall pray for him," she told Père Couturier.[23] His reaction, as expressed to friends was less sanguine: "Elisabeth is leaving us because we have disappointed her."

De Miribel remained at the Carmelite convent only four years, departing shortly before she was to take her perpetual vows. De Gaulle, not knowing of her decision to quit, had sent her a letter saying she would be in his thoughts on that day, and that they had been through experiences that would "burn [in our memories] forever, even after our deaths." He added, "You will have a prayer, isn't it so, for me, for your friends, for the priests?"[24]

We do not know if they ever saw each other again. While at the convent, Elisabeth de Miribel wrote a biography of Edith Stein, the Jewish-born German nun who died at Auschwitz and was later canonized. De Miribel had been in poor health at Nogent-sur-Marne and spent months recovering in Switzerland. She later took up a career in the French diplomatic service.

These were the years in which the world became caught up in the Cold War. The "Iron Curtain" spoken of by Winston Churchill in his famous address of March 5, 1946, at Fulton, Missouri, became bywords for the division of Western and Eastern Europe, with "all the capitals of [these] ancient states ... subject, in one form or another, not only to Soviet influence but to a very high and in some cases increasing measure of control from Moscow." The next year, President Truman enunciated the Truman Doctrine by which the United States extended armed aid to Greece and Turkey and set out on a program of military containment of the Soviet Union. It saved those two countries from communism but did not prevent the USSR from taking control of Czechoslovakia in 1948. The same year, Moscow imposed an embargo on road and rail traffic from West Germany into Berlin, giving rise to the Berlin airlift and fear on the part of de Gaulle that a third world war was imminent. In response, NATO — the North Atlantic Treaty Organization — had come into being by 1949. By then, the Marshall Plan of American aid to Europe, named after Secretary of State George C. Marshall, had poured billions of dollars into the rebuilding of France and other European countries.*

Charles de Gaulle welcomed the arrival of NATO, but observed that France should reserve final judgment "until she knows under what conditions she will be getting the arms she needs ... and what her commitments

* Officially the European Economic Recovery Plan. Marshall had served as chief of staff of the U.S. Army in the Second World War.

would be." He opposed Jean Monnet over the creation in 1950 of the European Coal and Steel Community — forerunner of the Common Market — arguing that it was ridiculous for France to give up control of its heavy industry in a scheme that would ultimately benefit Germany. He still held the view that Germany should be reformulated as a loose confederation. De Gaulle also watched anxiously as a battalion of French engineers fought in Korea as part of the United Nations response to the invasion from the north.

The long hours de Gaulle spent working on his memoirs took a toll on his eyesight and he suffered pain that he wouldn't have wished "on my worst enemy." He had an operation in 1952 for a cataract, leading him to wear at first dark glasses, and then glasses with very thick lenses. He did not take well to this, commenting that one couldn't review troops with "thick spectacles on his nose." The affliction did not stop de Gaulle from travelling widely. In four overseas trips between 1953 and 1957, he visited France's central African colonies, toured Madagascar and Ethiopia, where he visited his friend Emperor Haile Selassie, touched down on France's island colonies from the Caribbean to Tahiti, and travelled across the Sahara desert in Algeria.

These were years of spreading unease throughout the French Empire. During de Gaulle's eighteen months in power, he had begun to develop the concept of a French community in which former colonies would assume autonomy while still linked to Paris. His successors carried that over into creation of the French Union, an idea that met with varying responses, ranging from cautious acceptance to resentful rejection. French Indochina, where Ho Chi Minh's Communists had proclaimed the Democratic Republic of Vietnam in 1946, posed the biggest problem. De Gaulle had sent off Admiral d'Argenlieu, appointing him high commissioner to Saigon with the advice, "There's a big piece for us to take back, a great game to play."[25] Seeing rising Communist strength in the north, d'Argenlieu arbitrarily ordered a naval bombardment of Haiphong, in which thousands of civilians were killed or wounded. Later, also without reference to Paris, he recognized the southern part of the peninsula as the State of Vietnam. That spurred Ho Chi Minh to intensify his insurrection.

The French Expeditionary Force, led initially by General Leclerc, fought bravely but suffered a painful defeat at Dien Bien Phu on May 7, 1954. The resulting crisis led to a new government headed by Pierre

Mendès France, the one leader of the Fourth Republic who had the respect of de Gaulle. Scion of a family of well-to-do Sephardic Jews, Mendès France shocked the country with an agenda that within a month brought independence to Vietnam, produced a formula for self-determination of Tunisia and Morocco, and launched a new plan of economic reform in France. The Indochina war was over, but at a cost to the French of seventy-five thousand dead.

Trouble was brewing in other French colonies as well. Of all the domains over which the Tricolour flag of France had flown, no region was seen as more truly woven into the fabric of the nation than Algeria, since 1830 the cornerstone of the French Empire. The fact of *Algérie française* was by now an indisputable reality, a consequence of the colonizing efforts of a million Mediterranean — mostly French — *colons* (also called *les pieds noirs**) under whose sun-blackened feet the malarial swamps of coastal Algeria had been turned into rich farmland drenched in the scent of orange blossoms in the spring and vivid with the sight of vineyards of plump grapes in the fall. Aside from a brief uprising centred on the market town of Sétif in 1945, a five-day madness that led to the deaths of more than one hundred Europeans and resulted in the wanton slaughter by the French army of several thousand Muslim civilians, the colony staggered lethargically into the 1950s. However, a militant new Arab underground revolutionary force, encouraged by the success of Ho Chi Minh and the transition to independence of neighbouring Tunisia and Morocco, was rising to challenge French control. Charles de Gaulle's gamble that France would again have need of him would soon play out to its final resolution.

---

* Other theories for the origin of this term stem from the coal-blackened feet of firemen on Mediterranean ferries, to the black shoes favoured by settlers.

U.S. National Archives

D-Day landing of Allied forces in Normandy put 155,000 men ashore from the U.S., British, and Canadian armies. The Free French 2nd Armoured Division was held in reserve until August 1944.

U.S. National Archives

General Eisenhower mingles with American troops after the Normandy landing.

Ray Argyle

Relics of a burned-out vehicle lie scattered beside walls of houses destroyed in the German atrocity at Oradour-sur-Glane, June 10, 1944.

Universal History Archive / UIG / Bridgeman Art Library

Charles de Gaulle walks through Bayeux, France, on June 14, 1944, accompanied by an ecstatic crowd of adults and children.

U.S. National Archives 208-MFI-5H-1

General de Gaulle speaks from l'Hôtel de Ville in Cherbourg shortly after return of the Fighting French, August 1944.

Ray Argyle

General de Gaulle paused at Chateau Rambouillet before entering Paris on Liberation Day, August 25, 1944.

THE LIBERATION OF PARIS
August 25, 1944

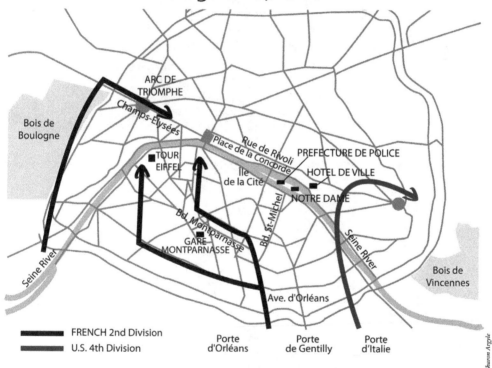

FRENCH 2nd Division

U.S. 4th Division

Bois de Boulogne

ARC DE TRIOMPHE

Champs-Elysées

TOUR EIFFEL

Place de la Concorde

Rue de Rivoli

Île de la Cité

PREFECTURE DE POLICE

HOTEL DE VILLE

NOTRE DAME

Bd. St-Michel

Bd. Montparnasse

GARE MONTPARNASSE

Seine River

Seine River

Ave. d'Orléans

Bois de Vincennes

Porte d'Orléans

Porte de Gentilly

Porte d'Italie

Sharon Argyle

After more than four years of German occupation, the Fighting French and American forces liberate Paris on August 25, 1944.

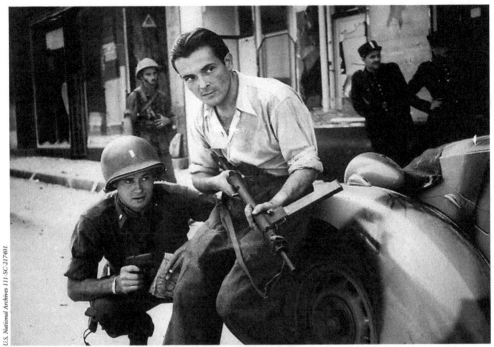

U.S. National Archives 111-SC-217401

An American soldier backs up a French Resistance fighter in Paris on the day of liberation.

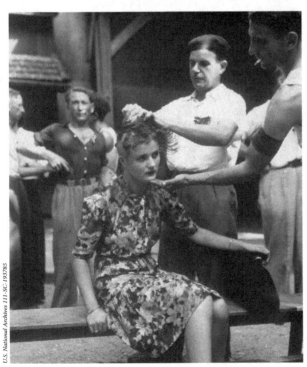

U.S. National Archives 111-SC-193785

A French girl pays the penalty for having fraternized with German soldiers.

A TOUS LES FRANÇAIS

La France a perdu une bataille!
Mais la France n'a pas perdu la guerre!

Des gouvernants de rencontre ont pu capituler, cédant à la panique, oubliant l'honneur, livrant le pays à la servitude. Cependant, rien n'est perdu!

Rien n'est perdu, parce que cette guerre est une guerre mondiale. Dans l'univers libre, des forces immenses n'ont pas encore donné. Un jour, ces forces écraseront l'ennemi. Il faut que la France, ce jour-là, soit présente à la victoire. Alors, elle retrouvera sa liberté et sa grandeur. Tel est mon but, mon seul but!

Voilà pourquoi je convie tous les Français, où qu'ils se trouvent, à s'unir à moi dans l'action, dans le sacrifice et dans l'espérance.

Notre patrie est en péril de mort.
Luttons tous pour la sauver!

VIVE LA FRANCE !

GÉNÉRAL DE GAULLE

Ray Argyle

Historic words from General de Gaulle's Appeal of June 18, 1940 are inscribed in this plaque.

Archives de Gaulle, Paris, France / Giraudon / Bridgeman Art Library

General de Gaulle and General Jacques Leclerc together at the liberation of Paris. Leclerc's 2nd Armoured Division led the Allies into the city.

Ray Argyle

The memorial to Jean Moulin in Salon de Provence symbolizes mankind's reach for freedom.

This memorial in Annot, hear Nice, is one of thousands throughout France where ceremonies are held every year on November 11, Armistice Day, marking the end of First World War.

Ray Argyle

Deborah Windsor

This majestic Cross of Lorraine dominates the site of the de Gaulle Memorial in Colombey-les-Deux-Églises.

Charles de Gaulle issued his incendiary "Vive le Quebec Libre" proclamation in Montreal, 1967.

Canadian Press / Charles Mitchell

V

Days of Glory: The Wager Is Won

It is only in times of crisis that nations throw up giants.
They don't need them in normal times.

— Charles de Gaulle
Interview with Cyrus L. Sulzberger
An Age of Mediocrity, 1973

CHAPTER 19
The Crisis and the Call

In the Paris of the 1950s — unlike the Paris of the twenty-first century — the presence of visible minorities was slight enough to be hardly noticed or remarked on. The city's North African population, preponderantly men, led hidden lives in the squalid conditions of the *bidonvilles* — shanty towns — that took root on the outskirts of the capital. The "Algerian Paris" of the twenty-first century, with upwards of a million African labourers, servants, and shop assistants crowded into blighted suburbs like Clichy-sous-Bois or in the more livable Goute d'Or area of the 18th arrondissement, was something yet unseen. These harbingers of a distant future would take form only in the long shadow to be cast by *la guerre d'Algérie*, that most brutal war of decolonization that would plunge France into a new crisis, put an end to the Fourth Republic, and issue the call that would return Charles de Gaulle to power.[1]

If the French brought anything to Algeria during their long years of colonization, it was education, although not every young Algerian got to go to school. Those that did were inculcated with fidelity to the Republic, having been taught to honour "[o]ur ancestors, the Gauls...." It was true that only one in every five native boys — and one girl in sixteen — were being educated at the end of the Second World War. The classrooms of Muslim Algeria, however, would prove as adept at graduating young revolutionaries as in fulfilling what the French saw as their primary purpose: to provide literate workers for industries catering to the markets of the Mediterranean.

In a territory almost four times as large as Metropolitan France, nine million Muslims outnumbered Europeans nine-to-one, but it was the wealthy European bourgeoisie, the *grands colons*, who owned the best land and employed most of Algeria's workers. Alastair Horne, in his magisterial account of the country's troubles, *A Savage War of Peace,* describes figures such as Henri Borgeaud, owner of four hundred hectares of the country's best vineyards from which flowed four million litres of wine per year. Borgeaud also made a fortune in food production and cigarette manufacturing. Laurent Schiaffino, the wealthiest man in Algeria, brought his Italian personality to local business and became owner of the country's largest shipping fleet as well as a newspaper, *Dépéche Algérienne*. Georges Blachette, scion of a pioneering French family, completed Horne's trio of Algerian entrepreneurial heavyweights. His alfalfa fields generated 20 percent of Algeria's foreign earnings, but his workers drew the poorest wages.

Young Algerian men, the sons of *pieds noirs* and Muslims alike, enrolled in the French army by the thousands in the 1930s. The pattern continued under General de Gaulle after the Fighting French dislodged Vichy from control following the Anglo-American invasion of 1942. Ahmed Ben Bella, a husky young Arab born in 1918 into a family of mountain peasants in Maghnia, on the Algeria-Morocco border, stood out among these recruits. His family had migrated across the border from Marrakesh and Ahmed's father had managed to assemble a farm of thirty hectares, three times that of the typical Arab farmstead. Ahmed's eldest brother had died of injuries received serving in the French army in the First World War. The racial discrimination Ahmed encountered at school did not deter him from twice enlisting, first as a draftee in 1937. He rose to become a sergeant and emerged from the Battle of France with the Croix de Guerre. Demobilized after the Armistice, and not wishing to return to the back-breaking work that marked life on his father's farm, he enlisted in a Moroccan regiment and served with the Fighting French in the Italian campaign. There, his skill and bravery gained him the Médaille Militaire. It was personally pinned on his chest by General Charles de Gaulle, both quite unaware that their lives were destined to become entwined in events that would decide the fate of France and Algeria.

After the war, Ben Bella's superiors urged him to go to officers' school, but he turned them down, as he did several offers to play professional soccer. The incident at Sétif on the day the war ended and the heavy reprisals suffered by Algerians turned him against the French. Returning home, Ben Bella won a seat on the municipal council in Maghnia, but his career in the ruthless game of Algerian politics ended with an altercation over the inheritance of his father's farm. According to Ben Bella, European rivals on the local council had manufactured false papers giving a stranger ownership of the property. Ben Bella shot and wounded his adversary, after which he had to go underground. He joined one of the splinter revolutionary groups that were springing up in Algeria and became a leader of the Organization Spéciale, pledged to fight French rule by "all means possible," legal or otherwise.

Like other revolutionaries, members of the OS resorted to robberies to raise funds, and in 1950 Ben Bellla was captured after an amateurish attempt to raid the central post office in Oran. He was sentenced to eight years in prison, but in 1952 he and another prisoner had a saw smuggled to them, hidden in a loaf of bread. They used it to cut through the bars of their cell in the Blida Prison and Ben Bella escaped to Tunisia, from where he made his way first to France and then to Cairo.

He arrived in Cairo virtually penniless. Speaking only French and a local Arabic dialect, he was unable to communicate in the literary Arab spoken among educated revolutionaries in the Egyptian capital. Travelling on a passport issued by a sympathetic Pakistani government, Ben Bella was in Switzerland in 1954 for the founding of the main Algerian revolutionary movement, the Front de Libération Nationale (FLN). It was born in Berne under cover of the World Cup tournament that saw West Germany beat Hungary by a score of 3 to 2.

To build a unified revolutionary movement took brains, determination, and money. Ben Bella's mission in Cairo was to gain the financial support of Egypt's Revolutionary Council that had overthrown the regime of King Farouk in 1952. He was told to start the revolution and that aid would follow. The FLN began by inundating the countryside with pamphlets demanding "restoration of the Algerian state, sovereign, democratic and social, within the framework of the principles of Islam." Its authors were no modern jihadists. Their goals, while consistent with their religious scruples, were the expulsion of the French and the assumption of power by native Algerians.

The FLN's first large-scale operation called for simultaneous attacks on seventy targets the night of *La Toussaint* — All Saints' Day — November 1, 1954. The date was chosen for its religious significance to the French Catholics of Algeria. Most police would be on leave and army officers would be dining with their families after leaving flowers at the headstones of their loved ones. The operation, involving homemade bombs and a variety of weaponry scrounged from the Second World War, was to begin at 3 a.m., while Algeria's villages slept.

From the beginning, everything went wrong. Premature attacks that started as early as midnight tipped off the police that something was up. In most cases, the rebels either had to withdraw from their targets or were shot and captured. The occasion might have been quickly forgotten except for one tragic occurrence. Although the FLN had given orders that no civilians were to be attacked, rebels who stopped a bus as a chilling dawn broke across the Aurés Mountains failed to calculate the consequences of their actions. The bus passengers included a *caid* — a local governor loyal to the French — and when he reached in his jacket for a gun, he was shot and killed. Also killed were two young French schoolteachers, Guy Monnerot and his wife, who were returning to their duties after their honeymoon. The death of the *caid* traumatized the Algerian *évolués** who had co-operated with the French, while the killing of teachers dedicated to educating Muslim children shocked Europeans. Beyond that, the amateurishness of the assaults brought its own ironic success. The French failed to realize how wide and deep the revolutionary movement had spread.

When Premier Pierre Mendès France addressed the National Assembly on November 12, he repeated the conventional French line that "the departments of Algeria are part of the French Republic ... between

---

* Africans viewed as having "evolved" through education to accept French values and practices.

them and Metropolitan France there can be no conceivable secession." His minister of the interior, François Mitterrand, agreed that "Algeria is France." Yet Mitterrand was cautious in his response, ordering that no napalm or high explosives be used against native villages. Algerian police were incorporated into the French national police and troops of the 25th Parachute Division were sent to patrol outback roads. Many FLN rebels were hunted down and killed or jailed, including the killer of the French schoolteachers. By the New Year, Pierre Mendès France concluded that what was really needed was a new man who could apply to the problems of Algeria the skills that had enabled the French Resistance to survive the German Occupation. He was convinced he had just such a man in Jacques Soustelle, an intellectual, a soldier, a *résistant* who knew the ways of armed insurrection, and therefore would understand how to combat one.

Jacques Souselle had been one of Charles de Gaulle's closest companions during the war, described by the general as "this gifted man, this brilliant intellectual, this passionate politician."[2] When offered the post of governor general of Algeria, he asked de Gaulle if he should take it and got the answer, "Why not?"[3]

Forty-three in 1955, Soustelle had been trained as an ethnologist and had served with distinction as the deputy director of the Musée de l'Homme. The son of a railway worker and a native of Montpelier, Soustelle headed an anti-fascist league in Paris in the 1930s while working as a university professor. He studied pre-Colombian native life in Central and South America and was on a cultural mission to Mexico when France was invaded in 1940. Out of his travels came several books, including *la Vie quotidienne des Aztèques (Daily Life of the Aztecs)*. After the fall of France, Soustelle joined the Free French, becoming de Gaulle's intelligence chief in Algiers in 1943. After the war, he was elected to the National Assembly and de Gaulle made him his minister of information before asking him to head up the general's Rally of the French People.

The problems of Algeria did not come as any great surprise to Charles de Gaulle. Officially out of public life, he travelled to Paris most Wednesdays from Colombey-les-Deux-Églises and was well aware of the tensions developing in France's remaining North African colony. He also knew that France was haunted by the fear of another Indochina. With the sad experience of the Rally now behind him, de Gaulle was preoccupied in the last months of 1954 with the publication of the first volume of his *Mémoires de guerre*. It sold one hundred thousand copies in five weeks. Eight months after All Saints' Day, de Gaulle told a press conference in Paris that he was retiring from public life. His departure came with a prescient warning that France must prepare itself for a "great shock" in North Africa. He called for "integration, providing it can be sincere." François Mauriac attended the carefully staged event and he came away "with a secret, poignant regret for what might have been, for what has not been."[4] De Gaulle would busy himself with the planting of red, white and blue flowers at Colombey, laid out in the shape of a Cross of Lorraine. He also had time for an extended trip by steamer from Marseille to Tahiti.

The shock that de Gaulle had foreseen for France came on a stifling Saturday, August 20, 1955, in the "season of storms" and under a leaden sky. When Muslims gathered at their mosques for holy day services on Friday, FLN cell leaders passed word to followers to attack Europeans wherever they found them. The killings began in Constantine, where the first victim was an évolué, Allouah Abbas, a municipal councillor and the nephew of the famed Algerian moderate leader, Ferhat Abbas. The worst slaughter took place in the mining village of El-Halia, near the port city of Philippeville. FLN gangs led by mineworkers who knew each alley of the small community, went from house to house slitting the throats of European mothers and dashing their babies against walls.

Alastair Horne described the butchery that took place at Ain-Abid, a tiny settlement east of Constantine: "... an entire *pied noir* family called Mello perished atrociously; a seventy-three-year-old grandmother and eleven-year-old daughter, the father killed in his bed, with his arms and legs hacked off. The mother had been disembowelled, her five-day-old baby slashed to death and replaced in her opened womb."[5] When the French 18th Parachute Regiment arrived — with orders to shoot every Arab they met — they found Arab children rushing about, finishing off the dying. Suspected rebels were rounded up and machine-gunned. A

346 · THE PARIS GAME

paratrooper wrote that "There were so many of them they had to be buried with bulldozers."[6]

Jacques Soustelle had arrived in Algiers with ambitious plans for reform. He thought he understood the aspirations of the indigenous population. Seeing widespread poverty on his first tour of the Aurès, he deplored the use of such army tactics as sending in tanks to destroy village houses. His solution would be modelled on de Gaulle's policy of "integration." The teaching of Arabic would be made mandatory in Muslim schools, spending on education and infrastructure would be greatly expanded, and land reform would begin. A new military corps — the Sections Administrative Specialisées or SAS — was created to afford protection to remote communities. Soustelle flew to Constantine as soon as he heard of the outbreak. A final tally of the deaths would show 123 Europeans killed by the mobs with 1,273 officially admitted deaths among the "insurgents." The FLN would issue a casualty list bearing the names and addresses of close to twelve thousand Muslim dead.

Soustelle's reform plans could hardly survive such ferocious attacks. Under the Socialist government of Guy Mollet that took office following French elections in December 1955, Soustelle was ordered back to Paris. Thousands of Europeans filled the street as he drove to the harbour to board the ferry for France. "*Soustelle, Soustelle, avec nous,*" they shouted, but it was too late. The French now realized they had a full-blown revolution on their hands.

By 1956, Soustelle's successor, Robert Lacoste, a Resistance hero turned politician, had abolished the Algerian Assembly and was ruling by decree. In a candid moment, he issued a document that listed six thousand deaths due to terrorism, but nearly twenty thousand killed in military action, most of them non-European. The use of torture now had become endemic throughout the French army in Algeria, with what would become known as "water boarding" a favourite tactic to extract confessions, genuine or contrived. Muslim hatreds hardened when two FLN members were guillotined, one for killing a gamekeeper and the other for engineering an ambush in which eight members of a *pied noir* family died, including an eight-year-old girl. The FLN promised to kill a hundred Frenchman for every guillotined Algerian.

The French were well aware that Ahmed Ben Bella was by now playing a critical role in the FLN rebellion. He was still based in Cairo, but he flew frequently to other points. When French intelligence got word in October that Ben Bella would be flying from Rabat, Morocco to Tunis, the Ministry of Defense made arrangements to intercept the flight. A radio message to the French pilot of the Air Maroc DC3 carrying Ben Bella ordered him to put down in Algiers instead of Tunis. After some arguing, he complied, and when the aircraft arrived at the terminal, Ben Bella and his companions thought they had landed in Tunisia. All five were taken to France and held in a series of prisons for the next five and a half years. Tentative peace talks that the French had opened in Rome had already been disrupted when the FLN reaffirmed its intention of using violence to secure independence. The abduction of Ben Bella, a clear violation of international law, created what seemed an unbridgeable gap between the two solitudes.

In the fall of 1956, the world's eyes were diverted to issues of greater global concern. Egypt's Gamal Abdel Nasser had nationalized the Suez Canal — an affront to the British and French who had financed its building, and the Israelis who used it for shipping to much of the world. All three countries attacked Egypt but were forced to withdraw within a few days in the face of bitter international criticism. The United Nations adopted a plan for the use of peacekeepers that had been devised by the Canadian foreign minister, Lester Pearson.* At the same time, student protests in Hungary brought on a rebellion against its Communist government. The entry of Soviet tanks into Budapest on November 4 put an end to the uprising, prolonging for another thirty years Hungary's fate as a Communist satellite. Watching these events, General de Gaulle saw the Suez fiasco as another example of France having relied too heavily on Britain. He said he would have sent paratroops into Cairo and it would all have been over "within two hours."

In the weeks after Suez, the FLN's leader in Algeria, Saadi Yacef, found a new technique for spreading terror among the civilian population. After a French attack in the Casbah that left sixteen dead in the rue de Thebes,

---

* Pearson received the Nobel Peace Prize, thereby gaining Canada its reputation as a "peacekeeper."

Yacef recruited young women as bomb carriers, sending them on deadly missions into the heart of European Algiers. Unlike today's jihadists, these unveiled, often smartly dressed young women planted their bombs and escaped before they exploded. They chose such targets as the Milk Bar on Place Bugeaud, filled with children and their mothers, or the Cafétéria on rue Michelet, where students were dancing to juke-box music. The bombs detonated with lethal force, claiming scores of victims. FLN assassination squads were going about the country killing almost at will. The vortex of disorder into which the country was plunging reached a boiling point on January 28, 1957, when the FLN called for a general strike.

Governor Lacoste had already made the decision to use whatever force might be needed to maintain order. He called in the army's commander-in-chief in Algeria, General Raoul Salan, one of the most experienced officers in the French army. His instructions were to crush the general strike and end the rebellion. Salan had been commander-in-chief in Indochina, but did not bear the stain of the defeat there, having been withdrawn in 1953. With Salan came General Jacques Massu, head of the crack 10th Paratroop Division. Massu, one of the most skilled and disciplined senior officers in the French army, was fiercely determined to enforce law and order. He'd seen action with colonial units during the war and had performed heroically when he led a regiment of General Leclerc's 2nd Armoured Division into Paris on Liberation Day. After the war, he helped break the French miners' strike and served a tour of duty in Indochina.

Massu and Salan were fervent supporters of the *"Algérie française"* school, insistent on maintaining the privileges of the *colons* and making the territory safe for évolués and *pieds noirs*. With the strike underway and the streets of Algeria largely deserted, Massu sent armoured cars to rip open the closed steel shutters of Arab shops. Their owners rushed back to protect their goods from looters, who included the paratroopers as well as civilians. Army trucks, meanwhile, collected workers from their homes and delivered them to their places of employment. Within forty-eight hours, the strike was broken. Salan escaped death in an attempted assassination when a bazooka shell fired at his office killed his military attaché. The French army had won the "Battle of Algiers," and the air force followed up with an attack on a frontier village in neutral Tunisia near where sixteen French soldiers had died in an FLN ambush. The retaliatory attack took sixty-nine lives, but it was merely one more incident in the long chain of killings and counter-killings. What had more impact on French public opinion was the announcement early in May that the French army had lost more than fifteen thousand men since the beginning of the year.

Visitors to Colombey were now returning to Paris with pessimistic accounts of General de Gaulle's take on the Algerian situation. De Gaulle had broken his arm in a fall, making more difficult his work on his memoirs. Concerned about the impressions being spread as to his views on Algeria, he issued a statement. "When General de Gaulle considers it useful to make known what he thinks, one knows that he will do it himself, and publicly. That is the case, in particular, on the subject of Algeria."[7] In revealing himself as he did, de Gaulle was letting it be known that he would be a player as the Algerian episode unfolded. He had a network of supporters in the territory and was kept well informed on developments. De Gaulle foresaw that settlers could tolerate only so much turmoil and disruption, and that if Paris could not bring the situation under control, the *colons* — with the help of the army — would do so themselves. Told that an army revolt was being planned in Algeria under de Gaulle's name, the general replied, "If there is no government, the army will seize power in Algeria … and I shall seize power in Paris, in order to serve the Republic."[8]

The secret planning had gone on for months, but it took the fall of another French government and the determination of General Salan, convinced that only Charles de Gaulle could save Algeria for France, to pull the trigger. On May 9, 1958, while the politicians were trying to find someone to head up the twentieth government in France since the end of the Second World War, Salan sent a telegram to the chief of the army general staff in Paris, General Paul Ely. "The army in Algeria," he said, "is … risking a useless sacrifice if the representatives of the nation [the politicians] are not determined to maintain *Algérie française*." He added a blunt warning: "One cannot predict how it would react in its despair."

Salan took the telegram to Governor Lacoste that night, arriving as the governor was departing for Paris. Algeria now had no governor, just as France had no government.

On May 13, at an Algiers ceremony to honour three French soldiers killed by insurgents, a crowd that may have reached one hundred thousand cheered as Salan laid a wreath and a student leader, Pierre Lagaillarde, called for a settler uprising. It was all General Massu, hailed by the assembled *pieds noirs* as the hero of the Battle of Algiers, needed. He drew up names for a committee of public safety to be headed by Salan. While the mob marched on the governor's office, Massu dispatched a telegram to President Coty advising that the committee had taken power for the purpose of maintaining order. The message urged "creation in Paris of a government of public safety ... capable of preserving Algeria as an integral part of the mother country." General Salan backed it up with a second wire. He appealed for the presence of "a national arbiter" whose "high authority" would ensure the re-establishment of order. No name was mentioned, but it was clear Salan had only one person in mind: Charles de Gaulle.

In Paris, the National Assembly sat most of the night. Shortly before three a.m., by a vote of 280 to 186, Pierre Pflimlin of the Mouvement républicain populaire (MRP) was elected premier. The news brought howls of outrage in Algiers. Why had not de Gaulle stepped forward? When de Gaulle arrived at his Paris office on the rue de Solférino for his weekly visit, his supporters pleaded permission to ask President Coty to request his return. At six o'clock, de Gaulle put out a ten-line statement that made it clear he was ready for a final roll of the dice. For twelve years, his statement read, France had been on the road to degradation. "Not so long ago, the country, in its depths, trusted me to lead it in its entirety to its salvation. Today, with the trials that it faces once again, let it know that I am ready to assume the powers of the Republic."

There things rested nervously for another week, while crowds of Arabs demonstrated in support of de Gaulle in Algiers. Clearly, he was the only man who could unite all factions. Jacques Soustelle, ordered to stay in France, eluded his gatekeepers and caught a flight to Switzerland, from where he flew to Algiers for a delirious welcome. "At last we have a chief," crowds shouted.

On May 19, de Gaulle held a press conference in Paris, at the Hôtel d'Orsay adjoining the old railway station. Those who hadn't seen him for years noted how much older he was, with a noticeable paunch and hair that was streaked with grey. He was out of uniform, wearing a dark double-breasted suit. "I am a man who belongs to nobody and who belongs to everybody," he asserted. Then he suggested the crisis in Algeria might lead to "a sort of resurrection." As to what he would do, he was not ready to say. De Gaulle preferred to allow people to make whatever interpretation they might wish of his intentions. If the French army chose to inject itself on his behalf, he would not object. But he had no desire to become a dictator. "On the contrary, I … re-established freedoms when they had disappeared." He concluded with a simple pronouncement: "Now I will return to my village and remain there at the disposal of the country."

While de Gaulle waited at Colombey, General Massu took the first step toward a *coup d'état*. He landed a paratroop force in Corsica that quickly took control of the island. Premier Pfimlin, outraged, wanted a counter-invasion, but was told the fleet was out on manoeuvres. De Gaulle phoned Georges Pompidou, his old friend from the Rothschild Bank, and asked him to start drawing up a list of Cabinet members. De Gaulle then let it be known he was ready to meet with the premier. Late on May 26, Pfimlin left the Hôtel Matignon and following a devious route, arrived at midnight at the home of the warden of parc Saint-Cloud, a one-time royal hunting domain. Pflimlin and de Gaulle talked for an hour and a half. De Gaulle assured the premier he would not take power in a military coup, but he refused to condemn the generals who were said to be planning one. The next day de Gaulle issued an astounding statement. It declared he had "set in motion the regular procedure necessary for the establishment of a republican government capable of ensuring the unity and independence of the country." He called on the military to observe "exemplary behaviour" and said he would be in touch with its leaders. Was he signalling the military that a *coup d'état* would have his backing?

On the strength of de Gaulle's statement, General Massu, supported by other key army figures, drew up plans — "Operation Resurrection" — for the very action that de Gaulle had promised Pfimlin he would not support. Paratroops from Algeria and the south of France would land in Paris, occupy the National Assembly, l'Hôtel de Ville, and other government centres, including the Préfecture de police. There would be a march by supporters on the Champs Élysée, all leading to "the fall of the present government and the setting up of a republic government of public safety under the leadership of General de Gaulle." A military message to Algiers carried de Gaulle's approval for the action. The likelihood of a coup had become so widely discussed that President Coty, in a special message to Parliament, warned that France was on the brink of civil war. He was turning, he said, "towards the most illustrious of Frenchmen, towards the man who, in the darkest years of our history was our chief.... I ask General de Gaulle to confer with the head of state...."

This was the call for which Charles de Gaulle had been waiting, but it left Yvonne perplexed and troubled. "After all," she told her husband, "it is they who have created this problem, not you. They let you down in 1946; you owe them nothing. So now they come for you!" When de Gaulle heard her out in silence, Yvonne admonished him: "Sixty-seven years! At that age, generals do not go into battle."[9]

On the afternoon of May 29, de Gaulle again made the three-hour drive from Colombey to Paris. He travelled in a six-cylinder Citroën, one of two he owned. Arriving at the Élysée Palace just after seven o'clock, he found President Coty waiting to ask him to form a government. A deal was quickly struck. De Gaulle would address the National Assembly and ask for special executive powers for six months while a new constitution was being prepared. The general issued a statement in which he said he would propose a referendum on separating executive power from the legislature. Then he drove back to Colombey. In Algiers the next day, three hundred thousand people roared their approval of de Gaulle. The army cancelled its plans to drop paratroops on Paris. A message noted the operation would be restored in case of difficulty for the general. Over the next two days de Gaulle met with members of the various parties, and by the time he arrived at the National Assembly on Sunday afternoon, June 1, 1958 — amid a terrible thunderstorm — Premier Pflimlin had submitted his resignation to President Coty. In his memoirs, de Gaulle recounts his brief remarks to Parliament:

> I summed up the situation: French unity threatened; Algeria plunged in turmoil; Corsica in the grip of the conta-

gion; the [a]rmy, having come through long and bloody trials with merit, led astray by the dereliction of the civil authorities; the international position of France undermined even among her allies.... As I spoke, there was total silence on all the benches, as befitted the occasion.[10]

Now it was time for de Gaulle to collect on his great gamble. It had taken twelve years and a crisis of shattering consequences, but the country was finally calling him back. The vote in the National Assembly was 553 to 329 for de Gaulle's return. The opposition, consisting of 147 Communists and 49 Socialists, cited fear of dictatorship as their reason for voting against him. Pierre Mendès France, the former premier and one of twelve Radicals who refused to endorse de Gaulle, complained that the Assembly had been blackmailed by the threat of a military coup. For the Socialists, François Mitterrand complained bitterly that de Gaulle had become partners with "force and sedition."

After the vote, de Gaulle returned to the Hôtel La Pérouse, where a small staff headed by Georges Pompidou was already at work on transition matters. De Gaulle could have chosen a no more capable confidante: Pompidou had served on the general's personal staff in 1944 and after a brief career as a schoolteacher he'd entered the banking profession. From assisting de Gaulle with his Colombey mortgage, Pompidou had negotiated the contract for the publication of the general's memoirs and had set up the trust fund for the Anne de Gaulle Foundation. He'd also become de Gaulle's personal financial advisor.

De Gaulle had been a frequent guest at the Hôtel La Pérouse on his forays from Colombey. Tonight would be the last time he would stay here; in a few days he would move into the Hôtel Matignon, official residence of French premiers. A few hours before, de Gaulle had encountered Léon Delbecque, head of his network in Algeria. The general complimented Delbecque on the way he had handled things. "You haven't made a single mistake! But you must admit that I too have played my cards well!" That night, as de Gaulle readied himself to return to his room for the last time, he exchanged a few words with the hotel's night porter. Tapping the porter on the back, de Gaulle chuckled, "Albert, I've won!"[11]

CHAPTER 20
The Last Battle

The bonds of blood and emotion that bound France and Algeria brought wealth and status to the *pieds noirs,* benefits that were the result — as Charles de Gaulle would record in his memoirs — of French money, French technology, and local labour. But they also came, he had to concede, at the price of terrible "agonies and indignities" inflicted on a rebellious native population.[1]

When de Gaulle flew on June 4, 1958, to Algiers, travelling in a French-made Caravelle jetliner, he was making his first voyage as prime minister after being out of office for a dozen years.[2] He had no "strictly predetermined plan" to deal with what was rapidly evolving into a "French tragedy," other than the conviction that no policy short of "replacing domination by association … would be worthy of France."[3] De Gaulle's emotional attachment to Algeria stemmed not only from all he had absorbed as a youth who had feasted on the romance of empire and the grandeur of France's attainments. Fresh in his memory, too, was the fact that it was in Algiers that he had won the undisputed leadership of Free France and that it was there he had established the Provisional Government that he later transferred to Paris. De Gaulle recognized that the French in Algeria, long secure in their privileged status and wealth, were now haunted by the fear of being "submerged, dispersed, and driven out" of their idyllic *Algérie française*.[4] He was in it "up to the eyes," but he was firm in his mind that France had no choice but to grant its wealthiest colony the right to self-determination.[5]

De Gaulle's plane had been escorted by French air force fighters flying in a Cross of Lorraine pattern. On his arrival at Maison-Blanche airport outside Algiers he was met by a clutch of officials led by General Raoul Salan and General Jacques Massu, key figures in the Committee of Public Safety that had been formed as part of their intrigue to bring de Gaulle to power. Their chief sympathizer, Jacques Soustelle, who would soon become de Gaulle's minister of information, was also there.

De Gaulle was wearing a plain uniform without medals and on the drive from the airport to the harbour, he stood in an open Citroën to receive the cheers of *pieds noirs* and Arabs alike. *Le Monde* described the reception as a "spectacle [that] resembled both an American-style triumph and the Tour de France."[6] A reception on the cruiser *De Grasse* followed, and then it was on to a mass meeting at the Place du Forum with thousands of Algerians cheering their new chief.

De Gaulle entered the government offices at the Palais d'Été around seven o'clock, and his party made its way to the big balcony overlooking the square below. When de Gaulle stepped forward he paused, raised his arms in the V gesture that was by now a familiar sight, and only then began to speak. His first words — *"je vous ai ..."* — were drowned out by the welcome of the crowd, but the third word that he uttered — *"compris!"* — fell like a lighted match on dry tinder, setting the square afire. He had told the *pieds noirs* that he understood them — and they took it to mean he was with them in their determination to hold on to Algeria.[7]

Had the crowd listened more carefully to what else de Gaulle said, their excitement might have been muted: "... in less than three months' time, all the French, including the ten million French citizens of Algeria, will have an opportunity to decide their own destiny." But more incendiary words were to follow. Two days later, at the prosperous farming town of Mostaganem, de Gaulle finished his remarks with the phrase that had become sacred to the *pieds noirs* cause: *"Vive l'Algérie française!"*

Alastair Horne has written: "The crowd went wild. Men as well as women wept; Muslims gesticulated with V signs."[8] We have no way of knowing whether de Gaulle had become caught up in the emotion of the moment, or was simply exasperated by relentless cries of "Soustelle! Soustelle!" that preceded his talk. The official draft of his text contains no such words. But it was all that Soustelle, Salan, and Massu needed to convince themselves de Gaulle would support a massive repression of the rebel Front de Libération Nationale. In fact, they were half right: while de Gaulle was convinced Algeria must eventually be given the option of independence, he insisted its freedom was a privilege that could only be granted by a benevolent victor; it could not be a concession extracted from a defeated ruler. By example, de Gaulle the very next week signed agreements that withdrew French forces from Morocco and Tunisia, affirming the independence of those former colonies.

The advent of de Gaulle and his talk of "true equality" for all in Algeria demoralized some sections of the FLN, but brought no halt to attacks by its military wing, the Armée de Libération Nationale (ALN). Based largely in Tunisia, the ALN suffered heavy losses when it attempted to crack the Morice Line of fences and minefields that the French had set up to resist its incursions. On de Gaulle's last day in Algeria, the FLN attacked the police station in the city of Bone.

The rebels then turned to political action and, in September, from a safe haven in Cairo, the FLN announced the formation of a provisional government. Ferhat Abbas, for long considered by the French a moderate among Arab leaders, took up the presidency. In doing so, he was forgiving the FLN for having killed his nephew during its attack on Philippeville three years earlier. He also was demonstrating that Arabs could overcome their differences to present a united front to the French. Arab nations throughout the Middle East hastened to recognize the Abbas regime. In turn, they carried to the United Nations a call for the independence of

Algeria. The next step for the FLN was to extend the war to France, with the intention of spreading fear among the civilian population that would lead to demands for withdrawal of the French army. During August and September, the FLN carried out more than four hundred bombing attacks in French cities, mostly aimed at military targets. In Paris, Jacques Soustelle miraculously escaped injury when gunmen raked his car as it drove down the avenue Friedland. On the same night, on the rue de Rivoli, rebel gunmen fired at police cars. Then, as suddenly as they started, the attacks in France were called off.

On September 4, de Gaulle presented his constitution for the Fifth Republic in a ceremony at the Place de la Republique. In a referendum on September 29, it won the approval of 78 percent of the voters, an endorsement that was helped along by news broadcasts on the state radio and TV networks that were heavily slanted in favour of the Yes side. De Gaulle went on the air (a privilege denied the Opposition) to say he was entrusting "the fate of France" to its citizens.

A week later, de Gaulle travelled again to Algeria to present a five-year plan for development of the country. When the FLN announced formation of its provisional government, de Gaulle responded with a press conference at the Hôtel Matignon. With three hundred journalists in attendance, he offered a "peace of the brave" to the Algerian rebels. All they had to do was ask for a meeting to discuss the end of hostilities. Rooms were booked at the Hôtel de Crillon for Ferhat Abbas and his Alsatian wife, but no one ever came. The FLN simply rejected de Gaulle's overture.

If a settlement was to be reached in Algeria, de Gaulle decided, it would take the intervention of a new military chief. He brought General Salan back to France to become military governor of Paris and sent to Algiers the pipe-smoking General Maurice Challe, a veteran of the French air force. Challe had worked with the Resistance and in 1944 he had obtained the Luftwaffe order of battle in advance of D-Day and transmitted it to the British. In 1956, he had been instrumental in gaining the backing of British prime minister Anthony Eden for the French-Israeli attack on Egypt. By now a strong supporter of de Gaulle, Challe went to Algeria with a basic win-the-war strategy: carry the fight to the enemy. The Challe Plan, as it came to be known, brought thousands of Algerians into the native militia, enrolling 250,00 *harkis* as support to the French army. Using attack helicopters, the army devastated rebel encampments in operations that claimed thousands of Algerian lives. The French then herded a million Muslim civilians into "regroupment" camps. Torture was widely used in questioning prisoners.[9]

The FLN also unleashed terror attacks; in one village, Melouza, more than one hundred *pieds noirs* were massacred, their throats cut in an atrocity that came to be known as égorgement.

Approval of the constitution of the Fifth Republic paved the way for de Gaulle's election as president, which came on December 21, when the electoral college — an elite body of eighty thousand leading citizens — chose him over several rivals, including a Communist senator and a centre-left candidate. As in the referendum, de Gaulle won 78 percent of the votes. On January 8, 1959, de Gaulle went to the Élysée Palace to be sworn in as president of the Fifth Republic. "The first of Frenchmen," outgoing president René Coty told him, "is now the first man in France." They rode up the Champs-Élysée together, paid tribute to the Unknown Soldier in a ceremony at the Arc de Triomphe, and joined in singing "La Marseillaise."[10] De Gaulle described his feelings in his memoirs:

> On my return, henceforth the prisoner of my high duty, I heard all the doors of the palace closing behind ne. But at the same time I saw the prospect of a great undertaking open up before me ... it must be done! If France in the depths of her being once more called upon me to serve as her guide, it was surely not, I felt, in order to preside over her sleep. After the terrible decline which she had suffered for more than a hundred years she must use the respite which chance had accorded her to re-establish her power, her wealth, and her influence in tune with the spirit of modern times. Failing this, a catastrophe on the scale of the century might one day crush her forever.... My duty was thus laid down, for as long as the people would follow me.[11]

President de Gaulle returned many times to Algeria, but nine months passed before he was ready to show his hand. He spoke on television and radio to declare that the time had come for Algeria's "self-determination." Algerians would be given the opportunity to choose between complete secession — which would mean loss of French benefits and economic support — and either full "Francization" (integration into France), or association with France in a federal regime. His offer was widely applauded in Metropolitan France. *Le Monde* declared that "de Gaulle has given France back her old prestige as the great Liberal nation."[12] The National Assembly voted 441 to 23 to support de Gaulle's policy. From Cairo came word that the provisional government was ready to consider preliminary talks.

In Algeria, de Gaulle's scheme drew a bitter response from French settlers and the *ultras* — the advocates of *Algérie française.* The chief organ of the *pieds noirs,* the *Echo d'Alger,* expressed its hostility in sharply critical editorials. A militant body calling itself the Front National Français (FNF) turned out 1,500 uniformed men to escort Georges Bidault, the Resistance leader who now was campaigning against Algerian self-determination.

The FNF was the brainchild of Joseph Ortiz, a rabble-rousing saloon-keeper of decidedly fascist views. Ortiz ran a *brasserie,* the Bar du Forum, where he catered to an eclectic crowd of the Algiers French. Ortiz had been born in Algeria of Spanish stock and was a veteran of the Free French expeditionary force that had helped liberate Italy. He was known as "the king of tomatoes" after having supplied the tomatoes used to pelt French premier Guy Mollet on his 1956 visit. Many saw him as little more than a thug, but he described himself as simply a follower of the right-wing philosopher, Charles Maurras. He adopted as the symbol of the FNF a Celtic cross that had long been used by extreme right-wing groups. "The determination of the French will conquer the self-determination of de Gaulle," Ortiz declared when he welcomed Bidault to the Forum. "Algiers may become Budapest, but we shall remain.… For us, it's either the suitcase or the coffin!"[13] De Gaulle, he was suggesting, had left them no choice but to abandon Algeria or be killed by the rebels.

As the killings went on day after day, resentment toward Paris mounted. Not only had the army, despite some successes, failed to quell the rebellion, but now de Gaulle was ready to hand over Algeria to the Arabs. It was a difficult time for the new president on both political and personal matters. Just before Christmas, de Gaulle's brother, Pierre, collapsed while visiting the Élysée, apparently from strain brought on by difficulties he was having in organizing France's participation in Expo '67, the World's Fair to be held in Montreal. The president rushed to his side and tried to comfort him. Pierre recovered consciousness and was taken to a hospital, but he died in hospital on December 26. De Gaulle took a break from his duties with a short vacation in the Var department in the south of France.

De Gaulle was back in Paris when he heard that General Massu, head of the 10th Paratroop Dvision that had been carrying the brunt of the fighting against the FLN, had given an incendiary interview to a West German newspaper, Munich's *Suddeutsche Zeitung.* "We no longer understand the policy of President de Gaulle," he told the newspaper's reporter, who had been a paratrooper like himself. "The government should help us to see the future clearly, in order that we can succeed in maintaining *Algérie française.*"[14] Massu was challenging de Gaulle directly, but, by now, too many hands had been played. Too volatile a figure to be allowed to remain in Algeria, he was ordered back to Paris before being reassigned as the military governor of Metz, the city where de Gaulle had served in the 1930s.

Massu's departure infuriated the *colons.* Within hours of learning of his banishment, Joseph Ortiz and his *pieds noir* rival, Pierre Lagaillarde, hatched plans for a general strike and uprising. Lagaillarde, a lawyer and ex-paratrooper, had led student demonstrations that helped bring de Gaulle to power and was now a member of the National Assembly. While Ortiz was announcing plans for the strike, Lagaillarde had already seized a university building that he promised to hold until de Gaulle had yielded. Protecting him were 1,500 men of the FNF carrying weapons "liberated" from an army depot. On January 24, 1960, General Challe threw up roadblocks across the city while *pied noir* insurgents huddled behind their barricades. Thirty thousand protesters filled the Place de la Forum, chanting anti-de Gaulle slogans and vowing never to abandon Algeria.

The counterattack, when it came, was deadly. Police splayed the square with tear gas and a gun battle broke out. While the police engaged the strikers, the paratroopers mysteriously held back. As the echo of gunshots faded, sympathetic paratroopers and rebels were seen talking together at the barricades while women handed out croissants with coffee and wine. By the time the casualties had been totalled up, the count was twenty dead on both sides, and more than two hundred wounded.

Joseph Ortiz thought he had won: "Tomorrow, in Paris I shall be the ruling power," he announced.

Paris had other ideas. De Gaulle had been at Colombey when the troubles began. He rushed back to Paris, arriving at midnight, and met with his Cabinet and army commanders. The next day, a new detachment of troops was ordered to Algiers to take over from the reluctant paratroopers. De Gaulle also dispatched his premier, Michel Debre, to Algiers with orders to end the insurrection. Everything Debre heard pointed to an imminent takeover by a junta of colonels and a *pied noir* rabble. The civilian governor, Paul Delouvrier, convinced General Challe that the two of them should leave the city and take refuge at an air force base twenty miles to the east. Delouvrier made an emotional radio broadcast in which he said he was leaving behind as hostages his wife and a newborn son. In Paris, there were rumours of a shadow government in the making. Work began on plans to move the government to Belgium in event of a military takeover of the capital.

President de Gaulle had been scheduled to broadcast to the nation on January 29. He was urged to move up the date but refused to do so. When de Gaulle appeared before television cameras dressed in his uniform, he appeared pale and under great strain. He told the nation he was wearing military garb in order to show it was "General de Gaulle who speaks, as well as the Head of State." He made it clear that "the Algerians will have the right to decide their own destiny" and that "self-determination … is the only possible outcome." He warned the army that it was he who bore "the supreme authority" and that he was giving the order for the rule of law to be maintained. Then, asserting all the emotional power of which he was capable, de Gaulle addressed himself to the people:

> Lastly, I address France. Well, my dear old country, here we are together once again, facing a grave trial. By virtue of the mandate that the people have given me and of the national legitimacy that I have embodied for twenty years, I ask you all to give me your support. While the

> guilty men, who dream of being usurpers, use as a pretext
> the decision that I have taken with regard to Algeria, let
> it be known everywhere that I shall not go back on it. To
> cede on this point … would also be to abase the state.…
> France would be no more than a poor, dislocated toy
> floating on the oceans of adventures.[15]

Few in France could resist such a powerful appeal to both sentiment and reality. Within minutes of de Gaulle's address, telegrams of support were flowing into the Élysée. In Algeria, where the broadcast was heard during a pounding downpour, one army unit after another declared its loyalty. By Monday morning, February 1, the streets were bare of paving stones and while littered with debris, were otherwise empty. Joseph Ortiz disappeared, apparently having taken refuge in Spain. Pierre Lagaillarde, after threatening to blow up the building he held, marched out with a band of followers, flags flying, and was immediately arrested. He was flown to Santé Prison in Paris. Allowed out on bail during his trial for sedition, he also fled to Spain. De Gaulle shook up his Cabinet, dropping Jacques Soustelle, who had continued to support the Algerian protest. He also, relieved General Challe of his post. The battle of "Barricades Week" had been won, but the last battle, to win peace in Algeria, still eluded de Gaulle.

Suddenly, in the spring of 1960, new hope for a settlement of the Algerian revolution appeared in the form of an overture from a field commander of the FLN, Colonel Si Salah. Word conveyed to Paris via mysterious intermediaries suggested that de Gaulle's offer of a "peace of the brave" was not dead after all. If France would promise an amnesty, the revolutionaries would turn in their arms. De Gaulle, ready to gamble on the possibility of a breakthrough, agreed to meet Si Salah and two aides at the Élysée Palace. They met, and de Gaulle revealed he was about to issue a new appeal to the FLN for peace talks. The idea of an amnesty was put aside for the moment. The interview over, de Gaulle declared: "Because we are fighting each other, I will not shake your hand, but I salute you."[16]

Si Salah's reward for his efforts was his arrest by the FLN; he later died in an ambush by a French patrol while being transferred to Tunisia.

De Gaulle's offer to talk peace with the Algerian rebels included the firm commitment that "we await them here in order to find with them an honourable end to the fighting." This time, the rebels answered with the assurance that they, too, wanted to "put an end to the conflict." They were ready to send a delegation headed by Ferhat Abbas, their provisional president, to meet de Gaulle. Despite this promising overture, when delegates of the two sides met in the Paris suburb of Melun to negotiate a summit meeting, their talks collapsed in mutual suspicion. The promised referendum on allowing Algeria self-determination went ahead on January 8, 1961, and it produced satisfactory results, although the *yes* vote was far from overwhelming. Across France, 75 percent voted approval, but in Algeria, where the FLN told people to abstain, only 55 percent voted for self-determination. Two weeks later, the Algerian provisional government declared its willingness to "engage in negotiations with the French government."

With peace an imminent prospect, the stubborn supporters of *Algérie française* saw that any hope of staving off defeat would require a change in government in Paris. No price, including the assassination of de Gaulle, would be too high to pay. The first steps were taken by two colonels, Antoine Argoud and Joseph Broizat, who found a sympathetic response among higher-ranking officers. They formed themselves into the Organisation de l'Armée Secrète (OAS). The conspiracy was joined by General Challe, who had resigned following his dismissal from Algiers, and was now ready to mount an armed coup. With him came General Salan, the former inspector general of the army, Edmond Jouhaud, the air force commander, and others who had been critical of de Gaulle's policies.

The "generals' putsch" was touched off on April 22, a Saturday. It began with the arrest of the top officials of the French government in Algiers, including General Fernand Gambiez, the army commander-in-chief; Jean Morin, the delegate-general and civilian governor; and René Jannin, the prefect of police. Among those taken prisoner was a Cabinet minister visiting Algiers, Robert Buron. By dawn the conspirators, joined by several paratroop regiments, were in control of the chief government buildings in Algiers.

De Gaulle was awakened at 2:30 a.m. and told of the situation. He ordered his minister for Algeria, Louis Joxe, to fly immediately to Algiers, along with General Jean Olié, chief of the General Staff. They took off as General Challe was broadcasting a proclamation of the uprising. "A government of abandonment is preparing to hand over Algeria to the rebellion … the army shall not fail in its mission." Despite Challe's call, most army units remained loyal, as did the navy and the air force. No effort was made to move on Paris.

"Fidel Castro would already have been here," de Gaulle remarked. "But that poor Challe isn't Fidel Castro."[17] De Gaulle took to the air on Sunday night to declare that "an insurrectional power has been set up in Algeria by a military junta." He went on:

> Their enterprise is leading straight to national disaster. The State is flouted, the nation defied, our power shaken, our international prestige abased, our place and our role in Africa compromised. And by whom? Alas! Alas! By men whose duty, honour, *raison d'être* is to serve and to obey. In the name of France, I order that every means, I say every means, be used to close the road to those men, until they are crushed. I forbid any Frenchman and, above all, any soldier to carry out any of their orders. The only leaders, civil and military, who have the right to assume responsibilities are those who have been properly appointed to do so. French men and women, help me.[18]

Once again the de Gaulle words had worked their magic. Biographer Jean Lacouture considers this speech the greatest of de Gaulle's career: "Already undermined by their divisions and by their lack of vision," he has written, "the Algiers rebels were to be swept aside by these words."[19]

By the next morning, General Challe knew his cause had failed. He surrendered, as did General Zeller. Others escaped and living underground, then joined with the OAS to plot further against de Gaulle. Challe was tried and sentenced to fifteen years imprisonment. Undeterred, OAS plotters began a vicious wave of attacks that would go on for years. On

May 19, the OAS bombed nineteen buildings in Algiers and on May 31 Police Commissioner Roger Gavoury was stabbed to death. An escalating series of bombings later spread to France.

The long-delayed peace talks with the Algerian provisional government finally got underway in Evian, on the French side of Lake Geneva, on May 20. The OAS assassinated the mayor of the town and stepped up its attacks in Algeria. In September in Paris, an attempt was made to bomb de Gaulle's car as he was driven with his wife to Colombey. Ten kilograms of plastic concealed in a pile of sand exploded, sending a sheet of flame across the road, but no one was injured. In October, thirty thousand Muslims staged a demonstration in Paris in support of the FLN. It was not the kind of showing likely to be tolerated by the Paris police chief, Maurice Papon. His officers beat back the demonstrators, killing at least thirty and perhaps as many as three hundred.

The endgame of the peace talks was finally played out ten months after their beginning, with the announcement on March 18, 1962, that an accord had been reached. The ninety-three-page document covered everything from the cessation of hostilities to the treatment of civilians. French voters gave the accord 90 percent backing, and on July 1, voters in Algeria added their support — by more than 99 percent. Two days later, France recognized an independent Algeria. Ahmed Ben Bella, the young soldier on whose chest Charles de Gaulle had pinned a Médaille Militaire in 1945, would become its first president.

Within a few months of Algerian independence, nine hundred thousand of the slightly more than one million *pieds noirs* had packed their suitcases and abandoned their homes and businesses. One in three of the quarter of a million Algerian Muslims serving in the French army — regulars and *harkis* alike — also took refuge in France. The return of such large numbers brought both economic dislocation and heavy social cost to France. The FLN estimated in 1964 that the war had taken 1.5 million Algerian lives. The French army lost more than twenty-five thousand men, and after the war, large numbers of pro-French Muslims were murdered by vengeful revolutionaries. In addition, France was left with a dirty residue of the war in the form of the OAS, which continued to carry out attacks and to attempt assassinations in France. The most notorious OAS leader, General Salan, was tried in absentia and sentenced to death. After his arrest in Algiers in April 1962, his sentence was commuted to life imprisonment. He and others involved in the coup were given amnesty in 1968.

Some understanding of the immense psychic trauma that the war caused in France can be gained by comparing what the United States might have suffered had its defeat in Vietnam occurred under similar circumstances. Jean-Benoit Nadeau and Julie Barlow offer such a perspective in their book, *Sixty Million Frenchmen Can't Be Wrong: Why We Love France but not the French*:

> Imagine, if at the time of the Vietnam War, there had been one million [American] settlers who had lived in Vietnam for four generations. Imagine if Vietnam had not been "foreign territory" but part of the United States, a fifty-first state — and if North Vietnamese terrorists had killed twenty-five hundred American civilians in the United States. And just imagine the scenario of the U.S. Army becoming so displeased with its own government's conduct in Vietnam that it attempted to overthrow the American government by staging a coup in Washington. That is exactly what happened in France during the war in Algeria.[20]

The seven-year Algerian War of Independence, pitting some 1.3 million French troops against 330,000 Algerian revolutionaries, was the last colonial battle fought by any empire anywhere in the world. There would be other wars around the globe, waged over economic or political interests — Vietnam, Afghanistan, Iraq, the Falkland Islands — but the Algerian struggle marked the end of empires.

It would take years for Algeria to restore the economy left derelict by the departure of the *pieds noirs*. Ahmed Ben Bella was overthrown in 1965 by one of his military chiefs, Houari Boumédiéne.[21] Beginning in 1992, when the Algerian army cancelled run-off elections in fear of a victory by Islamic extremists, Algeria underwent a long and bloody civil war that took 150,000 lives. Armed Islamic groups had carried out indiscriminate slaughter, wiping out entire villages. Never entirely suppressed, they would become known as Al-Qaeda in the Islamic Maghreb. This force remains a continuing source of terror attacks.

Charles de Gaulle pondered the consequences of the war in his memoirs: "The end of colonization was a chapter in our history. France felt a mixture of regret for what was past and hope for what was to come."[22] As the curtain descended on *Algérie française,* his only certainty was that General de Gaulle (as he sometimes referred to himself) would remain in the game, resolute in his determination to "pursue his path and his vocation," even at the risk of his own life.

CHAPTER 21
The Republic of de Gaulle

The destiny of France is to irritate the world.

— Jean Giraudoux, author and diplomat

C harles de Gaulle's return as head of the government of France brought a rapid shift in the country's status in the world. Suddenly, this almost mythical figure out of the Second World War was casting a long shadow as he stood abreast the ramparts of France. As the world faced the new decade of the 1960s, the Big Three — the United States, Britain, and the Soviet Union — quickly became the Big Four, as France reclaimed a position of global influence. From setting off nuclear explosions in the Sahara, to extricating the nation from Algeria, blocking Britain's entry to the European Common Market, and withdrawing French forces from the North Atlantic Treaty Organization (NATO), de Gaulle began the decade playing what François Mauriac described as his "trump card" — his declaration of independence from American foreign policy.[1]

For all de Gaulle's determination to recast France in the world, however, he realized when he moved into the Élysée Palace that the country was economically "on the verge of disaster."[2] It would take a series of economic plans to get France growing again. In just three years, the country would achieve "a triumph of expansion and stability," with annual growth having nudged the 8 percent mark — the strongest in French history.[3]

De Gaulle's return brought a collective sigh of relief to France. The general's opponents, including the Communists, were tempered in their response. His insistence that he rule with direct powers while a new constitution was being written left no doubt that the Republic of de Gaulle would be very different than anything known in the past. The First Republic, established in 1792, lasted only twelve years before devolving into the Napoleonic Empire, and the Second Republic of 1848 met a similar destiny after only four years. The Third Republic, born in the defeat of 1870 and destined to be remembered as *"La Gueuse"* (The Slut), was the longest lasting, but died in the ashes of the Pétain regime after the defeat of1940. Its successor, the Fourth Republic, survived de Gaulle's retreat to Colombey, and then expired unmourned. "The Fourth French Republic died quietly today in its twelfth year," the *New York Times* reported on October 4, 1958. "The funeral services were private." It was a marvel, especially to Americans, inheritors of a constitution written in 1787 that had endured a civil war and remained intact after twenty-seven amendments, that a country that produced the brilliance of a Le Corbusier, a Matisse, or a de Maupassant could not, until the advent of Charles de Gaulle, devise a system of government to survive the mismanagement of those entrusted with it.

Perhaps the new Republic's main difference from past manifestations of French republicanism was that it reduced the power of a squabbling Parliament — the National Assembly and the Senate — to an emanation of the presidency. De Gaulle's insistence that the president be elected by direct vote of the people, an innovation that required a referendum that won overwhelming support, demonstrated his unique capacity to use this tool of presidential popularity to gain his ends. The fact a referendum would ultimately bring about his resignation was not something that he or anyone else could foresee.

Memories of the liberation and an appreciation of de Gaulle's determination to turn around a conquered people lay at the root of his support. However, as Janet Flanner would write, "it was by his words that de Gaulle took control of France."[4] The peculiar de Gaulle style that combined the image of an autocrat with the dedication of a servant worked as effectively on radio as it did on television. The renowned literary figure André Malraux, de Gaulle's minister of culture and intimate admirer, saw the change de Gaulle brought to the nation as "a revolution of French institutions — accomplished without the shedding of a drop of blood."[5] Malraux, whose six-hundred-page reflection, *Antimémoires*, had been the hit of the fall literary season, was perhaps overlooking the loss of life in Algeria that had brought de Gaulle back to power.

Neither Charles de Gaulle nor Yvonne were enamoured of living in the Élysée Palace, the eighteenth-century mansion at 55 rue du Faubourg Saint-Honoré that King Louis XV had given to his mistress Mme de Pompadour, and that had been used as a dance hall during the Revolution. They were assigned a suite of five large rooms outfitted with heavy, dark furniture. It overlooked a well-manicured garden, but Yvonne complained they could never take a quiet walk there because of the constant presence of the Gardes Républicains. She also worried that their neighbours could see into their windows, which she ordered shuttered. Most of their meals were cold when they were served because of the great distance they had to be brought from the palace kitchen. In desperation, Yvonne bought a kettle that she used to boil water for tea. She complained about the scantily clad cherubs depicted in frescoes on the walls of the general's office, and also about the popular new mini skirts worn by young women. When she asked her husband to have them banned, he had to patiently explain there was nothing he could do.[6]

One of Yvonne de Gaulle's few pleasures came in choosing the recorded music that was played during receptions; she particularly liked Vivaldi and opted for selections by him or by Handel. Receiving state visitors, however, left her cold. When the president of the Congo Republic, Fulbert Youyou, a defrocked Catholic priest arrived wearing a white cloak designed by Dior, she couldn't help but notice that beneath his robe he carried a revolver. She refused to pose for pictures with such a "miscreant."

De Gaulle tired of having state visitors to his home and ordered that the nearby Hôtel de Marigny be bought to accommodate them. "I do not like encountering kings in pyjamas in my corridors," he is said to have commented. As often as possible, the de Gaulles retreated to Colombey, using a government aircraft that took them there in about an hour. At Colombey, he received his family, wrote his speeches, read books, walked under the "immensity of the sky," and restored his "peace of mind."

De Gaulle's first task as president was to name a prime minister and assemble a Cabinet. Their seating around the Cabinet table reflected their influence. Opposite de Gaulle sat Michel Debré, his prime minister. On his right he placed André Malraux. Couve de Murville, who had been ambassador in Bonn, Germany, and had been called back to become minister of foreign affairs, sat nearby. De Gaulle's *chef du cabinet* was the reliable Georges Pompidou, while his aide from London days, Geoffroy de Courcel, headed a staff of forty-five as secretary-general to the Presidency. De Gaulle ran his Cabinet meetings with a firm hand. He concedes in his *Mémoires d'espoir* that anyone could ask to speak in Cabinet and the requests were always granted, but after hearing them, he would "give [his] own view of the matter and formulate a conclusion." Later, he would draw up a "summary of decisions" and would tell Malraux, his minister of culture, what should be released to the public.[7] Between Cabinet meetings, all the ministers visited de Gaulle in rotation, "each of them giving me an account of what he was doing and taking cognizance of my intentions." In de Gaulle's mind, the system he'd set up ensured that "relations with my government were continuous and extensive." He kept himself "at a distance, but by no means in an ivory tower."

De Gaulle worried about "the Parisian monster" that had emerged since the war — a capital whose population had increased by a million and a half. "A decision had to be made. I made it."[8] The Paris Region was created, subdivided into seven *départements*, with unified planning to be applied over all districts, especially the "problem-ridden" suburbs. Although by no means a one-man government, de Gaulle showered his ministers with notes on every conceivable subject. His interests ranged from plans to move the food market of Les Halles — "the stomach of Paris" — out of its age-old location, to establishing admission standards for overcrowded universities.

The economy was also an issue. Earlier, de Gaulle had devalued the franc by 17.5 percent (its twelfth devaluation since the war) and instituted a new, "heavy franc," equivalent to one hundred old francs. Economic issues would always be close to de Gaulle's heart as he sought to strengthen the country's economy and upgrade its global standing. Not all his initiatives were successful. When he called for reform of the international monetary system and a return to the gold standard, he was met with opposition from nearly every capital and his scheme went nowhere. At home, he deplored "the anxiety of the employers, the revolt of industrial workers, the anger of farmers, the irritation of shopkeepers, the fury in the public services, the distress of the civilian population, and the poverty of the military."

Economic rejuvenation and the war in Algeria may have dominated discussions in de Gaulle's Cabinet, but it was the larger world stage with which he was preoccupied. His return to power restored for the moment the unique Second World War triumvirate of de Gaulle and Harold Macmillan, now prime minister of Britain, and Dwight D. Eisenhower, since 1953 the president of the United States. Both had been steadfast supporters of the general during the difficult years when the Free French movement was asserting its birthright as the only legitimate French opposition to a common foe, and as the future government of France. De Gaulle realized, however, that the world situation was very different from what it had been in the immediate postwar years. For all the West's obsession about the aggressiveness of Moscow, it would be "madness" for Moscow to launch a global conflict that would end in "wholesale destruction." France, rather than acting with the "docility" it exhibited during de Gaulle's absence, needed now "to act on its own in Europe and the world."[9]

The foreign visitors were not long in making their way to the Élysée Palace. Macmillan came in June 1958, and the two argued about Britain's wish to open up the European Common Market, then emerging out of earlier economic agreements between France, Germany, and the Benelux countries.* The Italian prime minister followed.

---

* Belgium, the Netherlands, Luxembourg.

The American Secretary of State, the redoubtable John Foster Dulles, architect of containment and advocate of the *cordon sanitaire* behind which Russia would be confined and constrained, came that summer. Dulles reported back to Washington that the general was determined to demonstrate that France was still of "considerable importance" in the world. "The proof is that you are here today and I am also here," de Gaulle told Dulles. He recognized that the United States could not alone defend the world against a hostile Soviet Union and that "all the nations of the free world had to contribute." For that reason, de Gaulle urged, the scope of NATO should be extended to Africa and the Middle East.* After lunch, he returned to the subject of France's role in the world. The French people must feel they were citizens of a world power, de Gaulle told Dulles, or "France would quickly degenerate." On the subject of Algeria, de Gaulle recognized that the age of colonialism was past but that it was necessary to move slowly; it might take another ten years to resolve things there. (In fact, the French would be out of Algeria in just four years.)[10]

What was probably de Gaulle's most important meeting with a foreign head of government, however, came that fall when West German Chancellor Konrad Adenauer arrived at La Boisserie to spend the night. Adenauer had asked for the meeting and de Gaulle told his son, Philippe, it was safer for the German to come to the general's country home rather than risk riots in Paris. After all that Germany had done to France, it was time for reconciliation.

Adenauer, fourteen years older than de Gaulle, a Catholic like his host, had been dismissed as mayor of Cologne by the Nazis. He had been twice jailed, and had been forced to rely on the welfare of friends when he was denied the right to practise law. He'd built the German Christian Democratic Party almost from scratch after the war and had come to ask de Gaulle if either country could "reach a genuine long-term understanding." De Gaulle, for all the traditional French fear of a revived Germany, saw that it was time "to reverse the course of history." It was too soon, however, to think of German reunification; more pressing was the need to begin integration of the European community under the leadership of France and Germany without in any way extinguishing "their individual personalities."[11] (Both countries had signed the Treaty of Rome in 1957

---

* As later occurred with NATO involvement in Afghanistan.

that established the European Common Market.) De Gaulle and Adenauer would exchange some forty letters in the coming years and meet on fifteen occasions. Their most poignant moment saw the two Catholics come together in the ancient cathedral of Rheims, France — damaged by German shellfire in the First World War — to pray that "the deeds of friendship might forever supplant the miseries of war."

De Gaulle reached the apex of his foreign policy offensive when he conceived the idea of calling together the leaders of the Big Four — Eisenhower, Macmillan, and Soviet chief Nikita Khrushchev, with himself as host — to a summit meeting in Paris. It would provide the opportunity to tackle what de Gaulle saw as the great questions of the day: nuclear disarmament, the future of Germany, and the provision of aid to under-developed countries. Putting the four most important players in the world around the same table and on French soil would be a diplomatic coup for de Gaulle and would also ensure that France's view was heard and taken into consideration.

De Gaulle laid the groundwork for the summit by inviting President Eisenhower to Paris in September 1959. Huge crowds turned out for the president's visit. De Gaulle told Eisenhower that France would remain faithful to the Atlantic alliance but that it had to have its own nuclear *force de frappe* and would soon be exploding an atomic bomb. As well, France had to maintain control of its own armed forces and therefore could not accept their integration into NATO. Eisenhower returned in December for a pre-summit meeting with de Gaulle, Macmillan, and German chancellor Konrad Adenauer. De Gaulle visited London and in March played host to Khrushchev for a ten-day state visit to France. April saw de Gaulle travel to Canada and the United States and he was back in Paris in time to prepare for the first session of the summit meeting on May 16.

Things started to go wrong even before the opening of the summit. On May 1, a United States U2 photo-reconnaissance plane was shot down over the Soviet Union and its pilot, Gary Powers, was taken prisoner. The State Department maintained that Powers had strayed into Russsian air space due to a navigational error, but it was clear he had been on a spying mission. Khrushchev reacted with fury. When he arrived at the Élysée Palace, he handed de Gaulle the text of a statement announcing he could take no part in the conference unless Eisenhower made a public apology to the Soviet Union. He also insisted the president undertake to punish those responsible, and promise there would be no more such flights.

The next day, the four delegations eyed each other warily as they met in a high-ceilinged chamber next to de Gaulle's office. De Gaulle had put President Eisenhower and his aides opposite him, the Soviets on his left, and the British on his right. Khrushchev took the floor and repeated his demands, adding that a planned visit by Eisenhower to the Soviet Union would have to be cancelled. Eisenhower looked contrite, and read a long statement in which he said the flight of the U2 plane had been a defensive measure, and in any case it would not happen again.

De Gaulle tried to smooth things over; he noted that two weeks had elapsed since the U2 incident, giving ample time to settle things before the summit meeting. In any case, "At this very moment a Soviet satellite is passing over France eighteen times in every twenty-four hours. How do we know it is not taking photographs?"[12]

Khrushchev retorted: "What devil drove the Americans to commit this heinous act?"

De Gaulle told him there were many devils in the world. He then proposed that the Russian and American sides meet privately to settle the issue, in the hope the summit could resume the next morning. When the three Western leaders arrived the next day, there was no sign of Khrushchev. The Russian leader was busy holding a press conference in which he again denounced the Americans. The summit was finished, an international fiasco that foreshadowed the further tensions that would arise as the Cold War heated up. Despite the disappointing outcome, no one attached blame to de Gaulle. Neither would any leader attempt again to organize such an ambitious gathering of world figures.

"The successor was John Kennedy." On this laconic note, Charles de Gaulle introduces us to the man who replaced General Eisenhower as president of the United States. We might think from the brevity of de Gaulle's words that the two had a cool relationship, but such was not the place. While de Gaulle disdained Franklin Roosevelt and felt gratitude to Eisenhower for his wartime support, he looked on John Fitzgerald Kennedy as a man who, but for "the crime which killed him, might have had the time to leave his mark on our age." A few weeks after disastrously intervening at the Bay of Pigs, Kennedy arrived in Paris "brimming over with dynamism, he and his dazzling and cultivated wife forming a remarkably attractive couple."[13]

Soon after meeting Kennedy, de Gaulle became aware that "the attitude of the United States towards France had undergone a very decided change." The day had passed when Washington insisted on regarding Paris as "just another of its proteges." Kennedy acknowledged France's independence and offered de Gaulle "a share in his projects." Their one area of disagreement was Vietnam, where de Gaulle was advising the president that "he was taking the wrong road." Having been brutally bled in that Far East state, de Gaulle cautioned Kennedy that if he persisted in escalating operations there he would "sink step by step into a bottomless military and political quagmire."[14] As events would prove, de Gaulle was unable to deter him.

During the visit, JFK famously referred to himself as the "man who accompanied Mrs. Kennedy to Paris," acknowledging the attention Jacqueline Kennedy had received for her beauty, sophistication, and her fluency in French. In conversations recorded later, Jackie Kennedy intimates that de Gaulle "came on" to her. However, he remained politically discreet when she asked him whether he had gotten along best with Churchill or Roosevelt. "With Churchill I was always in disagreement but we always reached an accord," he told her. "With Roosevelt I was always in agreement but we never had an accord." Of Yvonne de Gaulle, Jackie Kennedy found a woman who was uncomfortable in her role of hostess. She found Yvonne "sweetly going through" the formalities, but tired of having to bear her official duties. When Jackie commented on how beautiful the tablecloth was at their state banquet, Yvonne replied, "the one at lunch was better."

After Paris, President Kennedy travelled to Vienna for his first meeting with Nikita Khrushchev. The Russian premier's truculent behaviour, begun in Paris a year before, continued; the Soviet leader did everything he could to intimidate the president, treating him as little more than an errand boy. Their future dealings would be on a far more equal level. De Gaulle concluded that Kennedy was a man "who inspired immense hopes." He seemed to be "on the point of taking off into the heights, like some great bird that beats its wings as it approaches the mountain tops."[15]

✝

Both Kennedy and de Gaulle were to become the objects of hatred and violence, although history would carry them to different destines. In de Gaulle's case, the end of the war in Algeria had left the proponents of *Algérie française* more fiercely determined than ever to exact revenge on the architect of their betrayal. At a secret meeting in Rome of the commanders of the Organisation de l'Armée Secrète (OAS), Georges Bidault took over its leadership, Colonel Antoine Argoud was put in charge of operations in France, and Jacques Soustelle took on responsibility for operations abroad. A series of bank robberies followed, and on July 3, 1962, playing in deadly earnest, a "military court" of the OAS handed down a death sentence on General de Gaulle for "the crime of high treason."

A light rain was falling on the evening of August 22, a Wednesday, when de Gaulle emerged from a day-long meeting of his Cabinet where the Évian Accords and the resettlement of the *pieds noirs* had been discussed. De Gaulle stood briefly atop the steps outside the Élysée Palace before descending to a black Citroën DS parked at the curb. Yvonne de Gaulle was with him, as was his son-in-law, Alain de Boissieu. De Gaulle's driver, Francis Marroux, a former policeman who had been at the wheel when an attempt had been made to blow up the car the previous September, waited, his motor idling. De Boissieu got in beside him while the general and Yvonne took their places in the back seat. Unnoticed across the street from the Élysée, a man carrying a motorcycle helmet interrupted his examination of an antique shop window to observe the departure. The presidential car drove off, followed by its escort vehicle flanked by two motorcycle outriders.

Marroux was following the same route, in reverse, that he had driven that morning when he'd brought the de Gaulles in from the airport at Villacoublay, sixteen kilometres to the southwest. They'd flown in from Colombey and would be returning home by the same means. The drive out of Paris was uneventful, the streets nearly empty with most Parisians still enjoying their August vacations. After crossing the Pont Alexandre III bridge and passing through the Porte de Châtillon, Marroux approached the crossroads at the Avenue de la Libération in the grungy industrial suburb of Petit-Clamart. It was eight minutes after eight and cars were turning on their headlights in the reduced visibility of the approaching dusk and the light drizzle that was falling. Observing their approach, a man later identified as Jean-Marie Bastien-Thiry, a disillusioned army colonel, waved a copy of the right-wing newspaper *L'Aurore* from the window of his Simca 1000. It was a signal to the dozen men, ten of them armed with automatic rifles, who lay in wait in four vehicles two hundred metres down the road.

When the assassins opened fire, de Boissieu shouted to Marroux to speed up. "Straight ahead, in the middle, Marroux, straight through!" Looking back at his in-laws, he screamed, *"Pere, baissez-vous!"* ("Father, get down.") The fusillade of bullets had blasted the Citroën's windows, blown out two tires, and smashed its gearbox. De Gaulle and Yvonne were covered with shards of glass and the smell of burning rubber filled the vehicle. De Boissieu caught sight of the last of the attack vehicles, its windows lowered with two gunmen who were shooting at them with their pistols. With the car "swaying dangerously like a motor-boat on the sea," he asked Marroux if they could make it to the airport. The driver said he would try.

Three minutes later, the car pulled up beside the tarmac at Villacoublay. De Gaulle got out and calmly inspected a waiting army guard of honour before boarding the plane. "It was touch and go this time!" he remarked.

Yvonne de Gaulle, worried about the brace of chickens she had bought for lunch in Colombey the next day, said "Don't forget *les poulets*. I hope they're all right." Policeman standing nearby wondered if she was referring to them; *poulets* being the Parisian nickname for police.[16]

That evening, de Gaulle phoned his prime minister, Georges Pompidou, to say "My dear friend, these people shoot like pigs."

Miraculously, none of the nearly two hundred bullets fired at General de Gaulle's car had touched any of its occupants. Fourteen bullets had entered the vehicle, some passing within centimetres of the heads of de Gaulle and his wife.* De Gaulle had merely nicked his fingers as he

---

* The car has since been exhibited at the Musée Charles-de-Gaulle in Lille, the General's birthplace.

brushed glass from his suit, leaving a spot of blood on his collar. That evening, one of the assault cars containing guns and ammunition was found nearby. A bomb that had been set failed to go off. By mid-September, all but three of the would-be killers were under lock and key.

Bastien-Thiry compared himself to the officers who had tried to kill Hitler, but claimed he had intended only to take de Gaulle prisoner so he could be tried. His argument convinced no one and he was condemned to death. De Gaulle refused clemency, on the grounds that the gunmen had fired on a car containing a woman, they had endangered the lives of innocent people in other cars at the scene, and that Bastien-Thiry had taken no personal risk in the affair, merely raising his newspaper to alert his accomplices. On March 11, 1963, Bastien-Thiry was shot at the prison in Ivry-sur-Seine, clutching his rosary. The general wrote but briefly of the incident in his memoirs: "So let de Gaulle continue his course and his vocation."[17]

Less than a month after being fired on at Petit-Clamart (in what by one count was the eighteenth attempt on his life), de Gaulle took to the air to announce plans for a referendum to provide for election of the president by popular vote. "When my own seven-year term is over ... the President of the Republic will thenceforward be elected by universal suffrage."[18] De Gaulle had extended the vote to women in the first election after the war, and now he was further stamping the Republic of de Gaulle in his own image. "As always," he told the people of France, "it will be for you to decide." The Communists and others, objecting to further empowerment of the office of president, again attacked de Gaulle with the charge that he wanted a dictatorship. The referendum carried by a 62 percent *Yes* vote — not the triumph de Gaulle had wished, but approval by a substantial margin.

The French — and the people of the world — were caught up by a far more worrisome prospect once the heat of the referendum campaign had died away; the possibility of a nuclear holocaust. On October 14, an American U2 aircraft returned from a flight over Cuba with photographic evidence that the Soviet Union was building missile bases in Cuba. Resisting the urging of his war hawks to send attack planes, President Kennedy ordered a naval embargo of the island. When Kennedy's emissary, Dean Acheson, arrived at the Élysée Palace on October 22 with maps and photographs of the installations, de Gaulle told him, "Put your documents away; the word of the President of the United States is good enough for me."[19] De Gaulle's reaction demonstrated his high degree of confidence in Kennedy.

A year later, John F. Kennedy was dead, assassinated by a gunman in Dallas, Texas on November 22, 1963. There had been discussions before Kennedy's death of another meeting with de Gaulle. Speaking the day after the assassination to his Cabinet, de Gaulle said that Kennedy "was one of the very few leaders of whom it may be said that they are statesmen." De Gaulle flew to Washington for the funeral. His tall, gaunt figure was seen in the front line of the funeral march. De Gaulle was the first foreign visitor to be received by the president's widow. She impulsively snatched a white marguerite from a bouquet and held it out to him. He kept it in his pocket until his return to Paris.[20]

Along with that flower, de Gaulle was also forced to abandon his thoughts of Kennedy and of what the American president might have achieved in the future. France's present needs, in particular, the needs of its economy, demanded his attention. A series of French economic plans, designed by de Gaulle's economics advisor Jacques Rueff and backed enthusiastically by the general, brought rapid improvement in French living standards that by 1964 were one-third above their 1959 level. No longer was de Gaulle deploring the disaffection of the population. A "stabilization plan" introduced in 1963 had cut inflation in half (from 6 to 3 per cent) and would help France move toward a balanced budget. As Janet Flanner would tell her New Yorker readers:

> This year's end finds President de Gaulle on a peculiar pinnacle of lonely leadership — lonelier by far than the isolated eminence he has always contrived for himself. In a little more than a twelvemonth, through the brutal loss of President Kennedy, the unexpected sacking of Nikita Khrushchev, and the sequestration into old age of Sir Winston Churchill, de Gaulle has emerged as the unique familiar, powerful political and historical figure

left on the Western world's governing scene. As encouragement, the miraculous fiscal prosperity of his Fifth Republic, now entering its seventh year, has reached new amplitudes. Today, France is one of the richest nations.[21]

The year was notable for de Gaulle for one other event: his prostate operation. At seventy-three, he was beginning to suffer the inevitabilities of passing years, but he recovered quickly and was ready, in 1965, for the ultimate test of political gamesmanship: winning office via the ballot box. This was the first and only time that de Gaulle would submit himself to a vote of the people; his previous attainments of high office had come through appointment by the French Committee of National Liberation (1944); appointment by President Coty (1958); and approval by an elite college of electors (1959). He stood above party politics, refusing to become personally involved in the Gaullist Union pour la Nouvelle République (UNR) that protected his interests in the National Assembly. De Gaulle faced two competitors in 1965 and he expected to win handily in the first round of voting on December 5. The result, however, gave him but 44 percent of the ballots. François Mitterrand, benefitting from the backing of the Socialist Party, collected 32 percent, and 16 percent had voted for Jean Lecanuet of the Mouvement républicain populaire (MRP). Stunned by the results, de Gaulle spoke of resigning. In the second round campaign, he went on television but refused to hold public rallies, while Mitterrand was drawing large crowds across France. On December 19, however, de Gaulle was safely re-elected with 54.5 percent of the vote.

Following his re-election, de Gaulle told his cabinet that "The regime had to go through the trial by fire. It has emerged well-tempered."

Yet another conflagration, entirely of de Gaulle's own making, lay not far in the future. Charles de Gaulle considered that France's surrender of Canada to the British in 1763 had been an abandonment of its children, and that it was now "France's duty to help" Quebec, the home of the French in that country, become "at last master of its own fate."[22] Like distant, unheard trumpets, Quebec and France had said little to each other in the centuries since the Treaty of Paris. That was about to change.

Following the conquest, Britain, by the Quebec Act of 1774, had confirmed the rights of the French *"habitants"* to their Catholic religion, language, and civil laws and customs. From the time the British North American colonies joined in Confederation to create modern Canada in 1867, French-speaking citizens have formed a majority in Quebec. As a result of their "revenge of the cradle" — compensation for their defeat by the British on the Plains of Abraham at Quebec City — the French-speaking population grew from sixty thousand to six million by 1967.

In 1960, travelling to Canada for the first time as president of France, de Gaulle was welcomed by Prime Minister John Diefenbaker and his old wartime comrade General Georges Vanier, who had become governor general. On his earlier visits, de Gaulle had poured praise on Canada for its wartime achievements. This time, as he went to Quebec City and Montreal, he was more conscious of the profusion of Quebec flags adorned with the fleur-de-lis symbol, "beside the very rare Federal flags."[23] De Gaulle's meeting with Diefenbaker, a populist Conservative from the western plains who spoke no French, gave him the opportunity to highlight the need for Canada to "solve the problem posed by the existence within her borders of two peoples, one of which was French and must, like any other, have the right to self-determination."[24]

De Gaulle debated for months whether he should accept the invitation of the Canadian government to travel to Montreal for the opening of the World's Fair in 1967 — known as Expo '67 — that coincided with celebrations marking the centennial of Confederation It was finally the prospect of a sea voyage and the opportunity to remind Canada that it had a French minority in need of liberation, that convinced him. "I will hit hard," de Gaulle told his son-in-law, Alain de Boissieu. "Hell will happen, but it has to be done."[25] After a stopover in St. Pierre, de Gaulle arrived in Quebec City aboard the French cruiser *Colbert* on July 23, a Sunday. He spoke that night at a formal banquet, saying France had come to assist "at the advent of a people who want, in every domain, to make up their own mind and to take its fate in its own hands."[26] The next day, he travelled 270 kilometres from Quebec City to Montreal along the old

Chemin du roi of French Canada. Huge crowds gathered along his route, often bursting into the singing of "La Marseillaise." He repeated the same message in every town: "It is France's duty to help you. She has owed you something for a long time."

In Montreal, half the population of the world's second-largest French city turned out to welcome de Gaulle. People filled every street leading to the Hôtel de Ville. Signs proclaiming *"Vive le Québec Libre"*— the slogan of a small nationalist party — were prominent in the crowd. Buoyed by the boisterous welcome, de Gaulle felt the weight of his seventy-seven years lifting from his shoulders.

He asked the mayor, Jean Drapeau, a confirmed federalist, if he could speak from the balcony. "No," Drapeau said, there was no microphone. An aide appeared mysteriously and led the general to the balcony where a microphone that Drapeau had ordered disconnected, had been hooked up again by a radio broadcaster. As de Gaulle looked out into the twilight of the Champs-de-Mars below him, the crowd cheered and then fell silent.

"I am going to tell you a secret that you will not repeat," he began. "This evening, here, and all along my route, I found the same kind of atmosphere as that of the liberation." The crowd roared. After a few more remarks, he ended abruptly: *"Vive Montréal. Vive le Québec!"* Then he was to repeat himself, adding just one word: *"Vive le Québec ... libre!"* It was the addition of that single word, *libre,* the slogan, Mayor Drapeau would remind de Gaulle, of an opposition separatist party, that would transform the visit into an international incident. Overlooked by the Canadian media was the fact that during his speech de Gaulle had four times cried out, *"Vive le Canada."*[27]

The prime minister of Canada, Lester Pearson, watched de Gaulle on television that night. "I could hardly believe my ears when I heard the words he uttered," he wrote later.[28] The next day Pearson issued a statement and went on TV to assert in French that "some of the President's declarations tended to encourage the small minority of our population whose aim is to destroy Canada and, as such, they are unacceptable to the Canadian people and her government." The people of Quebec needed no liberation, he added, recalling the blood Canada had spilled in helping to rescue France in two world wars.

Pearson said he was still looking forward to talking to de Gaulle, but the general had other plans. Told of Ottawa's reaction, he attended a lunch in his honour, wrapped up a quick visit to the French pavilion at Expo, and embarrassed but defiantly proud, boarded a plane to fly back to France.

De Gaulle's comments caused consternation across Canada. The *Winnipeg Free Press* headlined: "DE GAULLE SHOUTS SEPARATIST SLOGAN." The next day, the *Lethbridge Herald* bannered across its front page: "DE GAULLE GOES HOME."

In Paris, even de Gaulle's own Cabinet, accustomed to the calculating politics played constantly in France, were largely critical of him. "He's crazy," said one minister. "This time he's gone too far," said another. Others blamed de Gaulle's advancing years, recalling his characterization of Marshall Pétain: "Old age is a shipwreck." Some observers noted that France also had separatists in its midst — Basques in the south and Bretons in the north. France's two most important newspapers were critical. *Le Monde* called de Gaulle's Canadian visit "a humiliating misadventure" and *Le Figaro* criticized his interference in the internal affairs of another country.

De Gaulle told his Cabinet that things in Canada were not yet settled. "They're only just beginning. It's a great matter … a generation determined to become its own boss in its own country." At a press conference later that year, de Gaulle continued to defend his remarks. Problems between the French and English in Canada would only be solved, he said, with the "advent of Québec as a sovereign State, master of her own national existence." To bring that about would require "solidarity of the French community on both sides of the Atlantic."[29]

Seen from the perspective of the decades that have since passed, de Gaulle's comments of 1967 might hardly be considered prophetic.* But given the circumstances of that era, his words represented nothing less than an intellectual shot across the bow. They fuelled the nationalistic spirit of a rapidly changing Quebec, a region that was throwing off its old sectarian culture (as France had already done) and through its "Quiet Revolution" was transforming itself into the most socially liberal region of Canada. The Parti Québécois, dedicated to independence under the guise

---

* In the Quebec election of April 7, 2014, the separatist Parti Québécois suffered its most crushing defeat since its first election in 1970, gaining only 25 percent of the popular vote and losing power to the federalist Liberal party.

of "sovereignty," would arise to take power in 1976. It would conduct two vaguely worded referendums, one in 1980 and the other in 1995. Both would fail — the latter by a breathtakingly small margin of 50.6 percent "No" to 49.4 percent "Yes." In the meantime, Canada had become officially a bilingual country. It also brought its constitution home from the United Kingdom, with inclusion — at the insistence of Prime Minister Pierre Elliot Trudeau — of a Charter of Rights and Freedoms.

After the 1995 referendum, the federal government adopted a Clarity Act that recognized the right of a province to leave Canada, but only after a referendum with a "clear question" had won the support of a "clear majority." A later federal government, seeking reconciliation between English and French, enacted a law recognizing the Quebecois population as representative of "a nation" within Canada. The extent to which de Gaulle's *Vive le Québec Libre* cry may have foreshadowed or influenced these events is arguable. What cannot be denied is that the Gaullian intervention marked one of the few occasions when a head of state had knowingly injected himself into an internal debate of a friendly nation.

CHAPTER 22
The Final Days

Old Earth, worn by the ages … Old France, weighed down
with history … Old man, exhausted by ordeal, detached
from human deeds, feeling the approach of the eternal cold,
but always watching in the shadows for the gleam of hope!

— Charles de Gaulle, *Mémoires de guerre*

Student rebellion and labour insurrection, twin progeny of a decade of global social turmoil, reached France in 1968, the tenth year of General de Gaulle's return to power. Where there had been riots against the Vietnam War in the United States and the celebration across the West of a new youth culture memorialized in the music of the Beatles and the slogan, "Make love, not war," young people in France turned against what they saw as the ossification of their universities. Their protests against overcrowded classrooms and assorted other dissatisfactions

— including the sexual segregation of their dormitories — were quickly matched by demands from industrial workers for better working conditions and higher wages. With the Communist trade unions nervously adjudicating labour strategy, Charles de Gaulle found himself confronting the greatest challenge to his authority since the "revolt of the generals" that followed the crisis in revolt-torn Algeria.

Ten years after Algeria, France was a much different country and Paris a vastly different city from that for which de Gaulle had been the instrument of liberation in 1944. Streets had been renamed in honour of the liberators, old buildings demolished, trees cut down, and entire blocks transformed into shopping centres. New government buildings had gone up in every city across France. At the same time, almost everyone agreed that the stilted academic bureaucracy of France's universities needed to be shaken up. Student enrolment had more than doubled to five hundred thousand, but because university study in France was free, there was little money to build the new facilities such numbers demanded. Professors lectured to classes of fifteen hundred students. The sexual permissiveness of the new youth culture found itself in conflict with bourgeois dictates of chastity and modesty. Male students enjoyed raiding female dormitories in intrusions that met little resistance from their occupants. The young people who had most benefitted from France's economic progress had become its sharpest critics.

In January 1968 the French minister for youth and sport, François Missoffe, had been insulted when he went to the Nanterre branch of the University of Paris to open a swimming pool. His German-born adversary, Daniel Cohn-Bendit — soon to be known as "Danny the Red" for both his politics and his hair — assailed him for having failed to make any mention, in a six-hundred-page report on education, of the sexual concerns of young people.[1] Students were not allowed to have visitors in their rooms or hang pictures on their walls. Nanterre was typical of the new French universities — a structure of concrete slabs built for two thousand students, now occupied by some fifteen thousand.

Students at other universities had similar complaints. In Bordeaux, five thousand boycotted the university canteen. When Nanterre students went into Paris on March 22 to protest the Vietnam War, their demonstration ended in the smashing of windows in the American Express office at the Place d l'Opera. Two thousand young people paraded through the Latin Quarter on April 19 and the next week a right-wing organization attacked student headquarters. Nanterre was closed, reopened after two days, but had to close again when classes descended into anarchic talkfests and argumentative debates. Danny the Red was arrested after having put out a bulletin that contained instructions on how to make a Molotov cocktail.

The protests — and the government's reaction, which included police repression — quickly escalated. At the Élysée Palace, President de Gaulle exhibited little patience for student agitation. Accustomed to military discipline, he could not understand why the university authorities — who he agreed were exceedingly conservative — could not keep things in hand. Added to his natural authoritarian bent was a strict moral code inherited from his family and buttressed by Mme de Gaulle. His main interest in educational matters was in changing the selection system for university admission by requiring merit testing of applicants. When his education minister, Alain Peyrefitte, announced plans for just such a change, howls of protest came from students all over France. *"Dix ans, c'est assez"* (Ten years, that's enough) became the cry, along with *"Au revoir, de Gaulle!"*

Prime Minister Pompidou did his best to play down the significance of the student turmoil. "Let them sleep together," he told guests at a lunch in the Matignon. "When they're doing that, they won't cause us any worries."[2] Deciding to free Cohn-Bendit, he remarked, "I'm not the man to put French youth into barracks."[3] He then got on a plane and flew off to visit Iran and Afghanistan.

The prime minister's approach may well have worked if the Communist Party had not abandoned its early opposition to the student strikers, whom it had put down as "false revolutionaries." After raucous May Day demonstrations by the Communist-led Confédération Général du Travail (CGT) on Europe's traditional day of labour, a one-day token strike at Sud Aviation escalated into a countrywide general strike. Before it was over, ten million workers were off the job and stores were running short of food and other essentials. Rising unemployment and inflation had been eating away at the gains of the working class; labour's concerns were suddenly to be married to the youthful revolt against government authority.

On May 13, the day that peace talks between the United States and North and South Vietnam opened in Paris, ten thousand demonstrators marched on the Sorbonne. That night, students erected barricades and pelted police with stones. Police responded with tear gas, and after hand-to-hand fighting, the student barricades were demolished. In Kabul, Prime Minister Pompidou received word of the violence and booked a quick passage home. His first move was to get de Gaulle's approval for the reopening of the Sorbonne. He won it, reluctantly, and Pompidou went on the air to express "deep sympathy" for the students. He assured de Gaulle that he could safely reopen the universities and deal with student concerns.

"If you win, so much the better, France will win with you. If you lose, too bad for you," de Gaulle warned him.[4] The Sorbonne reopened the next morning and was immediately occupied by students. Red flags were flown from statues and plans were made for a "people's tribunal" to try the police. A mass march to the Place de la République was matched by similar parades in other cities. The police made hundreds of arrests.

Why did Charles de Gaulle choose this moment to embark on a long-scheduled visit to Romania? He had been assured by Pompidou and others that the prime minister's soft line would eventually bring the students around. More important, de Gaulle saw an opportunity to strengthen ties with Romania, where dictator Nicolae Ceausescu was tugging at his Moscow tether. On May 14, the day of de Gaulle's departure, walk-outs flared throughout the country and, with the support of the Communist-led CGT, a general strike was underway. In Bucharest, de Gaulle got word that the Odéon, the national theatre on the Left Bank, had been occupied by demonstrators. After making speeches calling for "the end of opposing blocs" in Europe, de Gaulle decided to head home, a day early.

In Paris, de Gaulle met with his key ministers and made it clear he was furious over what had happened. He wanted the police to clear demonstrators out of all sites they'd occupied. Told this could lead to deaths, he agreed to limit action to the Odéon. Then de Gaulle dropped an expression that has been debated for its true meaning ever since: "*La reforme, oui; le chienlit, non.*" In common usage, the term "*chienlit*" refers to "shitting your bed," but de Gaulle biographer Jonathan Fenby believes the president was using it in its classical sense, to mean a carnival or masquerade.[5] In either case, de Gaulle was fed up. He made a seven-minute broadcast promising workers and students more "participation" in decisions affecting them. A referendum on such matters was promised for June 16, but the speech changed no one's mind. The first fatality occurred when a young man died after being hit by a tear gas canister in Lyon. It was time to settle. Encouraged by the minister of social affairs, Jacques Chirac, the employers' federation agreed to a 35 percent rise in the minimum wage and a 10 percent across-the-board wage increase. None of this was good enough. Demonstrations continued throughout the country. The bitterness of the workers came home to de Gaulle when Mme de Gaulle returned from a shopping trip to say she'd been shouted at and insulted.

Charles de Gaulle was bored with the minutiae of government and his health was beginning to trouble him. He suffered from a distended stomach and tired easily. At the height of the crisis, he had to take time out to reflect. Cancelling a Cabinet meeting, he passed word that he was going home to Colombey for a day. Instead, he made a secretive flight to Baden-Baden, the French base in Germany, where he met with the one-time commander of forces in Algeria, General Jacques Massu. The president's absence threw his Cabinet into turmoil. Where had de Gaulle gone and what was he up to?

De Gaulle wanted to be sure he had the support of the military; otherwise, he would have to resign. He told Massu that if the Communists stormed the Élysée Palace they would find no one there. De Gaulle must have felt as depressed and hopeless as the day he had withdrawn Free French forces from Dakar. He might step down and go far away — as far as Canada, perhaps? General Massu told de Gaulle he could count on the army, and that he should fight on. An understanding was possible; de Gaulle agreed to a pardon for General Salan and other outcasts from Algiers. Then Massu added the decisive pronouncement: "Go back. There is nothing else to do. You are still in the game; you've got to stay in it."[6]

It was all de Gaulle needed. Reassured, his spirits bucked up, he returned to Colombey by plane. He walked the grounds of La Boisserie with Mme de Gaulle, enjoyed a good dinner, and set about writing a speech for broadcast the next day. He flew to Paris in the morning. At half past four on May 30, a Thursday, he went on the radio to tell the nation that he was not quitting, that he was dissolving the National Assembly and new elections would be held, and that he was postponing his promised referendum. De Gaulle spoke with authority and conviction. His speech called for "civic action ... everywhere and immediately to assist the government." De Gaulle followers sprang to work. Within an hour, the streets of Paris began to fill with his supporters. A vast assemblage marched down the Champs-Élysée from the Arc de Triomphe, headed by André Malraux and Michel Debré. There was no sign of Prime Minister Pompidou, but other admirers were there, including eighty-two-year-old François Mauriac. Estimates placed the crowd at half a million. Outside the presidential palace, fifty thousand stood to chant, "De Gaulle, you are not alone!" The legend lived; the man of June 18 had spoken once again, and the people listened.

✝

By the middle of June, the last of the strikes and student demonstrations, claiming four lives in all, had petered out. In the elections that month, the Gaullist party — the Union des Démocrates pour le République (UDR), as it was now known — won a historic victory. By securing 354 of the 487 National Assembly seats, the UDR gained the biggest majority ever attained in France. The economy would have to absorb the costs of the raises won by the workers.

De Gaulle, true to his admonishment to Pompidou about failure, chose a new prime minister. He settled on Maurice Couve de Murville, former minister of foreign affairs, briefly minister of finance. Pompidou continued to let it be known he was available for the presidency whenever de Gaulle might choose to retire. To de Gaulle, Pompidou seemed to be pushing a bit hard. The fissure between the two of them widened in the wake of scurrilous talk about Pompidou's wife. There had been rumours linking her to a sex scandal. Investigation showed there was nothing to the allegations, but Pompidou would never forgive de Gaulle for what he felt was the general's complacence in dealing with the rumours.

Faced with unemployment approaching the million mark, the government in the fall of 1968 set out to achieve economic growth through easy credit and an increase in the money supply. The franc was held at parity. When these policies threatened to set off a flight of capital, the budget was slashed, but for the first time, more money was allocated to education than to defense. De Gaulle, however, was not satisfied. His goals became the framework for the postponed referendum. Workers would be given the means to participate in the management of their companies. Regional governments would be reformed throughout France. And the Senate would be reorganized, with membership to be drawn from business, cultural organizations, and community groups. This Gaullist view of democracy held but one problem: it would be bitterly opposed from every power base in the country, from trade union chieftains to corporate executives and their boards, to say nothing of most of the political leadership.

Amid this turmoil, de Gaulle kept his focus on France's international relations. He had twice rejected Britain's application to enter the Common Market, and now watched with satisfaction the strengthening economic ties between its six members. The invasion of Czechoslovakia by Soviet troops following a brief "Prague Spring" gave him further evidence that his hoped for European détente would take a long time to be realized. In the Middle East, where de Gaulle had strong memories of France's protectorate role in Lebanon and Syria, the rise of Israeli influence had become a concern to him. When an Israeli commando unit destroyed Lebanon's commercial air fleet in a raid on the Beirut airport, de Gaulle felt compelled to act. The raid had been in retaliation for an attack on an El-Al airliner in Athens carried out by Palestinians based in Lebanon. De Gaulle, without consulting any of his ministers, ordered an embargo on all arms shipments to Israel. He also approved sending arms to the breakaway region of Biafra in Nigeria, perhaps seeing a breakup of the former British colony as an advantage to France's African interests. The revolt, however, was put down.

De Gaulle began 1969 with a tour through Brittany. He hoped to relight the flame of enthusiasm that previous tours of French regions had brought, but there was little excitement among his audiences. Breton separatists chided him about his remarks in Quebec, shouting they wanted to be free, too.

Returning to Paris, he announced that his much-promised referendum would be held on April 27, a Sunday. From the beginning, it was evident that so many groups had become disaffected with the general that the referendum would prove a hazardous venture. Business was alarmed at the increasingly socialist bent of the government, the proponents of *Algérie française* would never forgive de Gaulle, and the Jewish community was shocked and frightened by his position on Israel. Three days before the referendum, the general told Michel Debré, "The dice have been rolled. I can do nothing more. I have no more illusions."[7]

He went on television to appeal for a yes vote, but told viewers that a defeat would make it impossible for him to carry on. "Your reply is going to determine the destiny of France," he said in a sonorous but aging voice. "If I am disavowed by the majority of you, my present task as chief of state would obviously become impossible [and] I would immediately stop exercising my functions."

On the weekend of the referendum, de Gaulle went home to Colombey-les-Deux-Églises. It rained that Sunday, a cold spring day, and he and Mme de Gaulle bundled up to go to vote at the municipal office. Late that night, Bernard Tricot, the long-serving secretary-general in de Gaulle's office, phoned with the results. The referendum had been defeated, 53 percent to 47. The general would not have been surprised; he had prepared a resignation statement for just such an eventuality. At ten minutes after midnight, Agence France-Presse carried the bulletin: "I am ceasing to exercise my functions as President of the Republic. The decision takes effect at noon today."[8]

The fact de Gaulle had been able to hold nearly half of the vote was impressive, considering the wall of opposition that had built up against his policies. There has never been a satisfactory explanation as to why de Gaulle insisted on this fourth referendum. The issues were largely of the general's own making, and could have been dealt with in other ways. Was de Gaulle acting out an unconscious political death wish? His old contemporaries were all dying off, one by one — Churchill in 1965 and Paul Reynaud in 1956 — and he was not only tired, but lonely.

In the days after the referendum, de Gaulle took only a few visitors at La Boisserie, preferring to spend his time going over his files and planning the next volume of his memoirs, to be called *Mémoires d'Espoir*. Eighteen days after the vote, he finally left Colombey for an unannounced overseas visit. He and Mme de Gaulle were bound for Ireland for a recovery vacation that would also give the general the opportunity to meet with his distant Celtic relatives, the MacCartans. Landing in Cork, they stayed, in all, at three different resorts, concluding their trip in Dublin.

De Gaulle was received by the president of Ireland, Eamon de Valera, eighty-five years old and blind. They were joined by about thirty of de Gaulle's "cousins," who confirmed that he was indeed a descendant of the MacCartans killed at the Battle of the Boyne in 1690. "I raise my glass to a united Ireland," de Gaulle said in toasting his relatives and his native country.[9] He had done it again, speaking out on the internal affairs of another country, Ireland having been divided between the independent south and its northern counties, Ulster, that remained part of the United Kingdom. That night, de Gaulle was feted at the French Embassy. By the time the de Gaulles returned to France, the Republic had a new president. Georges Pompidou led the first round ballot on June 1 with 45 percent of the vote and on June 15 he handily beat the centrist candidate, Alain Poher, collecting 58 percent of the vote.

As if unable to settle his feet or his spirits, de Gaulle and his wife soon set out on a second trip, this time to Spain. June found them travelling from the verdant north of Spain to the arid south of a country that de Gaulle had always wanted to see. Finally, it was home to La Boisserie, this time to stay. It was as it was when he was awaiting the call. Silence filled the house and he wandered the grounds, staring at the stars at night, steeped "in the insignificance of things." He encouraged family visits, and the voices of his son, Philippe, daughter, Elisabeth, their spouses, and children often filled the house.[10]

In August, the de Gaulles took a brief trip through the Vosges, returning to learn on September 1 of the death of another old friend, François Mauriac. His passing saddened the general, Mauriac being one of the two men — the other being André Malraux — whom de Gaulle felt best knew and understood him.

De Gaulle spent a third of each day in his study — where visitors were forbidden to disturb him — and within a year he had finished the next volume of his memoirs, *La Renouveau, 1958–1962 (The Renewal)*. While far less dramatic than his earlier volumes, it quickly sold out its first printing of 750,000 copies when it appeared in October 1970. He had promised one last volume, to consist of seven chapters, but completed only two. He was to have given, in his final chapter, his "personal view on the situation of France, Europe and the world."[11]

On the morning of November 9, 1970, only thirteen days before his eightieth birthday, de Gaulle rose as usual, put on a dark grey suit, took breakfast, and worked until noon on his memoirs. He and Mme de Gaulle went for a stroll after lunch, having dressed warmly against the cool, windy weather. De Gaulle received his last visitor at 2:30, a young farmer with whom he had exchanged some land. Alone in his study, he wrote a half dozen letters, including one to his son, asking to confirm the cost of land Philippe wished to buy in the south of France. De Gaulle had promised a gift of 400,000 francs to go toward the building of a house. They could work out the details on Philippe's visit to Colombey at Christmas.

After a quiet supper, de Gaulle went to his study to close the shutters, then moved into the library where Yvonne was at her desk, writing letters. De Gaulle pulled up a chair to the green baize bridge table, picked up a deck of cards and began to play a game of solitaire. He had dealt only a couple of hands when he suddenly put his right hand on his back and cried, "Oh, it hurts here."[12] As he slumped in his chair, Yvonne and two servants struggled to stop him from slipping off. A doctor was called, while de Gaulle's driver, Francis Marroux, was summoned from a house opposite La Boisserie. When Dr. Lacheny arrived from the village, he found de Gaulle still breathing, lying on a mattress on the floor. The doctor recorded de Gaulle's last breath at 7:25 p.m. He concluded he had died of a rupture of the abdominal aorta, the result of an aneurism. A priest rendered the last rites. "He suffered so much these last two years," Mme de Gaulle remarked. The general had dealt the last hand of his life and perhaps fittingly, he had played it alone.[13]

Mme de Gaulle took charge. The first thing was to call the family. Only then could the news be made public. On hearing of his father-in-law's death, Alain de Boissieu phoned the Élysée Palace to inform President Pompidou. Philippe de Gaulle left his office at the naval station in Brest, travelled by train to Paris, then by car to Colombey in the morning. At 9:40 a.m., the news agencies broadcast word of de Gaulle's death. The French Cabinet met and declared November 12 a day of national mourning. President Pompidou went on the air to confirm the general's death.

> *Françaises, Français,*
> *Le Général de Gaulle est mort*
> *La France est veuve …*

✝

In declaring France a widow, Pompidou was evoking the spirit of a motherland desolate at the loss of its father and mentor. Beginning the next day, a stream of prominent personages made the pilgrimage to La Boisserie. Pompidou arrived in early afternoon and he and Jacques Chaban-Delmas, the premier, spent sixteen minutes in the parlour with de Gaulle's coffin.

In his will, a copy of which he'd given Pompidou, de Gaulle had insisted on a simple funeral. He was to be buried in the Colombey churchyard beside his daughter Anne. There was to be no national funeral and no speeches were to be made. These dictates were respected, but that did not stop forty thousand people from descending on Colombey on November 12. At four o'clock, twelve young men of the village carried de Gaulle's white oak coffin to the graveyard beside the church and de Gaulle was laid to rest. A simple pale gravestone read, "Charles de Gaulle 1890–1970."

France came almost to a stop that day, and the rest of the world paused to take notice. In Paris, the theatres shut down. "All of France has been plunged into mourning," the Associated Press reported.[14] On the day of the funeral, eighty world leaders, ranging from President Nixon to Soviet premier Kosygin, attended a memorial service at Notre Dame. Cyrus Sulzberger of the *New York Times* noted in his diary: "I am glad for the old man's sake that death was swift. He had a horror of the gradual decline. There is a peculiar hollowness in France this afternoon."[15]

The consecration of de Gaulle to the ages began even before the general had been laid to rest. The illustrated weekly *Paris Match* published a 150-page memorial edition, "l'Adieu a de Gaulle," to record that the heart of France had stopped beating. "He had fought with all his strength, fervently, sometimes angrily … caught in the vortex of history." The Man of June 18 was gone, but the nation that he had transformed would forever bear the imprint of his presence.

CHAPTER 23
The Legend and the Legacy

Charles de Gaulle attained a legendary status during thirty years as a defiant defender of his country in war and a bold leader in peace. His departure from the presidency deprived France of its most noble personality; even his death could not erase a powerful presence that would endure and grow, made the more memorable by its narrative of historic accomplishment. The period of Gaullist leadership largely coincided with *les Trente Glorieuses*, the thirty glorious years from 1945 to 1975 in which France's population, economy, and standard of living grew exponentially.[1] The extent that de Gaulle's policies contributed to this growth may be arguable, but their legacy is felt in every area of French life, from education to commerce, technology, and social welfare.

The strength of the de Gaulle legend has grown in the years since his death, sustained by successive French governments whose policies have continued to reflect the ideas he espoused. His views remain largely the views of the French today. Nearly half a century after his death, he is almost universally regarded among his countrymen as their greatest historic figure.

General de Gaulle's personality and achievements were shaped by war. No one would expect a leader of his stature to arise in peacetime — as de Gaulle had observed, the country would have no need of one. Successive presidents, from Georges Pompidou to François Hollande in the twenty-first century, have brought distinctive qualities to the Élysée Palace, but none faced such life and death issues as those which confronted de Gaulle. History would prove de Gaulle to have made the right decisions on all his major challenges — the fight against Nazi Germany, unifying the Resistance, replacing the splintered party politics of the Fourth Republic with the presidential stability of the Fifth, decolonization of the Empire, and pursuit of an independent foreign policy. His voice was in many ways that of the prophet, whether in his prescience on the inevitability of war between Germany and Russia, or on the ultimate retreat that the United States would be forced to make from Vietnam.

De Gaulle's nationalism was the product of a long history of nation states marked by interminable wars. Such sentiment seems out of place in what has become an interdependent world characterized by a global economy, free trade agreements, and instant technological communication. But de Gaulle's insistence on a foreign policy independent of the United States — a doubtful proposition in his time — is now widely emulated under the more flexible conditions of a post–Cold War era. Had he lived to finish his memoirs, de Gaulle would have left us with a more complete understanding of his view of a post-Gaullist world. Without that, we must struggle with what we have in trying to understand how he might have reacted to the realities of succeeding years. In view of the new global relationships of the twenty-first century, he might well have agreed, for example, with the decision of President Nicolas Sarkozy in 2009 to reintegrate France's armed forces with NATO, or the actions of President François Hollande in 2013 in support of the United States' criticism of the policies of the Syrian regime of Bashar al-Assad.[2]

As a consequence of de Gaulle's determination to reconcile France and Germany, a European war of the kind his generation experienced is unimaginable today. De Gaulle's greater vision of a "Europe from the Atlantic to the Urals" has been substantially realized, although the West's attempt to bring Ukraine into the European orbit has been stalled, at least for the time being. Historians may debate whether his attitude to European integration was motivated by a desire to protect France's great power status or, as argued by a more current and revisionist school of thinking, to support French business and commercial interests. More important is the fact that while de Gaulle never abandoned his primary loyalty to the nation state, he saw and acted on the need for states to work together in their mutual self-interest.

The *New York Times* devoted an unprecedented six thousand words to de Gaulle's obituary, observing that "he could not resist shocking American opinion." Because of this, he "generated strong resentments among many Americans, some of whom even refused to visit France or purchase French-made goods while he was in power."[3] Such reaction has persisted beyond the de Gaulle era, as in the American anger over France's refusal to support its attack on Iraq in 2003. Campaigns to rename French fries as "Freedom fries" and dump French wine down sewers were among the more inane responses to that episode. De Gaulle's encouragement of Quebec separatism earned him the disapproval of many Canadians who otherwise admired his wartime courage and shared his reluctance to accept every eccentricity of American foreign policy.

General de Gaulle's greatest legacy to his country and the world has to be the Fifth Republic. It has given France stable government and enabled it to deal with the inevitable crises of national and global affairs. His legacy also embraces the rule of law and democracy, both sorely lacking in France during the years of the Vichy regime and never securely anchored in the Fourth Republic. There can be no doubt of de Gaulle's enduring commitment to democratic values. He extended the vote to women in the first postwar election and insisted on changing the constitution to provide for election of the president by popular vote. He was not the first military leader to take power in France; he assumed power twice, in 1944 and in 1958, by edict rather than by popular vote. The circumstances were too grave to permit the choice of the ballot and there was no demand for it from the public. However, he also was twice democratically elected as president — the first time by a college of electors and the second time by popular vote. He won three of four referendums and respected the public's will in each case, even at the price of his ultimate resignation.

Charles de Gaulle is the father of two other constructs that endure in France: the heroic French Resistance, part myth and part reality, which he idealized in rescuing the country from a slough of despair and recrimination; and the social welfare state, which, despite its cost and its attendant discouragement of entrepreneurial initiative, has provided the French people with one of the world's most comfortable standards of living.

De Gaulle encouraged multi-racial participation in government, appointed black Africans to senior positions, and worked seamlessly with colleagues of varied ethnicity. Although critical of the policies of the "warrior state of Israel," he relied heavily on Jewish colleagues, including his first prime minister, Michel Debre, who was a grandson of a chief rabbi of France. He also spoke approvingly of another Jewish premier, Pierre Mendes France, who held office in 1954–55. De Gaulle had grown up at a time of deep-rooted anti-Semitism. While his remarks on this subject reveal an occasional acceptance of prejudicial conventions, they give no evidence of anything more. When de Gaulle referred to Jews in a 1967 news conference as "self-confident and dominating," he was speaking in his usual blunt style.

The most difficult decision de Gaulle faced involved France's last major colony, Algeria. No issue was more emotive in France, and he rose to power in the vortex of forces that, had they been left to whirl relentlessly, would have led to civil war, probably ending in a military dictatorship. His decision to permit Algeria to opt for independence demonstrated that he was no prisoner of the past and showed that he had the courage to make tough decisions, no matter the personal risk that might ensue. In the case of Algeria, de Gaulle put his life on the line and it is a miracle that he survived so many attempts to take it.

Regrettably, de Gaulle was less decisive in dealing with Vietnam in 1945–46. At the time, France was determined to regain control of its Empire and public opinion opposed letting go any of the colonies. For a long time, de Gaulle was equally intransigent on the issue of colonial independence. He had reversed his position by the time of the Algerian crisis and was by then willing to have the colony go its own way. It was a short step from this change of attitude to his staunch conviction that neutralization was the only solution to the Vietnam quagmire, even at the risk of Communist supremacy in that country. That this was the ultimate outcome anyway, even after massive U.S. military involvement and its horrendous death toll, proved the soundness of his analysis.

While Vietnam in 1946 and Algeria in 1958 represented grave challenges to the Republic, it was the Second World War that threatened the country's very existence. By rallying the French people to the support of a united and effective resistance, de Gaulle made a significant contribution to Allied victory. Without a de Gaulle — or if the general had lost his life from the hazardous risks he took during the war — France would have experienced a far more traumatic passage to peace. Others would have tried to take de Gaulle's place, but the Communist Party would likely have been the only effective counterweight to Vichy. The French, largely unaware at that time of the vileness of that regime, might even have countenanced its re-establishment in Paris.

Had President Roosevelt's deluded plan to foist an American military government on France been implemented, it would have drawn universal opposition from the French and would likely have led to a Communist *coup d'état*. De Gaulle's vigorous opposition to that scheme, supported at a critical time by General Eisenhower, was fundamental to averting such a destiny. Thus the "Man of June 18" entered into his country's history as an indissoluble link with its honoured past. The text of his famous Appeal of that date is inscribed on the Arc de Triomphe, and since 2006, the date has been declared a "national day of commemoration of General de Gaulle's historic appeal to refuse defeat and continue the fight against the enemy."

Faults? Like any man, Charles de Gaulle had many. His reputation for arrogance, vanity, and self-absorption is too well-known to need further recounting. Less obvious is the realization that a man less sure of himself, less convinced of his destiny, and less committed to his cause would also have been less likely to overcome the disaster of 1940.

Do a Google search of "de Gaulle" and you get twenty million hits. This notoriety raises the question of what other historic figures might be compared to de Gaulle. De Gaulle's faithful make no pretension to a comparison with Napoleon Bonaparte. Franklin Roosevelt claimed de Gaulle had a Joan of Arc complex, but this theory can be dismissed as political hyperbole. Realizing that comparisons can be invidious, one is compelled to recognize that Charles de Gaulle came to prominence as the result of a unique set of circumstances. No contemporary leader evokes a credible comparison, although psychologically there may be a parallel between de

Gaulle's personality and that of Pierre Elliott Trudeau, the Canadian prime minister described in British Cabinet documents as a "complex personality" who combined "great charm with brutal insensitivity." Shades of de Gaulle!

De Gaulle would have realized that the arrival of large numbers of Muslim immigrants after the Algerian war would present France with a difficult confluence of cultures. The presence of six million Muslims, most of whom are economically and socially segregated from the larger society, is severely testing the French model of *laïciti* — securalism — that has it roots in the 1905 Law on the Separation of Churches and the State. The emphasis the French have placed on the banning of such religious symbols as *hajibs* and *burkas* in schools and public spaces has helped deter integration of Muslim faithful. Combined with economic deprivation, the resulting social tension has led to riots and social unrest. If France can better integrate its youthful Muslim population into mainstream French society, it will also be well on its way to solving its greatest economic problem: the aging of its working population which, as in every Western country, threatens the viability of social security programs.

Charles de Gaulle's service to France is enshrined in the thousands of streets, squares and other sites that carry his name. Charles de Gaulle Airport and Place Charles de Gaulle in Paris are known to every traveller, but virtually every city in France has its own tribute to the general. Not all de Gaulle memorials are grand affairs; the city of Arles which came through the war relatively unaffected by Vichy rule or the Occupation has dedicated but a few metres of sidewalk on its main street, avenue des Lices, as Esplanade Charles de Gaulle.[4] Globally, there are Charles de Gaulle avenues in New Orleans, Berlin, and Cairo, and other memorials in cities around the world. Five American states have named public squares or streets after the general.

Charles de Gaulle's great admirer, François Mauriac, saw the general's life in terms of its dedication to France. Because of him, wrote Mauriac, "France, if she is no longer *the* great nation, remains the irreplaceable nation, and ... to serve France is to serve the world."[5] Charles de Gaulle played the game well. His country — and the world — has been the winner for it. The Man of June 18, the founding father of the Fifth Republic, lives in history as not just a citizen of his homeland, but the world.

Acknowledgements

There are many people in France and elsewhere whose interest and support has made *The Paris Game* possible. To all those who have over many years helped me learn about and understand the history, character and culture of France, I owe a great debt of gratitude. I wish to express my appreciation to Professor Maurice Vaïsse of Sciences Po, University of Paris, for his invaluable assistance and for contributing the Foreword to this book. I also am grateful to William D. Irvine, Professor Emeritus, Department of History, York University, Toronto, who read the manuscript and made helpful suggestions. I wish to thank Emily Heppner of the Université de Caen Basse-Normandie for her timely research assistance. Sharon Argyle contributed the maps, for which I am grateful.

I also want to thank the staffs of a number of institutions — Archives de France and the Bibleothèque Nationale de France in Paris; the U.S. National Archives, College Park, Md.; the British Library, London; Library and Archives Canada, Ottawa; Bibleothèque et Archives nationale, Québec; and the Stauffer Library, Queen's University, Kingston, Ontario.

My thanks especially to Diane Young and her team at Dundurn Press, without whose support *The Paris Game* might not have seen the light of day. Dominic Farrell's careful editing contributed vastly to the final product.

My thanks also go to the Ontario Arts Council for its financial support toward the research and writing of this book.

Finally, to my partner, Deborah Windsor, my undying gratitude for her constant support.

Notes and Sources

Introduction

I have titled this book The Paris Game because the struggle it depicts reflects in many ways the "Great Game" that was played out between Russia and Britain for influence in Central Asia in the late nineteenth and early twentieth century. The Great Game, a term popularized by Rudyard Kipling in his novel *Kim*, was played out between 1813 and 1907 as Russia and Britain, in the words of Meyer and Brysac, competed in "bestowing the benefits of a Christian civilization and economic progress on less fortunate peoples." It ended when Russia agreed to recognize Afghanistan as a British protectorate.

The demise of colonialism following the Second World War removed Britain from the scene; the vacuum was eventually filled by the Soviet Union, which succeeded in setting up an Afghan puppet regime. In support of it, Moscow invaded the country between 1979 and 1989; in the end, though, it was forced into a Vietnam-like retreat. The empires that had spawned the Great Game for supremacy in Central Asia ended in dissolution; I would argue that the Paris Game eventually produced reconciliation rather than rupture.

For an account of the Great Game, see Karl Meyer and Shareen Brysac, *Tournament of Shadows: The Great Game and the Race for Empire in Asia* (New York: HarperCollins, 1999).

1. Irwin Shaw, in Hynes, Samuel, comp., *Reporting World War II*, Vol. 2, *American Journalism, 1944–1946* (New York: Library of America, 1995), 251.

2. Jean Lacouture, *De Gaulle: The Ruler, 1945–1970* (London: Harvill, 1991), 181.

Chapter 1 — The Débacle of Paris

In a book largely centered on the life of Charles de Gaulle, one must inevitably rely on the general's observations and judgments of the events and personalities of his time. The three volumes of de Gaulle's *Mémoires de Guerre* are critical to an understanding of his thoughts and motivations. The first, published in English as *The Call to Honour: 1940–1942* (New York: Simon & Schuster, 1955), was followed by *Unity, 1942–1944* (New York: Simon & Schuster,1959); finally, *Salvation, 1944–1946* (New York: Simon & Schuster, 1971), was published after his resignation as president of the Fifth Republic. Three of de Gaulle's pre-war books were published in English: *The Army of the Future* (London: Hutchinson & Company, 1940), *France and Her Army* (London: Hutchinson & Company, 1945), and *The Edge of the Sword* (London: Faber & Faber, 1960). Nine volumes of *Lettres, Notes, et Carnets*, de Gaulle's official records from the period 1905 to 1968, have been published in French under the direction of his son, Philippe de Gaulle. Philippe's book, *De Gaulle: Mon Père*, 2 vols. (Paris: Plon, 2003), is also a useful reference but must be read with a skeptical eye, like de Gaulle's own works, because of its intrinsic personal bias.

De Gaulle composed most of his *War Memoirs* at his desk in his study at La Boisserie, in Colombey-les-Deux-Églises, after first leaving office in 1946. He wrote in longhand with a fountain pen, drawing on documents and diaries close at hand, while chain-smoking incessantly. He was a fussy editor, doing much rewriting and making so many changes to his text that his daughter Elisabeth, who typed his manuscripts, had difficulty deciphering his words. He was happy during this time, according to Yvonne de Gaulle, "because he was doing what he likes best: writing." He would work from nine o'clock until about noon, and again between four and six o'clock.

When the first volume of *War Memoirs* was published, de Gaulle had the first four copies sent to the Pope, Queen Elizabeth, the Comte de Paris, and the president of the Republic. He viewed his memoirs as important historical documents. "What I am doing here," biographer Jean Lacouture reports him telling journalist Michel Droit a few months before his death, "is much more important for France than anything I could be doing at the Élysée if I were still there" (Lacouture, *De Gaulle: The Ruler* (London: Harvill, 1991), 583). Author Charles Williams, in *The Last Great Frenchman: A Life of Charles de Gaulle* (London: Little, Brown, 1993), 336, considers de Gaulle's *Mémoires de Guerre* as "without doubt a major work of French literature in their own right. The language is noble, the analysis profound and the sweep heroic."

1. Margaret Collins Weitz, *Sisters in the Resistance: How Women Fought to Free France, 1940–1945* (New York: Wiley, 1995), 52.

2. Simone de Beauvoir, *Mémoires d'une jeune fille rangée (Memoirs of a Dutiful Daughter)* (Paris: Gallimard, 1958).

3. Yann Fouéré: *La Patrie Interdite (The Forbidden Homeland)* (Paris: Éditions France-Empire, 1987). Fouéré worked for the Ministry of Information in Paris and took part in the government's flight from the capital. A Breton separatist, he was charged with collaboration after the Liberation and sentenced to life imprisonment, but fled to Britain two days before his trial. Acquitted at a retrial in 1955, he established the Mouvement pour l'Organisation de la Bretagne, which advocated greater autonomy within a federated Europe. He died in 2011, aged 101.

4. In Paul Valery's *Cahiers/Notebooks* (New York: Peter Lang, 2000). People outside France often view the Académie française as the ultimate arbiter of French literary life, but

this is not the case — although its members (forty at any one time) are referred to as "the immortals." Its official function is to produce a French dictionary, of which it has managed to issue eight editions since 1694. However, it eschews technical and scientific terms and is not widely used as a result. Its main purpose, write Jean-Benoit Nadeau and Julie Barlow in *The Story of French* (New York: St. Martin's Griffin, 2006), is to serve as "a kind of museum of ideal French."

5.   C. de Gaulle, *Call to Honour*, 55.

6.   *Ibid.*

7.   *Ibid.*, 4.

8.   The defeatist and pro-fascist elements that influenced French policies in the years leading up to the Second World War were also present in other countries. Britain had its share of Nazi sympathizers, including Sir Oswald Mosley's British Union of Fascists and the Anglo-German Fellowship that included MPs and members of the nobility. Mosley was interned in May 1940 along with his wife, Diane Mitford, but was later released and spent the war under house arrest. Members of the Anglo-German Fellowship included the Duke of Wellington; Lord Redesdale, the father of the Mitford sisters; London *Times* editor Geoffrey Dawson; press baron Lord Rothermere; and Montagu Norman, governor of the Bank of England.

German Ambassador Joachim von Ribbentrop (hanged after the Nuremberg trials for war crimes) escorted many upper-class Britons on trips to Germany where they would meet Adolf Hitler. Many daughters of the British upper class were sent to German finishing schools in the 1930s. Rachel Johnson described her experiences and those of her friends in "You Must be that Marvelleous Mr. Hitler" (*Sunday Times*, October 28, 2012). "They were self-absorbed teenagers and, anyway, it was not until after the war that the true horror of Hitler's regime was made plain, and even then, people still didn't believe it." In *The Remains of the Day*, Kazuo Ishiguro's novel of an English butler serving British nobility, the German ambassador

Joachim von Ribbentrop is pictured in the 1930s as "a well-regarded figure, even a glamorous one, in the very best houses."

9. Ernest Renan (1823–1892) was a philosopher and writer noted for his historical works on Christianity and his studies of nationalism and national identity.

10. France, as seen by the editors of an early twentieth–century edition of the *Encyclopaedia Britannica*, was a "nation formed of many different elements. From the Celts has been derived the gay, brilliant, and adventurous temperament easily moved to extremes of enthusiasm and depression, which combined with organizing faculties of a high order, the heritage from the Latin domination, and with the industry, frugality, and love of the soil natural to an agricultural people, go to make up the national character." *Encylopaedia Britannica*, 11th ed. (London: 1910), 10: 778.

   Serge Berstein's *La France des années 30* (Paris: Armand Colin, 1988), 8, provides a clear picture of France's social structure during the 1930s, including its continued loyalty to the land. Henri Dubief's *Le Déclin de la IIIe République: 1929–1938* (Paris: Éditions du Seuil, 1976) is informative of French social and economic life prior to the Second World War.

11. Barry Williams, *Modern France, 1870–1976* (London: Longman, 1980), 33.

12. United States, Department of State, *Foreign Relations of the United States: Diplomatic papers, 1940* (Washington, DC: GPO, 1955–61), I: 240–41.

13. Confiance, *Le Temps* [Paris], May 11, 1940.

14. C. de Gaulle, *Call to Honour*, 61.

15. Lacouture, *De Gaulle: The Rebel, 1890–1944* (London: Harvill, 1991), 195.

16. C. de Gaulle, *Call to Honour*, 61.

17. The use of "hotel" in French can be confusing for English readers, as the term relates not to a hotel for travellers, but to an aristocratic residence, or town home, such as the eighteenth-century building known as l'Hôtel Matignon.

Most of these buildings have since been converted to purposes such as that of the Hôtel Matignon, a residence and office for the premier.

18. C. de Gaulle, *Call to Honour*, 195–96.

19. Cited in Eleanor Gates's *The End of the Affair: The Collapse of the Anglo-French Alliance, 1939–40* (Berkeley, CA: University of California Press, 1981), 411.

20. C. de Gaulle, *Call to Honour*, 63.

21. William L. Shirer attributes the débacle remark to de Gaulle in *The Collapse of the Third Republic: An Inquiry into the Fall of France in 1940* (New York: Simon & Schuster, 1969), 758.

Chapter 2 – A Rebel at Heart

The siblings and children of Charles de Gaulle all contributed to French history, each in their own way. De Gaulle's eldest brother, Xavier, won the Croix de Guerre in the First World War and was forced to flee France in 1942, finding refuge in Switzerland where he later served as consul general in Geneva.

Xavier's daughter Geneviève followed up her service in the Resistance with work on behalf of survivors and in 1995 published *La Traversée de la nuit (The Crossing of the Night)*. She testified at the trial of Klaus Barbie and in 1988 became a member of the French Economic and Social Council. She was awarded the Médaille de la Résistance, the Croix de Guerre 1939–45 and the Grand Croix de la Légion d'honneur, becoming the first woman so honoured.

Pierre, de Gaulle's younger brother, sat as a member of the National Assembly for the Rally of the French People (RPF) from 1951 to 1956. He died from a heart attack while on a visit to the Élysée Palace on December 26, 1959.

Philippe, de Gaulle's son, enlisted in the Free French navy after the family's escape to England. He served as a platoon commander with the 2nd Armoured Division during the liberation of Paris and took part in the French offensive in the Vosges during the winter of 1944–45. Following a succession of promotions in the French navy after the war, he became an admiral in 1980 and finished his military career as inspector general of the navy, retiring in 1982. He served as a member of the French Senate from 1986 to 2004. Philippe inherited La Boisserie from his father and members of his family continue to reside there.

Charles De Gaulle's daughter Elisabeth married Alain de Boissieu in 1946. Boissieu worked closely with the general and himself became a general, appointed army chief of staff (*chef d'État-major de l'Armée de Terre*) for the period 1971 to 1975.

The many biographers of Charles de Gaulle agree he had a traditional upbringing as the eldest son of a respected conservative family that adhered to Catholic values yet also accepted that France needed to modify many aspects of its society if it were to persevere in the twentieth century. Because there is general agreement of the essential facts of de Gaulle's early life — his schooling, military training, and army experience — these notes reference only the most critical of these details.

1. Alden Hatch, *The de Gaulle Nobody Knows* (New York: Hawthorne Books, 1960), 16, 33.
2. Pierre Galante, *The General!* (New York: Random House, 1968), 39.
3. Jonathan Fenby, *The General: Charles de Gaulle and the France He Saved* (New York: Skyhorse Publishing, 2012), 44.
4. *Ibid.*
5. Theodore Zeldin, *A History of French Passions*, Vol. 1, *France, 1848–1945: Ambition and Love* (Oxford: Oxford University Press, 1979), 19.
6. *Ibid.*, 91.
7. Hatch, *The de Gaulle Nobody Knows*, 30–31.
8. Lacouture, *De Gaulle: The Rebel*, 20.
9. *Ibid.*, 21.
10. *Ibid.*, 35.
11. Don Cook, *Charles de Gaulle: A Biography* (New York: G.P. Putnam's Sons, 1983), 31.
12. Fenby, *The General*, 72.
13. Lacouture, *De Gaulle: The Rebel*, 70.
14. *Ibid.*, 82.

15. Hatch, *The de Gaulle Nobody Knows,* 60.

16. Weitz, *Sisters in the Resistance,* 22.

Chapter 3 — Into the Abyss

1. Pierre-Étienne Flandin, *Politique française* (Paris: Les Éditions Nouvelles, 1947), 317. Poland met the German and Russian invasions with half a million men in arms but most were poorly equipped, including an outdated cavalry. Polish airmen fought the Luftwaffe bravely but were overcome by larger German numbers. Many Polish airmen escaped to Britain and served valiantly with the Royal Air Force.

2. Lacouture, *De Gaulle: The Rebel,* 170.

3. *Ibid.*

4. C. de Gaulle, *Call to Honour,* 26.

5. *Le Petit Parisien,* Dec. 24, 1939.

6. Geneviève Moll, *Yvonne de Gaulle* (Paris: Éditions Ramsay, 1999), 105.

7. Lacouture, *De Gaulle: The Rebel,* 171.

8. C. de Gaulle, *Call to Honour,* 6.

9. *Ibid.,* 30.

10. *Ibid.,* 31.

11. *Ibid.,* 34.

12. Shirer, *The Collapse,* 559.

13. Fenby, *The General,* 123–24.

14. P. de Gaulle, *De Gaulle: Mon Père,* 110.

15. *Ibid.,* 109.

16. C. de Gaulle, *Call to Honour,* 37.

17. Kenneth Macksey, *Guderian: Panzer General* (London: Macdonald and Jane's, 1975) 114–15.

18. C. de Gaulle, *Call to Honour,* 40.

19. Paul Huard, *Le Colonel de Gaulle et ses Blindès, Laon, 15–10 Mai 1940* (Paris: Plon, 1980), 172.

20. *Espoir,* été 2010, 140.

21. Cook, *De Gaulle: A Biography*, 59.

22. C. de Gaulle, *Call to Honour*, 47.

23. Shirer, *The Collapse*, 611.

24. Winston Churchill, speech to House of Commons, June 4, 1940. See *www.winstonchurchill.org/learn/speeches/speeches-of-winston-churchill/128-we-shall-fight-on-the-beaches*.

25. Lacouture, *De Gaulle: The Rebel*, 188. Paul Reynaud's decision to call General de Gaulle into his Cabinet is arguably the most important decision he made during his short period as premier. After recovering from injuries sustained in the accident that killed Hélène des Portes, Reynaud was arrested and held at Fort du Portalet in the Pyrenees before being turned over to the Nazis. He was liberated by Allied troops from a prison in Austria on May 7, 1945. After the war, Reynaud was elected to the National Assembly and supported the concept of a United States of Europe. He opposed de Gaulle's abolition of the Electoral College and election of the president by popular vote. His death on September 21, 1966, brought generous tributes for his patriotism and honesty.

26. C. de Gaulle, *Call to Honour*, 52.

27. P. de Gaulle, *De Gaulle: Mon Père*, 110.

28. C. de Gaulle, *Call to Honour*, 57.

29. C. de Gaulle, *Lettres, Notes, et Carnets*, Vol. 4, *Juillet 1941–Mai 1943* (Paris: Plon, 1982), 225.

30. Winston S. Churchill, *The Second World War*, Vol. 2, *Their Finest Hour* (Boston: Houghton Mifflin, 1949), 145.

31. C. de Gaulle, *Call to Honour*, 57.

32. In 1981, General de Gaulle's son-in-law, Alain Boissieu, disclosed that when he reached the Berchtesgarden ("eagle's nest") of Adolf Hitler on May 6, 1945, he found in the Fuhrer's private library "a lot of books on military tactics, strategy, and the use of weapons." He recounts in *Pour Combattre Avec de Gaulle* (Paris: Plon, 1981), 316, that among them was a copy of a German translation of de Gaulle's *Vers l'Armée de Métier*. "I thumbed feverishly through the pages

until I discovered, with astonishment, annotations that were undoubtedly in the hand of Hitler." An American guard took the book from him and threw it into the fireplace.

Along with de Gaulle, the British military analyst Liddell Hart argued in the interwar years that future battles would be decided by the strength of combatants' mechanized columns. General Heinz Guderian translated Liddell Hart's work into German, but concedes he also paid close attention to de Gaulle's writings. Guderian elaborated on the theories of Liddell Hart and de Gaulle in *Achtung — Panzer! die Entwicklung der Panzerwaffe, ihre Kampftaktik und ihre operativen Möglichkeiten* (Stuttgart: Union Deutsche Verlagsgesellschaft, 1937).

33. C. de Gaulle, *Call to Honour*, 63.
34. *Ibid.,* 64.
35. Edward L. Spears, *The Fall of France: June 1940* (London: William Heinemann, 1954), 138.

Chapter 4 — The Collapse of the Third Republic

1. C. de Gaulle, *Call to Honour*, 64.
2. Spears, *The Fall of France*, 140.
3. C. de Gaulle, *Call to Honour*, 64.
4. Spears, *The Fall of France,* 139.
5. *Ibid.,* 165.
6. *Ibid.,* 170.
7. Churchill, *Their Finest Hour*, 178.
8. Spears, *The Fall of France,* 195, 293.
9. C. de Gaulle, *Call to Honour*, 68.
10. Churchill, *Their Finest Hour*, 182.
11. Spears, *The Fall of France,* 241.
12. Shirer, *The Collapse*, 777.
13. C. de Gaulle, *Call to Honour*, 71.
14. Julian Jackson, *The Fall of France: The Nazi Invasion of 1940* (Oxford: Oxford University Press, 2003), 141.

15. *Ibid.,* 72.

16. Victor Vinde, *La fin d'une grande puissance? la France depuis la déclaration de guerre jusqu'à la révolution nationale,* (Lausanne: Jean-Marguerat, 1942), 138.

17. C. de Gaulle, *Call to Honour,* 73.

18. H. Amouroux, *Paris-Match,* November 15, 1970.

19. P. de Gaulle, *De Gaulle: Mon Père,* 111–12.

20. C. de Gaulle, *Call to Honour,* 74.

21. *Ibid.,* 77.

22. Spears, *The Fall of France,* 292.

23. The de Havilland DH89 Dragon Rapide in which de Gaulle flew from London to Bordeaux and back to Britain had come into service in 1934 as a short-haul, eight-seat passenger plane. The plane Churchill made available to de Gaulle had been fitted out luxuriously with fewer seats and comfortable amenities. The twin-engine biplane had a wingspan of 14.6 metres, a top speed of 253 kmh, and a range of 920 kilometres. It has been flown by air forces and commercial airlines all over the world. Seventy years after de Gaulle's fights, one was still in use carrying sightseers over London and the English countryside. For a video of a flight, see *www.youtube.com/watch?v=mFLLPUT6NIw.*

    Edward H. Fielden served as pilot to two kings, Edward VIII and George VI, and on the accession to the throne of Queen Elizabeth II, was promoted to Air Commodore and became Captain of the Queen's Flight. He retired in 1962.

24. Lacouture, *De Gaulle: The Rebel,* 204.

25. P. de Gaulle, *De Gaulle: Mon Père,* 114–15.

26. *Ibid.,* 120.

27. Spears, *The Fall of France,* 311–12.

28. Galante, *The General!,* 96.

29. C. de Gaulle, *Call to Honour,* 80.

30. Hatch, *The de Gaulle Nobody Knows,* 97.

31. C. de Gaulle, *Call to Honour,* 80.

Chapter 5 — The Appeal of June 18

1. Agnès Humbert, *Resistance: A Woman's Journal of Struggle and Defiance in Occupied France* (New York: Bloomsbury, 2004), 7. Originally published as *Notre Guerre: Souvenirs de Resistance: Paris 1940–41* (Paris: Éditions Émile-Paul Frères, 1946).

2. For a country light on both industry and population (11.5 million by the 1941 census), Canada made a contribution to the Allied cause in the Second World War well in excess of its relative size. More than 1.1 million men and women served in its armed forces and conscription was imposed for homeland defence. Canada trained thirty-one thousand pilots from Commonwealth countries, converted factories to the production of planes, tanks, and ships, and ended the war with the world's third largest navy (after the United States and Britain). The country's record in both world wars is examined in Tim Cook's *Warlords: Borden, Mackenzie King, and Canada's World Wars* (Toronto: Penguin, 2012).

3. William Lyon Mackenzie King, *The Mackenzie King Diaries, 1893–1950: The Complete Manuscript Entries* (Toronto: University of Toronto Press, 1980), 1940: 685.

4. C. de Galle, *Call to Honour*, 83.

5. Eric Roussel, *Jean Monnet* (Paris: Fayard, 1996), 243.

6. Elisabeth de Miribel, *La liberté souffre violence* (Paris: Plon, 1989), 30.

7. *Ibid.,* 37–38.

8. There are great inconsistencies in various accounts of de Gaulle's visit to the BBC for his Appeal of June 18. Did de Gaulle speak live or was his address recorded? Did he speak at six o'clock, eight o'clock, or ten o'clock? The official history of BBC has it that the message was announced at 8:15 and aired at 10 p.m. Did the BBC forget to make a recording, or was the recording discarded? Did de Gaulle broadcast from Studio 4C or 4D? Did de Gaulle furnish a draft of the speech

to Duff Cooper at lunch, as Cooper always insisted? I have relied on personal reminiscences of those present, including testimonials appearing in the Summer 2010 issue of *Espoir*, published by the de Gaulle Foundation. Such details will forever remain murky, and are perhaps of little consequence in comparison to the mythic status the Appeal has attained. See Asa Briggs, *The History of Broadcasting in the United Kingdom* (Oxford: Oxford: 1965), 4: 242.

Studio 4C was badly damaged from a delayed-action German bomb dropped on Broadcasting House on October 15, 1940. The bomb had lodged itself in the music library on the fifth floor. Seven people died when it exploded as a crew attempted to push it onto the street.

9. The translation of the Appeal is by the Gilder Lehrman Institute of American History: *www.gilderlehrman.org*.

10. Galante, *The General!*, 105–06.

11. Lacouture, *De Gaulle: The Rebel*, 240.

12. According to René Cassin's memoir, he posed a second question to de Gaulle: "I take it we are not a legion but allies re-forming the French army?" De Gaulle answered, "The French Army? We are France itself!" René Cassin, *Les hommes partis de rien* (Paris: Plon, 1975), 76.

Cassin went on to work with the Canadian legal scholar John Humphrey in writing the United Nations Declaration on Human Rights, proclaimed in 1948, for which Cassin won the Nobel Peace Prize. Humphrey was serving as director of the UN's Division of Human Rights.

13. C. de Gaulle, *Call to Honour*, 90.

14. Lacouture, *De Gaulle: The Rebel*, 241.

15. Details of the de Gaulle family evacuation to England are from Moll's *Yvonne de Gaulle*, 116–36.

16. The German and Italian Armistice Terms are contained in *Private Diaries of Paul Baudouin*, translated by Sir Charles Petrie (London: Eyre & Spottiswoode, 1948), 301–06.

17. Extracts of UK National Archives files on Mers-el-Kebir can

be read at *www.hmshood.org.uk/reference/official/adm234/adm234-317.htm.*

18. Lacouture, *De Gaulle: The Rebel,* 249.

19. Robert Mengin, *No Laurels for de Gaulle* (New York: Farrar, Straus and Giroux, 1966), 95.

20. C. de Gaulle, *Call to Honour,* 91.

21. *Ibid.,* 92.

Chapter 6 – Surviving the Swastika

1. Claire Fauteux, *Fantastic Interlude* (New York: Vantage Press, 1961), 17.

2. Jean-Paul Sartre, "Paris sous l'Occupation," *Sartre Studies International* 4, No. 2 (1998). This article was first published in *France libre* (London: 1945).

3. *Life* correspondent Sherry Mangan was an eye-witness to the German occupation of Paris. After he was expelled in August 1940 he made his way to Portugal and filed a first-hand account, published in the magazine's September 16, 1940 issue.

4. Charles Glass, *Americans in Paris: Life and Death Under Nazi Occupation* (New York: Penguin Press, 2010), 66–67.

5. Robert O. Paxton, *Vichy France: Old Guard and New Order, 1940–1944* (New York: Columbia University Press, 1972), 53.

6. Guderian's letter is cited in Kenneth Macksey's *Guderian Panzer General* (London: Macdonald and Jane's, 1975), 122.

7. Weitz, *Sisters in the Resistance,* 58.

8. The description of Vichy spa visitors is by Ted Morgan, *An Uncertain Hour* (New York: William Morrow, 1990), 84.

9. Various accounts of Reynaud's trip with Mme des Portes are in agreement on the details of their accident, if not the exact circumstances of either it or their flight from Bordeaux. The death of the Countess was reported in *Time,* August 5, 1940. The incident is also described by, among others, Mor-

gan, *An Uncertain Hour*, 53–54; Tom Shachtman, *The Phony War* 1939–1940, (New York: Harper & Row, 1982), 257; and Pertinax (André Géraux), *The Gravediggers of France* (New York: Doubleday, Doran & Company, 1944), 311.

10. C. de Gaulle, *Call to Honour*, 101.

11. Fenby, *The General*, 205.

12. Ian Ousby, *Occupation: The Ordeal of France, 1940–1944* (London: Pimlico, 1997), 147.

13. For an image of the poster, see Robert Belot, et al., *Les Résistants: L'histoire de ceux qui refusèrent* (Paris: Larousse, 2007) 13.

14. Jean Moulin's memoir *Premier Combat*, which covers the period from June to November 1940, was published in 1947 by his sister Laure. (Paris: Les Éditions de Minuit, 1965), 76–77.

15. *Ibid.*, 85–87.

16. *Ibid.*, 97–100.

17. *Ibid.*, 107–10.

18. *Ibid.*, 109.

19. Patrick Marnham, *The Death of Jean Moulin: Biography of a Ghost* (London: Pimlico, 2001), 122.

20. *Ibid.*, 123.

21. Jean-Paul Sartre, "Paris sous l'Occupation," *Situations, III* (Paris: Gallimard, 1949).

22. C. de Gaulle, *Call to Honour*, 155.

23. Apologists for Marshall Pétain have claimed he resisted German demands for anti-Semitic legislation, but recent evidence indicates Pétain was a willing advocate of Jewish harassment. A copy of the Statut des Juifs in the hands of the Holocaust Museum in Paris shows amendments in the marshall's handwriting that "completely redrafted" the bill to make its provisions more onerous. He also eliminated a caveat protecting "descendants of Jews born French or naturalized before 1870." In July 1941, the Vichy government of Pierre Laval instituted an "Aryanization" program that enabled authorities to seize Jewish property, leaving their owners destitute. Some seventy-seven thousand Jews were deported from

France to German death camps. See the *Guardian,* October 3, 2010, and *www.memorialdelashoah.org.*

24. Raymond-Raoul Lambert, *Diary of a Witness, 1940–1943* (Chicago: Ivan R. Dee, 2007), 23.

25. Jean-Raymond Tournoux, *Sons of France: Pétain and de Gaulle* (New York: Viking Press, 1964), 117.

26. Paxton, *Vichy France,* 47, 69, 77.

27. C. de Gaulle, *Call to Honour,* 139.

28. Lacouture, *De Gaulle: The Rebel,* 243.

29. *Ibid.,* 244.

30. Clermont-Ferrand was the setting for Marcel Ophüls's acclaimed 1969 documentary film *Le chagrin et la pitié (The Sorrow and the Pity),* which details the response of the French people to the collaborationist excesses of the Vichy regime under the Nazi occupation. It centres on the experiences of Pierre Mendès France, a *résistant* and later prime minister of France, and Christian de la Mazère, a fascist-minded aristocrat who fought for the Germans on the Eastern Front.

31. The indictment against de Gaulle and the verdict of the court appears as Appendix A in *The Trial of Charles de Gaulle,* by Alfred Fabre-Luce, (London: Methuen, 1963), 237–45. Originally published as *Haute Cour* (Paris: J.F.G. Lausanne, 1963). A fictional work, it depicts the equivalent of an impeachment trial of de Gaulle for having allowed Algeria its independence. Paris prefect of police Maurice Papon ordered seizure of the book on the grounds it constituted an insult to the head of state (de Gaulle was then in office). Fabre-Luce and publisher Mme René Julliard were each fined 1,500 francs.

32. Le general de Gaulle est condamnè à mort contumace, *Le Temps,* August 3, 1940.

33. C. de Gaulle, *Call to Honour,* 52.

34. Hatch, *The de Gaulle Nobody Knows,* 102.

35. Lacouture, *De Gaulle: The Rebel,* 574.

36. See *www.museemilitairelyon.com/spip.php?article54.*

Chapter 7 — Soldiers of the Empire

1. C. de Gaulle, *Call to Honour*, 95.
2. Hatch, *The de Gaulle Nobody Knows*, 109.
3. Lacouture, *De Gaulle: The Rebel*, 269.
4. *Ibid.*, 261. Charles de Gaulle was the author of a multitude of pithy remarks, many of which have been used to illustrate his supposed arrogance. Some of the more frequently quoted include: *"Moi, je suis en France"*; "If I want to know what France is thinking, I ask myself"; "I respect only those who resist me but I cannot tolerate them"; "The better I get to know men the more I find myself loving dogs"; "The graveyards are full of indispensable men"; "I am a man who belongs to nobody and who belongs to everybody"; "I am too poor to bow"; "Have you ever seen a dictator on a run-off ballot?"
5. Churchill, *Their Finest Hour*, 508. Pierre Dupuy made three extended trips to Vichy, but his reports to the British and Canadian governments revealed little understanding of what was actually happening in France. Mackenzie King had approved Dupuy's visits as a way of avoiding a break in Canada-France relations; he was quite willing to go along with the vain hope of encouraging Vichy resistance to Germany, especially if it meant keeping the French fleet out of German hands. By avoiding a premature break with Vichy, his Liberal Party was saving itself from an internal rupture with its Quebec francophone members of Parliament. King's policy on such issues was consistent: delay, delay, delay.

   Dupuy, who was virulently anti-de Gaulle, went well beyond his mandate and tried to negotiate the conditions under which the Allies would lift their Mediterranean boycott of French ports, thus allowing more food and resources from France's African colonies. This "infernal little chatterer" argued that "the Petain government was double-crossing Germany, buying time until it could resume fighting alongside Britain." Despite his poor insights diplomatically, Dupuy proved to be an able administrator, and after the war, served as Canadian ambassador to France from 1958 to 1963. He had a successful posting as Commissioner-General of Expo '67 in Montreal, where he succeeded in attracting a record number of foreign nations as participants in a world's fair. Oliver Courteaux, *Canada between Vichy and Free France, 1940–1945* (Toronto: University of Toronto Press, 2013), 83.

6. Félix Éboué is memorialized in the square that bears his name in eastern Paris. Éboué, born in the South American colony of French Guiana, was one of *les* évolués (the evolved), who came out of the educated class of colonial subjects. He attended the École Coloniale and after his death in 1949 became the only black to be interred in France's Panthéon of heroes in Paris.

7. Lacouture, *De Gaulle: The Rebel*, 272.

8. Williams, *The Last Great Frenchman*, 124.

9. C. de Gaulle, *Lettres, Notes, et Carnets*, 3: 76.

10. Mary Borden, *Journey Down a Blind Alley* (London: Hutchinson, 1946), 113.

11. Galante, *The General!*, 122.

12. Nigel West, *Secret War: The Story of SOE, Britain's Wartime Sabotage Organisation* (London: Hodder & Stoughton, 1992), 16.

13. Moll, *Yvonne de Gaulle*, 144–45.

14. C. de Gaulle, *Call to Honour*, 115–16.

15. Williams, *The Last Great Frenchman*, 129.

16. C. de Gaulle, *Call to Honour*, 125.

17. *Ibid.*, 127.

18. Lacouture, *De Gaulle: The Rebel*, 278.

19. Edward L. Spears, *Two Men Who Saved France* (London: Eyre & Spottiswood,1966), 147–48.

20. Tournoux, *Sons of France*, 127.

21. C. de Gaulle, *Call to Honour*, 128.

22. C. de Gaulle, *Lettres, Notes, et Carnets,* 3: 125.

23. Lacouture, *De Gaulle: The Rebel,* 278.

24. C. de Gaulle, *Call to Honour,* 98.

25. *Ibid.,* 165.

26. Raoul Aglion, *Roosevelt and de Gaulle: Allies in Conflict — A Personal Memoir* (New York: Free Press, 1988), 115.

27. *Ibid.,* 33.

28. De Miribel, *La liberté souffre violence,* 49. The Quebec in which Mlle de Miribel found herself was 80 percent French but dominated by an English economic elite. Its two and one-half million francophones, cut off from their ancestral homeland for nearly two hundred years, viewed modern France as corrupt and immoral, and harkened to the Vichy line for its support of church and hearth. The circumstances made it difficult to rally support for Charles de Gaulle, who was seen as dangerous republican and possibly a Communist.

    Contrary to popular belief, most French-Canadians were descended not from Breton or Norman peasants but from the labouring classes of Paris, Bordeaux, Nantes, and other cities. The first females in New France were the so-called *filles du roy,* girls of marriageable age sent from Paris orphanages. In the isolation of what would become Quebec, the settlers hewed to their Catholic faith, had large families, and kept their sons on the land.

    In the Treaty of Paris of 1763, Britain gave France the option of retaining either Canada or its Caribbean "sugar island" colonies; it chose the islands for the wealth of their plantations. The 1774 Quebec Act accorded the French language official status, allowed Catholics to hold civil office, and retained the French civil justice system.

29. De Gaulle's problems in Canada were complicated by the fact that rival committees had been established in support of Free France. Elisabeth de Miribel played a crucial role in overcoming these divisions. Meanwhile, Vichy's ambassador to

Canada, René Ristelhueber inundated the French-language media with Pétainist propaganda. "Why cry over the fate of the Third Republic, which confused liberty with licence?" Montreal's *La Patrie* asked. Olivier Courteaux recounts the episode in *Canada between Vichy and Free France.*

30. C. de Gaulle, *Lettres, Notes, et Carnets,* June 1940–July 1941, 272.

31. Dale Thomson, *Vive le Québec Libre* (Toronto: Deneau, 1988), 42.

32. Lacouture, *De Gaulle: The Rebel,* 241.

33. Moll, *Yvonne de Gaulle,* 179.

34. C. de Gaulle, *Call to Honour,* 214.

35. François Kersaudy, *Churchill & De Gaulle* (London: Collins, 1981), 175.

36. C. de Gaulle, *Call to Honour,* 215.

37. See *www.winstonchurchill.org/learn/speeches/speeches-of-winston-churchill/106-preparation-liberation-assault.*

38. *Mackenzie King Diaries,* July 29, 1940, December 30, 1941.

39. Dwight D. Eisenhower, *Crusade in Europe* (New York: Doubleday, 1948), 84.

40. *Ibid.,* 239.

Chapter 8 – Wild Cards in Play

Epic stories of how the French Resistance fought the German occupation have been told in countless non-fiction books, but are rare in English language fiction. An exception is *The Free Frenchman* by the British author Piers Paul Read (New York: Random House, 1987). Read, better known for the non-fiction *Alive: the Story of the Andes Survivors,* has produced a true *roman à clef* in his novel of the aristocratic and deeply Catholic Bertrand de Roujay's involvement with the Resistance in the south of France. If you can get through a saccharine opening episode on his romance and marriage to Madeleine Bonnet, you will be rewarded with a thoroughly authentic rendering of the personal and ideological struggles in which anyone touched by the war in France — French, German,

British, or American — found themselves entangled. Read is at his most powerful in his insights into the perplexing behaviour of his characters, illustrating that few in the Resistance were without sin themselves and that the rewards did not always go to the innocent. *The Free Frenchman* is a story of morality, greed, romance, and war, that testifies to the ability of a master of the novel to render truths of emotion, motive, and consequence that are rarely found in purely factual accounts.

1. Fenby, *The General,* 204. The Cabinet memo drafted by Neville Chamberlain said the new organization would "coordinate all action, by way of subversion and sabotage, against the enemy overseas." Lost for many years, the memo was published in *Secret War: The Story of SOE*, by Nigel West.
2. Julian Jackson, *France: The Dark Years, 1940–1944* (Oxford: Oxford University Press, 2001), 203.
3. C. de Gaulle, *Call to Honour,* 149.
4. The description is by the translator of *Resistance,* Barbara Mellor. It can be found at *http://news.bbc.co.uk/today/hi/today/newsid_7634000/7634154.stm.*
5. Humbert, *Resistance: A Woman's Journal,* 15.
6. *www.spartacus.schoolnet.co.uk/FRmusee.htm.*
7. Ousby, *Occupation,* 244.
8. C. de Gaulle, *Call to Honour,* 263.
9. Lacouture, *De Gaulle: The Rebel,* 376.
10. Daniel Cordier, *Jean Moulin: L'Inconnu au pantheon,* Vol. 1, *Une ambition pour la République* (Paris: Jean-Claude Lattès, 1980), 25.
11. Marnham, *The Death of Jean Moulin,* 129.
12. *Ibid.,* 130.
13. *Ibid.,* 141.
14. C. de Gaulle, *Call to Honour,* 269.
15. An English translation by the SOE appears in M.R.D. Foot's *SOE in France: An Account of the British Special Operations Executive in France* (Frederick, MD: University Publications of America, 1984), 489–98.

16. *Ibid.*, 136.

17. Until it was replaced by larger, four-engine bombers, the Whitworth Whitley served as the RAF's main long-range bomber, with the capability of attacking targets as far away as Italy. Early in the war, it was used to drop propaganda leaflets on Germany and the occupied territories. Later, the Whitley was assigned to patrolling the North Atlantic, where it sank many German U-boats.

    The Alpilles, "Little Alps," are a striking geological feature with ridges that rear up suddenly out of the Provençal plain, the Crau. Old Roman and Greek settlements abound in the region.

18. Of the three men who parachuted into Provence on January 2, 1942, only Hervé Montjarret would survive the war. Raymond Fassin went on to become a major but tragic figure in the Resistance. He took control of Allied airdrops of men and *materièl* in the south of France and was promoted to be General de Gaulle's military delegate in northern France. After his third return to France, he was betrayed in April 1944 and, with his wife, was arrested and sent to Fresnes Prison near Paris. Fassin was then moved to Lille and, on August 31, 1944, was put on the last train to take prisoners to Germany. He died in a concentration camp near Hamburg on February 12, 1945.

    Montjarret ran radio communication between the Resistance and the London headquarters of the Free French. He also was arrested by the Gestapo and was sent to the Mauthausen concentration camp in Austria. He was liberated by a Red Cross contingent that reached the camp on April 29, 1945. In a memoir, Montjarret wrote that his survival enabled him "to bear witness on behalf of my comrades in arms." The betrayal of all three men speaks to the weakness of Resistance security and the willingness of some of its members to resort to betrayal for personal gain or to settle political scores. See *www.france-libre.net/temoignages-documents/temoignages/retour-moulin-france.php.*

19. A mural depicting Jean Moulin adorns the wall of a building at the main intersection in St. Andiol. It was unveiled on May 27, 2012, with a mass parachute drop recording the seventieth anniversary of Moulin's landing. A plaque describes Moulin's farm as a *bergerie,* which translates to English as a sheepfold or enclosure. His farm, La Leque, has been swallowed up by a housing tract. St. Andiol is the beginning of the forty-two-kilometre Chemin de la Liberté that commemorates Moulin's travels in the district, winding through several villages before concluding at the site of an impressive Moulin memorial outside Salon de Provence. That city is the site of an important French air force base.

20. C. de Gaulle, *Call to Honour,* 81.

21. *Ibid.,* 242.

22. Fenby, *The General,* 182.

23. The old Velodrome, situated at boulevard de Grenelle and rue Nélaton near the Eiffel Tower, was demolished following a fire in 1959. An office building and apartments now fill the site. A sculpture of a pregnant women, children, and a sick man bears a plaque with these words (translated): "The French Republic in homage to victims of racist and anti-semitic persecutions and of crimes against humanity committed under the authority of the so-called 'Government of the State of France.'" Belot, et al., *Les Résistants,* 129.

24. Lambert, *Diary of a Witness,* 146.

25. Jacques Chirac, *My Life in Politics* (New York: Macmillan, 2012), 166. The Vel d'Hiv affair tortured the French for years, with officials obstinately insisting the atrocity was the responsibility of Vichy France, acting under the influence of the Germans. It was not until 1995, on the fifty-third anniversary of the roundup, that President Jacques Chirac accepted that the entire nation bore responsibility for what had happened on July 16, 1942: "France, home of the Enlightenment and the rights of man, a land of welcome and asylum, committed the irreparable that day. Failing to live

up to its word, it handed those whom it was meant to protect over to their oppressors."

26. German policy toward French art distinguished between national holdings such as those at the Louvre, which were left largely intact, and privately owned art held by Jewish collectors. Most Jews had to abandon their possessions, giving the Nazis the excuse to declare them "ownerless" and thus ripe for plucking. In Paris, collections seized from the Rothschild family, the David-Weill family, Lévy de Benzion, George Wildenstein, the Seligman family, and others, were picked over by Herman Goering on behalf of Adolf Hitler and himself. Between 1941 and 1944, 4,174 cases containing some twenty thousand works of art, were shipped from Paris to Germany. Most had been stored at the Jeu de Palme gallery, an adjunct of the Louvre adjoining the Tuileries Gardens, before being shipped to Neuschwanstein castle in Bavaria, the fairy tale–like creation of the mad King Ludwig. The Monuments, Fine Arts, and Archives unit ("Monuments Men") of the American army traced the looted art on advice from Rose Valland, a French curator who had spent the war years at the Jeu de Paume. She secretly recorded every item and turned over the information following the liberation of Paris. The search for plundered art still goes on; in 2012 some 1,400 works of art stolen by the Nazis were found in a Munich apartment during investigation of a tax case.

27. Dana Thomas, "The Power Behind The Cologne," *New York Times*, February 24, 2012.

28. Josephine Baker, cited in Alan Riding's *And the Show Went On: Cultural Life in Nazi-Occupied Paris* (New York: Knopf, 2010), 99.

29. *And the Show Went On*, 233.

30. The story of Quebec's wartime French publishers is told in R.O. Paxton, et al., eds., *Archives de la Vie Littëraire Sous l'Occupation: À travers le désastre*, (Paris: Tallandier, 2011), 340–41. The flirtation between French authors and Quebec

publishers failed to survive the war, despite postwar visits by such luminaries as Jean-Paul Sartre and Albert Camus. The revival of Parisian publishers rendered the Montreal houses irrelevant, but more damaging were the accusations of the French *Comité national des* écrivains. Led by Louis Aragon, the committee charged the Quebec houses with having published books by collaborationist authors. In addition, the Montreal publishers came under censure by the Catholic Church for "immoral" works of French republican writers. By 1948, all but a few of Montreal's twenty-two new wartime publishers had gone out of business. Quebec, according to the *Archives de la Vie Littëraire Sous l'Occupation,* quietly returned to its *grande noirceur* (great darkness).

Chapter 9 — Warriors at Odds

1. Movements of Task Force H can be read at *http://Naval-History.net.* The *Duke of York* had been based at Scapa Flow in the Orkney Islands off the north coast of Scotland. In December 1941 she had carried Winston Churchill to the United States for his second wartime meeting with President Roosevelt. The *Duke of York* took part in the pursuit of the *Tirpitz* in March 1942 and had a second encounter with the German battleship during the summer. Her active duty ended in 1951 and she was scrapped in 1957. The *Tirpitz* was sunk in a Norwegian harbour in 1944 following British submarine and air attacks.
2. Eisenhower, *Crusade in Europe,* 96.
3. Lacouture, *De Gaulle: The Rebel,* 397.
4. *Ibid.*
5. Churchill, *The Hinge of Fate,* 605.
6. *Ibid.,* 608.
7. C. de Gaulle, *Unity,* 46.
8. Anthony Verrier, *Assassination in Algiers: Churchill, Roo-*

sevelt, de Gaulle, and the Murder of Admiral Darlan (New York: W.W. Norton, 1990), 167.

9. *Ibid.*, 187.

10. *Ibid.*, 182.

11. Raymond Clapper, *Register Star-News* [Sandusky, OH] and other newspapers, November 18, 1942.

12. Lacouture, *De Gaulle: The Rebel*, 231.

13. Churchill, *The Hinge of Fate*, 635.

14. Simon Berthon, *Allies at War* (London: Collins, 2001), 135.

15. C. de Gaulle, *Call to Honour*, 233.

16. Kersaudy, *Churchill and de Gaulle*, 213.

17. Charles L. Robertson, *When Roosevelt Planned to Govern France* (Amherst, MA: University of Massachusetts Press, 2011), 183.

18. Lacouture, *De Gaulle: The Rebel*, 349.

19. C. de Gaulle, *Unity*, 50.

20. *Ibid.*, 55.

21. Verrier, *Assassination in Algiers*, 181.

22. *Ibid.*, 180.

23. *Ibid.*, 190, 192.

24. Lacouture, *De Gaulle: The Rebel*, 410–12, and Verrier, *Assassination in Algiers*, 226–43, offer details on the killing of Admiral Darlan.

25. *Verrier,*191.

26. London *Sunday Times*, January 4, 2004.

27. Interview with the author, Kingston, ON, 2013.

28. Details of General de Gaulle's visit to Greenock were reported in the *Greenock Telegraph* of December 24 and 26, 1942.

29. Verrier, *Assassination in Algiers*, 247.

30. C. de Gaulle, *Unity*, 75.

31. Moll, *Yvonne de Gaulle*, 190–91.

32. *Ibid.*, 191.

33. David Schoenbrun, *Soldiers of the Night: The Story of the French Resistance* (New York: New American Library, 1980), 230. On December 21, 1945, the Court of Appeal in Algiers rehabili-

tated Bonnier as a patriot, ruling that the killing of Admiral Darlan had been "in the interest of the liberation of France."

34. Churchill, *The Hinge of Fate*, 645.

35. Roosevelt had reached Casablanca following a trans-Atlantic flight in a Boeing 314, the *Dixie Clipper*, one of the famed Flying Boats of Pan American Airways. It took him from Miami to Trinidad and Brazil before crossing the Atlantic to Bathurst, British Gambia, where the president switched to a C54 U.S. Air Force transport plane for the final leg of the trip. Roosevelt celebrated his birthday on the return flight.

   Churchill, meanwhile, had an uncomfortable flight from London in an unheated B24 Liberator bomber. He slept on a mattress on the floor, protected only by a blanket and his usual nightwear, consisting of nothing more than a silk vest. Lord Moran remembered the prime minister: "On his hands and knees, he cut a quaint figure with his big, bare, white bottom."

   Pan American's Flying Boats provided a colourful, if brief phase in aviation history. The huge planes carried passengers in comfort over the Atlantic and Pacific Oceans between 1938 and 1941. The construction of longer airport runways that could be used by larger planes made the Flying Boats obsolete. Von Hardesty, *Air Force One: The Aircraft That Shaped the Modern Presidency* (Minneapolis: Tandem Library, 2005), 38.

36. *Ibid.*, 680.

37. *Ibid.*, 681.

38. Lacouture, *De Gaulle: The Rebel*, 423.

39. Robert Murphy, *Diplomat Among Warriors* (London: n.p., 1964), 223–24.

40. Kersaudy, *Churchill and de Gaulle*, 265.

41. C. de Gaulle, *Unity*, 102.

42. Marnham, *The Death of Jean Moulin*, 179.

43. Mlle Pons survived the war, married Philippe Dreyfus, and lived to the age of ninety-three, dying in 2007. She was a remarkably beautiful woman all her life.

44. Marnham, *The Death of Jean Moulin*, 184.

45. *Ibid.,* 186.
46. Cook, *De Gaulle: A Biography,* 203.
47. Klaus Barbie was arrested in Brazil in 1983 and extradited to France. He was convicted for crimes against humanity and was sentenced on July 4, 1987, to life imprisonment. He died of leukemia in 1991 at the age of seventy-seven.

    He was defended by Jacques Vergés, who also represented such notorious figures as Khmer Rouge leader Khieu Samphan, former Serbian leader Slobodan Milosevic, Iraqi dictator Saddam Hussein, and the Venezuelan terrorist Ilich Ramírez Sánchez, known as Carlos the Jackal. Vergés, born in Thailand of a Vietnamese mother and a French father, believed that "defending doesn't mean excusing ... a lawyer tries to understand." Vergés married an Algerian woman whom General de Gaulle spared from execution after she had been found guilty of setting off bombs in Algeria. He disappeared for eight years in the 1970s, never explaining his absence. Vergés died in 2013 in the house in Paris once occupied by Voltaire.

48. M.R.D. Foot, *Six Faces of Courage: True Stories of World War II Resistance Fighters* (London: Magnum/Methuen, 1978), 54.
49. Erna Paris, *Unhealed Wounds: France and the Klaus Barbie Affair* (Toronto: Methuen, 1985), 108.
50. Pierre Brossolette committed suicide by jumping from the sixth-floor guardroom of the Gestapo headquarters on avenue Foch in Paris on March 22, 1944. He chose to die rather than risk giving up information under torture.
51. Jean Moulin's ashes were transferred from Pére Lachaise Cemetery in Paris to the Pantheon on December 19, 1964. André Malraux, author and French cabinet minister, declared Moulin had "made none of the regiments; but he made the army." He is recognized today as the outstanding leader of the French Resistance.

    In his *Mémoires de guerre,* Charles de Gaullle declared that "The disappearance of Jean Moulin had grave consequences, for he was one of those men who incarnate their jobs and who therefore cannot be replaced." C. de Gaulle, *Unity,* 183.

Had he lived, Moulin would have no doubt played a prominent role in postwar French politics, possibly as a successor (or rival) to de Gaulle.

52. No Resistance unit was more active than the Manouchian Group. In a single day, September 8, 1943, its members derailed a train on the Paris–Reims line and executed seven soldiers in four different operations. The conscription of French workers into the STO may have helped increase German war output but it drove thousands of young men into various branches of the Resistance, especially the Maquis in mountainous central and southeastern France. The Germans attempted to exploit the Manouchian convictions by publishing a propaganda poster that came to be known as the *Affiche Rouge* (Red Poster). It assailed the group as a criminal army made up of Communists, foreigners, the unemployed, and especially Jews. The attempt largely backfired and brought increased sympathy for the Resistance. A 2009 film, *L'Armée du crime,* tells the story of the Manouchian Group. A Mémorial de la France Combattante at Mont Valerian commemorates the more than one thousand hostages and Resistants who were executed there.

53. Churchill, *The Hinge of Fate,* 891.

54. Cook, *De Gaulle: A Biography,* 186.

55. Eisenhower, *Crusade in Europe,* 414.

56. C. de Gaulle, *Unity,* 129.

57. Moll, *Yvonne de Gaulle,* 202.

58. Giraud survived an assassination attempt in Algeria on October 1, 1944. He was elected in 1946 to the French Constituent Assembly as a representative of the Republican Party and helped to create the constitution of the Fourth Republic. He died in 1949.

59. *Ibid.,* 208.

Chapter 10 – Débarquement at Dawn

1. Robert Aron, *De Gaulle Before Paris: The Liberation of France, June–August 1944* (London: G.P. Putnam's Sons, 1962), 12–14.

2. Raymond Dronne, *La Libération de Paris* (Paris: Presses de la Cité, 1970), 29–31. The raid on Dieppe was one of the worst Allied blunders of the war, resulting in the injury, death, or capture of 3,623 of the 6,086 men (almost 60 percent) of the Canadian 2nd Division who made it ashore. Canadian prisoners were marched through the streets of Dieppe in shackles and were generally mistreated during their wartime imprisonment.

   The attack on August 19, 1942, began at 6:00 a.m., and by 10:50 a.m. the assault was called off. The Royal Navy lost thirty-three landing craft and one destroyer, and the Royal Air Force ninety-six aircraft. The Germans defenses were much stronger than anticipated. There was no advance bombardment prior to the landings on six beaches, four of them within the town. The men on the beaches proved to be easy targets for German gunnery crews firing from cliffs above them.

   Winston Churchill (*The Hinge of Fate*, 511) wrote that the raid "shed revealing light on many shortcomings [including] the value of powerful support by heavy naval guns...."

   Allied propaganda presented the raid as a valuable learning experience for a later invasion, but there is no evidence this was the case. It has been argued that the main purpose of the raid was to facilitate a mission organized by Ian Fleming (later author of the James Bond stories) to capture a new German code machine, the four-rotor Enigma. If so, this too was a failure as no such machine was recovered.

3. P. de Gaulle, *De Gaulle: Mon Père*, 331–32.

4. *http://en.wikipedia.org/wiki/Avro_York*

5. Kersaudy, *Churchill and de Gaulle*, 341.

6. C. de Gaulle, *Unity*, 252.

7. *Ibid.*, 252–53.
8. Cited in a letter from U.S. Ambassador Winant to the Secretary of War, June 13, 1944. United States, Department of State, *Foreign Relations of the United States* (FRUS) (Washington, DC: U.S. Government Printing Office, 1944).
9. Lacouture, *De Gaulle: The Rebel*, 503.
10. C. de Gaulle, *Unity*, 240.
11. *Ibid.*, 241.
12. United Sates National Archives, RG107, ASW 3708, France.
13. *Ibid.*
14. United Kingdom Foreign Office 954/9, Halifax to Foreign Secretary, no. 550, 3/2/44, cited in Kersaudy, *Churchill and de Gaulle*, 323.
15. C. de Gaulle, *Unity*, 254.
16. *Ibid.*
17. *Ibid.*
18. Eisenhower, *Crusade in Europe*, 250.
19. C. de Gaulle, *Unity*, 265.
20. *Ibid.*, 524.
21. *Ibid.*
22. Cook, *De Gaulle: A Biography*, 216.
23. Eisenhower, *Crusade in Europe*, 253.
24. C. de Gaulle, *Discours et Messages* (Paris: Plon, 1946), I: 407.
25. Robertson, *When Roosevelt Planned to Govern France*, 155.
26. *Ibid.*
27. *Winnipeg Free Press*, June 9, 1944.
28. C. de Gaulle, *Unity*, 257.
29. Churchill, *Triumph and Tragedy*, 12–13.
30. Kersaudy, *Churchill and de Gaulle*, 355.

Chapter 11 — Return of the Fighting French

1. P. de Gaulle, *De Gaulle: Mon Père*, 334.
2. Lacouture, *De Gaulle: The Rebel*, 527.

3. P. de Gaulle, *De Gaulle: Mon Père*, 334.

4. Kersaudy, *Churchill and de Gaulle*, 358.

5. Lacouture, *De Gaulle: The Rebel*, 528.

6. *Ibid.,* 529.

7. C. de Gaulle, *Unity*, 260.

8. Lacouture, *De Gaulle: The Rebel*, 529.

9. C. de Gaulle, *Unity*, 260.

10. C. de Gaulle, *Discours et Messages,* I: 245–46. Bayeux is one of the most attractive of French towns, steeped in history and culture. Anyone who has visited there and walked through Place Charles de Gaulle or stood before the column commemorating de Gaulle's appearance in June 1944 is sure to come away with a feeling of having been touched by history. The region was the source of many colonists to New France and in the town's Place de Québec there is a statue of St. Catherine-de-Saint-Augustin, a native of Normandy who nursed French and native peoples in New France.

11. C. de Gaulle, *Unity*, 261.

12. Lacouture, *De Gaulle: The Rebel*, 532.

13. *Ibid.,* 531.

14. F. Coulet, *Vertu des temps difficiles*, 247–48, cited by Robertson, *When Roosevelt Planned to Govern France*, 160. Robertson asserts that "the menace of an AMGOT for France, perhaps real in the early years of the war, was in the end mainly a Gaullist myth, built on the foundation of President Roosevelt's unrealistic aim of installing a military government" (196). He argues that the Anglo-American military intended to allow Gaullist officials to administer liberated territories as soon as possible, and that de Gaulle's people knew this to be the case. This is a somewhat disputable assumption, given the authority and influence of the president and the uncertainty among the Fighting French regarding the Allied acceptance of their claim to governance. Robertson's very thorough recounting of President Roosevelt's tactics amply confirms the fact that

France's national sovereignty was at risk. His conclusion that Roosevelt "was in no way actually ready to install a military government in France in June 1944" (190) does not detract from the reality — as the title of the book indicates — that he had wished to do so.

15. Lynne Olson, *Citizens of London* (London: Bond Street Books, 2010), 332.

16. C. de Gaulle, *Unity*, 267.

17. Williams, *The Last Great Frenchman*, 264.

18. Cook, *De Gaulle: A Biography*, 229.

19. *Ibid.*

20. *Ibid.,* 269.

21. *Ibid.*

22. *Ibid.,* 271.

23. C. de Gaulle, *Discours et Messages,* cited in François Mauriac, *De Gaulle,* translated by R. Howard (New York: Doubleday, 1966), 127–28.

24. Roosevelt, "Inaugural speech, March 4, 1933," *The Public Papers of Franklin D. Roosevelt,* Vol. 2, *The Year of Crisis, 1933* (New York: Random House, 1938), 11–16.

25. Mauriac, *De Gaulle,* 45.

26. C. de Gaulle, *Unity,* 273–75.

27. The *Pocket Guide* has been reprinted as *Instructions for American Servicemen in France During World War II* (Chicago: University of Chicago Press, 2008).

28. C. de Gaulle, *Discours et Messages,* I: 47.

29. During the war Louis Ricardo had married a British nurse, Nadine Stuart, who had cared for him at the Beaconsfield Nursing and Convalescence Home. In 1946, she, with her infant daughter, Marie Louise, in tow, arrived at the home of Ricardo's parents in Marseille. They insisted their son could not have married as he had been killed in the war. According to Nadine's granddaughter, Catherine Christie-Luff of Ottawa, their doubts were erased when they saw the girl. She bore family traits that made them realize she had to be a child of

their son. Throughout her life, Nadine Ricardo took part in numerous commemorative events in England and France. She never remarried, and, according to Ms. Christie-Luff, always regarded Louis as "the love of her life." Interview with the author, 2014.

30. C. de Gaulle, *Unity*, 323.
31. Cook, *De Gaulle: A Biography*, 235.

Chapter 12 – To the Barricades!

1. C. de Gaulle, *Unity*, 324.
2. Schoenbrun, *Soldiers of the Night*, 446.
3. Willis Thornton, *The Liberation of Paris* (London: Rupert-Hart Davis, 1963), 128.
4. Michael Neiberg, *The Blood of Free Men: The Liberation of Paris* (New York: Basic Books, 2012), 84. Captured during the German collapse, Dietrich von Choltitz was held first in Britain and then in Mississippi, but was freed from Allied captivity in 1947. He settled in Baden-Baden, headquarters of the French army of occupation in Germany, and died in 1966 from a longstanding wartime illness.
5. Schoenbrun, *Soldiers of the Night*, 446.
6. Larry Collins and Dominique Lapierre, *Is Paris Burning?* (New York: Simon & Schuster, 1965), 46.
7. Neiberg, *The Blood of Free Men*, 134.
8. Aron, *De Gaulle Triumphant*, 50.
9. Neiberg, *The Blood of Free Men*, 143.
10. Collins and Lapierre, *Is Paris Burning?*, 119.
11. Neiberg, *The Blood of Free Men*, 148. Widely admired for his courage, Nordling was favorably depicted in the film, *Is Paris Burning?* His role was played by Orsen Welles. Nordling died in 1962.
12. A wealthy businessman, Pierre Taittinger had taken over a small Champagne vineyard in 1931 and set up Taittinger

Champagne, which soon became a brand known around the world. In August 1944, he used his office to try and convince General von Choltitz to withdraw without damage to the city. This effort won Taittinger the forgiveness of the Resistance and after the war he became an honourary member of the French National Assembly. He also authored a book, … *et Paris ne fut pas détruit* ("… and Paris was not destroyed").

13. It was later revealed that Bender had been a member of a Paris-based anti-Nazi German group and a double agent for the Resistance.

14. C. de Gaulle, *Unity*, 332.

15. *Ibid.*

16. Lacouture, *De Gaulle: The Rebel*, 564.

17. Cook, *De Gaulle: A Biography*, 239.

18. David T. Zabecki, *Ruckzug: The German Retreat From France, 1944* (Lexington, KY: University of Kentucky Press, 2012), 132.

19. Aron offers this insight on Otto Abetz in *De Gaulle Triumphant*, 51–52. The Abetz message may indeed have saved Paris, as it contributed to von Choltitz's survival long enough to allow him to surrender the city without destroying its bridges and monuments. Abetz was tried and jailed for war crimes in 1945. Released in 1954, the former SS colonel died in a car accident in 1958.

20. *Ibid.*, 64.

21. Neiberg, *The Blood of Free Men*, 190.

Chapter 13 – The Road to Paris

1. John Keegan, *Six Armies in Normandy* (New York: Viking, 1982), 283.

2. The Denfert-Rochereau station of the Paris Metro was later given the subtitle of Colonel Rol-Tanguy.

3. Sartre, "Paris sous l'Occupation," 8.

4. Cited in *Ruckzug: The German Retreat From France, 1944* (Lexington: 2012), 133.

5. Thornton, *The Liberation of Paris*, 171–72.

6. Albert Camus, *Actuelles: Chroniques, 1944–1948* (Paris: 1950), 20.

7. C. de Gaulle, *Unity*, 340.

8. *Ibid.*, 568.

9. *Ibid.*, 341.

10. Cook, *Charles De Gaulle*, 242.

11. *Ibid.*, 243.

12. De Miribel, *La liberté souffre violence*, 151.

13. Dronne, *La Libération de Paris*, 280.

14. *Ibid.*, 284.

15. *Ibid.*, 285. Dronne fought with the 2nd Armoured Division in Alsace and Germany. He was promoted to colonel in 1947 and served in Indochina with a French Army battalion of armoured infantry. He became the mayor of his hometown of Sarthe, served as a senator and a member of the National Assembly, and was the author of six books. He died in 1991.

16. Visitors to the Hotel Meurice can ask for a copy of the hotel's history which tells how Charles-Augustin Meurice opened his first inn in Calais in 1771 as a stopping point for upper-class British travellers. He followed with a Paris branch in 1817. "Its current clientele as well as its historical patrons speak for its significance in Paris." The history notes that just before the arrival of the Germans in 1940, staff hid the wine cellar, only unveiling its treasures at the end of the war.

17. There are no archival records of the conversation at this last German dinner in Paris, but fragments remembered by various sources have come to be accepted as generally accurate.

18. Galante, *The General*, 152.

Chapter 14 – Paris Liberated

1.   Jacques Massu, *Sept ans avec Leclerc* (Paris: Plon, 1974), cited in Laurent Fournier and Alain Eymard, *La 2e DB Dans La Liberation de Paris et de sa région* (Paris: Histoire et Collections, 2009), 144.
2.   Schoenbrun, *Soldiers of the Night*, 468.
3.   Simone de Beauvoir, *La Force de l'Age* (Paris: Gallimard, 1960), cited in Herbert R. Lottmann, *The Left Bank: Writers, Artists, and Politics from the Popular Front to the Cold War* (Boston: Houghton Mifflin, 1982). 211.
4.   AP dispatch by Don Whitehead, *Winnipeg Free Press*, August 26, 1944.
5.   Fauteux, *Fantastic Interlude*, 109.
6.   De Miribel, *La liberté souffre violence*, 159.
7.   Lacouture, *De Gaulle: The Rebel*, 568.
8.   General von Choltitz published a memoir in 1950 entitled *"Is Paris Burning?"* The title was borrowed for the popular book and film of the same name. Whether Adolf Hitler actually ever uttered these words is in doubt, and von Choltitz has denied ever hearing them. The film was neither a critical nor a popular success. Its mixture of actual footage with dramatic episodes proved confusing to many viewers and its timing — in a year when President de Gaulle withdraw French forces from NATO and criticized the United states for its involvement in Vietnam — worked against its box office success.
9.   Statements attributed to Karcher are from Collins and Lapierre, *Is Paris Burning?*, 297–98.
10. AP dispatch, *Lethbridge* (AB) *Herald*, August 26, 2013.
11. C. de Gaulle, *Unity*, 342.
12. *Ibid.*, 343.
13. *Ibid.*
14. *Ibid.*
15. *Ibid.*, 344.
16. *Ibid.*

17. Aron, *De Gaulle Triumphant,* 89.
18. C. de Gaulle, *Unity,* 346.

Chapter 15 – Paris Exultant

1. C. de Gaulle, *Unity,* 325.
2. De Miribel, *La liberté souffre violence,* 160. After witnessing Charles de Gaulle's arrival at Gare Montparnasse, Mlle de Miribel drove to her parents' home on rue de Bellechasse and parked in the courtyard while her father waited at the front door. The telephone message announcing her return had reached her family.

   Her father, even before embracing Elisabeth, demanded to know: "Why did General de Gaulle send his soldiers to fight against other French in Syria?" He was referring to the British and Free French invasion of the Vichy-held French protectorate.

   She tried to give her father "the explanation he wanted," then went inside where "the joy of reunion hid all the misunderstanding." Deciding not to go to l'Hotel de Ville, she lost herself "in the sweetness of seeing my family again, before falling to sleep, completely exhausted."
3. Collins and Lapierre, *Is Paris Burning?,* 326.
4. Ernest Hemingway, *Collier's,* October 7, 1944. Reprinted in Samuel Hynes, comp., *Reporting World War II,* Vol. Two, *American Journalism, 1944–46.* (New York: Library of America,1995).
5. Picasso applied for French citizenship on April 3, 1940, but was turned down because of his "extremist ideas" and the belief he was "moving toward Communism." *Guardian,* London, May 2, 2004.
6. Jean-Paul Sartre, "Paris sous l'Occupation," *Situations, III.*
7. François Mauriac, *Le Figaro,* August 25 1944.
8. C. de Gaulle, *Unity,* 346.
9. *Ibid.,* 347.

10. Collins and Lapierre, *Is Paris Burning?*, 332.

11. C. de Gaulle, *Unity*, 348.

12. Lacouture, *De Gaulle: The Rebel*, 577.

13. Mauriac, *De Gaulle*, 577.

14. C. de Gaulle, *Unity*, 350.

15. Graham Robb, *Parisians: An Adventure History of Paris* (New York: W.W. Norton, 2010), 319.

16. C. de Gaulle, *Unity*, 354.

17. Collins and Lapierre, *Is Paris Burning?*, 336.

18. Aron, *De Gaulle Triumphant*, 79.

19. C. de Gaulle, *Unity*, 356.

20. A. de Boissieu, *Pour combattre de Paris* (Paris: 1981), 259, cited in Lacouture, *De Gaulle: The Ruler*, 17.

21. C. de Gaulle, *Salvation, 1944–1946* (New York: 1959), 7.

22. *Ibid.*, 2.

23. C. de Gaulle, *Lettres, Notres et Carnets*, 5: 297, cited in Williams, *The Last Great Frenchman*, 276.

24. Mauriac, *De Gaulle* (Paris: B. Grasset, 1978), 65, cited in Lacouture, *De Gaulle: The Ruler*, 6.

25. *Ibid.*, 7.

26. Paul Valéry, *Oeuvres completes* (Paris: Gallimard, 1957), 1544, cited in Lacouture, *De Gaulle: The Ruler*, 7.

27. C. de Gaulle, *Salvation*, 23.

28. Charles de Gaulle always maintained a certain distance between himself and the Resistance. He never capitalized the term in his writings. We have done so in recognition of its central role in our narrative.

29. C. de Gaulle, *Salvation*, 50.

30. La Couture, *De Gaulle: The Ruler*, 26.

Chapter 16 – Getting Even

1. In 2013, Oradour-sur-Glane was the setting for a symbolic act of reconciliation when German president Joachim Gauck joined

President François Hollande and survivor Robert Hebras, 88, in an emotion-laden visit. The three men held hands as they paused in the charred wreckage of the village church. "We will never forget Oradour and the other sites of barbarity," President Gauck said. (Agence France-Presse, September 4, 2013.)

One cannot visit Oradour, as the author did on a bleak October day, and fail to be caught up in this awful testament to human bestiality. One wanders unescorted through the village; no guides or guardians are visible to block the way. Despite the thousands of visitations over the years, very few acts of vandalism have been reported. The events of June 10, 1944 become more vivid when viewed against the panorama of what had been a vigorous and self-sufficient community boasting all manner of activity — bakeries, butchers, cafés, tailors, hairdressers — and served by a range of professional and trades people from the doctor to the lawyer to the local auto mechanic, with the inevitable spire of the Roman Catholic church dominating its modest skyline. The tranquil life of Oradourians had vanished in a few moments of terror and rampage. The broken remnants of the village are all that remain to bear silent witness to its people's destiny.

In 1953, twenty-one members of Der Fuhrer Regiment, including thirteen French Alsatians, went on trial in Bordeaux, charged with murder of the Oradour civilians. One was acquitted, two sentenced to death, and the rest given lengthy jail terms. The Alsatians were freed when, a few days after the trial, the National Assembly passed an amnesty for persons convicted of crimes while serving the Germans under duress.

General de Gaulle urged acceptance of the amnesty, arguing that France needed to avoid "the infliction of a bitter injury to national unity." De Gaulle also played down any responsibility of the Resistance for having carried out acts that had led to the German reprisals. He sought, and largely succeeded, to impose on the French a collective memory of a nation united in struggle against German oppression.

As late as 2014, charges remained pending against six former members of Der Fuhrer Regiment who had been arrested in Dortmund, Germany in 2011. There seemed little likelihood of these now aged men ever going to trial.

2. Interview with the author, Kingston, ON, 2013. Ms. Manquet's father, Louis, also was an active member of the Resistance. A former gendarme, he was employed as a guard at the Annecy prison and used his position to organize the escape on August 18, 1944, of seventy-six prisoners who had been scheduled for execution the following day.

3. Alfred M. de Zavas, *The Wehrmact War Crimes Bureau, 1939–1945*, (Omaha, NB: University of Nebraska Press, 1989), 152.

4. Michel Germain, *Le Prix de la Liberté, Chronique de la Haute-Savoie de la bataille des Glières à la Libération et au-delà, 26 mars 1944–19 août 1944*, Vol. 4, *Chronique de la Haute-Savoie pendant la deuxième guerre mondiale.* (Montmélian: La Fontaine de Siloë, 1993), 337.

5. C. de Gaulle, *Salvation*, 11.

6. C. de Gaulle, *Unity*, 75. He was speaking in reference to the assassination of Admiral Darlan.

7. Albert Camus, *Combat*, October 20, 1944.

8. C. de Gaulle, *Salvation*, 204.

9. *Ibid.*, 121.

10. Aron, *De Gaulle Triumphant*, 269.

11. Lacouture, *De Gaulle: The Ruler*, 77.

12. C. de Gaulle, *Unity*, 361.

13. C. de Gaulle, *Salvation*, 284.

14. Fenby, *The General*, 295.

15. C. de Gaulle, *Salvation*, 127.

16. Papon became prefect of the Paris police in 1958. He was the central figure in what became known as the Paris massacre of 1961, in which somewhere between one hundred to three hundred people died as a result of police oppression of a peaceful demonstration in support of the Algerian National Liberation Front. In the same year Papon received the

Legion of Honour from Charles de Gaulle. Other flagrant acts of repression by the police occurred under Papon's leadership, leading to his forced resignation in 1965.

Papon was elected to the National Assembly and it was not until 1995 that he was charged with crimes against humanity over the deportation of 1,600 Jews from Bordeaux when he was in charge of police there. He was sentenced to ten years imprisonment but fled to Switzerland, from where he later was extradited and returned to La Santé prison in Paris. Papon was paroled in 2002 and died in 2007 at the age of ninety-six.

17. See *http://en.wikipedia.org/wiki/Mitterrand_and_the_far_ right*.
18. C. de Gaulle, *Salvation*, 200.
19. *Ibid.*
20. C. de Gaulle, *Salvation*, 56.
21. *Ibid.,* 57.
22. Fauteux, *Fantastic Interlude,* 115. Claire Fauteux spent the rest of her life in Canada painting and teaching art at the École des beaux-arts de Montreal. She died in 1988, aged ninety-seven, never having married.

Marie Claire Christine Fauteux came from a distinguished Quebecois family and could trace her ancestry back to the kings of France through Robert I of Dreux, the fifth son of Louis VI. Her maternal grandfather, Jean-Antoine Panet, had been the first Speaker of the Legislative Assembly for Lower Canada; a distant relative, Abbe Jean-Antoine Aide-Créquy (1749–1780), was Quebec's first Canadian-born painter.

Chapter 17 – From Rebel to Ruler

1. C. de Gaulle, *Discours et Messages*, I: 488.
2. C. de Gaulle, *Salvation*, 21.
3. Janet Flanner, *Paris Journal: 1944–1965,* 2 vols. (New York: Athaneum, 1965), I: 15.

4. Jean K. Chalaby, *The de Gaulle Presidency and the Media: Statism and Public Communications* (London: Macmillan Palgrave, 2002), 14, 81.

5. C. de Gaulle, *Salvation,* 130.

6. Nancy Mitford was separated from her husband, Peter Rodd. She was delighted when Palewski moved to within a few doors of her home at 20 rue Bonaparte. Their love affair was largely one-sided and they never lived together. The relationship ended when Palewski married Violette de Talleyrand-Périgord, the Duchesse de Sagan, in 1969. Ms. Mitford's life cannot be separated from that of her equally famous sisters, Pamela, Diana, and Unity, who was an admirer of Hitler. Nancy Mitford, Paris-born, died at her home in Versailles, aged sixty-eight, in 1973.

7. C. de Gaulle, *Salvation,* 68.

8. *Ibid.,* 88.

9. *Ibid.,* 99.

10. *Le Monde,* April 14, 1945.

11. C. de Gaulle, *Salvation,* 156.

12. *Ibid.,* 166.

13. *Ibid.,* 169.

14. Eisenhower, *Crusade in Europe,* 414.

15. Flanner, *Paris Journal,* I: 25.

16. Kennedy's scoop embarrassed his agency and AP president Robert McLean apologized, saying: "The Associated Press profoundly regrets the distribution on Monday of the report of the total surrender in Europe which investigation now clearly discloses was distributed in advance of authorization by Supreme Allied Headquarters." Kennedy was expelled from France and was fired by the AP. He later became the editor and publisher of newspapers in California and died in a car accident in 1963, at the age of fifty-eight. "The absurdity of attempting to bottle up news of such magnitude was too apparent," he had written. In 2012, the Associated Press apologized for the way it treated Kennedy. "It was a terrible

day for the AP. It was handled in the worst possible way," said president and CEO Tom Curley.

17. C. de Gaulle, *Discours et Messages*, I: 545.

18. C. de Gaulle, *Salvation*, 230.

19. *Ibid.*, 240.

20. *Mackenzie King Diaries*, August 28, 1945, 828.

21. C. de Gaulle, *Salvation*, 246.

22. *Ibid.*, 104.

23. *Ibid.*, 117.

24. Lacouture, *De Gaulle: The Ruler*, 101.

25. *Journal Officiel*, January 1, 1946 (Paris: 1946), 732.

26. C. de Gaulle, *Salvation*, 319.

Chapter 18 – The Gamble for France

1. C. de Gaulle, *Salvation*, 319.

2. *Cette chance que j'ai eue*, cited in Lacouture, *De Gaulle: The Ruler*, 117.

3. Jules Moch, *Une si longue vie*, cited in Lacouture, *De Gaulle: The Ruler*, 118.

4. *Ibid.*

5. *Ibid.*,119.

6. C. de Gaulle, *Discourses et Messages*, (Paris: Plon, 1970), I: 720. As prime minister from 1917 to1920, Georges Clemenceau carried France through the First World War, helped frame the Treaty of Versailles at the Paris Peace Conference in 1919, and was largely responsible for the heavy war reparations imposed on a defeated Germany. He took a bullet in the ribs in an attempted assassination. Clemenceau failed to win the presidency in 1920, was unable to get the United States to forgive France's war debt, and died in 1929. He is remembered for his famous statement, "War is too important to be left to the generals."

7. Flanner, *Paris Journal*, I: 53.

8. *www.charles-de-gaulle.org/pages/espace-pedagogique/le-*

point-sur/les-textes-a-connaitre/discours-de-bayeux-16-juin-1946.php.

9. Mauriac, *De Gaulle,* 33.

10. The Charles de Gaulle Memorial Museum was inaugurated in 2008 by French president Nicolas Sarkozy and German Chancellor Angela Merkel. One of its main exhibits deals with the rapprochement between France and Germany engineered by de Gaulle and Konrad Adenhauer, then chancellor of the West German Federal Republic. The main exhibition covering two floors is organized chronologically, with different periods showing highlights of the general's life. The museum also contains a library and research facilities.

11. P. de Gaulle: *De Gaulle: Mon Père,* 471. De Gaulle's descendants continue to live at La Boisserie, although it is open for public viewing.

12. Galante, *The General!,* 6.

13. Lacouture, *De Gaulle: The Ruler,* 144–45. Jacques-Philippe Leclerc de Hauteclocque, one of the most brilliant of French army officers, was posthumously named a marshall of France. Born Philippe François Marie, comte de Hauteclocque, product of an aristocratic family descended from the nobility of pre-revolutionary France, he had his name officially changed after the war to incorporate his Resistance alias.

    Leclerc-Hauteclocque joined the French Army in 1924 after graduating from Saint-Cyr, rising to the rank of captain by the Second World War. Wounded and captured during the Battle of France, he escaped, made his way to Perpignan, near the Spanish border, and, with the help of a false passport produced on a child's printing press, entered Spain. In a letter to his wife on June 27, 1940, he wrote, "I will overcome all difficulties, putting all my strength in the service of the country until the final victory. I embrace you,..." With the help of the British Embassy in Lisbon, Leclerc caught a ship to England and reached Liverpool on July 21, an early volunteer to the Free French. Two Parisian streets bear his name: Avenue du Général Leclerc in the 14th arrondissement and rue du Maréchal Leclerc in the 12th arrondissement near the Bois de Vincennes.

14. *Ibid.*, 145.

15. *Ibid.*, 135.

16. Williams, *The Last Great Frenchman*, 325.

17. Cyrus Sulzberger, *A Long Row of Candles: Memoirs and Diaries, 1963–1972* (New York: Macmillan, 1969), 343.

18. Soustelle, *Vingt-huit ans de gaullisme*, 65, cited by Lacouture, *De Gaulle: The Ruler*, 150.

19. C. de Gaulle, *Discourses et Messages*, II, 582.

20. Mauriac, *De Gaulle*, 15.

21. Robert Speaight, *Vanier: Soldier, Diplomat and Governor General* (Toronto: Collins, 1970), 339.

22. De Miribel, *La liberté souffre violence*, 211.

23. Speaight, *Vanier*, 339.

24. De Miribel, *La liberté souffre violence*, 224. De Miribel wrote a second book and ended her career as consul general of France in Florence, Italy. She died, aged ninety, in 2005.

25. Lacouture, *De Gaulle: The Ruler*, 87.

Chapter 19 – The Crisis and the Call

1. As French law does not permit enumeration by race or ethnicity, it is difficult to determine the precise number of persons of North African origin in the country. The population of France in 2011 was 65,821,885, up from 40,506,639 in 1946. In 2004, the Institut Montaigne estimated that France had six million people of North African origin, two million blacks, and one million of Asian origin. Significant immigration occurred after the Algerian war. In addition to the million European *pieds noirs* who moved back to France or other countries in Europe, several hundred thousand North African Jews joined the migration. Residents of French colo-

nies were considered subjects but not citizens of France until passage of the Statute of Algeria in 1947 granted Algerian men full citizenship in Metropolitan France and permitted unregulated passage between Algeria and France. The Évian Accord of 1962 bringing the war to an end also provided for freedom of movement between Algeria and France. Migration accelerated as conditions became chaotic for many while others left in search of economic opportunity.

The presence of Algerians in large French cities has given rise to considerable social friction and issues relating to their presence rank among the most serious social challenges facing the country. Riots in 2005 in Paris involving North African immigrants and native-born youths of Algerian descent led to imposition of a state of emergency. The riots, focused on Clichy-sous-Bois, involved burning of cars and public buildings. French laws that restrict the wearing of Muslim dress — hijabs (head scarves) and burqas are banned in the civil service and state-run schools — cause deep resentment in the Muslim population. Meanwhile, right-wing parties such as the National Front have flourished through opposition to Muslim rights and non-white immigration. The family I stayed with in Paris in 2012 employed a Tunisian refugee who had arrived on one of the many small boats that ferry North African refugees to Italy and France. She managed to "regularize" her status after her arrival. Her position is typical, as there is widespread acceptance of North Africans in service jobs in France, similar to the pattern in the United States where Hispanic "illegals" are knowingly employed in homes and small businesses.

2. C. de Gaulle, *Memoirs of Hope: Renewal and Endeavor* (New York: Simon & Schuster, 1971), 85.

3. Alistair Horne, *A Savage War of Peace: Algeria, 1954–1962* (New York: New York Review of Books, 2006), 106.

4. Mauriac, *De Gaulle*, 36.

5. Horne, *A Savage War of Peace*, 123.

6. *Ibid.*
7. C. de Gaulle, *Discours et Messages, 1946–58,* 654.
8. Tournoux, *La Tragédie du Général* (Paris: Plon, 1967), cited in Lacouture, *De Gaulle: The Ruler,* 163.
9. P. de Gaulle, *De Gaulle: Mon Père,* 544.
10. C. De Gaulle, *Memoirs of Hope,* 29.
11. Lacouture, *De Gaulle: The Ruler,* 181.

Chapter 20 – The Last Battle

1. C. de Gaulle, *Memoirs of Hope,* 43.
2. Introduced in 1955, the Caravelle was the first medium-range jet built by France's SUD Aviation. A total of 282 were produced. The plane's unique aft-mounted engine and clear wing design was copied by many other manufacturers. SUD formed a consortium with British Aircraft Corp. (BAC) to build the supersonic Concorde. The company, headquartered in Toulouse, was later merged into Airbus, the civilian aircraft manufacturing branch of the European Aeronautic Defence and Space Company NV (EADS).
3. *Ibid.,* 44.
4. *Ibid.,* 42.
5. *Ibid.,* 44.
6. *Le Monde,* June 5, 1958.
7. Lacouture, *De Gaulle: The Ruler,* 189.
8. Horne, *A Savage War of Peace,* 301.
9. The extent that French forces practised torture in Algeria did not become generally known until 2000, when *Le Monde* published a memoir by an Algerian woman, Louisette Ighilahriz, detailing her rape and abuse at the hands of French captors. *Le Monde* also published in the same year an interview with General Paul Aussaresses, a wartime Resistance hero, who confessed to have personally tortured and murdered many Algerian prisoners. Aussaresses then wrote a book, "Ser-

vices spéciaux, Algérie 1955–1957," in which he alleged that General Massu had approved of the use of torture. Aussaresses escaped prosecution by virtue of a general amnesty that had been passed in 1968, but the French president of the day, Jacques Chirac, ordered Aussaresses stripped of his rank and his Legion of Honour medal. Aussaresses was later convicted of "trying to justify war" but the European Court overturned the verdict, primarily on grounds of free speech. Timing of the 1968 amnesty suggests the legislation had the general's prior approval. Significantly, there is little indication of the prevalence of torture after 1958, when de Gaulle assumed office. Aussaresses died in 2013. For his obituary, see *New York Times*, December 4, 2013. For a discussion of amnesty for war crimes, see *www.crimesofwar.org/a-z-guide/amnesty/*.

10. The French national anthem "La Marseillaise" is surely one of the world's most stirring songs, appealing to national spirit to a degree matched by the hymns of few other countries. It was born, not as its name suggests in the French city of Marseille but in Strasbourg, where the composition by Rouget de Lisle was first played in the city's Place d'Armes on April 30, 1792. This was a war song, written to boost the morale of French troops fighting Prussia and Austria. It was popularized, and given its name when volunteers from Marseille sang it as they marched from that city to Paris. "La Marseillaise" was proclaimed as France's national anthem on July 14, 1795. No English translation can do justice to its poetic call to arms:

> *Aux armes, citoyens*
> *Formez vos bataillons*
> *Marchons, marchons!*
> *Qu'un sang impur*
> *Abreuve nos sillons!*

11. C. de Gaulle, *Memoirs of Hope*, 36.

12. *Le Monde* September 17, 1959.

13. Horne, *A Savage War of Peace*, 351.

14. *Ibid.,* 357.
15. Lacouture, *De Gaulle: The Ruler,* 260.
16. Horne, *A Savage War of Peace,* 392.
17. Lacouture, *De Gaulle: The Ruler,* 283.
18. *Ibid.*
19. *Ibid.,* 284.
20. Jean-Benoit Nadeau and Julie Barlow, *Sixty Million French-men Can't Be Wrong: Why We Love France but Not the French* (Naperville, IL: Sourcebooks, 2003), 102.
21. Would the Algerians have won their revolution without the leadership of Ahmed Ben Bella? They doubtless would, but during his prolonged confinement, he continued to share in the leadership of the FLN and to inspire his followers. Ben Bella was elected president of Algeria in a democratic vote in 1963, and led his country in defence of a Moroccan invasion known as the "Sand War." He promoted the concept of "self-management" and conducted a widespread but disorganized program of land reform. Increasingly eccentric and arrogant, he was deposed in 1965 and lived under house arrest until 1980. On his release, he moved to Lausanne, Switzerland, and was allowed in 1990 to return home, where he died in 2012. He was given a state funeral and Algeria declared eight days of national mourning.
22. C. de Gaulle, *Memoirs of Hope,* 130.

Chapter 21 — The Republic of de Gaulle

1. Mauriac, *De Gaulle,* 54.
2. C. de Gaulle, *Memoirs of Hope,* 137.
3. *Ibid.,* 149.
4. Flanner, *Paris Journal,* II: 411.
5. André Malraux, quoted in Flanner, *Paris Journal,* I: 377.
6. Moll, *Yvonne de Gaulle,* 331–40.
7. C. de Gaulle, *Memoirs of Hope,* 272–74.

8. *Ibid.,* 370.

9. *Ibid.,* 201.

10. United States, Department of State, *Foreign Relations of the United States 1958–60,* Vol. II, Part 2, *United Nations and General International Matters* (Washington, DC: GPO, 1958–60), 64–67.

11. C. de Gaulle, *Memoirs of Hope,* 174–80.

12. *Ibid.,* 251.

13. *Ibid.,* 254–55.

14. *Ibid.,* 256.

15. *Ibid.,* 258.

16. Christian Fouchet, *Au service du general de Gaulle.* Vol. 1, *Mémoires d'hier et de demain* (Paris: Plon, 1971), 175–77.

17. C. de Gaulle, *Memoirs of Hope,* 130.

18. C. de Gaulle, *Ibid.,* 312.

19. Lacouture, *De Gaulle: The Ruler,* 175.

20. *Ibid.,* 378.

21. Flanner, *Paris Journal,* I: 591.

22. Lacouture, *De Gaulle: The Ruler,* 453.

23. C. de Gaulle, *Memoirs of Hope,* 241.

24. *Ibid.*

25. Fenby, *The General,* 556.

26. Lacouture, *De Gaulle: The Ruler,* 452.

27. Thomson, *Vive le Québec Libre,* 205.

28. Lester B. Pearson, *Mike: The Memoirs of The Rt. Hon. Lester B. Pearson,* Vol. 3 (Toronto: University of Toronto Press, 1975), 267.

29. Lacouture, *De Gaulle: The Ruler,* 461.

Chapter 22 – The Final Days

1. Daniel Cohn-Bendit became a symbol of youthful rebellion in the 1960s by his involvement in the French student strike. He was born in Montauban, France, to German-Jewish parents who had fled Nazi Germany in 1933. Schooled in

Germany between 1956 and 1968, he returned to France to study at Nanterre. His spirit of rebellion led him to a brief involvement in anarchist organizations. After the student strikes of 1968, he went back to Germany, became involved for a time in radical left-wing and Marxist organizations, but in 1989 he became deputy mayor of Frankfurt and in 1993 was elected to the European Parliament. He is the leader of the Green Party parliamentary group. In the 1970s, Cohn-Bendit published articles claiming he had engaged in sexual activity with children as young as six; he later denied actually have carried out such acts and said the articles "shouldn't have been written that way."

2. Fenby, *The General*, 568.
3. Lacouture, *De Gaulle: The Ruler*, 530.
4. Fenby, *The General*, 579.
5. *Ibid.,* 585.
6. *Ibid.,* 600.
7. *Ibid.,* 621.
8. *Agence France-Presse*, April 28, 1969.
9. Lacouture, *De Gaulle: The Ruler*, 582.
10. C. de Gaulle, *Salvation*, 328.
11. Pierre-Louis Blanc, letter to his editor, May 30, 1970, cited in *Memoirs of Hope*, 378.
12. Fenby, *The General*, 630.
13. *Ibid.,* 631.
14. *Associated Press*, November 12, 1970.
15. Sulzberger, *A Long Row of Candles*, 685.

Chapter 23 — The Legend and the Legacy

1. The term *les Trente Glorieuses* was first used by French demographer Jean Fourastié in his *Les Trente Glorieuses, ou la révolution invisible de 1946 à 1975*. From the mid-1970s, France suffered, as did other countries, from the oil crisis

and a period of stagflation. After 2000, France found itself facing serious unemployment and high national debt. A trenchant observer of French affairs, Erna Paris wrote of the country's economic and social problems in the Toronto *Globe and Mail* of August 14, 2013:

> Industry remains strong in some areas, such as technology, but there is an underlying resistance to globalization that is largely cultural. Significantly, the French view basic capitalism, the motor of globalism, with skepticism. France is not a land of entrepreneurs, but a country where wealth and privilege have historically been inherited through property and preferred access to elite schools. To enrich oneself through personal effort remains suspect.

2. The mellowing of Franco-American relations under de Gaulle's twenty-first-century successors represents one of the more interesting turns in global geopolitics. One observer, Rem Kortewag of the Centre for European Reform in London, described Mr. Hollande as "the last man standing in Europe ... the unquestioned leader of Europe on defence and securities issues." (Toronto *Globe and Mail,* September 4, 2013). Recognition of France as the dominant European player in foreign affairs would have delighted Charles de Gaulle. Kortewag's remarks, picked up by many observers, followed French action in Mali to repulse al-Qaeda-backed rebels and President Hollande's support of the United States's desire to "punish" the Syrian government for the use of chemical weapons. The French position was in sharp contrast with the reluctance of Germany — due to the ghosts of its Nazi past — to involve itself in foreign engagements, as well as the refusal of the British Parliament to support Prime Minister David Cameron's request for military ac-

tion against Syria. American Secretary of State John Kerry, no doubt recalling France's support of the United States in the Revolutionary War, was moved to describe France as "America's oldest ally."

3. *New York Times,* November 12, 1970.

4. The U.S. Air Force bombed the Rhone River bridges and railway yards of Arles prior to the city's liberation in 1944. The raid destroyed about two hundred dwellings, including the historic "yellow house" that Vincent Van Gogh had occupied during his sojourn in Arles between February 1888 and May 1889. There is a memorial in Place Lamartin, near the bombing site, to two U.S. fliers killed in a crash during the raid.

5. Mauriac, *De Gaulle,* 229. François Mauriac was born in Bordeaux in 1885. He studied literature at the University of Bordeaux and moved to Paris to pursue writing. He was elected to the Académie française in 1933, won the Nobel Prize for Literature in 1952, and was awarded the Grand Cross of the Légion d'honneur in 1958. Mauriac was strongly opposed to French rule in Indochina (Vietnam) and criticized the use of torture by the French Army in Algeria. After the war, he wrote for *Le Figaro* and *l'Express.* Mauriac had a bitter dispute with Albert Camus over punishment of collaborators; Camus called for stiff penalties but Mauriac argued that national reconciliation should take precedence. The moral themes of his novels reflected his strongly held Roman Catholic views. Mauriac's complete works were published in twelve volumes in the 1950s. He died September 1, 1970.

BIBLIOGRAPHY

Primary Sources

Archives nationales de France, Paris
Institut Charles de Gaulle, Paris
Library and Archives Canada, Ottawa
Mémorial Charles de Gaulle, Colombey-des-Deux-Églises, France
United Kingdom National Archives, London
United States National Archives and Records Administration, College
    Park, MD.

English Books

Aglion, Raoul. *Roosevelt and de Gaulle: Allies in Conflict — A Personal
    Memoir.* New York: Free Press, 1988.
Aron, Robert. *De Gaulle Before Paris: The Liberation of France, June–*

August 1944. London: G.P. Putnam's Sons, 1962.

———. *De Gaulle Triumphant: The Liberation of France*. London: G.P. Putnam's Sons, 1964.

Atkin, Nicholas. *The Forgotten French: Exiles in the British Isles, 1940–44*. Manchester, UK: Manchester University Press, 2003.

———. *The French at War, 1934–1944*. London: Pearson Education, 2001.

Atkinson, Rick. *The Guns at Last Light. New York: Henry Holt, 2013.*

———. *Instructions for American Servicemen in France During World War II*. Chicago: University of Chicago Press, 2008.

Badouin, Paul. *The Private Diaries of Paul Badouin*. Translated by Sir Charles Petrie. London: Eyre & Spottiswoode, 1948.

Barber, Noel. *The Week France Fell*. London: Macmillan, 1976.

Beevor, Antony, and Artemis Cooper. *Paris After the Liberation, 1944–1949*. New York: Penguin Books, 2004.

Bennett, G.H. *The RAF's French Foreign Legion: De Gaulle, the British and the Re-emergence of French Airpower, 1940–45*. London: Continuum, 2011.

Berthon, Simon. *Allies at War*. London: HarperCollins, 2001.

Blumenson, Martin. *Liberation*. New York: Time-Life Books, 1976.

Borden, Mary. *Journey Down a Blind Alley*. London: Hutchinson, 1946.

Briggs, Asa. *The History of Broadcasting in the United Kingdom*. 5 vols. Oxford: Oxford University Press, 1995.

Buchwald, Art. *Art Buchwald's Paris*. London: Chatto and Windus, 1955.

Chirac, Jacques. *My Life in Politics*. London: Palgrave Macmillan, 2012.

Churchill, Winston. *The Second World War.* Vol. 2, *Their Finest Hour.* Boston: Houghton Mifflin, 1949.

———. *The Second World War.* Vol. 4, *The Hinge of Fate.* Boston: Houghton Mifflin, 1950.

———. *The Second World War.* Vol. 5, *Closing the Ring.* Boston: Houghton Mifflin, 1951.

———. *The Second World War.* Vol. 6, *Triumph and Tragedy.* Boston: Houghton Mifflin, 1953.

Clinton, Alan. *Jean Moulin, 1899–1943: The French Resistance and the Republic*. London: Macmillan Palgrave, 2002.

Cobban, Alfred. *A History of Modern France*. Vol. 3, *1871–1962*. London: Penguin, 1965.

Collins, Larry, and Dominique Lapierre. *Is Paris Burning?* New York: Simon & Schuster, 1965.

Cook, Don. *Charles de Gaulle: A Biography*. New York: G.P. Putnam's Sons, 1983.

Cook, Tim. *Warlords: Borden, Mackenzie King and Canada's World Wars*. Toronto: Penguin, 2012.

Courteaux, Oliver. *Canada Between Vichy and Free France, 1940–1945*. Toronto: University of Toronto Press, 2013.

Craley, Aiden. De *Gaulle: A Biography*. London: Collins, 1969.

de Beauvoir, Simone. *Memoirs of a Dutiful Daughter*. Reprint. New York: Harper Perennial Modern Classics, 2005.

de Gaulle, Charles, *The Army of the Future*. London: Hutchinson, 1940.

———. *The Edge of the Sword*. London: Faber and Faber, 1960.

———. *France and Her Army*. London: Hutchinson, 1945.

———. *Memoirs of Hope: Renewal and Endeavor*. New York: Simon & Schuster, 1971.

———. *War Memoirs*. Vol. 1, *The Call to Honour, 1940–1942*. New York: Simon & Schuster, 1955.

———. *War Memoirs*. Vol. 2, *Unity, 1942–1944*. New York: Simon & Schuster, 1959.

———. *War Memoirs*. Vol. 3, *Salvation, 1944–1946*. New York: Simon & Schuster, 1959.

de Gramont, Sanche. *The French: Portrait of a People*. New York: G.P. Putnam's Sons, 1969.

de Zavas, Alfred. *The Wehrmacht War Crimes Bureau, 1939–1945. Omaha, NB: University of Nebraska Press, 1989.*

Eisenhower, Dwight D. *Crusade in Europe*. New York: Doubleday, 1948.

Erlich, Blake. *Resistance, France, 1940–1945*. Boston: Little, Brown, 1965.

Fabre-Luce, Alfred. *The Trial of Charles de Gaulle*. Translated by Antonia White. Introduction by Dorothy Pickles. London: Methuen, 1963.

Fauteux, Claire. *Fantastic Interlude*. New York: Vantage Press, 1961.

Fenby, Jonathan. *The General: Charles de Gaulle and the France He Saved*. New York: Skyhorse Publishing, 2012.

Flanner, Janet. *Paris Journal, 1944–1965*. 2 vols. New York: Atheneum, 1965.

Foot, M.R.D. *Resistance: 1940–1945*. London: Eyre Methuen, 1976.

———. *Six Faces of Courage: True Stories of World War II Resistance Fighters*. London: Magnum/Methuen, 1978.

———. *S.O.E. in France: An Account of the Work of the British Special Operations Executive in France*. Frederick, MD: University Publications of America, 1984.

Friesen, Karl-Heinz. *The Blitzkrieg Legend: The 1940 Campaign in the West*. Annapolis, MD: Naval Institute Press, 2005.

Gates, Eleanor M. *The End of the Affair: The Collapse of the Anglo-French Alliance, 1939–40*. Berkeley, CA: University of California Press, 1981.

Glass, Charles. *Americans in Paris: Life and Death Under Nazi Occupation*. New York: Penguin Press, 2010.

Haskew, Michael E. *De Gaulle: Lessons in Leadership from the Defiant General*. New York: Palgrave Macmillan, 2011.

Hatch, Alden. *The de Gaulle Nobody Knows*. New York: Hawthorne Books, 1960.

Hazareesingh, Sudhar. *In the Shadow of the General: Modern France and the Myth of de Gaulle*. Oxford: Oxford University Press, 2012.

Horne, Alastair. *A Savage War of Peace: Algeria, 1954–1962*. New York: New York Review of Books, 2006.

———. *Seven Ages of Paris*. New York: Alfred A. Knopf, 2002.

———. *To Lose a Battle: France, 1940*. New York: Penguin Books, 2007.

Humbert, Agnès. *Resistance: A Woman's Journal of Struggle and Defiance in Occupied France*. New York: Bloomsbury, 2008. (Originally published as Notre Guerre. Paris: Éditions Émile-Paule Frères, 1946.)

Hynes, Samuel, comp. *Reporting World War II*. Vol. 2, *American Journalism, 1944–46*. New York: Library of America. 1995.

Jackson, Julian. *The Fall of France: the Nazi Invasion of 1940*. Oxford: Oxford University Press, 2003.

———. *France: The Dark Years, 1940–1944*. Oxford: Oxford University Press, 2001.

Jahier, Alice. *France Remembered*. Introduction by T.S. Eliot. Translated by J.G. Weightman. London: Sylvan Press, Nicholson & Watson, 1944.

Karnow, Stanley. *Paris in the Fifties*. New York: Random House, 1997.

Kedwood, H.R., and Nancy Wood. *The Liberation of France*. Washington: Berg Publishers, 1995.

Keegan, John. *Six Armies in Normandy*. New York: Viking Press, 1982.

Kersaudy, François. *Churchill and De Gaulle*. London: Collins, 1990.

King, William Lyon Mackenzie. *The Mackenzie King Diaries, 1893–1950: The Complete Manuscript Entries*. Toronto: University of Toronto Press, 1980.

Lacouture, Jean. *De Gaulle: The Rebel, 1890–1944*. London: Harvill, 1991.

———. *De Gaulle: The Ruler, 1945–1970*. London: Harvill, 1991

Lambert, Raymond-Raoul. *Diary of a Witness, 1940–1943*. Chicago: Ivan R. Dee, 2007.

Laval, Pierre. *The Unpublished Diary of Pierre Laval*. London: Falcon Press, 1948.

Liebling, A.J. *The Road Back to Paris*. Garden City, NJ: Doubleday, Doran, 1944.

Lottman, Herbert R. *The Fall of Paris*. London: Sinclair-Stevenson, 1992

———. *The Left Bank: Writers, Artists, and Politics from the Popular Front to the Cold War*. Boston: Houghton Mifflin, 1982.

Louizillon, Gabriel J. *The Bunau-Varilla Brothers and the Panama Canal*. Raleigh, NC: Lulu.com, 2008.

Macksey, Kenneth. *Guderian: Panzer General*. London: Macdonald and Jane's, 1975.

Mahoney, Daniel J. *De Gaulle: Statesmanship, Grandeur, and Modern Democracy*. Westport, CT: Praeger, 1960.

Marnham, Patrick. *The Death of Jean Moulin: Biography of a Ghost*. London: Pimlico, 2001.

Marshall, S.L.A. *Battle at Best.* Nashville, TN: Battery Classics, 2007.

Mauriac, François. *De Gaulle.* Translated by R. Howard. New York: Doubleday, 1966.

McCullough, David. *The Greater Journey: Americans in Paris.* New York: Simon & Schuster, 2011.

Mengin, Robert. *No Laurels for de Gaulle.* New York: Farrar, Straus and Giroux, 1966.

Meyer, Karl, and Shareen Brysac. *Tournament of Shadows: The Great Game and the Race for Empire in Asia.* New York: HarperCollins, 1999.

Morgan, Ted. *An Uncertain Hour.* New York: William Morrow, 1990.

Murphy, Robert. *Diplomat Among Warriors.* London: Collins, 1964.

Nadeau, Jean-Benoit, and Julie Barlow. *The Story of French.* New York: St. Martin's Griffin, 2006.

Neiberg, Michael. *The Blood of Free Men: The Liberation of Paris, 1944.* New York: Basic Books, 2012.

Olson, Lynne. *Citizens of London.* London: Bond Street Books, 2010.

Ousby, Ian. *Occupation: The Ordeal of France, 1940–1944.* London: Pimlico, 1997.

Paris, Erna. *Unhealed Wounds: France and the Klaus Barbie Affair.* Toronto: Methuen, 1985.

Paxton, Robert. *Vichy France: Old Guard and New Order, 1940–1944.* New York: Columbia University Press, 1982.

Paxton, Robert, and Nicholas Wahl, eds. *De Gaulle and the United States: A Centennial Reappraisal.* Oxford: Berg Publishers, 1994.

Pearson, Lester B. *Mike: The Memoirs of The Rt. Hon. Lester B. Pearson.* Vol. 3. Toronto: University of Toronto Press, 1975.

Perrault, Gilles. *Paris Under the Occupation.* London: André Deutsch, 1989.

Pertinax (Géraud, André). *The Gravediggers of France.* Garden City, NJ: Doubleday, Doran, 1944.

Pryce-Jones, David. *Paris in the Third Reich.* New York: Holt, Rinehart and Winston, 1981.

Reynaud, Paul. *In the Thick of the Fight: the Testimony of Paul Reynaud.* New York: Simon & Schuster, 1955.

Riding, Alan. *And the Show Went On: Cultural Life in Nazi-Occupied Paris*. New York: Alfred A. Knopf, 2010.

Robb, Graham. *Parisians: An Adventure History of Paris*. New York: W.W. Norton, 2010.

Robertson, Charles L. *When Roosevelt Planned to Govern France*. Amherst, MA: University of Massachusetts Press, 2011.

Rosenman, Samuel. *The Public Papers of Franklin D. Roosevelt. Vol. 2, The Year of Crisis, 1933*. New York: Random House, 1938.

Ryan, Cornelius. *The Longest Day*. New York: Simon & Schuster, 1959.

Schapiro, J. Salwyn. *Anticlericalism: Conflict Between Church and State in France, Italy, and Spain*. Princeton, NJ: Van Nostrand, 1967.

Shachtman, Tom. *The Phony War, 1939–1940*. New York: Harper & Row, 1982.

Schoenbrun, David. *Soldiers of the Night: The Story of the French Resistance*. New York: New American Library, 1980.

———. *The Three Lives of Charles de Gaulle*. New York: Atheneum, 1966.

Scobie, Steven. *The Measure of Paris*. Edmonton: University of Alberta Press, 2010.

Shirer, William L. *The Collapse of the Third Republic: An Inquiry into the Fall of France in 1940*. New York: Simon & Schuster, 1969.

Simon, Berton. *Allies at War: The Bitter Rivalry Among Churchill, Roosevelt, and de Gaulle*. New York: Carroll & Graf, 2001.

Speaight, Robert. *Vanier: Soldier, Diplomat and Governor General*. Toronto: Collins, 1970.

Spears, Sir Edward L. *The Fall of France: June 1940*. London: William Heinemann, 1954.

———. *Two Men Who Saved France*. London: Eyre & Spottiswood, 1966.

Sulzberger, Cyrus L. *An Age of Mediocrity: Memories and Diaries, 1963–1972*. New York: Macmillan, 1973.

———. *A Long Row of Candles: Memoirs and Diaries, 1934–54*. New York: Macmillan, 1979.

Thomson, Dale. *Vive le Québec Libre*. Toronto: Deneau, 1988.

Thornton, Willis. *The Liberation of Paris*. London: Rupert-Hart Davis, 1963.

Tornoux, Jean-Raymond. *Sons of France: Petain and de Gaulle*. New York: Viking Press, 1966.

United States, Department of State. *Foreign Relations of the United States: Diplomatic Papers, 1940*. Washington, DC: GPO, 1955–61.

———. *Foreign Relations of the United States: Diplomatic Papers, 1958–60, Vol. II, Part 2, United Nations and General International Matters*. Washington, DC: GPO, 1958–60.

Valéry, Paul. *Cahiers/Notebooks*. 5 vols. Editor-in-chief, Brian Stimpson. Translated by Paul Gifford. New York: Peter Lang, 2000.

Verrier, Anthony. *Assassination in Algiers: Churchill, Roosevelt, de Gaulle, and the Murder of Admiral Doran*. New York: W.W. Norton, 1990.

Weitz, Margaret Collins. *Sisters in the Resistance: How Women Fought to Free France, 1940–1945*. New York: Wiley, 1995.

Werth, Alexander. *The Last Days of Paris*. London: Hamish Hamilton, 1940.

West, Nigel. *Secret War: The Story of SOE, Britain's Wartime Sabotage Organisation*. London: Hodder & Stoughton, 1992.

White, Edmund. *The Flaneur: A Stroll Through the Paradoxes of Paris*. London: Bloomsbury, 2001.

Wieviorka, Olivier. *Divided Memory: French Recollections of World War II from the Liberation to the Present*. Stanford, CT: Stanford University Press, 2012.

Williams, Barry. *Modern France, 1870–1976*. London: Longman, 1980.

Williams, Charles. *The Last Great Frenchman: A Life of Charles de Gaulle*. London: Little, Brown, 1993.

Zabecki, David T., ed. *Ruckzug: The German Retreat From France, 1944*. Lexington, KY: University Press of Kentucky, 2012.

Zeldin, Theodore. *A History of French Passions*. Vol. 1, *Ambition and Love: France 1848–1945*. *The Oxford History of Modern Europe*. Oxford: Oxford University Press, 1979.

French Books

Belot, Robert, et al. *Les Résistants: L'histoire de ceux qui refusèrent. L'oeil des archives.* Paris: Larousse, 2007.

Bergheaud, Edmond, et al. *La France Libérée; Histoire Inconnue de la Libération de Paris.* Geneva: Éditions de Crémille, 1994.

Berstein, Serge. *La France des années 30.* Paris: Armand Colin, 1988.

Bourget, Pierre. *Paris année 1944.* Paris: Plon, 1944.

Camus, Albert. *Actuelles: Chroniques, 1944–1948.* Paris: Gallimard, 1950.

Cassin, René. Les homes partis de rien: le réveil de la France abattue, 1940–41. Paris: Plon, 1975.

Dansette, Adrien. *La France Libérée: Histoire de la Libération de Paris.* Geneva: Éditions de Crémille, 1994.

de Beauvoir, Simone. *La Force de l'Age.* Paris: Gallimard, 1960.

———. *Mémoires d'une jeune fille rangée.* Paris: Gallimard, 1958.

de Boissieu, Alain. Pour Combattre avec de Gaulle. Paris: Plon, 1981.

de Gaulle, Charles. *Discours et Messages. 2 vols.* Paris: Plon, 1946.

———. *Lettres, Notes, et Carnets.* Vol. 3, *Juin 1940–Juillet, 1941.* Paris: Plon, 1981.

———. *Lettres, Notes, et Carnets.* Vol. 4, *Juillet 1941–Mai 1943.* Paris: Plon, 1982.

———. *Lettres, Notes, et Carnets.* Vol. 5, *Juin 1943 – Mai 1945.* Paris: Plon, 1983.

———. *Lettres, Notes, et Carnets.* Vol. 6, *May 1945–Juin 1951.* Paris: Plon, 1984.

———. *Lettres, Notes, et Carnets.* Vol. 7, *Juin 1951–Mai 1958.* Paris: Plon, 1985.

de Gaulle, Phillippe. *De Gaulle: Mon Pere. 2 vols.* Paris: Plon, 2003.

de Mirabel, Elisabeth. *La liberté souffre violence.* Paris: Fayard, 1996.

Dronne, Raymond. *La Libération de Paris.* Paris: Presses de la Cité, 1970.

Dubief, Henri. *Le déclin de la IIIe République: 1929–1938.* Paris: Éditions du Seuil, 1976.

Flandin, Pierre-Étienne. *Politique française, 1919–1940.* Paris: Les Éditions Nouvelles, 1947.

Fouéré, Yann. *La Patrie Interdite*. Paris: Éditions France-Empire, 1987.

Fournier, Laurent, et Alain Eymard. La *2e DB Dans La Liberation de Paris et de sa région*. Paris: Histoire et Collections, 2009.

Galante, Pierre. *Le Général*. Paris: Presses de la Cité, 1968.

Germain, Michel. *Le Prix de la Liberté: Chronique de la Haute-Savoie de la bataille des Glières à la Libération et au-delà, 26 mars 1944–19 août 1944*. Vol.4, *Chronique de la Haute-Savoie pendant la deuxième guerre mondiale*. Montmélian: La Fontaine de Siloë, 1993.

Huard, Paul. *Le Colonel de Gaulle et ses Blindés: Laon, 15–20 mai 1940*. Paris: Plon, 1980.

Michel, Henri. *Paris Allemand*. Paris: A. Michel, 1981.

Moll, Geneviève. *Yvonne de Gaulle: Biographie*. Paris: Éditions Ramsay, 1999.

Moulin, Jean. *Premier Combat*. 1947. Paris: Les Éditions de Minuit, 1965.

Paxton, Robert O., et al., eds. *Archives de la Vie Littëraire Sous l'Occupation: À travers le désastre*. Paris: Tallandier, 2011.

Renan, Joseph. *Qu'est-ce qu'une nation?* Paris: Mille et une nuits, 1997.

Roussel, Eric. *Jean Monnet*. Paris: Fayard, 1996.

Sartre, Jean-Paul. *Situations, III*. Paris: Gallimard, 1949.

Storck-Cerutty, Marguerite. *J'étais la femme de Jean Moulin*. Roanne, France: Éditions Horvath, 1976.

Touzé, Christine Levisse. *Paris libéré, Paris retrouvé*. Paris: Gallimard, 1994.

Vaïsse, Maurice. *Alger le Putsch. Paris: Éditions Complexe, 1983.*

———. *La grandeur: Politique étrangère du general de Gaulle 1958–1969*. Paris: Fayard, 1998.

———. *Mai–Juin 1940: Défaite Française Victoire Sous l'oeil des Historiens Étrangers*. Paris: Autremont, 2010.

———. *La Puissance ou l'influence? La France dans le monde depuis 1958*. Paris: Fayard, 2009.

Vidalenc, Jean. *L'Éxode de Mai–Juin 1940*. Paris: Presses Universitaires de France, 1957.

Vinde, Victor. *La fin d'une grande puissance? La France depuis la déclaration de guerre jusqu'à la révolution nationale*. Lausanne: Jean-Marguerat, 1942.

French Periodicals

Espoir, Revue de la Fondation Charles de Gaulle, [Paris]

France Libre [London]

Journal Officiel, Gouvernment de France [Paris]

Paris Match

Le Temps [Paris]

Selected Web Sites

1944 The Liberation of Paris in Color
www.youtube.com/watch?v=skGQ0fVx75o

The Paris Story from the U.S. National Archives
www.youtube.com/watch?v=GOkZkjf6itg

INDEX

MORE GREAT BOOKS FROM DUNDURN

FIGHTING TO LOSE
by John Bryden

Based on extensive primary source research, John Bryden's *Fighting to Lose* presents compelling evidence that the German intelligence service — the Abwehr — undertook to rescue Britain from certain defeat in 1941. Recently opened secret intelligence files indicate that the famed British double-cross or double-agent system was in fact a German triple-cross system. These files also reveal that British intelligence secretly appealed to the Abwehr for help during the war, and that the Abwehr's chief, Admiral Canaris, responded by providing Churchill with the ammunition needed in order to persuade Roosevelt to lure the Japanese into attacking Pearl Harbor. These findings and others like them make John Bryden's *Fighting to Lose* one of the most fascinating books about World War II to be published for many years.

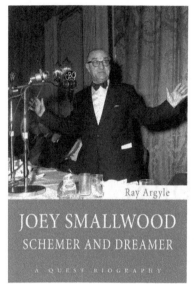

Ray Argyle

JOEY SMALLWOOD
SCHEMER AND DREAMER

A QUEST BIOGRAPHY

JOEY SMALLWOOD
Schemer and Dreamer
A Quest Biography
by Ray Argyle

Born in Gambo, Newfoundland, Joseph ("Joey") Smallwood (1900–1991) spent his life championing the worth and potential of his native province. Although he was a successful journalist and radio personality, Smallwood is best known for his role in bringing Newfoundland into Confederation with Canada in 1949, believing that such an action would secure an average standard of living for Newfoundlanders. He was rightfully dubbed the "only living Father of Confederation" in his lifetime and was premier of the province for twenty-three years.

During much of the last part of the twentieth century, Smallwood remained a prominent player in the story of Newfoundland and Labrador's growth as a province. Later in life he put himself in debt in order to complete his *Encyclopedia of Newfoundland and Labrador*, the only project of its kind in Canada up to that point.

In *Joey Smallwood: Schemer and Dreamer*, Ray Argyle reexamines the life of this incredible figure in light of Newfoundland's progress in recent years, and measures his vision against its new position as a province of prosperity rather than poverty.

VISIT US AT

Dundurn.com
@dundurnpress
Facebook.com/dundurnpress
Pinterest.com/dundurnpress